Thinking Ecologically

Thinking Ecologically

Environmental Thought, Values and Policy

Bruce Morito

Fernwood Publishing • Halifax

Editing: Donna Davis
Cover Design: Margaret Anderson
Production: Beverley Rach
Printed and bound in Canada by: Hignell Printing Limited

A publication of:
Fernwood Publishing
8422 St. Margaret's Bay Road
Site 2A, Box 5
Black Point, Nova Scotia
B0J 1B0

This book has been published with the help of a grant from the Humanities and Social Sciences Federation of Canada, using funds provided by the Social Sciences and Humanities Research Council of Canada.

Fernwood Publishing Company Limited gratefully acknowledges the financial support of the Department of Canadian Heritage, the Nova Scotia Department of Tourism and Culture and the Canada Council for the Arts for our publishing program.

NOVA SCOTIA
Tourism and Culture   Le Conseil des Arts   The Canada Council
                       du Canada   for the Arts

National Library of Canada Cataloguing in Publication

Morito, Bruce
Thinking ecologically: environmental thought, values and policy /
Bruce Morito.

Includes bibliographical references.
ISBN 1-55266-092-3

1. Human ecology—Philosophy. 2. Environmental ethics. 3. Environmental policy. 4. Environmental responsibility.
I. Title.

QH540.5.M66 2002   304.2'01   C2002-903644-5

Contents

Acknowledgments vii
Preface 1
Introduction 5

1. **Animistic and Classical World Views** 13
   Animism and Teleology 14
   Animism Denied 20
   The Ptolemaic Universe 21
   The Greco-Christian Influence on Environmental Thought ... 28
   The Greco-Christian Pursuit of Knowledge 32
   The Legacy of Greco-Christian Environmental Thought 34

2. **The Copernican Revolution, Mechanism
   and the Modern World View** 39
   Transition from the Finite Cosmos to the Infinite Universe ... 39
   Knowledge and the Materio-mechanism 45
   The New Attitude of Dominance 48
   Fragmenting Spheres of Inquiry 51
   Observer Status 52
   The Modern Era's Pursuit of Knowledge 56
   Conclusion 58

3. **The Challenge of Evolutionary and Ecological Theories** 61
   The Rise of Evolutionary Theory and the New Physics 61
   A New Take on Rationality 69
   Ecology Beyond Science 71
   Ecology as Process and Units of Analysis 80
   Influences on Contemporary Thought 86
   An Ecologically Directed Pursuit of Knowledge 93

4. **Values and World View** 97
   The Universality of Value Commitments 97
   The Advent of Liberal Democratic Values 99
   Utility 105

An Ecological Approach to Value Theory:
    The Inverted Scheme 108
A New Set of Problems 117
A New Way to Think About Anthropocentrism 121

5. **Ecology and Ethics** 131
    Liberal Ethics and Ecology 134
    Freedom 142
    The Harm Principle 147
    The Ethics of Deep Ecology 148
    Thinking Ecologically Toward an Environmental Ethic:
        Further Directions and Tensions 154
    Judgment and Decision 157
    The Land Ethic 163
    Ecosystem Health 168
    Ecosystem Integrity 173
    Ethics, Humility and the Great Mystery 179

6. **Ethics and Policy** 185
    Ethics and Analytical Failure 185
    Systems of Marginalization 190
    Environmental Policy as an Instrument
        of Dominance and Eradication 192
    Stakeholder Approaches 195
    The International Joint Commission 202

7. **Sustainable Development, Conservation and Sustainability** 211
    Rationale for Sustainable Development 212
    Business and Sustainable Development 214
    A Perverse Assumption 216
    Lip Service to Holism and Tolerance for Contradiction 221
    Strong and Weak Sustainability 224
    The Ethics of Cost-Benefit Analysis 226
    Risk-Benefit Analysis 230
    Sustainable Development and the Third World 234
    Sustainability: Some Necessary Inversions 238
    Conditions Necessary for Full Values Analysis 243
    Conservation 247
    Muktuk and Terms of Reference 254
    Conservation for Whom and for What Values? 257
    Conclusion 258

Bibliography 261
Index 275

Acknowledgments

I wish to thank my aboriginal friends and teachers. In no intended order of importance, they are Winona Arriaga, (the late) Ross Waukey, Paul Jones, Eric Johnston, Karlene Elliott, Linda Bull, Darlene Johnston and Chief Ralph Akiwenzie. I wish also to thank the one whom I know only as Geishi La, a Tibetan Buddhist, and Aryne Sheppard, both of whom may not know how much they have taught me about attunement.

Many thanks go out to Donna Davis for her excellent copy editing. For the cover design, I wish to thank both Margaret Anderson and Beverley Rach (whom I also thank for designing and laying out the pages). Wayne Antony, my publisher, has been a tremendous support. I have benefited greatly from his advice and from his suggestion that I rework the title into its present form.

I wish to thank the Office of the President of Athabasca University for the President's Award for Research and Scholarly Excellence, which afforded me the time to complete the manuscript. This book has been published with the help of a grant from the Humanities and Social Sciences Federation of Canada, using funds provided by the Social Sciences and Humanities Research Council of Canada.

To my children Sarah, Andrew and Gavin, and their children

Preface

Writing philosophically about ecological approaches to environmental thought and ethics has, in part, been motivated by my experience with and sometimes against policy and decision makers. This experience has taught me much about ecology and its application to ecosystem-based management. Gradually, however, I became uncomfortable with the way I was expected to think about ecology, e.g., as an add-on to the more primary scientific disciplines (especially biology). Eventually, my discomfort led me to investigate possibly deeper and wider meanings of ecology and its implications. Andrew Brennan's *Thinking About Nature* and its distinction between scientific and philosophical approaches to ecology (1988: 31) helped evoke my discomfort and motivate this inquiry. While I am principally interested in philosophical ecology, my history of working through my discomfort with scientific ecology and its application has influenced the approach I take. This will be especially evident in the last two chapters on environmental policy, which should make this essay of interest even to more technically oriented ecologists.

While my interest in ecology was developing, other influences— among them aboriginal voices, exposure to the plight of outport fishing communities in Newfoundland, James Lovelock's (1987) Gaia hypothesis and, indeed, my own "wilderness" experiences—planted the seed of thinking differently about ecology and, in turn, environmental problems. Struggling to criticize the limits placed on what could count as meaningful statements about ecology, I began questioning even the manner in which I have been trained in analytic and continental philosophy. Principles of clarity, logic, parsimony of predicates and the like work well on well-defined problems and in simple contexts. But where faced with environmental management and justice problems, which are ill-defined because they are multifaceted and multilevelled, these principles fell short of enabling me to think through to solutions that felt sufficient and appropriate. For instance, dealing with other cultures and including their perspective and concerns in how we think about solving environmental problems, together with a commitment to democracy, led me to conclude

1

that the system of thinking we typically adopt is often arbitrarily truncated and sometimes undemocratic.

It may be well and appropriate for the scientific community to limit the purview of ecology, as long as the limits are acknowledged to be stipulated for specific purposes. But for the philosopher to insist on limits, where those limits can be shown to be stipulated or arbitrary, is to violate the spirit of critical inquiry, which seems to have no limits. With this in mind, my understanding of the history of ideas, especially those taken to be true, certain or self-evident, began to appear to me as a path to greater inclusion of perspectives, as shifts in world view seemed to undermine former world views, while building on them. Evolutionary theory and ecology, for instance, have shown how some fundamental assumptions about human nature have had to be abandoned, while adding to a richer sense of what it means to be an individual in relation to the earth. Connections between ecology and Eastern/aboriginal perspectives have challenged my attempts to be inclusive to the point where what I count as knowledge has had to expand. Ultimately, these challenges have constituted a deeper challenge to my assumptions about what it means to think and to think well. Questions about standards of legitimacy or truth can no longer be put aside in the face other cultural anticipations and especially in light of the types of understanding and knowledge I need when in the bush. But it was reflecting on the idea of ecology itself that gave me the direction for this work. "Ecology" is one of those terms that, upon reflection, has a self-referential and self-critical moment. Like "philosophy" or "reason," "language" or "thought," ecology directs thought to both a subject matter and to the fact that that subject matter explains itself. To illustrate, when a philosopher stipulates what thought or reason is, critical inquiry immediately exposes the fact that thought is not only what is stipulated, but it must also stand outside that stipulated definition to be able to judge the legitimacy of that stipulation. When we use thought to limit the meaning of thought, we are already at a vantage point that is beyond that limit. Similarly, ecology is the study of the systems from which we all derive and from which our thinking about ecology derives. So, however we want to think about ecology, it is the product of ecological processes, so that there remains something about those processes that remains outside or uncontained in the study of them.

Even philosophical inquiry, then, becomes an expression of ecosystem process. It is this reflection that lies at the foundation of what I mean by "thinking ecologically" and why I think it insufficient to leave to environmental thought the task of thinking about ecology. So, the idea of thinking ecologically is an attempt to articulate what it means to adopt a world view that takes ecological process to be the more comprehensive process from which thought emerges.

While questioning the standards of legitimacy and knowledge in which I was trained, I found myself, at the same time, resisting the more romantic proponents of ecology as a new form of consciousness. So much of this movement appeared to me to be a leaping to conclusions about ecology in the fervour of protecting Gaia (Mother Earth). The association with the abandonment of rules of evidence and standards of rigour in analysis, which this movement sometimes seems to have adopted, struck me as equally inappropriate and one-sided, ignoring the danger of abandoning standards of legitimacy and critical inquiry.

The process leading to this essay has concluded with what I have long resisted, namely, believing that to think well is to be inclusive of diversity and opposites, whether metaphysical, epistemological, valuational, ethical, social, etc. Opposites must be thought and addressed together. The question "How deeply do we take this principle?" arises. This essay does not attempt to answer the question but is written in full awareness that it might not have penetrated deeply enough.

Practical concerns have concurrently affirmed the need to think in terms of opposites. Failing in diversity and inclusiveness results oftentimes in overlooking and systemically dismissing important information (e.g., ignoring local knowledge about an ecosystem, the opposite of universal knowledge; failing appropriately to give disadvantaged and marginalized people a voice, the opposite of dealing efficiently with a problem). Accepting opposites obviously results in conflict. But conflict is inherent in the democratic process of recognizing a plurality of voices. Accepting conflict, then, presents an even deeper challenge to thought to become more inclusive, more comprehensive and more penetrating. If a just way of thinking, deciding and writing policy is our goal, then we need to be prepared to balance these directives against the need for efficiency, parsimony and immediate clarity. Insisting on simplicity and efficiency, while good values in appropriate contexts, appeared to lead decision-making processes to conduct superficial analyses of environmental problems and, in fact, to occlude from view deeper violations and injury to people and the planet.

The idea of attunement as a goal to which we are to aspire and as an integrative tool for synthesizing the many facets of thought arose in this process. It was helpful that I had earned a living using low-impact logging techniques, fishing in the west coast salmon fishery and building for the rural Ontario community. Coming into conflict with loggers using clearcut techniques, technologies using industrial seine fishers and developers who seemed to have no concern for protecting ecosystems forced me to think through economic constraints over and against where my more detached philosophical reflection was leading me. At the same time, my silent and non-economically focused time spent hiking, skiing, canoeing and tripping with inner-city children has brought me to an immediate awareness of the spiritual dimension and healing power of the land.

Having lived with much cognitive and emotional dissonance, which, earlier in my life, appeared to have produced nothing more than chaos and indecision, now enables me to dialogue with marginalized people and to listen to the land without dismissing the dominant and those who either cannot or will not listen to the land.

In any work there are many biases and assumptions operating, sometimes explicitly, but mostly implicitly. In *Thinking Ecologically* a strong bias operates, but I am uncertain how to identify it without distorting it. I should then have to be satisfied with describing it as a function of my experience with "dysfunctional inner-city" children and their healing experiences in the bush. Initially, responding to the need to avoid error and liability in working with these children led me to restrict their activity. But as time wore on and their obvious need to explore and engage in somewhat more dangerous situations arose, a sense of wrongness came over me. As I allowed them more opportunity to engage, an unanticipated consequence describable perhaps as an "awakening" or "opening up" of these children amazed me. When I realized that it was happening to me as well, I began to understand that it was a process of healing through becoming attuned to my nature and the environment. While I cannot properly describe this consequence, this essay would not have been written as it is without this experience as background. In this way, it forms an assumption that knits together what might, at first glance, appear to be disparate elements.

When citing classical philosophical texts (e.g., Plato and Aristotle), I have included the critical edition referencing method either exclusively or after the page reference in the translation used. I do this because there are many translations of these texts. Most translations include side-bar referencing to the critical edition, so that the appropriate text can be found in almost all translations.

A further note on the use of language is in order. Gendered language, when treating historical material, is intentional because it accurately represents the mode of thought during these periods. "Man," for instance, is used rather than "humanity," during discussion of historical periods, where the historical record is being referenced.

Introduction

"Thinking ecologically" is to be attuned to the multiple facets of our environmental relationships and our capacities that have evolved to deal with these facets. "Attunement" represents a mode of thought that, among other things, synthesizes more specialized modes of thought (e.g., rational analysis, deliberation, intuition, reflection on experience), especially in acts of judgment. The relationship between these specialized modes is often seen as oppositional and exclusionary. Owing to our tendencies to prefer one mode of thought over others and to devalue those in apparent opposition to it, environmental thought is divided into camps— those more analytical and science-based versus those more intuitive and experience-based. I argue against this division, partly because each mode is valuable for understanding ecology and its implications and, therefore, for developing ecological approaches to environmental thought. Becoming ecologically attuned, i.e., bringing our capacities into accord with the multiple modes of our relationship with the environment, is best illustrated in relation to wilderness. It is during wilderness experience that our primary capacities for survival are the most exercised and the sharpest. In this context, not only must our bodies be brought into accord with the exigencies of life, but our intellectual capacities of perception, understanding, analysis, decision making and strategizing must also be brought into accord with what we must face. Wilderness experience demands the full employment of our capacities. Hence, it serves as a good model for how we need to attune these capacities to operate in concert in order to understand and interact with the ecological conditions that can provide for, heal, kill or harm us.

The idea of attunement is raised for consideration in the context of criticizing more well-received ways of thinking about solutions to environmental problems. It is also raised in relation to conservative ways of thinking about ecology, which I argue are inadequate. Better-received and "conservative" approaches tend toward the strategy of retaining as much of the conceptual and methodological status quo as possible, so that the development of ecology is appropriated into already well-established modes of thinking, rather than allowed to challenge these modes at their foundations. Part of my effort is to demonstrate that such approaches have either missed or dismissed the deeper implications of ecology. The vehicle for advancing the argument is the concept of world view. Where "world view" refers to a comprehensive set of assumptions that shape ways of understanding, knowing and valuing, it serves to capture the level of critique for which ecology calls. By using historical shifts in world view—e.g., that between Ptolemaic and Copernican systems—as models for how a systematic rethinking can occur at a fundamental level, it is possible to structure how concepts, explanations and values can be reshaped in an orderly manner.

An historical approach is also used, particularly in Chapters One and Two, to explain why shifts in world view need to take place. Systematically criticizing each mode of thought and exposing its weaknesses allows us to advance to more adequate ones. As such, the approach is both radical, in that it attempts to get at foundational issues, and somewhat conservative, in the sense that it is directed by what has gone before. It does not try simply to replace the preceding system, but develops by superceding concepts one by one until a need for a new conception of the whole becomes evident.

The focus is on the dominant Western European world views, starting with animistic world views and progressing through Greek Antiquity, through the Modern Era (seventeenth and eighteenth centuries) and finally through the contemporary challenges to the Modern as formulated in evolutionary theory and ecology. Contemporary issues with ecology are thereby situated in a wider developmental context. Chapters One, Two and Three describe several features key to the erosion of world views. This erosion is owing to logical problems, anomalies in explanation, and promises of both greater powers of prediction and control and more elegant or simple explanations. Shifts also occur because of other powerful forces at work, such as economic forces (e.g., the Industrial Revolution) or political movements (e.g., the advent of democracy and the rejection of the monarchy), but focusing on the philosophical dimension (metaphysical, epistemological and axiological) can serve as a spearhead for thinking through these other dimensions as well. This work is, therefore, not irrelevant to economic and political concerns. It is in fact intended to address fundamental environmental policy issues (Chapters Six and Seven) and relevant economic and political concerns. Although it does not offer particular policy recommendations, it addresses fundamental policy principles, such as sustainability and conservation, to show where thinking ecologically can be effective in environmental policy making and management.

The historical perspective also helps to model how world views become normalized and how normalization sometimes leads to appropriation, enabling us to see how resistance to change influences the formulation of new concepts and moral principles. This, what might be considered the ugly side of conservatism, forms a foundation for cooptation, which constitutes an important focal point for the application of thinking ecologically. This theme of appropriation and cooptation of ecological concepts is emphasized in Chapters Six and Seven.

When we consider the manner in which we have come to acknowledge and act on environmental problems, we witness a pronounced lack of attunement to the needs of the land and of people. Over the last century, environmental problems have taken the shape of deforestation and irresponsible forest management, land, air and water pollution, ozone layer depletion, global warming, landfill siting, nuclear waste disposal, depletion of fish resources, genetic mutations, diminishing fresh water supplies, etc. These problems continue and sometimes even appear to have become normalized, that is, we have come to accept and expect to have to manage these problems as part of daily life. More effort is being directed today at helping people adapt to environmental problems by, for example, helping people cope with ozone layer depletion by reporting danger levels. With this information, people can determine how much time they can spend in the sun without being dangerously exposed to ultraviolet radiation. We attempt to regulate damage through systems of fines or tax incentives to reduce pollution, which encourages business to view pollution as a cost of doing business. International agreements or protocols such as the Montreal protocol, designed to reduce CFCs, and the Kyoto agreement, designed to reduce greenhouse gas emissions, often adopt a trade-off system, according to which nations negotiate a right to pollute. Moreover, they can acquire an increased right to pollute, if they can get the international community to consider measures that have already been taken (e.g., replanting deforested areas) as credit toward the right to pollute. The U.S. resistance to the United Nations' resolve to protect biodiversity at the 1992 summit in Rio de Janeiro was demonstrated when then president of the United States, George Bush, refused to sign any agreement that would demand the sacrifice of many American jobs.

Our hunger for energy continues to place demands for damming rivers and constructing coal-burning electricity generators. We seem not to know when to stop exploiting fish resources, unless they are depleted beyond the point of financial feasibility, as has occurred in the east coast fisheries of Canada. Rather than learning to conserve water resources and curbing the obsessions of California's rich, which has so drained the Colorado River that water no longer reaches the Gulf of Mexico, we entertain lobbying efforts to divert Canada's fresh water resources to service this insatiable thirst. Rather than addressing the mismanagement and pollution of other countries' water systems, we entertain and lobby for shipping water from the Great Lakes as an export commodity. In other words, we are trying to manage our environmental disasters by describing and analyzing them to accord with a particular view of the world and humanity's place in it.

But where the focus is placed on resources and economic viability, morbidity and mortality are seen as costs to the system. The destruction of communities engendered by these environmental problems is treated as an issue to be managed through retraining and relocation programs. Our methods of analyzing environmental problems and constructing solutions are determined by our perspective, which in turn determines how we understand problems, set standards of knowledge and identify our values. These assumptions, i.e., how we understand problems and respond to them belong to a world view that promotes both intellectual and emotional detachment from the local effects that environmental degradation has on the land and on people. In other words, they detach decision and policy making from being attuned to the particular effects of environmental degradation and, therefore, to particular places and people.

This effect of detachment is, in many respects, a product of the Modern world view. Concern for particular places, people and communities marks a particularly important feature of ecological attunement, requiring the same fullness of access to our capacities as is necessary in wilderness experience. Hence, ecological attunement is as relevant to the concerns of justice, cross-cultural communication and gender relations as it is to wilderness experience and healing. Since nuclear waste facilities, landfills and environmentally dangerous projects are more often than not sited near disempowered and poor communities, it is fairly obvious that a lack of attunement to particulars is endemic to dominant environmental policy and legislative systems. Many aboriginal and Third World peoples feel that the dominant economic influence of the Western European-based and industrialized countries has been imposed on their communities, so as to make culturally appropriate environmental practice impossible. Many women, especially in Third World countries, feel that their work on and knowledge of the land in the new economy are marginalized and devalued as monocultural, export-oriented agriculture replaces their traditional practices. But all of this unattuned intervention is "justified" by those in dominant positions through appeal to "development" initiatives under foreign aid programs.

It makes sense, then, to treat the array of environmental problems as world view issues. But there is yet another reason to focus on world views. Environmental managers and policy makers today increasingly are having to face a wide array of perspectives and stakeholders as they attempt to write sound environmental or resource policy to satisfy the values represented by this wide array. Finding a way to include all of these concerns requires a more comprehensive and holistic approach than specialists are trained to provide. Ecological approaches, as holistic and inclusive, hold out the promise that we will be able to envision a means to satisfy the demands of this multidimensional environmental problem. Each of these perspectives can count as a world view, as long as it involves comprehensive ways in which people understand and direct their lives and not just momentary opinions. Given that, it is becoming ever more clear that environmental management is about managing for world views as much as anything else.

A primary reason for the focus on world views is to help prevent the appropriation and cooptation of ecological attunement. Thus, analysis and the reconceptualizing of personhood (i.e., our identity as persons) are tied to thinking ecologically. Since what we take to be persons affects thought at fundamental levels, as I will argue, effecting change in our conceptions of personhood that is in line with ecological attunement will also create a mode of thought that resists cooptation.

As mentioned, the central intent of this book is to advance what I am calling "thinking ecologically," which is in contrast to thinking about ecology.[1] Ecology is treated not as one among many fields of inquiry nor as a separate discipline. When we begin to think ecologically, we begin to understand ourselves, perceive, judge, analyze, formulate concepts and assume responsibilities differently. The underlying thought process is fundamentally different from that of the now-present dominant mode of thought, when determining conditions of significance and legitimacy. Thinking ecologically and holistically may appear less determinate, less clear and less committed to finality in the methods of enquiry it adopts, but it owes this lack of determinacy to its commitments to being inclusive and comprehensive—principles that require a respect for oppositions—which, in turn, affects standards of inquiry in epistemology and ethics. The argument, as a result, moves from a critique of clear and determinate standards to a gradual shaping of less clear and indeterminate standards, as far as the majority of the audience I am addressing is concerned.

The first three chapters of the book address the historical develop-ment of Western world views, starting with the pre-Socratic era (i.e., pre-500 BCE). Environmental thought in this era is based on the belief that the natural world has both a purpose and a life force. Chapter One examines key conceptual and valuational features of this mode of thought and how it is supplanted by the emerging rational approach to explanation and knowledge in the Greek tradition. It serves two purposes: to characterize the nature of the rational and to examine why its development is such a powerful force in Western history; and to characterize the animistic and to examine why, in its early version, it could not withstand the onslaught of rational thought. At the same time, it helps to characterize the animis-tic and teleological, so as to prepare for a more generalized version to be reintroduced later in the discussion of ecology. Chapter Two leaps past the Dark Ages and the medieval period to examine the Modern world view and its assertion of the strictly material character of nature, its inertness and its mechanical properties. This leap is justified in part because of the fact that the Greek cosmological commitments, captured in what is known as the "Ptolemaic cosmology," reigned for well over a thousand years, including the medieval period. This chapter examines the confrontation between the Ptolemaic and the emerging Copernican or Modern world view, which takes the world to be a mechanically organized and inert place, rather than the divinely ordered and controlled place of its predecessor. Reason is seen as coming into its own, eliminating any remnants of a personality-driven cosmos. Chapter Three examines the more recent conflict between this Modern mechanistic world view and the emerging ecological world view with respect to ecological ideas in biology, politics and philosophy. We find a shift in thinking that takes wholes to be significant in explanations, as much as the mechanical relations between parts. But in so taking, the reductive and tidy forms of explanation acclaimed by Moderns are challenged by more complex and obscure forms of explanation, as different levels of explanation are invoked and what Moderns called "occult" qualities (e.g., animistic purposes or teleological explanations) begin to re-enter the explanatory scheme. Here, argument for the tolerance of less clear and less precise formulations of ideas and central concepts begins to develop.

Chapter Four examines value theoretical questions: what is of value, how are values formed, how is non-human nature to be valued? It utilizes the framework established in Chapters One through Three to show how value theory has been influenced and, indeed, limited by the world view in place, by showing how various metaphysical and cosmological commitments determine how nature can be valued. Chapter Five applies what has preceded in developing an ethical approach to how our understanding of environmental values established in Chapter Four should be acted upon. It does this by examining and criticizing the main ethical approaches in environmental ethics in a process of shaping an ethic of attunement and formulating a harm principle. It develops an ethical approach based as much on experiential (later to include cultural) awareness as on theoretical rigour. Chapter Six tests contemporary policy commitments ("sustainable development" and "conservation") against this ethic and against an ecologically grounded value theory. Each is examined principally for its failure to take the implications of ecology adequately into account and for its use as a tool of cooptation. This chapter, consequently, is designed to illustrate how the distinction between thinking ecologically and thinking about ecology matters. It addresses the principle of inclusion in relation to traditional aboriginal, Third World and other disenfranchised communities. Without offering final solutions to the problem of inclusion, it nevertheless attempts to guide thinking about the policy process toward resolution of conflict between divergent perspectives by examining how an ecologically informed harm principle should direct the policy development process.

A common thread running through all chapters is the role and formulation of reason as central to the human-environment relationship. Modeling world view shifts is, at the same time, a modeling of how reason has to be both conserved and radicalized in the process of transformation to thinking ecologically. Each chapter forms a component in the project to transform our understanding of reason; we will come to view reason not as a condition of superiority and privilege but as a tool of attuned understanding and decision making. Rationality is attached to hegemony, but unlike the Modern conception of hegemony—a view toward dominance and superiority—ecologically attuned reason is attached to the responsibility of leading by following. Appeal to Taoism (an Eastern philosophical tradition) is used to help shape this idea. In the end, leading by following through attunement is a means for integrating ways of knowing (perceiving, cognizing, emoting, intuiting, remembering) in the process of protecting all members of the ecological community.

A contemporary illustration of why attunement needs to become a guiding force in developing an ecological world view is provided by Michael Hough (1990: 69). He describes how paradigm orientation is significant for the professional. As a landscape architect, he has become quite concerned about how we perceive and analyze our environment because our perceptions and analyses determine how we value and how we act toward the environment. He cites Robert Newbury's study on stream hydrology. Students from various academic and professional backgrounds were asked to describe a stream in a way that the others in the study group could understand, by drawing pictures. The biologists drew representations of habitats, food sources, a diversity of vegetative life and other features pertinent to life-sustaining conditions. The engineers focused on hydrological properties as they pertained to erosion and drainage problems. A carefully constructed system of grids and symbols indicated possible correction sites. For the sake of simplicity, the waterway was represented by a straight and uniformly wide drawing. Landscape architects drew an aesthetically pleasing coursing of the waterway as it wound its way through the terrain. They saw trees of uniform shape and size occupying spaces along the river bank and adjacent areas. These trees did not actually exist. In Hough's words, "the landscape architects saw very little but did a nice drawing" (1990: 71). The technicians attempted to represent the diversity of elements. Their drawing was the most crowded of the group. It was also the most empirically accurate of the four drawings. Hough concludes from the differences between these drawings that professional "world views" determine what exists for members of these professions and what should be identified as relevant. Specialized training, then, leads to fragmentation in the sense of responsibility each group adopts.

James Karr (1993: 84–85) also shows how specialization can lead to inappropriate modes of understanding. In attempts to determine the parameters of water quality and the impediments to improving that quality, hydrologists trained in chemistry have traditionally considered little more than chemical properties when analyzing water quality. Karr likens this specialized approach to determining the health of the nation's economy to taking the salaries of university professors as key indicators. Something as complex as a nation's economy requires a multiparameter evaluation, which is more than looking at the incomes of one occupational group. Evaluating water quality on the basis of chemical analysis alone is similarly insufficient; it is misleading or misrepresentative of our interest in maintaining water quality. Evaluating the health of an ecosystem, something even more complex, requires inclusion of an even greater number of parameters.

Professional training, like all forms of training, not only determines what we take as real and what is noteworthy; it also forms what we take to be a problem and what falls outside the realm of our responsibility. Limiting professional perspective tends to support ignorance of social and moral injustices and justifies this ignorance on the grounds that such understanding falls outside the purview of the professional. Of importance and value to the engineer *qua* engineer, for instance, are the technical conditions concerning water management. Concern for possible effects on aboriginal or other burial grounds falls outside the realm of concern; it is seen as external to the management agenda, a political matter. What responsibility, then, is there to address the general impacts on human health? Clearly, world views, or when applied to narrower contexts, paradigm issues, have wide-ranging relevance. Preparing ourselves to deal with them is a basic building block of environmental thought.

Note

1. I wish to express my appreciation to Wayne Antony, my publisher, for helping with the articulation of what is distinctive about the approach I am taking. During conversation, he pointed out this implicit distinction.

Chapter 1

Animistic and Classical World Views

Introducing the concepts of animism and rationality historically helps characterize basic conceptions of both and how they are involved in understanding how world views operate. It allows for a gradual increase in complexity of these concepts, as they will be used later on, and in the complexity of our understanding of how world views operate. It also allows for a gradually increasing complexity in conceptual analysis as we move from somewhat simple transitions in the use of concepts, such as "reason," "person" and "knowledge," to more nuanced ones. We also move from somewhat straightforward problems to more complex ones. The historical approach, in this manner, helps structure the development of key concepts and problems as they will be used in constructing an ecological approach to environmental thought.

Describing the shift from animistic to early Greek philosophical views of the world (roughly pre-500 BCE) by emphasizing the centrality of rationality is meant to capture how the emergence of reason effects fundamental change in world view. With the coming of the "age of reason," thought becomes increasingly systematic, ordered and formal; each step in thinking is related to previous and succeeding ones; ideas become both open to argument and defeasible because they are subject to standards of evidence and rules of inference. Ancient animistic modes of thought, in contrast, were based more on sensory acuity, intuition, revelation and authority. I hope to show in the next two chapters that the role of reason in the shift away from animism is important because it commits thought to clarity (precision), simplification and analytical rigour in ways that are not supported under animistic systems. Examining the 2000-year period between animistic and ecological world views is helpful for understanding how these aspects of reasoned thought get drawn out and how they progressively result in a devaluation of animistic elements. Since there are aspects of animistic thinking that I hope to reintroduce to ecological approaches, it is important to begin shedding unsupportable aspects of animism in order to clear the path to admit elements that can be supported. My strategy is to show how Western culture is drawn increasingly into a one-sided embracing of reason, which overemphasizes reductive, mechanistic and exclusionary ways of thinking. A critique of this application of reason and defence of how certain animistic elements remain necessary for explaining ecosystem processes help sort out which elements of animism can be reintroduced.

As we examine the shift away from animism toward mechanism and then to more holistic ways of thinking about the environment, we also are examining the relationship between humanity and the land as it moves from one of intimate connection to increasing detachment and back again to connection. As reason becomes associated with the divine, non-physical and atemporal—and becomes identified with the essence of "man"— the relationship becomes more antagonistic. The peak of this detachment occurs during the Enlightenment (the seventeenth to the nineteenth centuries) in what is called the Modern Era. It reverberates in almost all aspects of Western culture, including the development of modern science, the emergence of modern democracy (politics) and the onset of the Industrial Revolution (economics).

The idea of detachment is developed along the three major themes (two of which are discussed in Chapters One through Three, the other in Chapters Four and Five): metaphysical understanding of the human-nature relationship, the epistemological shift to the idea that we can be objective/disinterested knowers and the axiological shift to excluding all but rational agents from the class of the intrinsically valuable. This last theme stresses the status of rational agents as inherently valuable, morally superior beings. When ecology emerges, arguments supporting these spheres of detachment lose their force. Ecology and evolutionary theory show us that we fundamentally misunderstand the foundations of detachment and so wrongly formulate it metaphysically as an expression of the fundamental separateness between rational and natural beings. As a result, we need to reform our understanding of the relationship between rational creatures and nature, adapt our ways of knowing about this relationship to fit better with this reformation and shift value theory accordingly.

Animism and Teleology

Two concepts central to the ancient Greek (pre-500 BCE) conception of the environment are "animism" and "teleology." "Animism" captures the idea that the world is filled with spiritual powers or "agents," who, like people, have intentions and wills. "Teleology" refers to a principle of design or purpose according to which the world is ordered and created. Debate over whether teleological explanations are sound or even meaningful came to a head in the 1800s in a debate between Christianity (represented by William Paley) and evolutionary theory (represented by Charles Darwin). Whether the world is a divinely designed unity or an accidental configuration of

matter and energy continues to be debated among creationists and evolu-
tionists, but it also finds expression in scientific debates, for example,
over the Gaia hypothesis (see Lovelock 1987), which assumes that the
Earth is a living organism that orders the balance of chemicals in the
biosphere to make life possible. What is at issue morally is whether we
should treat the environment as having purpose or as nothing more than a
purposeless object.

Animism and teleology are distinct concepts; one does not imply the
other. We can believe that the Earth is alive without believing that it has
an ultimate purpose. The Earth can also have a design or purpose without
being alive, as is the case with watches or automobiles. In the early
development of Western civilization, however, the two were closely connected. Animistic beliefs preceded teleological beliefs, since evidence of
teleological thinking does not arise until around 500 BCE, whereas animistic beliefs are characteristic of almost all peoples of prior eras. Clarence
Glacken (1967: 39) traces the origins of teleological thinking to Anaxagoras,
a pre-Socratic philosopher who theorized that Mind arranges the cosmos.
The seeds of Anaxagoras' idea can likely be traced to the development of
crude tools in the Stone Age, when humans began to see that they could
shape and design their environment. Gradually, a conception of a supreme power likely arose as humans extrapolated from their own limited
powers to a notion that a supreme power must be responsible for the
shaping of the environment as a whole.

Animism can be associated with the emergence of almost all civiliza-
tions and is likely based on natural inclinations to think about other
objects as having feelings or intentions. As far back as we can trace
recorded Western and Mid-Eastern history (Mesopotamia and Egypt),
there is evidence of deeply held beliefs in the gods, who were associated
with forces of nature and who held no special regard for humanity (see
Haywood 1971: 26). Rome understood itself as having been nurtured by a
she-wolf. Eliade (1978: 38–39) traces the development of religious consciousness to the development of plant cultivation during the neolithic
age. Using evidence from New Guinea, he describes the development of
religious myths by showing how primitive peoples treated plant foods as
sacred, since plants were seen as derived from an original murder of a
divine being whose parts subsequently transformed into various plants.
Animism, then, connects the ultimate powers of the cosmos with person-
alities or agents of creation and order.

A more contemporary illustration of an animistic and teleological
conception of the environment can be found in aboriginal societies. Earth
and its elements are living beings infused with the same spark that
"animates" all conscious or sentient creatures. North America's aboriginal cultures, for instance, typically retain elements of animism (see Booth
and Jacobs 1993; Momaday 1997). All creation, the sum total of that

which exists, is formed from a community of living beings who live together in reciprocal moral relationships. It is becoming clearer that indigenous cultures around the globe hold similar views about the world and the non-human elements constituting it. Earth's inhabitants, accordingly, have interests, aspirations and responsibilities. Each individual has a role to serve within its own community (species) as well as within the larger geographical community of interrelated communities (see Overholt and Callicott 1982; McPherson and Rabb 1993).

Consider the Anishnaabe (Ojibway) creation "myth" as told by Basil Johnston (1994: 12–15), a teacher of the Anishnaabe culture and language. After the original creation as envisaged and effected by Kitche Manitou (the Great Spirit or Mystery), during which period all manner of creatures were created and life was breathed into them by the Great Spirit, an Earth-covering flood ensued. Sky-woman, who then lived alone, was sent a series of consorts, some of whom destroyed each other, but one group eventually worked to establish Turtle Island or North America. In a way reminiscent of many ancient cultures, the original water environment was penetrated by a being (in this case, a muskrat) who brought mud up from the bottom of the waters and placed it on the back of a turtle, forming Turtle Island. At this point, Sky-woman gave birth to one male and one female human, who were nurtured by the other animals. According to this story, everything stems from the Great Spirit such that everything depends on the other members of the Earth's community for existence and identity.

Such views can be described as moral, since they ascribe "agency" and responsibility to all beings, not just humans. To be an agent is to possess powers of self-determination and to be motivated by interests and desires. More importantly, it is to have a sense of responsibility and the ability to choose. Many aboriginal myths and stories describe non-human creatures precisely in this way. Beavers, coyotes, ravens, salmon and moose are seen to have special roles in the development of the Earth's communities and even of the human race. Sometimes, through struggling to find a homeland and sometimes through disobedience, these agents create situations suitable to the development of human culture. Often and for various reasons, transformation from one form to another (e.g., from beaver to human) occurs. This intimate connection among all creatures, which extends in many aboriginal cultures to rocks, indicates that all that takes place in the world is an act of some agent. Goulet (1998: 136) uses the expression "every event is a deed" to describe this way of understanding. It implies that we cannot always explain events because each event is a product of an intention of some moral agent, a freely determined act. The idea that all beings are agents means that they have a will and an ability to form intentions.

A myth should not be construed as something akin to a fairy tale.

They are different, especially with respect to how myth relates to world view. Usually, fairy tales such as Beauty and the Beast and the Frog Prince frame the transformation of a human being into a beast in the context of magic. A wicked witch or the like casts a spell in revenge and turns the poor soul into an animal (a "lower" form of life) as a punishment. The human soul is left captive in the skin of another creature until rescued by a hero. Heroes, traditionally, are pure of heart and represent some basic virtue that we hope to promulgate in society. The point of a fairy tale is to teach a lesson.

Aboriginal myths, in contrast, rarely portray shifts to a different form as punishment, an entrapment of the human soul within the skin of another species. Shifts in form are shifts in power and perspective. Typical Western fairy tales place little emphasis, if any, on the moral responsibilities of the non-human creature. In contrast, aboriginal myths show that all creatures are moral agents who not only deserve respect but who protect and guide us. The result is that aboriginal myths teach us to understand the world, not just how to behave.

Myth does not mean "pure fabrication," either. It does not refer to a false but perhaps meaningful story that is fabricated merely to enforce belief. It is not a graphic crutch created for the immature mind and then discarded once the principles are learned. Myth, in the sense employed here, is a way people have of entering into a world view, a way of seeing and knowing. It is a mode of representing deeper underlying beliefs, commitments and feelings of individuals in communities. Myths enable the believer to enter into a world view by directing thought and action toward appropriate recognition of the loci of power and meaning upon which a people or community depends.

The underlying world view promulgated in aboriginal myths is that all of creation is unified. "Oneness" has been used to describe the relationship between humans and nature. To be one with the environment is to be inseparable, but not indistinct. Each individual is different from others, as is each species. All, however, are members of larger, more comprehensive communities from which individual identities are taken. All individuals are nested within these larger communities. This notion of individuality clearly does not mean that individuals are unimportant or irrelevant. According to the aboriginal world views that I have studied, individuals and communities exist in mutually dependent relations.

Since the world is constituted of agents, it is, to a large extent, inscrutable. For the animist, it is difficult to make claims about how the world works and why events happen because the reasons for an agent's actions involve choices. Just as we remain unsure about what each of our human acquaintances will do when faced with a difficult choice, the aboriginal person remains open to what the members of the world community will do. This openness is part of what it means to respect other agents. Each individual's sphere of privacy and autonomy is recognized and respected. And to respect this sphere is to remain open to the possibilities that the other agent will present to you. The hunt, for instance, is an act of the prey-animal offering itself to allow humans to survive (Johnston 1994: 16).

To know what others are thinking and why they make their decisions, we require privileged access to their thoughts. Privileged access is typically given only to close friends and relatives in whom we can place our trust. Likewise, insight into the workings of the world requires privileged access. Thus, the seer or shaman, someone with special gifts of insight, is recognized as a locus of knowledge. A contemporary example of the role of the shaman can be found in the writings of Black Elk[1] (Black Elk and Lyon 1991). The shaman in Lakota tradition is a gifted person who, through ritual and special talents, is able to access spiritual dimensions of the world and communicate with beings in this dimension. Sometimes the spiritual dimension is described as having places, like the world of space and time in which we normally live, but at other times it is not so clear that the spiritual dimension has the same space-time properties. Some experiences are considered to be ineffable.

Where description does seem possible, however, distinctions between the notions of space and place are apparent. Space, for most contemporary adults, is empty, inert and divided into coordinates according to which objects can be located. In animistic belief systems, space is more a place having efficacious properties, where different regions (e.g., east, west, south, north) have different characteristics (see, for example, Kuhn 1985: 97–98). The four directions in most aboriginal societies have different characteristics and powers, as they do in much of Chinese and other Asian cultures.

From a scientific point of view, animism is based on superstition and has nothing to do with knowledge. But for many aboriginal people, the route to knowledge necessarily involves a spiritual dimension, accessed sometimes only through dreams. According to Goulet's research among the Dene Tha in Northern Alberta, dreaming is vital for knowledge, especially for knowing who one is, but also for knowing in general (1998: xxix, 181).

Other animistic belief systems share some but not all of the concepts found in aboriginal world views. The Eastern religions of Taoism (see Ip 1998) and Buddhism (see de Silva 1998), for example, share the notion that an elemental spiritual power (*ch'i*, or *ki*) animates the universe. Since all creatures are formed by this universal power, individuality is of secondary importance; unity is primary. Indeed, some Buddhist sects take this view to its farthest reaches, claiming that individuality is nothing more than illusion (*maya*); it is the product of superficial perception and experience. From the perspective of *ch'i*, all difference disappears or becomes insignificant. Martial arts and many of the healing arts are based on this conception of the spiritual power of the universe. This power may not be personal or associated with agency, as in aboriginal perspectives, but it is the source of agency, much like the Great Mystery in aboriginal thought is the source of individuals. It is that which we attain when we overcome all dualism, including the dualism between self and other. Individuals "are merely so many points of reference, the meaning of which is not at all realizable when each of them is considered by itself and in itself apart from the rest" (Suzuki 1985: 277). Individuals are expressions of the whole, the Great Mystery from which all else gains its existence.

Knowledge of these deeper truths is non-intellectual. Neither careful logical thought nor scientific experimental investigation can determine the nature of the great spirit or aid us in becoming aware of it. Meditation and personal discipline, sometimes through a vision quest, a ritual and chanting or dreaming, are required to attain knowledge. In Zen Buddhism, the *ko-an*—a logically unsolvable or unintelligible saying that one must, nevertheless, try to decipher—is used to take thought past reliance on concepts and step-by-step logical (discursive) thought to a point of seeing into this power (enlightenment). It involves a direct penetration into the nature of things.

Animistic world views presuppose a non-dualistic ontology. What exists for the aboriginal are spiritual agents, emanating from the one spirit; everything has an internal motivation and is capable of intentional behaviour. What exists for the Buddhist is *ch'i* (a fundamental energy). All else that we experience and perceive is explained in terms of these fundamental elements. If we accept the Taoist, Buddhist or aboriginal perspective, we believe that there can be no ultimate separation nor distinction between ourselves, objects in the world and spiritual entities/ energies. There is no duality, no fundamental separation between humans, non-humans, nature and God. Everything is fundamentally connected, such that everything that exists is constituted of the same basic power. Those who insist that humans or God are essentially different from the Earth are said to be in a state of delusion or error. Even when we feel that our experience tells us that we are separate and alien, an animistic perspective would have us interpret these feelings as errors in perception, thought and judgment.

Where there is no distinction between the ultimate animating spirit (God) and nature, the term "immanence" is used to indicate that the fundamental spirit or power of God/Nature is not essentially different from the spirit and power in human beings. The claim that God is in all and is all things (pantheism) indicates that humanity is at home in the world, and it is this world that provides not only sustenance and shelter, but identity, value and a sense of belonging.

It is worth noting that animistic cosmologies can entertain forms of dualism, but they are not ontologically dualistic. Humanity's function may be to balance and integrate functions in nature, as the aboriginal idea "Keepers of the Land" would suggest. The story of the roses and the rabbits (see Borrows 1997: 459–61; Johnston 1994: 44–45) tells of the near extinction of the roses. While the rabbits are initially blamed and punished for eating the roses, the lone remaining rose casts much of the responsibility on the Anishnaabe, who failed to keep the balance between the roses and rabbits, indicating humanity's special responsibility to maintain ecosystem balances. Other creatures also live in communities and can be said to be "peoples," but human people have a special stewardship function.

Animism Denied

In Western thought, the attack on animism began with the pre-Socratic philosophers of ancient Greece. Homer's *Iliad* and *Odyssey* took first steps toward divorcing Greek thought from animism. The Greek classics almost entirely ignore the chthonic gods—those related to the Earth and worshipped by the "simpler people"—focusing, rather, on the Olympic gods. Homer represents these gods as the powers controlling the environment (e.g., Demeter as the god of the earth, Poseidon as god of the sea); they are not of the environment (Haywood 1971: 114–15). The Olympian gods control the heavens, the seas, the earth and the underworld; they are detached from them. The Olympian gods, however, are not primary gods; according to Hesiod, in the beginning there was Chaos or the Abyss from which arose Gaia (earth) and Eros (desire) (Eliade 1978: 247). From Gaia was born Uranus (heaven). The Olympians did not come on the scene until two generations later. Hence, the Olympian gods are ultimately derived from more primordial elements. Chaos and the Abyss represent a primordial oneness, an inscrutable reality, the origin of all that exists. Elements of oneness with the chthonic gods and deep mystery, then, are retained, even as the chthonic gods decline in stature and are replaced by the more explicitly anthropomorphic Olympian gods. This tension between the retention of the old and the shaping of a new cosmology represents the sort of tensions experienced during shifts in world view. It also represents the belief in progress from the simpler and primitive to the more complex.

The Olympic gods are less idiosyncratic and mysterious than the chthonic, in part because they govern and are governed according to law. Eliade notes that despite the belief that Zeus, the father of the Olympian gods, is omnipotent (*Iliad* 8.17 ff., cited in Eliade 1978: 252) and can choose to do as he pleases, he nevertheless accedes to Hera's warnings that to do so (in some cases) would be to undermine the laws of the universe, namely justice (*Iliad* 17.322, cited in Eliade 1978: 261). We find, in the same general time period, a transition away from the belief that the gods mete out justice to humans rather than merely acting on their whims. The story of Orestes, who is pursued by the Erinnyes—the hounds of heaven, who deliver justice to those who violate the law of the gods—indicates how this transition is conceived. After pursuing Orestes for murdering his mother, the Erinnyes are placated by Athene. She offers them an opportunity to retire to a sacred place, where they can enjoy the worship of earthly followers in return for a renunciation of their right to mete out justice to Orestes. Human courts of justice subsequently replace the Erinnyes (see Graves 1996: 396–400). Aeschylus' *Oresteia*, in which the Erinnyes are given the name Eumenides, relegates these agents of justice to minor roles as the age of the rule by the gods comes to a close. The responsibility for upholding justice comes to rest in human institutions.

With the decline of the Erinnyes, who are matrons of the underworld, the matriarchal order of the universe gives way to a patriarchal system (Graves 1996: 399). As the animistic belief system erodes, so too does the primacy of the female element in the operations of the world. The connection, at this point, may seem circumstantial, but it is worth mentioning in light of the further historical connection between humanity's increasing power to control the environment, the pre-eminence of reason and male dominance. During this period, an increasing belief in a system of order as engendered through law emerges. An ambiguity in the concepts "law" and "justice" should be noted, however. Under the proprietorship of the Erinnyes, law was derived from the inherent order of the cosmos, such that the law that humans were to follow derived from natural law. As the function of meting out justice gets transferred to human institutions, the origin of law becomes increasingly obscure. But humanity is beginning to see itself as capable of determining law independent of natural agents and order.

The Ptolemaic Universe

Once the Greek philosophers came on the scene, animism came under much more severe attack. For this reason, ancient Greece is often cited as the birthplace of modern Western thought and science. With Pythagoras, the idea that the world is governed according to mathematical principles took hold, although the Egyptians had developed a practical and empirical mathematics much earlier. Unlike the Egyptians, however, the Greeks conceived of mathematics as housing comprehensive ordering principles according to which the world was ordered. The Egyptian practical conception of mathematics was a tool for the purposes of engineering. It was with the Greeks, then, that mathematics became progressively more abstract, as attempts were made to understand the world at the most general level. This characterization of mathematics and reasoning power illustrates how progress was, and still is, seen. Progressive thought is a matter of being able to reduce explanation to as simple a form as possible while being able to give as universal an account of as much as possible. The Ionian philosophers (600–400 BCE), who are sometimes known as pre-Socratic thinkers, perhaps best exemplify this attempt at reducing explanations of the world to the universally applicable relationships between primary elements (i.e., water, fire, earth and air), which in turn obviates the need for gods or agencies.

It should be noted that, during this period, the idea of the individual rational mind was also developing. The concept of mind as an expression of the rational, divine mind emerged: it began to substitute for the divine as the ordering power of the world. Bruno Snell (1982) traces the emergence of what we now call the "mind" or "soul" to this period in Western history.[2] He focuses on the idea that the Greeks recognized the mind as the locus of thought. They identified thinking as an operation distinct from natural or lower order processes (e.g., biological, emotional), so that people could, for the first time, think about themselves as objects of thought (Snell 1982: ix). This contribution of the notion of mind as an element transcending nature creates an array of problems with which the Greek philosophers begin to struggle and which become central to the detachment of the rational thinker from the natural order. Socrates spends much time on this, for instance, in the *Phaedo*, where he determines that the mind is distinct from the body. Later the problem of freedom of the will versus the determinism of the physical universe is to become a key problem in Western thought. The place of the rational intellect in an increasingly mathematically describable and less animated cosmos begins to rend the relationship between the rational intellect and the physical world more deeply apart.

Returning to the theme of reduction and simplification, the emerging Greek system—eventually to be formulated into what is known as the Ptolemaic system—gradually eliminated both animistic and anthropomorphic elements in explanations of world events. Initially, the Olympians were identified with the planets (Aries or Mars, Aphrodite or Venus, Uranus, etc.) and governing principles. But with the influences of Pythagoras, the materialists (e.g., Parmenides) and the atomists (e.g., Leucipus and Democritus) emerges the notion that the universe operates mechanically and, therefore, predictably, according to law, rather than according to spiritual forces. Rational principles and impersonal calculations now begin to take centre stage as the bases for explanation.

The Ionian philosophers[3] (e.g., Thales, Anaximenes) posited general principles to explain the nature and events of the world, principles that could be discovered through careful observation. Unlike former ancient systems of explanation, which required special insight and access to the gods, the new approach promised that intelligent persons could explain events by using their own perceptual abilities and their ability to recognize patterns. These patterns were ultimately attributable to some primordial "stuff" (substance). For Thales, this substance was water or moisture. For Anaximenes, air was the primordial substance. It does not matter, for present purposes, whether they were correct; what matters is the significance of the shift to a non-spiritual or non-animistic explanation of how the world operates. Human intellectual capacities of observation and reasoning began to supplant the seers and priests as the sources of knowledge. Impersonal substances were replacing agents as the inhabitants of the world. This new-found observer status allowed human beings to think of themselves as less subject to divine powers for instruction and more the authors of their own explanations.

At about the same time, the Eleatic school, with thinkers such as Parmenides and Zeno, formed the seeds of what can be called early "rationalism." Abstract deductive reasoning (logic), rather than observation, discovers the ultimate principles governing the world. Although the Ionian (empiricist) and Eleatic (rationalist) camps opposed one another, they had one thing in common; both undermined religious authority and created an intellectual atmosphere in which animism could not long survive. A framework developed according to which it was intelligible to believe that objects were inanimate and that they obeyed laws not derived from divine will. The world could be explained as a series of events, all of which were subject to universal laws of cause and effect. We have seen how Anaxagoras posited the existence of a controlling Mind over the cosmos. With the demise of the Erinnyes and the emergence of the idea of the human individual mind, then, a shift to a very different world view became irresistible.

New criteria of legitimacy were called into play. Evidentiary principles (e.g., public verification and repeatability) and logical principles (e.g., consistency and coherence) began to supplant the priests, shamans and seers as authorities. Under an animistic world view, coherence is not so important, since the gods can change their minds, and their desires or reasons for intervening (jealousy or revenge) are often irrational in the first place. Rational construction of explanations began to supplant ritual and ceremony as access points to knowledge. The rational inquiring mind became the locus of explanatory force.

Plato and Aristotle, although critical of the pre-Socratics, more systematically and completely formulated what their predecessors initiated: the problematic approach. They advanced the idea that understanding and knowledge are gained through formulating problems for explanation, which in turn the rational intellect solves. Rational intellect (*nôus*) is both problem formulator and resolver. For this to be possible, it must be assumed that the world is rationally ordered.

Earlier, the shift to the ancient Greek world view was identified with Ptolemy, an astronomer who lived hundreds of years after the great philosophical minds of ancient Greece. His cosmological system, however, has been treated as the principal expression of the Greek world view (Kuhn 1985: 66). It dominated European cosmology until the advent of the Copernican revolution over a thousand years later.

Ptolemy, like his predecessors—especially Aristotle (1939: 91, or 279a) in *On the Heavens*—placed the Earth at the centre of the universe (geocentrism) with the planets and the Sun revolving around it. This cosmological system was based on the results of observation. Since it appears that the Sun, Moon and planets revolve around the Earth, it seemed reasonable to conclude that the Earth occupies the centre. The stars form an outer sphere, because they appeared to be permanently placed there, and the planets travel within the sphere of the stars. Earth was also thought to be the stationary centre of the universe, partly because of a belief in a law that all heavy things seek the centre of the universe. Since all heavy things appear to seek the centre of the Earth, the proposition that Earth must be the centre of the universe seemed self-evident. Each planet's orbit was believed to circumscribe a perfect circle within the cosmos and the outer orbit circumscribed the limits of the cosmos (universe).

This notion of circularity as a perfection of sorts was articulated in a passage describing the creation of the Earth in Plato's *Timaeus* (1973: 1164, or 32c–34a). Here, the world created in the shape of a globe was deemed perfect because it is "the most perfect and the most like itself of all figures." This view, it turns out, had a profound and, in Edward Rosen's view (1973: 539), pernicious influence on European thought. The universe (or world) was considered to be of finite magnitude because, according to Aristotle, infinite space is a contradiction in terms and contradicts the "fact" that Earth is the centre of the universe: in an infinite space there can be no centre. Since the world is a perfect creation, the limits of the cosmos are equidistant from the centre.

Desire for the centre of the cosmos (universe) explains not only why it is that objects fall to the Earth, but why the planets continue to revolve around the Earth and not fly away from it. This power (*eros*) is reminiscent of animism. What we call "gravity" is close but not equivalent to *eros*, since the former does not refer to subjective qualities. Although all change was understood to be the result of some animating power, this power is no longer directly associated with will and agency. Furthermore, as Kuhn (1985: 94) shows, Ptolemy's move to mathematical descriptions and explanations of the movements of the heavens meant that both the celestial and terrestrial events could be explained by appealing to the same impersonal laws. This unified theory and the increasing success of using mathematics to describe and predict planetary motions made it only a matter of time before animistic elements would appear completely superfluous.

Law-governed or principled understanding also affected conceptions of the divine in increasingly profound ways. Rather than residing in the Pantheon, as Homer had them, gods in the Ptolemaic world view were transplanted to the perfect spheres around the Earth, since it is the most appropriate place for the most perfect beings. But the idea of perfection, here, is not based on making good and wise decisions; it is based on the idea of circularity, a property described and treated in mathematics, not in ethics nor religion. The gods were becoming mathematical entities. An example of this characterization is how perturbations or changes in the heavens (especially regarding eclipses and comets) were explained. Where once the will of the gods might have been the basis of explanation, Ptolemy's more mathematical explanations proved more efficacious, reliable and effective because of their greater predictive power. Insofar as the gods remained parts of the explanation, they became principles of order, without will or intent. The gods were becoming cosmic energies (Glacken 1967: 68–69).

According to Homeric animistic conceptions, the Earth is a dark place existing below the abode of the gods. The Ptolemaic system retained much of this view. The Earth remains the cold, dark centre, existing at a low level of reality. This dark and earthly body is driven by a low form of "love" (desire). Such love, being formed by appetite and driven by base needs, is irrational, corrupt and ill-suited to the high calling of humanity. The metaphysical and value hierarchy of the Homeric system, then, was retained in the Ptolemaic. Socrates was instrumental in establishing the belief that the highest level of existence is intelligence (*nôus*), which can be apprehended only by rational beings through the search for wisdom (*sophia*). Creatures lacking in intelligence are transitory, dependent (on the life-death cycle) and base (appetitive, passion-driven). While those in possession of intelligence enjoy the promise of an eternal, independent and contemplative (rationally ordered) life, the base (corrupt) are subject to death and degeneration. Bodily existence, the fact of aging and eventual decomposition of all physical living beings, was associated with incompleteness and inadequacy. It is only through striving to become like the gods that one can find genuine happiness (see Plato's *Phaedo* and his *Republic*, as well as Aristotle's *Nicomachean Ethics*, Book 10). By carrying this belief into the Ptolemaic system, the world remained a place where human beings worked out their moral vocation in life.

Since this vocation is predicated on the belief that reason is of the highest value, rational existence was identified as the highest form of existence. Indeed, reason became associated with the divine. Plato and Aristotle understood God to be the highest form of intelligence and thought (*nôus*). This highest form is, therefore, non-physical. It is pure intelligence or reason. This Platonic/Aristotelian world view espoused a deeper dualism than either the Ionians or the Eleatics imagined. Things physical and sensual were not only assigned a lower degree of importance than things intellectual and rational, they were also assigned lower degrees of reality.

Figure 1.1 Plato's Divided Line

GOOD	
(*Noesis*) Understanding	forms, dialectic
Intelligible	
(*dianoia*) reasoning	mathematical realities
(*pistis*) opinion	objects of sense
Physical	
(*eikasia*) image-making or imagination	images, reflections

Source: Plato, *Republic,* Book 6

Plato's famous "Divided Line" teaches that reality is divided into two major types (the physical and the intellectual) and four levels (two in the physical and two in the intellectual). The intellectual is the abode of rational beings. This abode is for morally significant beings capable of thought and decision. These alone share in divine-like properties. Animals and inanimate objects do not. The dawning of the Age of Reason, then, also marked the beginning of a belief in two modes of existence: one amoral, impermanent and base; the other moral, permanent and exalted. Nature, for the first time, was thought to be a place from which escape was both conceivable and desirable. It was negatively valued because its demands were thought to distract human beings from their aspirational ideals.

Since human individuals have both physical and intellectual properties, they were thought to have one foot in heaven and one foot on Earth, torn between the two. Human life is not a harmonious integration of intelligence and physical existence; it is a struggle to separate the intellectual from the corporeal. It is to overcome the lower elements of bodily life and exercise the higher. Plato's (1977: 67d) *Phaedo* argues:

And does purification not turn out to be what we mentioned in our argument some time ago, to separate the soul as far as possible from the body and accustom it to gather itself and collect itself out of the body and to dwell by itself as far as it can both now and in the future?

Later, Plato's student, Aristotle, continues to entrench this body/soul dualism in Book 7 of the *Nicomachean Ethics* (1962: 174, or 1145a): "The most fitting description of the opposite of brutishness would be to say that it is superhuman virtue, a kind of heroic and divine excellence." In Book 10 he argues:

A man who would live it [a life that completely follows the activity of intelligence] would do so not insofar as he is human, but because there is a divine element within him. This divine element is as far above our composite nature as its activity is above the active exercise of the other [i.e., practical] kind of virtue. (Aristotle 1962: 290, or 1177b)

Greek hierarchical structuring of reality, knowledge and moral life is based on the distinction between reason (soul) and the physical (body). The Greek philosophers formulated a duality of the most fundamental order, such that the soul and body were thought to be constituted of such different kinds of "stuff" that they could have neither common measure nor characteristics. Consequently, dualities of many sorts arose: superior/inferior, high/low, eternal/temporal, unconditioned/conditioned, intrinsic value/instrumental value.

Some aspects of this kind of dualism were generated by a tension between teleological explanations of the universe (e.g., Aristotle's final causes, which explained things in terms of purposes or design) and the new-found rational, moral status of human thinkers. Glacken (1967: 87) traces teleological explanations to Hippocrates and the medical model of the cosmos or *oikemene* ("inhabited world"), which is related to the universal ordering of the cosmos. Based on the apparent beauty, utility and productivity of the *oikemene*, the purposiveness of the world and humanity's place in it seemed obvious (Glacken 1967: 147). Over and against this teleological explanation of the world and humanity, the Stoics (e.g., Lucretius) took rational nature to be the basis for a fight against corporeal nature (Glacken 1967: 70), an idea to be taken up later (in the 1700s) and rigorously formulated as a dialectical relationship between moral agency and the mechanism of nature (see Kant's *Critique of Pure Reason*, The Third Antinomy). Debate over whether rational beings are free or determined has become intractable, owing in large part to this original tension between teleological explanations and moral freedom of the rational being.

Indeed, this great dilemma in human thought emerged as an issue of control. A dilemma concerning whether humanity can and should seek to control the environment later became an issue of whether human beings can control their physical/biological natures. Initially, the issue was about humanity opposing the gods and taking destiny into its own hands. Zeus' punishment of Prometheus for stealing fire was a warning against hubris, an announcement to humanity that it is not its place to have the power of the gods. Before one could alter the environment, guidance from the gods (e.g., for construction, agriculture) must be sought and accepted. Plotinus, after Plato, stretched the limits of human control further still by rejecting astrological and environmental explanations of human character, at least as total explanations, and he asserted the presence of something that is primarily ours, our personal holding which is free of such influences (Plotinus 1956: 1.5). This tension gradually acquired new dimensions, as moral and aesthetic qualities were seen to oppose the body's natural functions, especially in Stoicism and Christianity.

These tensions and conflicts mark the beginning of a long history of debate between ways of thinking about humanity's place in the world. How rationality and intelligence are related to the physical and non-human world has become a dominant theme. The emergence of reason as a cornerstone of thought affects everything from conceptions of self, justice, what counts as the moral community and what counts as knowledge to the portrayal of the divine and the universe.

The Greco-Christian Influence on Environmental Thought

Greek hierarchical cosmology, especially as articulated through Stoicism and Christianity, fostered a growing antagonism toward the natural world and a sense of licence to manipulate and exploit it. Stoics, although believing in the world as designed for humanity, nevertheless tended to view the world as opposed to human purpose. Lucretius, for instance, understood human life as a laborious fight against nature (Glacken 1967: 70). Reverberations of this attitude are evident in the Christian Bible. After Adam and Eve sin, God pronounces, "Cursed is the ground because of you; in toil you shall eat of it all the days of your life; thorns and thistles it shall bring forth to you" (Genesis 3:17, 18). While there is considerable debate over what the actual teachings of Christianity are,[4] clearly elements antagonistic to corporeal nature developed in Christian institutions.

Admittedly, Christian thought and practice typically treat the environment as having sacred places (e.g., Jerusalem, special mountains, cathedrals), which often are thought to be protected and valued by God. Sometimes there are indications that the entire creation is sacred or at least favoured by God (e.g., seeing creation as good, as in Genesis 1:10) and, ultimately, the possession of God (Job 38: 25–27). Indeed, in some biblical passages, it seems that humanity is to see the power and deity of the invisible God through the evidence of nature (e.g., Romans 1:20). Many of the saints embrace nature as the eternal creation of God (e.g., Canterbury, Assisi, Bonaventura). Contrary to the analysis of many thinkers (e.g., White 1967; McHarg 1970), tracing the sources of our environmental problems to Christian thought seems unwarranted. For instance, McHarg's hard line on Christianity—blaming the Judeo-Christian assumption of human superiority for the wanton destruction of nature and the present-day exploitive economic agendas—seems an overreaction. He asserts, "To this ancient view the past two centuries has added only materialism—an economic determinism which has merely sustained earlier views" (McHarg 1970: 25; also see White 1967).

But there is evidence for the McHarg/White complaint against Christianity. Origen, a church father, saw the soul—but not the body—as God's work (Glacken 1967: 184). Man (gender intended) is the ruler of nature whose task it is to complete and improve nature. Moreover, as ascetics, Christians should deny the body, its pleasures and its plentiful environments that foster bodily pleasure by entering into cloisters to concentrate on the soul. Here, Platonic dualism is clearly at work. The idea that senescence is an inherent property of the environment, one which was adopted in the Middle Ages, takes the notion of Earth's lower status a step further. The physical world is growing old and decrepit; therefore, it belongs to a lower order in the Great Chain of Being (Giraldus Cambrensis [1146–1220], cited in Glacken 1967: 279). Physical reality, unlike intellectual or mental reality, is temporal and subject to the process of generation and degeneration, life and death. Plato's *Phaedo* (1977: 65b-c) is a prime example of how the physical is denigrated as deceptive, as evil because it is distracting (1977: 66b-c, 79c); it is, in the end, subject to being ruled by the rational soul (1977: 94d).

It is not difficult to see how the Christian notion of an immortal soul takes root in the fertile soil of Greek thought. Greek philosophy readily offered a framework for the doctrine of an eternal spirit situated in a less than perfect or even corrupt physical world. The spirit, although trapped in the physical realm, can, through the appropriate exercise of spiritual capacities and the grace of God, transcend the physical realm and exist eternally in the spiritual. Plato argued that a return (reincarnation) to bodily form is the fate of those who do not reach the highest state (*Republic*, Book 10). Christian doctrine warns of eternal damnation for those who do not purify themselves from bodily desires or who do not enjoy the grace of God.

Treating earthly existence as a battleground on which the mind (soul) and body play out their opposition to one another makes alienation a central theme for environmental thought, which is in turn fostered by the doctrine of original sin. Owing to the sin of Adam, humanity is severed from the possibility of a harmonious relationship with the environment. The statement "We are in this world, but not of this world" illustrates that humans remain foreigners in the land.

The Christian idea of freedom from corporeal existence cannot be ignored. Plato's notion of philosophical life as a preparation for releasing the soul from the body has had effects on the Christian notion of salvation from sin that should not be ignored; it has been an important factor in determining the way in which the West has come to think about its relationship to Earth. The contribution of reason to the characterization of the soul has, as a result, been instrumental in the erosion and elimination of animistic sensibilities and a deepening of the sense of alienation from the *oikemene*.

Philo (1929: 88) states that the Creator made man the driver or pilot of all things, charging him with the care of all animals and plants, like a governor subordinate to the chief. This view was carried out in practice, for example, through the deforestation of Europe by the monks for the establishment of monasteries and places of refuge and worship and by secular agents for social and economic purposes (Glacken 1967: 311, 313). A gradual erosion of accountability to an authority ensued, first, in the form of freedom from accountability to the gods, as Platonism supplanted animistic beliefs; and second, in the form of release from accountability to the Christian God, as economic and political forces began to assert their independence from church authority. The deforestation of Europe continued to be encouraged by the church in the 11th, 12th and 13th centuries, as Christianity gained land from pagan Eastern Europe. To establish its authority, the church, in concert with the monarchy, granted rights to develop the land. This process is known as *aedifcare*: a process of erecting buildings and clearing forests to improve the land (Glacken 1967: 330–31). During this period, much of Europe was deforested and turned into "productive," arable land. With the shift in power relations, control over the political situation and the increase in technological devices (e.g., the hydrolic saw), Christian domination resulted in the alteration of the land at a grand scale.

Implicit in the Greco-Christian world view was the idea that the environment is an arena for testing spiritual mettle (e.g., testing resistance to temptation). Sovereignty and dominion apply as much to the body as it does to the land. Hence, corporeal nature is something to be overcome, conquered and suppressed. Lynn White Jr. (1967) argues that Christian environmental ethics is based on a doctrine of dominion, where "dominion" means "dominance." Such is his reading of Genesis. Thus, tying Christian social and political history to European exploitive and expansionist policy largely undermines the argument that Christianity supports a respect for the land as advanced by Canterbury, Assisi and

Bonaventura. The expansion of Christianity in concert with European economic dominance throughout the world has been an attempt to eliminate cultures that are philosophically and religiously closely tied to the earth (animistic cultures), as exemplified in the missionary zeal to convert the heathen and savage to Christianity. From the 1500s on, North American missionary movements (especially the Jesuit movement) were instrumental in eradicating much of the influence of the indigenous religions of aboriginal peoples. The animistic base of most aboriginal societies was particularly targeted for eradication on the grounds that it espoused demonic beliefs. In concert with legislators and the powers of the time, the church was instrumental in the banning of such practices as the potlatch on the west coast, the sun dance in the plains area and the sweat lodge of the central regions of North America.

The results of the legislation today are clear. Native communities are split over religious lines. Christian elements continue to struggle against the traditional elements as aboriginal peoples attempt reconstruction of traditional practices. Their sense of identity largely has been destroyed as a result of cultural genocide programs and forced parochial residential schooling.

The Crusades were motivated by a religious/political commitment to free the Holy Land from the "infidel" Muslim threat; expansion into Asia and Africa was to secure trade and expansion of empire as well as to convert the heathen population to Christianity. Dominance of the world by Western Europe, then, has involved a complete transformation of non-European societies' world views, a transformation that has been founded on assertions of inferiority of non-European belief systems. Hence, the connection between the metaphysical modes of thought and the will to dominate is strong.

The North American colonization process illustrates how this Greco-Christian belief system operates. European states during the colonization period were governed by a "right of discovery"—a pact between expansionist nations not to interfere with the nation that discovered a new land (see section 36 of R. v. Van Der Peet for a legal synopsis of the concept). The right of discovery, while accepting a limited sovereignty of First Nations, nevertheless asserted ultimate sovereignty for the European nation that "discovered" the land. This belief in the right of discovery either denies the existence of an aboriginal belief system or summarily dismisses it. It is also based on the assumption that, despite having lived on the land from time immemorial, aboriginal peoples had not yet discovered it. This denial of aboriginal political, legal and social systems was not, in fact, a denial that they were in place, because to recognize that these systems interfered with their imperialist designs, the colonizers had to presuppose their existence. On this matter, Olive Dickason (1997: xiii) cites the analysis of Joseph Jouvency, a Jesuit: changing the initial assumptions of the "Amerindians" will enable the hegemony of the European nations in colonizing the Indians. Because he recognized an extant Amerindian system of thought, he found it necessary to undermine that system to enable the colonization process. European belief in the Great Chain of Being (which is based on the Platonic and Ptolemaic hierarchies) provided support, since European man, as rational agent, could see himself as closer to the divine, under obligation to eliminate the wild and obliged to convert the savage into a civilized (Christian) person (Dickason 1997: 43–44).

Introducing this issue illustrates how the Western European world view and associated value systems were used to devalue existing systems by classifying them as inferior. Just as earlier it was noted how Christianity expanded its influence in Europe by improving the land, similar justifications were used in the colonization of aboriginal peoples.

It is not difficult to see how the Greco-Christian world view, a system of beliefs and assumptions foreign to aboriginal peoples, could be and was used to characterize aboriginal people as irrational because they espoused animistic belief systems. It is also not difficult to see how aboriginal people could be morally devalued (even though they were economically highly valued for the fur trade). The long-standing assumption in European society that human rational beings are intrinsically valuable (valuable and worthwhile in their own right), whereas non-human, non-rational animals are instrumentally valuable (valuable only insofar as they are of some use to human beings) comes into play. If we couple Plato's hierarchy with René Descartes' (1975b) argument in his *Discourse on Method,* we find a tradition in which animals cannot be considered intrinsically valuable because they have no linguistic capacity, a necessary condition for being considered rational. They are, therefore, to be treated as little more than sophisticated machines. And as they are machines, no violation of their interests and rights is possible since they are not the sort of beings capable of having interests and rights. Similarly, aboriginal people, although human, are not fully rational and cannot be accorded the same rights as Europeans. In this way, a world view is instrumental in excluding other cosmological and value systems, by definition, from being recognized as legitimate modes of thought. Since this exclusionary potential can and has been used for purposes of colonization, examining the effects of world views on people is socially, economically, politically and legally significant.

The Greco-Christian Pursuit of Knowledge

Pursuing knowledge under the Greco-Christian world view was likewise governed by the hierarchical structure of reality (see Plato's Divided Line, Figure 1.1). Knowledge gained through the senses (empirical knowledge) was assigned less value than that gained through reason because it apprehends objects lower on the scale of being than does the intellect. At the highest level, God and divine-like creatures contemplate higher-order eternal truths, the sort of truths that are unchanging and known only through pure acts of intellect. However, since the Greeks saw human beings as both intellectual and physical creatures with bodily needs, they acknowledged the value of other forms of knowledge. Scientific thinking (physics, or the study of the physical world), for instance, was deemed important for a practical understanding of how the world worked. How best to irrigate or navigate, to build a bridge or temper steel were considered forms of knowledge required for survival as physical beings. But their practical value could not compete with the value of pure rational knowledge (e.g., mathematics). Aristotle, for instance, drew a distinction between practical wisdom—having primarily to do with moral excellence—and wisdom born of pure reason. True wisdom and the associated happiness for man comes with exercising pure reason, the activity of the Divine. This form of intellectual activity is not shared with the animals but is the exclusive possession of man and God (see especially Aristotle's *Nicomachean Ethics*) (Aristotle 1962: 15–20, or 1177; and 20–25, or 1178). What is important here is not the doctrine of the divine but the exclusive privilege assigned to rational beings. They not only have an exclusive type of happiness; they are also capable of understanding in a qualitatively different way than those of a lower order. This doctrine, then, squares well with the idea that man is created as God's partner and that we were placed on Earth to complete and improve it. Gradually, rationality has become associated with the power to design and plan.

Plato's analogy of the Divided Line asserts that truth in the highest sense is to be found at the level of pure reason, completely divorced from the senses and practical reasoning. While different types of knowledge are possible at different levels of the line, none can boast the certainty, reliability and necessity of the highest level. Knowledge gained at lower levels offers no more than glimpses or shadows of truth. People who would take experiential knowledge as truth fall victim to illusion and delusion. Such "knowledge" is uncertain, unreliable and unnecessary.

Animistic and experience-based belief systems, according to Greek metaphysics and epistemology, are determined by lower forms of knowledge since they rely on divine intervention, signs and revelations or sense experience. Any claims to knowledge based on such experience, including dreams, visions and answers to prayer, are judged to be suspect, if not entirely false. In fact, they are not knowledge at all but mere opinion (*pistis*). True knowledge is not personal but is based on universal impersonal truths.

In his *Meditations* (1964), the Roman emperor Marcus Aurelius followed Aristotle in pursuing the contemplative life as the highest expression of human nature. He saw contemplation of the highest truths as the only pursuit worthy of the human spirit. Contemplation requires isolation from the earthly world and, therefore, requires a degree of insulation from its demands. The pursuit of knowledge has primarily to do with understanding eternal truths and then applying these truths to living in the world. Hence, knowledge flows one way, from the designing mind to the constructed world.

The rational mind, undoubtedly, is the *sine qua non* of intellectual, scientific and technological developments. What we count as greatness in humanity is largely owing to our rational capacities. As naked primates, bereft of the protective fur, swiftness and strength of other animals, our intellectual cum rational capacities have been our key adaption and survival tools. Denying that these capacities are central to how we have survived and come to be the dominant species in the environment is similar to denying that we need oxygen to breathe. The "discovery" of reason, then, has been a key factor in our identity as a species and in our evolutionary adaptiveness.

The Legacy of Greco-Christian Environmental Thought

Clearly, we continue to carry much of the Greco-Christian world view in our modes of thought. We have seen how the transformation from the fear of nature to the assumption of superiority over nature tends to result in deforestation, devaluing of natural systems and redesign of natural systems. Rather than thinking of ourselves as subject to the whims of divine powers, we now think of ourselves as designers of the natural world, rightfully placed because of our superior intellect. This assumption of our place in the world as creators and improvers carries through two thousand years until it finds perhaps its clearest expression in the pioneering attitude of the American frontier. Wilderness is something to be overcome, levelled and tamed as it is converted into productive land. A significant element in U.S. history is the vision of "Manifest Destiny," a call to expand the American way of life across the North American continent. Under this program, the United States has justified the conquering of aboriginal peoples, the liquidation of forests and the annexation of the entire continent from coast to coast. Manifest Destiny is based on the belief that God has ordained America to rule over the continent and perhaps beyond. It justified the Spanish-American War and the Mexican War as well as other acts of aggression during the 19th century.

Such imperialist programs rely on the distinction between "us" and "them." Like Greco-Christian justificatory systems, Manifest Destiny was supported by assumptions of a fundamental dualism between the rational and the non-rational and hierarchy. We see this logic operating as far back as Plato's *Republic* (1974: 373b–374e), especially in Book 2. Socrates justifies support for a standing army and a guardian class, partly to ensure successful annexation of land as the city-state expands. Assumed superiority justifies the redesigning of natural systems because they undergo development or improvement. Likewise, "backward indigenous peoples" are improved through colonization. The attitude is particularly noteworthy when considering the relationship between Manifest Destiny and the Monroe doctrine (1823) (*Reference Encyclopedia* 1998: 926). Monroe, the fifth president of the United States, issued a statement to the European powers to stay out of the western hemisphere, since it was the exclusive right of America to expand into and control it. Implicit in Monroe's statement was the belief that Europeans were at least equal to the Americans as imperialists and conquerors and, therefore, rational or of the same ilk. Aboriginals, deemed savages, were not accorded the same recognition and so could be classified as the colonized, eliminated or dislocated without moral culpability.

Europe's encounter with the new world was an encounter with "untamed nature." Eugene Hargrove (1989) does not describe the emerging America as a land of opportunity where new ideas could be envisaged and implemented; rather, he describes it as a place where aspiring freemen and persecuted Christians could come to exercise their preconceived notions. In tracing the land-tenure system that was promoted by Thomas Jefferson—the *allodial* rights system, in which land was held without obligation to a superior—back to the Saxon freemen of the Norman conquest era in Europe, Hargrove (1989: 57–63) demonstrates that the westward march across North America was principally about imposing European legal and political systems, not to mention agricultural and forestry systems, onto North America. While there are complicated legal and historical issues to consider in a full understanding of just what was assumed in Jefferson's land-tenure system, it is clear that the westward march was based on a system of thinking that assumed the land to be of value only after it was cultivated by farmers, God's chosen people (Jefferson 1975: 217). Just as Manifest Destiny was seen as a heavenly sanctioned duty, the taming of the environment and its wildness was seen as part of the vocation or purpose of the European and American conquerors. This view was largely responsible for the attitude toward predator species as well. Large predators, such as the wolf, were typically characterized as evil competitors and were eradicated from the American landscape; such predators in Europe had been eradicated long before. Forests were considered wasted unless exploited for lumber and agricultural land, as was the received view during the Roosevelt era (at the end of the 19th century) under the new Forest Service adviser, Gifford Pinchot. Rational management and use of forests meant that forests not used for timber were being abhorrently wasted (Hargrove 1989: 79–80). If resources could not be used for commodities, they were often used for sport or targeted for alternative development. The wanton destruction of the buffalo herds of the midwest prairies took less than ten years; they were slaughtered first for their tails and tongues but later simply for sport. As the railway went through the west, piles of buffalo bones could be seen lining the railway (Hargrove 1989: 112–14). Similarly, the wanton slaughter of sturgeon (a fish sacred to the Ojibway of the region) was carried out at around the same time in the Georgian Bay area of Southern Ontario.

An instruction to the lieutenant-governor of the Northwest Territories after the cession of Rupert's Land is noteworthy for the attitude that imperialism engendered.

> Turn attention promptly toward North and West assuring Indians of your desire to establish friendly relations with them, you will ascertain and report to His Excellency the course you may think most advisable to pursue, whether by treaty or otherwise, for the removal of any obstructions that might be presented to the flow of population into the fertile lands that lie between Manitoba and the Rocky Mountains. (Canada, Sessional Papers 1871: no. 20, pg. 8, cited in Berger 1988: 218)

Since imperialism was accompanied by a religious fervour to convert aboriginal people, the assumed sovereignty of British (later Canadian) and American governments was an expression of presumed superiority over whatever was indigenous. It justified the exclusion of aboriginal people from the moral, political and legal community in the minds of governors, policy makers, settlers and the military. Sovereignty was later used to justify the social engineering agenda of assimilation programs.

Ecofeminists view the subjugation of nature and the subjugation of women as being of the same sort. Karen Warren (1998: 472), for example, argues that the conceptual framework of the dominant system of thought is itself oppressive. A forced association between rationality and maleness operates in the same way as the forced association between rationality and European-based social and political systems. The presumptions of male superiority and privilege that this forcing is used to justify is closely tied to assumptions of superiority over things indigenous. The idea that women are closely connected to the earth, and therefore irrational and emotive, is tied deeply to this overall justificatory scheme. The ramifications of Plato's Divided Line, then, reach far into the political, social, ethical and philosophical sensibilities of Western culture.

This historical examination of the shift from an animistic to a Greco-Christian world view has introduced a number of key factors for later analysis. The main factor has been the emergence of reason as the foundation for understanding, knowledge, value and legitimacy. In this latter role, reason supplants individual authority, intuition, revelation, insight and the like. Religious, economic, social and political factors in this emergence have been introduced to indicate how different conceptions of reason and associations with these factors have had far-reaching effects, whether or not they are justified. This association sets the stage for a discussion on the nature of reason, with what it has been associated and how it has been used to exclude other forms of understanding and knowing that bear on the way people understand and direct their relationship with the environment. We have identified some of the roots of the detachment of "man" from nature through the detachment of reason from nature. This detachment has been tied to the ways in which the West has conceived and justified its dominance of nature and other cultures. We have also begun to identify the network of assumptions that have led to the presently deeply ingrained ideas of the right of humanity to control the environment, the tendency to objectify and commodify all but human, rational, male and European beings. At the same time, the emergence of reason has increased predictive powers and elegance (effective simplicity) in explanation and has planted the seeds of democratization. As we turn to examine the transition to the Modern world view, we see how the relationship between reason and superiority becomes extreme, resulting in a concomitant extreme in the sense of detachment.

Notes

1. There are two people who go by this name. Black Elk, sometimes cited as Nick Black Elk, and Wallace Black Elk, to whom I refer here, were both shamans of the Oglala Sioux.
2. While we focus on Western thought, even a cursory examination of Eastern thought, especially as it arose in India, clearly reveals that the concepts of mind, person and intellect were developed considerably earlier there than in the West. The distinction between *atman* (self) and *anatman* (the non-self) is a case in point. This "discovery" of the mind in the West is based on a different set of concepts than it is in the East and is far more focused on rational intellectual processes.
3. Just about any introduction to early Greek philosophy or the history of philosophy will provide a fuller account of the development of Ionian and Eleatic thought (below). John Burnet's *Early Greek Philosophy*, John Mansley Robinson's *An Introduction to Early Greek Philosophy* are good examples of the former; Frederick Copleston's *History of Philosophy: Vol. 1* is a good example of the latter.
4. Glacken (1967) spends a great deal of time demonstrating how the Christian tradition is far more in line with notions of an ecological community than is often acknowledged. Using biblical references and teachings of the saints and church fathers, he shows how a sense of solidarity with the "natural world" is in keeping with Christian doctrine. While debate lingers over what the actual Christian view is, my focus will be on the more general effects that dualistic and hierarchical metaphysical commitments had on the West's conceptions of the environment and the practices that these conceptions either motivated or supported.

Chapter Two

The Copernican Revolution, Mechanism and the Modern World View

Transition from the Finite Cosmos to the Infinite Universe

Nicholas Copernicus in writing *De Revolutionibus Orbium Coelestium* became a focal point for a cosmological revolution, which had effects as far-reaching as those of Ptolemy's system. Copernicus argued that placing the Earth at the centre of the cosmos is not the most suitable for astronomical explanations. It would be better and more elegant in the explanatory scheme to place the Sun at the centre and the Earth as one of the planets revolving around the Sun. For many technical reasons, Copernicus' own work does not achieve this elegance, since it requires as much complexity as the Ptolemaic system. Later students, however, did achieve greater elegance after making adjustments to Copernicus' theory. They placed the Sun at the centre of what was thought, during this time, to be the universe, which implies that the Earth is but one of the planets; they reasoned that, if the Earth is a planet, it does not remain stationary, but moves (Kuhn 1985: 181–82).

These Copernicans come to face strong opposition for reasons that become clear once we understand the implications of this new astronomical theory for other areas of inquiry. Ptolemy and Copernicus were primarily astronomers, not cosmologists. Cosmology, here defined as the explanatory concepts and principles for why things operate as they do in the cosmos, is contrasted with astronomy, which deals more with the mathematical description of the movements of the celestial sphere. What may seem a mere technical change in astronomy can engender a monumental change in cosmology, however, especially when the two are tied as closely as they were in the Ptolemaic system. Just as astronomy, astrology and cosmology were closely tied, so too were social theory, politics, epistemology and value theory tied to cosmology. A change in astronomy, then, could have a considerable effect on all other areas of thought. The move to a heliocentric system in astronomy had just such an impact on cosmology because, to accommodate the shift in centres, explanations of the structure and function of the cosmos also had to change. First, the centre, as under the Ptolemaic system, is supposed to be the lowest part of the cosmos, a dark, cold place; the Sun is not that. Second, the hierarchical ordering of the planets is now disturbed, undermining the neat correspondence between levels of reality and levels of knowing. Third, where the neat hierarchical structure comes under question, so too does the assumption of a limited cosmos. Copernicus himself did not accept the notion of an infinite universe, but his pupils and successors (e.g., Thomas Digges and Giordano Bruno[1]) saw few reasons to resist it.

By moving the Sun to the centre, the centre could no longer be assumed to be the cold, dark place nor the object of desire for heavy matter. Since the Sun was associated with the high and divine, neither could the centre be the location of the corrupt. With Ptolemaic assumptions under attack, the Great Chain of Being was threatened. By implication, so too were the social, political and ethical hierarchies connected to it.

The development of the concept of the infinite universe was even more damaging. According to the Greco-Christian world view, infinity is impossible because it is unintelligible. Aristotle argues that infinity is inconceivable. In an infinite series of events, he argues, there can be no initial starting point. But if there is no first point from which a series begins (e.g., movement), there can be no series at all. Thus, there must exist a first event or point from which all series begin. An infinite regress in a series is, therefore, impossible. Denying the possibility of infinity means everything has limits and everything is bounded. Thus, the only sensible way to speak about the cosmos is as a finite extension. All that exists in a bounded universe can be accounted for and explained, at least in principle. The idea of an infinite universe profoundly undermines such confidence. In an infinite universe, there are no bounds nor ultimate limitations; there can be no centre nor absolute point of reference for judging where things are situated.

As Kuhn (1985: 109) describes, for thinkers of the Middle Ages, the Aristotelian-Ptolemaic conception of the universe was the received view. Kuhn calls this view the "two-sphere universe," with the stars, planets and Sun forming the outer sphere of the gods, and Earth forming the inner sphere of man and corrupt matter. This cosmology lasted in some form or other for approximately eighteen hundred years. Unlike the resistance to animistic cosmologies, resistance to Copernican cosmology was owing to religious and scholastic rigidity. By this point in history, the universities, which had not been established at the time of the pre-Socratics and Socrates, had been established by the church. Consequently, the shift to a Copernican view was much more difficult and faced more powerful enemies than did the Ptolemaic view. Without the concerted effort of the intellectual community to develop the Copernican system into an intellectually coherent and better explanatory system than the Ptolemaic, the shift likely would have failed, or it would have happened much more slowly. Indeed, it took great effort on the part of those following Copernicus (who, himself, remained principally Ptolemaic) to work out the implications of Copernicus' writings (Kuhn 1985: 182–83).

Resistance came from every corner, from popular poets to the Protestant church fathers (Luther and Calvin) and the Catholic church (Kuhn 1985: 189–93). For criticism of the Ptolemaic world view to be effective, a combination of intellectual rigour, political savvy, courage and conviction and a network of supporters were needed. Suggestions that the Earth moves, either on its axis or in its orbit around the Sun, were viewed as nonsense and heresy, contradictory to both Aristotle ("The Philosopher") and the Bible. Some advocates of the idea, such as Giordano Bruno, a successor of Copernicus, were burned at the stake for such heresy. The degree of resistance to the Copernican Revolution indicates the depth and extent of the changes that were afoot.

Aristotle himself implicitly attempted to address the problems that were eventually to undermine his system. One such problem can be formulated as follows (see McKeon 1941: 417–18 (Aristotle 178b:23–279a:15)): "If one reaches the outermost limits of space and stretches one's hand through the outer casing, what happens to the hand?" Many solutions were considered, such as "the hand ceases to exist" or, better, "it is an impossible question to answer because no one can stretch beyond the limits of the universe by definition." Such replies try the patience of critical thinkers because they avoid addressing the question instead of offering a solution. "How," it might be asked, "should my hand simply cease to exist? If the universe is bounded, it must be bounded by something. And it would be into that something that I would be stretching my hand. My hand, therefore, would not cease to exist." Or if it were asked, "On what grounds can one claim that my question is unintelligible?" believers in the finite universe readily would find themselves caught in assuming what they needed to prove. To say that my question is unintelligible is to assert that only questions that assume the universe to be finite are intelligible. With the advent of the heliocentric universe, the time was ripe for the conception of an infinite universe to supplant that of the finite.

Discussing Aristotle shows how many of the reasons for paradigm shifts are contained in the paradigm itself. Anomalies, or unsolvable difficulties in explanation, together with what come to look like ridiculous solutions to problems, also pave the way for developing new explanatory concepts. An idea like the infinite universe dissolves the puzzle of sticking one's hand beyond the limits of the universe because the problem does not arise. In part, the Copernican shift owes much of its success to the elegance in explanation that an infinite universe affords.

Another problem that the new astronomy solves has to do with retrograde motion of the planets. Under the geocentric scheme, explanations of celestial movements was quite simple because stars, in particular, seemed consistently to repeat the same paths. They appeared to travel around the Earth in perfect circular orbits. The planets, or wandering stars, were a different matter. They did not travel in perfect orbits around the Earth but reversed their path (retrograde motion) periodically. If the circle is a perfect shape, and the gods who live in the outer spheres are supposed to be perfect beings, it should not be possible for the planets to deviate from travel in perfect circles. Ingenious explanations were attempted and accepted for the duration of the Ptolemaic scheme. One explanation has already been noted: deviations in the planetary paths reflect the activity of the gods as they act on the Earth. Deviations from perfect circularity were thought to be circles within circles, forming epicycles. These epicycles could be mathematically described and their occurrence predicted, which enabled Ptolemaic astronomers to provide a somewhat rigorous account of celestial motion. Even so, such explanations required stretching one's conception of perfection, since epicycles are, however mathematically predictable, nevertheless, deviations from perfect circularity.

Copernicus himself retains epicycles in his theory,[2] but his successors abandon the idea, since epicycle theory can be shown to be superfluous. Retrograde motion can be explained as a matter of perspective. If the Sun is assumed to be at the centre and the Earth is assumed to be one of the planets revolving around it, then the Earth travels in one of several spheres around the Sun. Since it takes longer for a planet farther from the Sun to travel through its revolution, the Earth will "catch up" to it during its cycle. During this catch up period, an observer on Earth will perceive that the outer planet (e.g., Mars) apparently slows down. As Earth passes Mars, Mars will appear to stop and then move backwards. The phenomenon is similar to looking out the window of a parked car and being tricked into believing your car is moving. Upon examining the situation, you realize that the other car is moving. You realize that it is your perspective that creates the sensation of moving. Similarly, planetary retrograde motion can be explained as an appearance of reversal that is owing to the position and movement of the observer relative to the observed planet. This explanation, then, is more elegant than the old geocentric cosmology because it simplifies the number of principles and causes involved in explaining planetary motion.

Once the idea of an infinite universe was accepted, no centre to the universe could be posited because an infinity has neither centre nor edge. An ultimate point of reference from which to determine the location of things could find no support in the new cosmology. Although some tried to argue that the Sun simply replaced the Earth as the centre, thereby retaining the idea of a finite universe, the argument was a feeble attempt at salvaging the old system. Because the concept of a finite cosmos could not do the explanatory work that the concept of an infinite system could, the finite cosmos came into disrepute. The implications for metaphysics, epistemology and axiology were profound, as the grand unified Ptolemaic system began to crumble.

Contributing to the diminution of the Ptolemaic system were Galileo's discoveries concerning the heavens using the recently invented telescope. New stars were discovered with the aid of magnification, as others were observed to disappear (what we now call "novas"); comets and meteors were observed crossing the skies in what appeared to be non-circular paths. New challenges to the Ptolemaic system had to be addressed. Under the established system, the stars were thought to be permanent and equidistant from the Earth; some were just smaller than others. These new observations made it difficult to explain how the supposed perfect sphere of the gods could admit changes (disappearance of stars) and non-circular pathways. Novas directly contradicted the permanence of the heavens; comets and meteors contradicted the completeness of the heavens.

Yet another factor in the demise of the old system was the problem of space. According to Aristotle, the notion of empty space, a vacuum, was unintelligible and inconceivable. The Greek's logic went something like this: that which is not cannot exist; empty space is that in which nothing exists, and so in itself, it cannot exist. The Ancients and, indeed, thinkers for centuries afterward rejected the existence of space as a void or a vacuum. For example, in the 1600s Descartes' *Principia Philosophiae* (1905: pt. 2, sect. 10) defined space as the relations between bodies, so that if bodies cease to exist, so too does space. Space must be filled with an invisible something or other, called "ether"; only according to such a conception can talk about space be free of self-contradiction. So, when an arrow is shot through the air, it literally cuts through the ether, which, as soon as the arrow passes, flows back around the arrow so as not to leave any emptiness behind.

If space is filled and solid, however, movement is difficult to explain because it logically should be impossible. Defenders of the old paradigm may suggest that the ether is thinner in some places than in others, which leaves room for solid objects to compress the ether, allowing for the displacement of bodies from one place to another. Like epicycles, however, ether theory strains the patience and invites a better theory to supplant it.

Galileo all but puts an end to the ether theory. His vacuum experiments demonstrate that it is possible for a coin and feather to fall toward the Earth at a uniform rate. The ether theory predicts that they should fall at different rates, since a coin is thicker and heavier than a feather and exerts greater force on the ether, compressing it more readily. Since it can be shown that coins and feathers fall at a uniform rate in these vacuum tubes, it is more intelligible to suppose that, when pumping the air out of a glass cylinder, one is actually creating a void, such that neither the coin nor the feather encounters anything to resist its motion. The absence of resistance implies that there is nothing in the bottle to offer resistance. Hence, the idea of a void finds residence in the realm of explanatory concepts and awaits a general theory to make sense of it.[3]

The idea of empty space did not enjoy ready acceptance. Even the great astronomer Johannes Kepler, a post-Galilean, refused to believe in space as a void, a "nothing." To be consistent with his Christian beliefs, he asserted that God created the world from nothing; it would have been pointless for Him to create nothing from nothing. Hence, space must be some "thing." Despite Kepler's considerable influence, the cumbersome explanations of the Ptolemaic system together with Galileo's counterexample planted the seeds for accepting the notion of a void in spatial relationships. Furthermore, the notions of empty space and infinity cohere. Together they make it possible to conceive of an infinitely extending void, even beyond the stars. An ether theory does not cohere well with the idea of infinity, since all known material things are bounded or have a limited extension. Their sum total would also have to be bounded.

Resistance to change and shifts in fundamental concepts on the part of Kepler and Descartes motivated proponents of the Copernican paradigm to articulate their arguments more clearly and forcefully, creating an atmosphere in which ideas were refined and developed more rigorously. Galileo was motivated to invent an experiment that would prove the possibility of vacuums. Sir Isaac Newton later developed the idea of an infinite space/time grid to describe his new view of the universe. This period in history is particularly illustrative of how we will invent the language necessary to house ideas when we are compelled by lacunae in our explanatory capacity. We might even characterize the motivation toward the invention of language as "rational desire." It is driven by the desire for greater explanatory power, which involves greater comprehensiveness, coherence, consistency, simplicity and correspondence to the facts of experience. Eventually, a new paradigm has to develop as the demands for including new concepts makes retaining belief in the old system intolerable. By Newton's time, the new ideas had been accepted, and it was virtually impossible to think of the universe as limited.

By this point, the Copernican system had almost completely replaced the Ptolemaic system among the scientific/philosophical community. A new way of understanding humanity and its relationship to nature was also under way. Since the Greco-Christian system was one in which metaphysics, epistemology and axiology were integrated, shifts in thinking in one area meant a shift in the others. Shifts in astronomy would likely require shifts in religious belief, alterations in the foundations of science (knowledge), political authority, ethical values and social relationships. This pressure is well illustrated in the effects on the theory of knowledge.

Knowledge and the Materio-mechanism

Galileo's vacuum experiments serve as paradigm cases for the emerging form of knowing characterized as "modern science." For the first time, appeal to textual authority (e.g., the Bible or the Philosopher) is rejected in favour of experimentation (Kuhn 1985: 95), undermining the authority of the Ancients and the church. Whereas the Ptolemaic system was upheld by two important pillars—observation of the heavens and religious authority—the emerging world view undermined naive observation and challenged authority. It brought with it the birth of new-found powers of explanation and a more democratic system of legitimating knowledge claims. The new approach to knowledge depended largely on technological developments, e.g., devices to create a vacuum and telescopes. It was not a passive form of observation, but one aided by devices that enabled controlled manipulation of the objects to be observed and expansion of observational capacity.

These developments, coupled with an ever-increasing ability to describe events mathematically, opened the door to the mechanistic theory of the universe, a geometrically ordered and mathematically describable machine. It was Sir Isaac Newton who placed the finishing touches on the Copernican cosmology and created a mechanistic picture of the universe. He described the universe in terms of mathematically describable sectors. Physical bodies were thought to be governed not by spiritual forces, but by impersonal laws of gravity and motion. Although Newton had difficulties trying to explain this force of gravity and could not entirely rid his theory of "occult qualities" (inexplicable properties, e.g., desire for the centre of the Earth) to which animism and the Ptolemaic system appealed, he did pave the way toward a purely mechanistic cum mathematical description of the universe. Insofar as his system was successful in predicting events (e.g., the path of the planets and other celestial bodies as well as terrestrial events) it suggested the possibility of a comprehensive, powerful yet elegant theory of reality based on a few simple concepts and principles.

The difference between the laws of the mechanistic universe and the principles of Greek philosophy rests on the meaning of cause and effect. For the Greek, cause and effect were matters of desire and following the Good or God in some ultimate sense. The Good in some way was seen to be the ultimate cause of coming into being and of motion. God's causal powers, however, were occult qualities. By definition, it was never entirely possible to predict how God would cause things to occur or how these causes operated. For the mechanist, laws could be mathematically described and events predicted, at least in principle, with mathematical precision. Occult qualities were not only no longer needed, appeals to them were considered bad thinking. Thinking about causality using mathematical formulae is law-like, precise, clearly formulated and powerful with respect to predictability. Appeals to occult qualities, such as motivations of spiritual agents or desire, simply could not compete against the growing success of the mechanistic model. Appeals to God in explanations, if they were to be made in a scientifically acceptable way, would see God as a watchmaker who may have created the universe and set it in motion but who since has left it running in accordance with the laws of physics.

An important step forward was taken during this period. It no longer seemed necessary to provide a metaphysical explanation for motion or for the workings of the universe (e.g., as in appeals to ultimate teleological causes and forms); the ability to predict events and control conditions made such appeals seem irrelevant. It became more important to explain how events occur, rather than why they occur. Today, in what might be called "normal" science, it is not important to know why laws are the way they are; it is important to know only what the laws are and how they are to be applied, once discovered and proven reliable. In a way, reliability and predictability replace truth, at least as it was conceived by the ancient philosophers. The shift to the Modern world view amounts to what may be called "a denial of metaphysics." This shift in effect substitutes questions that seek ultimate explanations for questions that seek to disclose the mechanics of motion and change, which is to define knowledge in terms of having power to manipulate, control and predict, without having to appeal to ultimate realities and authorities. Indeed, science is a body of forward-looking knowledge increments, which grows through the contributions of individuals as they experiment and develop predictive models on the basis of these experiments. In former times, knowledge was backward-looking to the wisdom of the past, as embodied in sages and authorities. In this way, progressiveness became associated with the new science, and regressiveness with the old.

One of the key figures who helped establish the Modern world view was Sir Francis Bacon (*The New Organon*). The English philosopher argued that the world, like human nature, does not yield information about itself until it is placed under duress or vexation. When it is troubled, or "placed under the vexations of art" (i.e., artisanry or technology), nature yields information; otherwise it remains silent. As we impose stress on nature, we can learn from its reactions (Bacon 1955: Aphorism, 98). Here, we see another aspect of the experimental method taking shape. Vexation is the classical term for what we call manipulation of variables. It is contrasted not only with passive observation as a method of inquiry, but with having to appease spiritual agents, whether animistic or theistic. Understanding nature has become a matter of manipulating variables and controlling initial conditions, a process best accomplished in the laboratory. Good mathematical descriptions depend on being able to provide accurate measurements of the effects of the vexations placed on nature. Hence, establishing well-controlled experimental conditions has become necessary for good science.

The Modern approach to knowledge is also materialist in the sense that it is based on the belief that matter is what fundamentally exists. Spiritual, non-measurable entities are irrelevant. Matter is made of discrete bits that somehow attach to one another to form composite bodies. Discovering how these attachments occur is important; figuring out why they occur ultimately is not. Although materialism had been entertained since well before Socrates (Democritus was the leading champion of the theory during ancient times), it lacked the methodological and technological approaches that Bacon, Galileo and Newton brought to it. Whereas under the Ptolemaic hierarchical system matter was considered a low form of reality, under the new system it was the only thing that counted. The last remnants of the Greco-Christian distinction between the heavens and the Earth were dissolved. This Modern system had its golden age during the Industrial Revolution in the 1800s, when monumental technological advances occurred, especially in relation to modes of production and medicine. For example, the invention of the microscope proved that bodies could be carved up into finer and finer parts, even to microscopic dimensions. Disease was revealed to be the result of germs (the so-called "germ theory") and not the will of God or some such occult explanation. The conceptual shift to materialism and the concomitant shift to technology-based knowledge acquisition advanced the treatment of natural systems as repositories of raw material for the purposes of production, the diagnosis of disease and the development of therapeutic techniques. After millennia of occult-based medicine (e.g., healing based on prayer, the royal touch and alchemy), the change to a mechanical theory of medicine proved irresistible.

The world now became a place in which the essential nature of the relationships between bodies was mathematically describable. Newton's three laws of physics are a prime example. They describe the "laws" of the universe according to which all events are to be described. Coupling the idea of lifeless matter and the explanatory power of mathematical description offered a way to describe the universe as a material mechanism operating according to strict laws. The model for this mechanism is the machine. Machines can be systematically broken down into component parts and reconstructed. Physical objects (e.g., iron ore) can be broken down into constituent elements and reconstructed to form new objects (e.g., steel). All motion and change can be explained using the relations between billiard balls as a model. The structure and functioning of all things, then, are assumed to be explicable in terms of the mechanism of nature.

The power of the emerging scientific paradigm led thinkers to believe that all forms of explanation could ultimately be "reduced" to one primitive level (typically to physics). Psychological events could be explained in terms of biology, which could be explained in terms of chemistry and finally physics. Chemistry and biology simply described higher levels of complexity of organized particles, much like the term "drive train" describes the part of an automobile from the motor through to the transmission gears that drive the wheels. Nothing is gained by calling the whole complex of parts a "drive train," other than economy of expression. We can explain what a thing is and how it works by examining the component parts and relating them one by one to see how they form the whole, but it is far more practical to use a larger unit of reference. Similarly, we can describe a complex object in terms of its atomic components, but it is far more convenient to talk about molecules, organisms and communities.

Often, the mechanistic approach is described as hard, rigorous, clear and reliable, while non-materialist theories are described as soft, subjective, confused and unreliable. Materialism promises to provide clearly defined problems and solutions based on quantification of data (e.g., statistics and formulae), rather than on qualitative explanation (e.g., authority and personal experience).

Mechanistic theories clearly assume the superiority of reason (which is modelled on mathematics) for knowledge acquisition. But in the transition to the Modern world view, the idea of reason took on a different meaning and significance. Consequently, reason is no longer principally the capacity to contemplate the divine or to see into deeper explanations for why the world is as it is. In part what has happened is that Modernity has retained the formal nature of reason—its rule-like, discursive and systematic properties—and rejected its more contemplative properties, which propel thought toward the penetration of ultimate truths. In a way, reason has lost some of its self-critical capacity as the success of the mechanistic model increases, seemingly obviating the need for self-criticism.

The New Attitude of Dominance

The development of the Copernican cosmology into a full-blown mechanistic view of the world involved a radical separation of what were once integrated areas of life under the Ptolemaic world view. Since knowledge in the scientific sense was taken as the basis for the empire of "man" and had little or nothing to do with religion and the authority of the Ancients

(Bacon 1955: Aphorisms 129 and 84, respectively), the coherence of the former system was lost. If anything was left of the ancient influence, it no longer had to do with knowledge. Consequently, knowledge about the environment, qua mechanism of nature, had nothing to do with religion or ethics. On the one hand, conceptions of the physical environment were freed from their classification as belonging to the low and corrupt. On the other hand, they now belonged to and were shaped by a system of thought that took the environment to be a lifeless object devoid of spiritual properties. Non-rational nature was seen as a value-neutral object, open to capricious exploitation. Its once ambiguous status—as both good in the eyes of God and as low and corrupt—had been transformed into something unambiguously valueless.

With the new mechanistic model and experimental method, the environment became an object to be studied, manipulated, controlled and subjected to human purpose. If we examine the underlying assumptions of scientific method, we see how deeply the environment becomes an object for manipulation. The scientific method is based on testing hypotheses by setting up experiments that should, in principle, be repeatable. If the experiment cannot be repeated or if knowledge claims cannot be tested, they are not open to falsification. Knowledge claims based on authority, in contrast, cannot be falsified, precisely because they are authority-based. Not just anybody can test the verity of authority-based claims. Hence, knowledge about the environment was associated with special status.

Scientific method accepts no special status and no ultimate barrier to forcing nature to reveal its secrets. Testing hypotheses and repeating experiments (vexations of nature) require that the experimenter qua scientist hold no obeisance to authority and no moral respect for the object of study. The experimenter must be free to manipulate the object of study to discover its properties. Where a problem of understanding arises, the experimenter needs to be free to do what is necessary to solve that problem, irrespective of any moral or religious feelings he or she might have toward the object of study. Hence, a radical split between the epistemological stance taken toward the object of study and the moral stance can arise. We have seen such splits in cases where experiments on prisoners of war (for example, in testing brainwashing or interrogation techniques) bring experimental objectives into conflict with moral restrictions.

Experimental method and the principle that a hypothesis must be open to falsification are responses to scepticism. Authority-based knowledge claims are not. No evidence can be brought to bear against such knowledge claims if those claims are based on assertions of privileged access, unless an authority of equal stature contests the initial authority. Even where knowledge claims prove to be false (e.g., where a prophecy concerning future events turns out not to occur), we would find a way to explain the failure (e.g., by claiming that the will of God cannot be fathomed or that the sins of the people caused God to change His mind). But here scepticism naturally arises, since such rationalizations are not answers to the questions posed. If they cannot be proven true or false (i.e., if they are closed to scrutiny), then they will be seen as arbitrary and fabricated, especially by those who stand outside the system of beliefs. And those who stand outside the system will not only doubt, but will have no reason to believe. This places the believer in a position where verification and producing evidence for claims becomes necessary if the unbeliever is to be made to believe. The unbeliever, in turn, will constantly try to falsify the claims of the believer by introducing contrary evidence or reasons to dismiss the evidence that the believer presents. An instance of the latter is the strategy of showing that there may be equally plausible alternative explanations for an event occurring (e.g., the fact that rain fell after it was prophesied to fall could be explained as the result of a low-pressure front coming through an area).

The experimental method responds to the sceptic by establishing the experiment as a possible tool of falsification and as a tool for eliminating other possible explanations. A well-designed and well-controlled experiment will show a hypothesis to be false if the predicted outcomes do not occur. Insofar as a knowledge claim must answer to the sceptic by always being open to falsification, openness to the types of experiments that might falsify a claim must be maintained. Controlling initial conditions ensures that the actual cause of an effect is identified, eliminating the possibility of alternative causes. In this way, the mode of inquiry in modern science is directed by scepticism.

Scepticism, supported by the experimental method, must then devalue other approaches to knowledge. Ways of knowing based on intimate familiarity with a region are deemed idiosyncratic and subjective because they are not the results of well-controlled experiments and methodologically rigorous testing. They are "soft" forms of knowledge, better characterized as intuitions or guess-work than as knowledge. What is worth knowing and what properties of nature are worth examining are determined by their ability to be tested against scepticism. It comes as no surprise, then, that the development of the scientific method has promoted the training of our epistemic sensibilities to accept measurable quantities as the basis for evidence. Non-measurable, qualitative evidence (e.g., people's experience) either cannot count, or it counts much less. The Modern Era has promoted acceptance of only this one type of knowledge and this one access point to knowledge (the experimental method).

As a system of thought that assumes the necessity of controlling and manipulating the environment in whatever manner is necessary to extract information, it implicitly requires dominance over the environment rather than passive acceptance of its conditions. Scepticism, when seen in the light of developments in modern science, then, requires domination over the environment without limit.

Fragmenting Spheres of Inquiry

Scientific modes of knowing have been separated from other ways of knowing (e.g., as in religion, ethics and spirituality) in a way that has deeply fragmented influences on environmental thought. According to the Ptolemaic system, all modes of thought were conceived under one grand scheme, but the shift to Modernity undermined the solidarity of areas of inquiry, dividing knowledge into distinct arenas. The separation of the epistemic and moral spheres is mirrored in the separation of church and state, wherein authority-based claims (called "beliefs") are confined to matters of religion and the private sphere, while science or empirically based claims (called "knowledge") are public. Moral sensitivity toward the land, consequently, is to be treated as private and idiosyncratic.

Fragmentation took other forms as well. No longer could one comprehensive epistemological system integrate all forms of knowledge as different methodologies and bodies of knowledge arose, and continue to arise, to address the many types of problems we wish to solve. Private problems were to be handled differently from those that were public, and problems concerning religion and morality were subject to different modes of inquiry than were the experimental sciences. Various areas of inquiry were either separated from philosophy (e.g., natural science and mathematics), or they were developed in response to particular informational needs (e.g., medicine). More and more areas of inquiry evolved in response to particular problems, developing their own methodologies, bodies of data and, to a more limited extent, criteria of legitimacy. The result has been that those who remain untrained in the discipline remain excluded from discussing the validity and significance of results, hence the emergence of the type of insularity and professionalized perceptions Hough describes (see the Introduction). Part of the reason for this fragmentation is that there is no compulsion to make each area and method of inquiry conform to a grand unifying theory.

This fragmentation is related to a more general enjoyment of freedom from a comprehensive system of accountability, something to which those under the Ptolemaic system were subject. This, coupled with the Modern neutralization of the value of nature, allowed various groups to see and treat the environment according to special interests with overall accountability neither to a central authority nor to criteria of legitimacy. It should be no surprise, then, that the "environmental problem" is identified in such diverse ways. Different sectors focus on different problems, resulting in different proposed solutions. Some see the problem principally as a technological problem requiring repair, while others see it as a moral problem requiring rectification. Some see it as an economic problem requiring fairer trade practices, and others see it as a moral problem requiring a new ethic to address environmental responsibilities.

Observer Status

Perhaps a more important effect of the emerging world view and approach to knowledge was the growing tendency of human beings to think of themselves as detached observers. The separability thesis initiated in Antiquity was taken to its extreme in the Modern Era. The idea that we as rational beings are capable of detached, unbiased observation and explanation of the environment was supported by the new-found powers of science. Describing events in the world in terms of formulae and mechanisms achieves this objectivity. The relationship between the human being who uses objects in the world and the objects themselves becomes more explicitly and clearly formulated as one between subject (person) and object (non-person). The use of Modern science's methodologies, which were complemented by the Greco-Christian idea of an ontologically distinct rational being, deepened the assumption of detachment. It began to seem obvious that no essential connection existed between rational observers and the physical bodies that are observed, experimented on and exploited.

This movement toward an increasing detachment from the earth destroyed all sense of purpose, meaning and value for many of the time period. As John Donne (1929: 365) remorsefully puts it:

> New Philosophy calls all in doubt.
> The Element of Fire is quite put out;
> The Sun is lost, and th'Earth, and no man's wit
> Can well direct him where to looke for it.
> And freely men confess that this world's spent,
> When the Planets and the Firmament
> They seek so many new, then see that this
> Is crumbled out again to his Atomies.
> 'Tis all in peeces, all cohaerence gone;
> All just supply and all Relation.

For others, however, the new order offered new opportunities. Belief in the ability to be objective as an observer in alliance with conceptions of nature as a mechanism allowed people to think of themselves as freed from authority and to define their own realities in their disciplines, private worlds and social groups. Freedom to exploit their environments in accordance with these realities came as a matter of course.

Even in the Christian tradition, often blamed for causing the exploitive attitudes of Modern society, separation and detachment are not absolute because ultimate accountability to a supreme being implies a responsibility to care for its creation. As noted, the idea that the earth is the Lord's ultimately limits and shapes exploitive interests. Even deforestation for the sake of growing vineyards resulted more in replacement ecosystems than in uncontrolled extraction. Most of the Modern and contemporary approaches to deforestation, mining and other forms of exploitation, however, are carried out without ever imagining a replacement ecosystem or accountability to a greater authority. The sense of detachment as observers has much to do with this attitude because it is shaped in response to becoming freed from authority and from attachment to the land.

The advent of the Modern period can be viewed as a time when humanity began to exercise fully its power of reason. Initially, humans saw themselves as having been given this new-found power over the universe by the Creator (see, for example, Bacon 1955: Aphorism 129). Sir Thomas Browne, in the 17th century, said that the world

> was made to be inhabited by Beasts, but studied and contemplated by Man; 'tis the debt of our Reason we owe unto God, and the homage we pay for not being Beasts; without this, the world is still as though it had not been, or as it was before the sixth day, when as yet there was not a Creature that could conceive, or say there was a world. (1956: pt. 1, sect. 27, 27 & sect. 13, 24)

Creation is given meaning by virtue of man's reasoning and study. Browne was saying that "nature" is virtually made by the rational mind. At first glance, this creation of nature may seem only an extension of the medieval program of deforestation to establish vineyards or to complete God's work of creation. It may appear more like *noblesse oblige* to improve and complete the otherwise brutish and meaningless nature (see also Sir Matthew Hale, 1677, *The Primitive Origination of Mankind*). But we must not lose sight of the fact that God is being removed from the picture and that the value scheme motivating the engineering of the environment is also undergoing change. The new engineering approach to the environment is both quantitatively greater and qualitatively different from the type of engineering hitherto seen. Massive development of canals for agriculture and land reclamation as well as deforestation for everything from shipbuilding (during the Age of Discovery and beyond) to smelting begins to occur during the Modern Era as Europe gains mastery over the world.

The distinctiveness and power of the rational mind implied in Bacon's and Browne's assertions speaks to an even more radical separateness of mind from the physical world. Indeed, it supports the belief that only human rational beings are capable of feeling, valuing and experiencing. Descartes (1975b: pt. 5, pgs. 116–17) asserts that non-human animals are incapable of feeling pain because they, like all bodies, are governed strictly by the mechanics of material nature. They are machines, and machines cannot feel. Experimentation on animals using vivisection techniques was thought to be like taking apart a clock to study its inner workings. Unlike Plato, who in his distinction between rational and non-rational beings held that even the lowliest in nature was imbued with spiritual elements, Descartes denied non-rational beings spiritual or subjective properties. He, therefore, widened the divide between human and non-human beings. In his sixth meditation (1975b: 190), Descartes explicitly argues: "It is this I [mind or soul] which is entirely and absolutely distinct from my body, and can exist without it." The human body is a material thing, but the mind is separate, directing the body like a pilot steering a ship. Descartes also helped establish the valuational difference between mind and body, the difference between seeing physical nature as a corrupted, lower level of existence and seeing it as value-neutral matter flowing in space and time. For the Modern, detachment was absolute. The rational mind was not only thought to be separate from the physical mechanism of nature, it was also believed to be the creator of the world's meaning and value. Observer status was tied closely to the capacity to create meaning and value.

Rising tensions, especially during the Enlightenment period (roughly the 18th century), were engendered by three great ideas: reason, nature and progress. Reason, as the universal capacity of humans to think logically and in accordance with natural philosophy (science), became the arch enemy of church authority. Human nature, seen mostly as good—although this view is certainly challenged by Hobbes' view that man is alone, afraid and greedy (1972: 186)—is discoverable by reason and is in no need of instruction from church authorities. The designs of the rational mind admit of continuous progress, a belief most strongly held by proponents of the Enlightenment in North America (seen especially in Manifest Destiny). With the new science, increasing technological innovation and the discovery of the New World, the idea of progress took firm root over and against the dictates of the church, which took its authority from backward-looking appeals to sacred texts. Reason, in effect, began to displace the divine in all public important matters of explanation and legitimation. Now, rather than appealing to the past and to the dictates of God or the authorities, reason encouraged a focus on the future and on the progress it can make through innovation and science. Nature became the raw material for innovation and, according to Darwin's analysis, became a mechanism of adaptation, not the design of God. As a result, the church lost authority over both political decision making and the institutions of knowledge. Nature, then, became the raw resource on which humanity could work its designs.

Lastly, the Copernican revolution may have destroyed Ptolemy's tidy hierarchy, but it did not entirely destroy the valuational hierarchical structure. Rational beings remained atop the hierarchy, while material beings remained at the bottom. God, for some, retained a place in the hierarchy (even Descartes and Newton retained God in their systems) but lost significance in science, politics and morality. A secular morality developed in the liberalization of Europe. Liberalization not only undermined the idea of an ultimate authority; it positively rejected such authority. Indeed, this was a new era of "natural law," which marked yet another transformation in the role of God. Under church rule, natural law was the law that God decreed, the one communicated to the people through His appointed ones. Under liberalism, natural law has to be discovered by the innate capacity of reason to know the basic good of man and what is essentially right. Jean Jacques Rousseau (especially as represented in *Discourse on the Origin of Inequality* [1976]) was among the main thinkers in this vein. His doctrine of natural sympathy and the ability of reason to see the natural goodness (virtue) that God implanted in human beings was central to this movement. The most influential thinker of the modern world, Immanuel Kant (1969), developed an ethical system based on reason and the capacity of reason to legislate its own moral dictates independent of any instruction from authority. Reason, for Kant, shows that we must act so that our actions conform to the principle of universalizability, that is, our actions must conform to what would be justified by any rational being. We also get from Kant the dictate that all rational beings are to be treated as ends in themselves and never merely as means to an end. "Rational man" occupies the top rung of the hierarchy, but now there is no solidarity between the rungs.

Together, the separateness of reason from nature, the development of scientific method and technology, the new-found observer status and the capacity to create meaning and value form a picture of "man" as dominant by virtue of his capacity to exercise power through reason. It is noteworthy that women are not considered as enjoying the same status, recalling points made earlier about ecofeminism. Women, like the earth, are given meaning and value by men through marriage and childbearing. This exclusion of women's perspective is symptomatic of the general exclusionary mode of thinking that prevails in the Modern world view, which in turn is shaped by the power vested in man as a rational being.

The Modern Era's Pursuit of Knowledge

The Modern Era spanned the Age of Reason and the Enlightenment. Overcoming authority and the church was associated with the rise of reason, which, it was believed, enabled man to see clearly. The shift to the scientific method as the primary mode of inquiry supplanted metaphysics, which was associated with the antiquated doctrinal commitments of the church.

Even though the pursuit of knowledge was freed from the authority-based Greco-Christian hierarchical system, the age-old debate between the empiricists, for whom sense experience was the foundation of knowledge, and the rationalists, for whom rational capacities were the foundation of knowledge, became central. Ionian and Eleatic spirits lived on. The great Modern proponents of empiricism were Bishop Berkeley, John Locke and David Hume. They believed that all knowledge begins with a series of sense experiences from which generalizations are formed. "Nature" is simply a pattern of experiences formed through a process of recognizing constant connections in experience. Observation and memory of these patterns allow us to formulate generalizations about what we can expect.

Rationalists, especially in the tradition of René Descartes, thought true knowledge to be founded on unchanging truths, independent of sense experience. The world of experience is a world of change, relativity and uncertainty, as Plato described it. The world of the intellect, as reflected in mathematics and logic, is a world of unchanging, absolute and certain truths. Since the world of intellect is a world of eternal objects, it is not essentially connected to the world of experience. Objects that we sense rather than intellectualize are imperfect and of a lower order. Indeed, according to Descartes, who thought that only indubitable or certain ideas can count as real, the world of change (nature) is "unreal" or at least always possibly illusory. Reverberations of Plato's Divided Line indicate a strong affinity between certainty and knowledge for the rationalist. Empiricism cannot offer certainty, only a degree of probability.

Descartes so denigrated the world of sense that he thought it to have no relation to the intellect. The world of sense is related to the world of physical objects. So, the status of perceived objects (as opposed to conceived objects) is equivalent to that of physical objects, which are always potentially deceptive. Knowledge about nature is suspect and of a lower order than knowledge about eternal, intellectual objects. Anything that can be claimed about observed nature is subject to doubt and uncertainty. This low status of sense perception reinforces the idea that body-dependent knowledge is of a lower order than intellect-dependent knowledge.

With the emergence of the new science, the clear lines of battle between empiricists and rationalists became obscure. Both sides had important contributions to make to the theory of knowledge as the scientific method developed. Gradually, lines of thinking began to merge to find unity in the hypothetico-deductive method.[4] This element of the experimental method invokes the intellect as the creative element that formulates a hypothesis. A hypothesis is a prediction about what results will follow from manipulating certain variables, given that initial conditions are known. One assumes certain properties to be true of the variables under consideration and, independent of observation, one predicts their behaviour. In the experiment, observation of what actually occurs either supports or falsifies the hypothesis. The rationalism-empiricism synthesis, then, is enabled through utilizing rational activity for building hypotheses and empirical activity for testing hypotheses.

In this synthesis, experimentation through observation and theory building are essentially impersonal and non-idiosyncratic. Hence, the individual thinker is largely discounted as essential to the credibility of the body of knowledge gained through the hypothetico-deductive method. Unlike an authority-based system, in which the individual, with his or her special insight or link to God, is critical, the Modern places testability and repeatability at the foundation of credibility and legitimacy. Any person properly trained in the methods of science should be able to come up with the same observations and conclusions as the original investigator. Although we esteem the inventors of theories, we have no reason to treat them as individually important to the production and dissemination of knowledge.

This debate and synthesis radically altered the pursuit of knowledge. Not only did science replace authority as the source of knowledge, but the meaning of knowledge changed. Knowledge gained through experimental testing and confirmation is not the same sort of knowledge that is gained through pure reason or simple observation. Its openness to falsification implies that such knowledge is never about the truth, as defined in the older system, but is a hypothesis not yet shown to be false. In the Ptolemaic system, explanation revolved around teleology, purposes and desire. In this new system of knowledge, they play no role because they are thought to add nothing useful to explanation.

Unlike the grand unified theory of Plato or Aristotle, original systems did not believe scientific knowledge to have implications for any other area of life. Furthermore, its domain was to be guarded against intrusions from political or social interests. Resistance to placing moral restrictions on experimentation illustrates this point. Thus, with the developed Modern world view came two fundamental changes in epistemology: 1) the nature of the object of study changed from that of an animated being to that of a mere machine; and 2) the concept of knowledge changed from apprehending the essence of things and their place in the cosmos to modelling how things operate according to mathematically describable laws.

Conclusion

Although science, in the Modern sense, claims not to inform matters of value or ethics, its development has had undeniable and monumental impacts on axiology. Some of these impacts should be mentioned here to give a more complete picture of how environmental thought has been shaped by the Modern world view.

Now that rational minds have become builders of theories and sole authorities for determining what can count as knowledge, it is a small step to assume that these same minds are also the sources of value. If the mechanism of nature is, in itself, valueless and God is no longer operative in the world to give it value, then rational minds must be the creators of value. Further, if the mind is distinct in kind from physical reality, it has a distinct value from whatever kind of value nature can have. Rational minds, accordingly, are both intrinsically valuable, that is, valuable in and of themselves, as well as being that through which nature acquires its value. Rational human beings confer value onto nature, according to their interest, desires, choices and agreements. This idea is discussed in greater detail in Chapter Four.

Consider also the impact of the demise of authority-based knowledge on social and moral life. Where knowledge claims are freed from authority, individuals can see themselves as private, isolated units of moral authority. Social goods determined by authorities are replaced by individual goods defined by personal interests and choices. Agreement or deal making between individuals determines what is of collective value. The way is paved, then, for market or economic values to replace religious or moral values as the determinants of collective values.

With the demise of the Ptolemaic system, there are many consequences for axiology, ethics, political life and social arrangements (in short, normative aspects of life). For one, the marriage between science and economics seems unavoidable. In this marriage, the newly embraced attitude toward the environment as a resource to be exploited and brought under control to yield to human design becomes a formidable force, unleashed especially during the Industrial Revolution. A comprehensive array of metaphysical, epistemological, political, moral, valuational and methodological upheavals work to transform man's conception of the environment from a divine creation to a commodity or resource for exploitation.

Shifts from the cosmological system to the Copernican system and then to the Modern Era engendered an expanding and deepening detachment from the "natural" environment. They also altered the received views on what could count as intelligible and rational. A problem of explanation, for instance, was treated in a fundamentally different way in the two systems. In the Ptolemaic system, asking what God's will must have been when explaining why a disease killed someone was entirely intelligible. In the new system, such an explanation was considered irrational and backward—a meaningless formulation—because it could not be answered within the terms of reference of the newly received system of knowledge.

This chapter prepares the way for the critique of detachment and the use of reason as a tool for excluding perspectives and other modes of knowing, but it also shows why the application of reasoning powers was directed in this way. The power to design and control the environment, especially when that control is associated with freedom from autocratic rule by the church and monarchy, involves a certain degree of legitimacy. It is for us now to separate what is legitimate and what is not legitimate in this development.

The Age of Reason and the Enlightenment are also closely related to the Age of Discovery, during which the New World was discovered and colonized. It was a time of tremendous upheaval in the way Europeans thought about themselves and the world. It was a time of war—the French Revolution, the American War of Independence, the American Civil War. Freedom from oppression and backward-looking authority had become a cornerstone of European and American thinking. The era was one in which thought forged new concepts, not knowing exactly where they might lead but nevertheless daring to consider them in the interests of freedom.

Notes

1. For Digges, see Johnson and Larkey 1934; for Bruno, see Bruno 1907.
2. To resolve the problem of retrograde motion, post-Copernicans had to make other adjustments to the astronomical theory of the time. For example, the placement of Mercury and Venus closer to the Sun than Earth and Mars, and Jupiter and Saturn farther from the Sun, was needed before epicycles could be eliminated.
3. The history of ideas is replete with such concepts waiting for a general theory to make sense of them. "Infinite universe" is one and, later, "holistic causality" will become another. Anomalies, in general, present a need for revisions in theory; but when something of the order of a vacuum needs to be explained and the system of concepts available to construct explanations cannot admit such needs, a new explanatory scheme becomes necessary.
4. For a detailed discussion, see Feibleman 1972, especially pages 90–93. There he describes the method as hypothetico-experimental. The key discussion for present purposes, however, is his explanation of how hypotheses aspire to become theories and the related importance of being able to provide something resembling a causal explanation. As such, the hypothetico-experimental method presupposes some capacity to deduce cause-effect relationships.

Chapter Three

The Challenge of Evolutionary and Ecological Theories

This chapter emphasizes some anomalies and developments in ecology that challenge the Modern world view. Discussion of evolutionary theory will be restricted to the function of characterizing the impact of ecology on contemporary thought. Central to this discussion is the critique of the Modern notions of reason in its role of fostering detachment, mechanistic explanations and a focus on freedom.

The Rise of Evolutionary Theory and the New Physics

In the late 1800s and early 1900s, biology and physics faced challenges that would eventually lead to shifts in fundamental beliefs about nature, including human nature. How things came to be the way they were, indeed the nature of matter itself, came under question. Darwin, in the mid-1800s, and Heisenberg, later in the 1900s, challenged Modern conceptions of the genesis of the present physical world, the nature of matter and the observational powers of human beings to know the world. This challenge, in conjunction with the development of ecology, with its holistic, integrative elements, has arguably become as much a stimulus for changing basic assumptions affecting world view as the ideas of Copernicus were a challenge to the Ptolemaic world view. Evolutionary theory began a slow erosion process of assumptions in geology, namely, that the earth has had a constant structure since its inception; it also eroded biological explanations and categorizations of species that had their roots in ancient Greek thought. Changes in physics deeply challenged the mechanistic model and the idea of the detached observer.

Three elements will be emphasized when describing the shift away from the Modern world view. The first is the idea of process, which, although not incompatible with mechanism in itself, is important in undermining Modern assumptions about cosmology. The second element concerns Darwin's attempt to develop a mechanistic explanation of the evolution of species. Even though, on the surface, mechanical explanations seem to dispose of teleological elements, it can be argued that they nevertheless presuppose something like a telos or purposiveness. When examining the possibility of a mechanistic interpretation of ecology, this deeper teleological element will be addressed. The third and related element is this: evolution presupposes an interrelationship between environment and that which evolves (whether individual or species). As it turns out this element undermines the mind/body dualities on which Modern theories of knowledge and human superiority rest.

Evolutionary theory challenged the Modern understanding of nature and, in turn, humanity's place in it. The long-standing biological categories, which essentially had not changed from the days of Plato and Aristotle, described species and genera as fixed types or forms (see Bowler 1989: 13). Both Ptolemaic and Modern world views held that all creatures belong to a strict type, which, according to Plato, caused individuals to be what they are. Owing to their participation in eternal forms, individuals acquired their characteristics. Things belong to classes or types that represent certain sets of properties. Types can be compared to blueprints, representing forms that are transferred to succeeding generations through procreation. Such explanations fit well with the mechanistic picture of nature. Reproduction takes place by replicating the parent in accordance with some strict rule or pattern, and individual behaviour is governed by the set of rules inherent in the individual (Bowler 1989: 5). Admittedly, this view did not go unchallenged (see Glacken 1967: 393–94), but this system of typing (taxonomy) remained dominant throughout the period. Although animals were considered peculiar machines because they reproduce, they were seen as machines all the same. What is important to note is the Modern belief that the world of matter contains no novelty. All processes and behaviour are simply replications of law-governed patterns. This view not only reinforces the theory of animals as mechanisms, it positively requires it. This uneasy marriage between Platonic forms and mechanistic theory could work for thinkers like Descartes because, for the casual observer of nature, individuals did seem to propagate according to strict patterns or types. Animals seemed to give birth to other animals that grew up to be just like them.

The structure of the world also appeared to remain constant over long periods of time, so it was relatively unproblematic to assume that it had always been structured more or less as it then appeared. Rock formations and mountains appeared to be permanent from the perspective of human history. The world, at the time, was thought either to have an eternal structure (Aristotle) or to have been created in just the way it was experienced (Christian belief). Gradually, however, more astute observers began to detect anomalies. Something as ordinary as a sedimentary rock, for example, proved extremely difficult to explain under these assumptions. Once the theory of sedimentary rock formation was developed—such rocks were formed underwater over long periods of time—a new anomaly arose. The anomaly was formulated as follows: sedimentary rocks are found on dry land. If these rocks were at one time submerged, the general structure of the earth (the land-ocean relationships) had to have changed. Great oceans would have had to exist, at one time, where dry land presently existed.

As geology continued to develop, the estimated age of the cosmos had to be extended from a few thousand years (as calculated from Biblical stories) to the present multibillions of years. Biblical authority, under continuous attack from cosmology, now faced the same from the emerging special sciences. Moreover, the idea that little bits of earth could form rocks when placed under pressure made possible a conception of the world as gradually adopting its present structure through accidental configurations of more basic parts (e.g., rocks from sand or clay), configurations devoid of purpose or design. Geology, then, seemed to support the mechanistic view, entrenching it even more deeply; at the same time, however, it undermined the Platonic and Aristotelian explanations of formal causality. If rocks could be formed from component parts in novel ways, then they were not formed by participating in some eternal form. The idea of evolutionary process began to supplant the ideal forms as a foundation for explanation. Forms or types, in fact, evolved as a result of interactions between natural components (e.g., eroded sand being placed under pressure from water for millions of years). Hence, the idea that things acquired their characteristics through their predecessors' interactions with others began to take shape.

In biology, astute observers saw that offspring could sometimes be more or less well-adapted to their environment than their parents, and that weaker or otherwise poorly adapted individuals died while the better adapted continued to procreate. Successive generations were observed to be different from their ancestors. Indeed, selective breeding had been practised for millennia prior to this period; a manipulation of forms that in effect created new forms of cats, dogs, horses, etc. Darwin focused on this phenomenon to support his theory of speciation (diversification of species from a single species). As evolutionary theory progressed through geology and biology, it began to articulate a radically new explanation for the structure of the earth and the existence of species, based on the idea of process. The knowledge that some species (e.g., dinosaurs) had become extinct (which became accepted as paleontology developed) and new ones had emerged disproved the idea of a complete and perfect system.

Today, the science of genetics shows how mutation creates new forms and that species often form through a process of selection of the fittest. Individuals better adapted to an environment, i.e., better able to take advantage of resources, are more likely to procreate. Their characteristics are more likely to carry through successive generations, while the characteristics of the less well-adapted will be eliminated. As such, not only is the development of species dependent on a process of adaptation, but the process itself and, therefore, the number of possible species that can evolve are open, not eternally set.

During this initial period, evolutionary theory attracted severe criticism from the church; Darwin's *Origin of Species* was scathingly rejected and he was labelled the "most dangerous man in England" (Bowler 1989: 187). To suggest that humans have but a ten thousand year history in a multimillion or perhaps multibillion year history of biological processes, which Darwin claimed spawned human exist- ence, is to suggest that humans are not created by God. Neither is humanity the namer of the animal kingdom, as Biblical dogma would have it. Humans, rather, are latecomers, part of a blind evolutionary process. Further, since human capacities have evolved in relation to the animal and non-animal kingdom, they are essentially connected to this kingdom. Granted, during the pre-Darwin years of evolutionary theory, it was fashionable to argue that God created the process of evolution, whereby humanity enjoyed status as the end-point of the process (Bowler 1989: Ch. 8). Evolution was assumed to be directed toward the development of "man." Lamarck's version of evolution— that individuals would adapt to changes in the environment and pass these adaptive responses to their offspring—was compatible with this view because it allowed for the idea of evolutionary progress toward an end-point. Since contemporary science attempts to rid itself of any residue of teleology, however, few remnants of the Lamarckian version remain. Even as the attack on teleology, one pillar of the mechanistic view of the world, was being undermined, another pillar—the assump- tion of human superiority and separateness from nature—was being assaulted.

Many other problems arose for the defence of religious belief over and against evolutionary theory. The idea of a benevolent Creator did not fit well with the idea of suffering in predator-prey and parasitic relation- ships between species nor with the extinction of species. But the critical effect of evolutionary theory was that it established an explanation of the living world in terms of a mechanism of selection, according to which no divine intention is needed. It was Darwin's intention (for example, in *The Descent of Man*) to argue that there is no fundamental difference between human beings and other life forms—from this springs the idea that we are related to the apes—such that all beings belong to the same mechanical, non-purposive process. While the debate over whether evolution is crea- tive, purposive and progressive or merely a series of accidental occur- rences raged in the 1800s (Bowler 1989: 240–42), the dust now has settled largely in favour of the latter. The reason is that explanations of evolution not only do not need to appeal to purposes, they positively reject them. Darwin's idea of mechanism, for instance, is based on the supposition that nothing more than a purely accidental set of circumstances makes one individual more adaptable than another. Under a different set of circumstances, a different individual would be better suited.

Despite supporting the Modern world view, especially with regard to the accidental and mechanistic nature of the selection process, evolutionary theory also challenges its very core. It challenges the doctrines of dualism at the heart of both Greco-Christian and Modern perspectives. All human capacities, including the capacity to observe and reason, now are to be explained as results of adaptive behaviour. No capacity nor function, however apparently detached, can be considered, in essence, so. Evolutionary theory has proven destructive of metaphysical assumptions that support the human superiority thesis and claims to detached objectivity.

Coupled with developments in physics, the undermining of metaphysical assumptions began to show that human observers are not separate; indeed, they are connected to the things they observe in fundamental ways. Heisenberg (1958: 24, 47–48) showed that the act of observation affects the observed object, an effect especially noticeable at subatomic levels. One of the purposes of his discussion was to establish the indeterminacy principle, that is, to show that there is an uncertainty in the microscopic behaviour of the world, an uncertainty that cannot be overcome (Heisenberg 1958: 57). Part of the reason for this uncertainty is that our very acts of observation affect the object being observed by changing its course. An observed electron, for instance, is altered from the course it would otherwise take when not being observed. Since the act of observation (seeing) is a process of photons reflecting from an object onto the retina, the act of observing an electron has a noticeable effect on the course of the electron. This effect can be noticed because photons are sufficiently large to effect measurable changes in the path of electrons. Observer and observed, therefore, are of a kind. The Modern doctrine that we are fundamentally detached from the objects we observe, then, is falsified. If wrong about detachment and the permanence of types (species), then Modern assumptions about the nature of rationality also demand rethinking. Even reason has now to be conceived as an evolved capacity intimately connected to physical processes. The world of the intellect and the world of physical process are not radically separate.

A closer examination of evolutionary theory discloses a deeper problem, since the attempt to provide a mechanistic explanation for species and organisms runs into difficulties. A straightforward, mechanistic account of organic entities is not to be found. Evolutionary theory tells us that living forms with complex functions arose through selective adaptation. Taking geological time as a measure, we are to understand that life forms have evolved ultimately from a state of extreme radioactivity, which eventually evolved to allow simple bacteria (and later more complex forms of life) to evolve. How do we explain this evolution? One possibility is to suppose that increasingly complex chemical configurations developed to a point of sufficient complexity to generate life (Haldane 1996). The effective means by which life was generated, however, remains vague. Somehow a random set of events must have given rise to appropriate life-generating chemical configurations.

Even if we put aside these more spectacular evolutionary events and examine more mundane phenomena, significant problems remain for this theory. Take the nerve cell, for example. How could it have evolved? Before attempting an answer, it is important to understand how the neuron works from a mechanistic perspective. Laws of chemistry allow us to predict reactions between the two primary elements, sodium and potassium; they eventually form a state of equilibrium. In non-organic situations, sodium and potassium will mix through a membrane to establish a balance. This is the inorganic rest state. The interactions between potassium and sodium in a neuronal context is different. In a rest state, sodium and potassium are in imbalance, a state created by a process called "active transport" of sodium to the exterior of the neuronal membrane. The device is a process known as the "sodium pump," which maintains the imbalance of sodium and potassium. If equilibrium between sodium and potassium is the inorganic rest state, but non-equilibrium is the rest state in certain types of cells (e.g., neurons), the law-like relation between sodium and potassium is somehow subordinated in organic relationships. Something in the function and structure of the neuron, then, must be a causal factor effecting the imbalance.

We could describe the situation as follows: higher-level determinants override, but do not negate, lower-level causal laws as they organize lower-level processes to satisfy certain functions. Lower-level laws (the mechanics of osmosis) are necessary for neuronal transmission to occur, but they must be controlled and invoked only under specific conditions. Higher-order laws, then, can be said to subordinate lower-level laws in the sense that lower-level laws become means to fulfilling higher-order functions. Higher-order laws are retentive of lower-level laws but cannot be explained in terms of them.

The first conclusion is this: the evolution of neurons could not have been predicted on the basis of knowing the mechanics of chemistry alone. We cannot account for the existence of neurons simply by knowing the properties of their component parts and the laws according to which they operate. A mechanist would have to say, then, that these higher-order laws emerge randomly as accidental configurations of chemicals give rise to new chemical relationships. The form of explanation, however, does not conform well to the scientific method (hypothetico-deductive approach), in which a hypothesis is formed and an experiment formulated to predict results. The attempt to predict the emergence of these higher orders or configurations would have to be reasoned on the basis of a probability analysis, not on strict deductions based on strict chemical or physical laws. We would have to hypothesize a certain probability that neurons would evolve given certain initial conditions. But from where would such a hypothesis come? It would have to come from our history of observed evolutionary patterns. From presently observed and analyzed patterns, we describe higher-order laws (such as those pertaining to neuronal transmission) and then predict backwards (retrodict) that, under certain conditions, these laws had a certain probability of emerging. Of course, such hypotheses are not rigorously testable, since we could never exactly replicate the conditions that existed at the time of neuronal evolution. We would not know how to control for all the possible factors that might have formed the context in which neurons developed. If the higher-order laws are mechanistically related to the lower ones they subordinate, then this mechanism remains obscure. The method of analyzing the relationship, moreover, must be unlike the method for analyzing the lower order alone. Different sorts of processes and causal factors need to be taken into account, once we introduce higher-order laws.

The effective means or the causal laws through which these properties emerged cannot be specified. Even if we could design an experiment in which a neuron was created from initial chemical conditions, we would not necessarily have discovered how they emerged in the first place. There may be many possible worlds in which neurons could have evolved. A laboratory experiment is just one. The actual effective means, then, remain unidentified and uncertain. We are close to reintroducing occult qualities.

We have established thus far that higher-order laws are necessary for neurons to function as information transfer mechanisms. Some higher-order need or function (for instance, information processing) must be presupposed in explanations of such emergent capacities. Some need or function of a whole, an organic unity, must be presupposed. Thus, evolutionary theory supports holistic "explanations." This, in part, is what it means for causal properties of wholes not to be reducible to the sum of the causal properties of the parts.

Some might attempt to be rid of even this minimal admission to holistic causality by appealing to other reductive modes of explanation, such as genetics. The idea that the organic world comes about through a genetic selection process argues that a genetic mechanism explains the emergence of new configurations. The problem of explanation, however, is simply pushed back one step. If we accept that certain genetic dispositions, either through gradual, catastrophic or mutative changes in the DNA molecule, have brought about the emergence of neurons, we still have not explained holistic causality. Adaptations at the DNA level may be entirely accidental, but they still give rise to wholes whose needs as wholes direct the functions of the new organism. To claim that a new DNA configuration arises in the adaptive process, even quite by accident, is still to presuppose a form of holistic causality as the new configuration subordinates lower-order laws to allow the organism as a whole to adapt better. The DNA molecule is itself a whole, whose parts together form a system that gives instructions to the body as it develops. One part of the molecule by itself does not give instructions. It is only in the context of or in relation to the other parts of the DNA molecule that individual parts of the molecule give instructions. This is no surprise. The basic biological explanatory categories, "structure" and "function," indicate that an organism does not function apart from having a certain structure. It is the structure of the organism or the DNA molecule as a whole, then, that enables the parts of the DNA molecule to give their instructions. No grand teleological scheme is involved here; nevertheless, there is an element of purposiveness involved. The occurrence of adaptations may have no explicit purpose, but every adaptation is, nevertheless, purposive insofar as it requires some suitable configuration of DNA before a mutation can serve as an adaptive change. Many mutations occur but generate maladaptive behaviour. Thus, the organism dies, together with its DNA configuration. The few that survive are suited to their environment because their DNA configuration, in part, directs the organism to behave suitably in its environment. Suitability of structure, function and behaviour of an organism are purposive in the sense that they direct the organism to conform to environmental conditions.

Let us examine the development of the retina to clarify this notion of purposiveness. We know that if retinas had evolved through a mutation, without an accompanying emergence of neurons and suitable brain functions (imagining that such an occurrence is even possible), no function of sight would have developed. A complex number of coordinated conditions or sub-functions within an organism are required before retinas can function as instruments of sight. Each mutation, to be adaptive, must fit into a complex set of functions structured in a way that enables the organism to behave suitably within its environment. Thus, the conditions of suitability are set both by the external environment and by the internal structure and function of the organism. Many higher-order functions can evolve to subordinate lower-order processes, but few will be successful because the evolution of an organism and the DNA that directs its development has established preconditions for successful subordination. Hence, mutations must satisfy a complex of conditions, which determines the possibility of success for mutations. Insofar as "purposiveness" suggests a pre-established direction and guidance of behaviour, even without assuming that direction to be intentional, it is a suitable term to capture the relation between higher- and lower-order functions and laws.

The import of the discussion so far is not to establish some mysterious causal force in the destiny of the world. It is to ask just how many laws, how many principles and how many types of causes need be invoked to explain the world. The Modern world view promised that only a few basic assumptions about the nature of the world and one type of cause would be needed to explain it. Evolution has made that promise difficult to keep. At the very least, it shows that several levels of explanation are necessary to account for the way things evolve and function: 1) lower-order mechanistic, physical and chemical laws; 2) higher-order purposive or organizational causes; and 3) ecosystems as wholes, which determine the conditions of suitability. This third level, between the organism and the environment, involves the exigencies of life, changing environmental contexts (e.g., food scarcity, invasions of different species), which impose demands for adaptation. So, however else we may want to conceive of the mechanism of nature and evolution, holistic relational factors are inextricably involved.

A New Take on Rationality

Revisiting the concept of rationality in light of evolutionary theory is to recast our understanding of rationality as an emergent function like any other function. At some point in history, the capacity to reason developed as an appropriately structured brain developed. The dependency of the reasoning capacity on a very narrow set of organic and environmental conditions connects rational animals with other animals in an intimate way, making us one of many types within a complex system. This system sets the conditions for the structuring of the brain, enabling it to function rationally. It is perfectly feasible to argue that, as a higher-order function, the reasoning capacity of the brain subordinates lower-order functions, much like the need for information transfer subordinates biochemical functions. By the same token, however, its relationship to the organism as a whole makes it a lower-order function relative to the whole. This is not to say that it does not have a special or peculiar function, but it is to say that its function, by nature, cannot be separated from the other functions of the organism and the relationship to its environment. I am not at all proposing that reason be subordinated to any other function for normative concerns. When the nature of reason is more closely examined, it will be clear that no simple subordination of its function is sensible. For the moment, the concept "subordination" serves a restricted purpose. It serves only to describe relationships between different levels of organization, not to indicate levels of value or worth.

Nevertheless, just as developments in science could not directly cross over into religion or politics but had indirect effects in these areas all the same, so do shifts in the conception of rationality have indirect effects on Modern applications of rationality. First, evolutionary theory and evidence for it falsify the doctrine of radical detachment, undermining assertions of privileged status for rational beings. Once again, the metaphysical assumptions supporting normative doctrines cannot stand. As the Greco-Christian, hierarchical, normative system was jeopardized by the demise of the Ptolemaic cosmological system, so are the Modern assumptions of hierarchical ordering between rational and non-rational beings likewise jeopardized.

Rationality, according to evolutionary theory, emerges as an adaptation function. As such, it is of instrumental value to the individual organism and the species; it does not imply intrinsic value, contrary to what the Moderns thought. At most, evolutionary theory suggests that reason equips human beings with superior survival skills. Neither does the direction of evolution toward more complex organizations suggest that higher levels of organization are better than lower ones. What it suggests is that complexity is a necessary condition for human survival and functioning. Our having evolved means that, to some degree, we are well suited to some complex environments and not to others. We know that we are not suited to extremely simple environments. Were the earth exclusively water-based, we would not have evolved. Were the atmosphere predominantly carbon monoxide, we would fail to exist. Were the balance of carbon dioxide and oxygen to shift radically, our ability to think rationally would be severely impaired, since the functioning of the circulatory and nervous systems depends on a particular balance of atmospheric oxygen and carbon dioxide. Anyone who has held a plastic bag over his or her head for extended periods knows just how much rational thought depends on this balance. In the end, evolutionary theory tells us far more about our dependency on the environment than it does about our superiority over it. It tells us that our survival depends on our conforming to suitability conditions.

Claiming separability of the rational mind from this highly specialized set of environmental conditions, upon which its functioning depends, carries with it a heavy burden of proof. Since evolutionary theory is now supported by other areas of investigation, such as neuropsychology, any separability thesis to be entertained must be narrowly defined and highly qualified. For one, where it was once unproblematic to exclude all but human rational beings from the moral community, that exclusion is now deeply problematic. Similarly, the assertion that non-human nature is value neutral becomes problematic because our value cannot be separated in any radical way from the non-human world. Our valuational status and capacity are fundamentally connected somehow to all others involved in the ecological context in which we have evolved.

Ecology Beyond Science

Turning now to discuss ecology as the third level of explanation, we can expand on the ideas of purposiveness and holistic causality and their effects on our understanding of rational persons. *Oikos logos* is the Greek etymological root of "ecology"; it means "household order and management."

Roszak (1972: 400) calls ecology the subversive science:

> Its [ecology's] sensibility—wholistic, receptive, trustful, largely non-tampering, deeply grounded in aesthetic intuition—is a radical deviation from traditional science. Ecology does not systematize by mathematical generalization or materialist reductionism, but by the almost sensuous intuiting of natural harmonies on the largest scale. Its patterns are not those of numbers, but of unity in process; its psychology borrows from Gestalt and is an awakening awareness of wholes greater than the sum of their parts.

This description represents an alternative set of sensibilities concerning ecology, which contrasts with the mathematical modelling and other attempts at explaining ecosystems that follow scientific methodology. Even though these approaches diverge and have become de facto norms for different commitments to ecology, part of my interest is to bring these two streams more closely together. Roszak's (1972: 400) non-orthodox views deserve attention because of the "wholistic" elements, which he believes demand an approach to analyzing and explaining natural processes that is different from the approaches of the so-called hard sciences. I will demonstrate why this greater synthesis is needed by first showing why it is difficult, if not impossible, to conduct the kinds of experiments on ecosystems that a rigorous scientific approach demands.

Good experiments require that initial conditions are known and controlled. Thus, the ideal location for conducting an experiment is a laboratory, where conditions can be controlled and variables isolated such that their manipulation allows the experimenter to identify how changes in initial conditions are related to resulting conditions. Studying ecosystems as wholes, however, is next to impossible because initial conditions cannot be controlled. The study of ecosystems involves such an enormous number of variables that they cannot all be identified, let alone put into an analytical scheme. Determining what brings about a change in weather patterns, for instance, is not like determining whether or not a chemical is instrumental in a rat's ability to run through a maze. In the latter case, the controlled variable (the amount of chemical) can be strictly monitored and the research subjects (the rats) can be highly engineered (through breeding) to ensure little variation between them. The effects produced after introducing the chemical, then, can be reliably traced to the introduction of that chemical, since other possible causes of the effect have been eliminated. With respect to ecosystems, by contrast, no such reliability can be expected because the initial conditions cannot be controlled without, at the same time, altering the conditions that one might want to study. Attempting to study the effects of the spruce budworm on a spruce forest, for instance, cannot be done without artificially restricting the initial conditions, if this can be done at all. We could try to study the impact of the worm on a spruce plantation, but that would not be studying the effects on a spruce forest, which has more diversity than a plantation. Moreover, since every forest, however identified, is different from every other, no guarantees of transferability from one experimental context to another can be expected (see Shrader-Frechette and McCoy 1993).

In part, initial conditions cannot be controlled and relevant variables cannot be identified because we cannot, with the degree of certainty to be found in rat experiments, limit the scope of the ecosystem to be studied. A rainforest does not exist in isolation from other ecosystems. It is affected by neighbouring systems and, indeed, by the global ecosystem. Once we begin to take celestial effects into account (obvious ones being the effects of the Sun and Moon on the Earth), we begin to understand that we not only have to take many variables into account, we also need to take many disciplines and their methods into account before we can claim to have even approximately identified initial conditions.

One response to these problems is that we do not need to match the reliability of the rat experiment to make the study of ecosystems scientifically valuable. Loose generalizations in describing and analyzing ecosystem processes can gradually become tighter until we have a fair degree of reliability. Waring (1989: 18, 21), for example, describes the state of ecology as having moved from a descriptive enterprise to one of a predictive character. He demonstrates how, especially in relation to hydrological cycles, a certain predictive reliability can be gained and is progressively being gained.

Roszak's view of ecology may be an overly romantic view of holism, too one-sided to count as a general view of ecology. I see no reason why ecology's holism cannot admit of predictive modelling, especially since predictive potential has always been an aspiration of any explanatory scheme, including animistic ones. People often performed rituals and ceremonies to reduce the chances of the gods visiting disasters on them or to increase the chances of beneficial action. Talk about predictability, however, must be engaged with caution. We may be raising a false idol. The behaviour of a neuron is predictable, given knowledge of initial conditions. But predicting the evolution of neurons is quite a different matter. Recall that the best approximation to predicting the emergence of neurons was retrodiction. That is, we might be able to explain the evolution of neurons, like retinas, after the fact. As will be seen in relation to chaos theory, the possibility of identifying all significant initial conditions in an ecosystem as a whole is extremely remote, if not impossible. Another problem of predicting evolutionary developments in ecosystems is that we cannot be certain which properties or capacities will emerge, which will change the conditions that need to be taken into account. Ecosystems as wholes, then, have causal and emergent properties that cannot be explained in terms of the causal properties of the parts or subfunctions, making predictions tentative and the basis for them incomplete.

Lovelock (1987: 11), in his Gaia hypothesis, argues that Earth is a complex entity, consisting of complex interactions and relations in feedback (cybernetic) relations. We have been misled, he argues, by explanations of life in terms of the distribution and configuration of matter. The distribution of matter does not explain life; rather, the fact of life explains the distribution of matter. Attempts at explaining life have assumed that we determine the conditions necessary for life as we know it, and then construct a theory about how life must have started. We analyze the conditions that seem necessary for life here on Earth and treat them as necessary for life everywhere else.

Lovelock finds this strategy wanting. As a NASA scientist, commissioned to design experiments that would determine whether there is life on Mars, he became critical of the assumptions he was expected to employ. The assumption in traditional science is that life can be supported only if there are indications of micro-organisms, bacteriological or fungal presence (Lovelock 1987: 2). Lovelock began to think this assumption perhaps too restrictive for determining the presence of life. Standard scientific indicators of life are useful relative to specific sorts of environment, he thought, but they are not the only possible indicators. Might it be possible to formulate a wider concept of life, that would not, by definition, make detection of other forms of life impossible?

Lovelock began to think that all life processes, whether aerobic or anaerobic, are associated with a reduction in entropy or randomness. Life processes engender order from within disorder. They seem to run contrary to the second law of thermodynamics, namely, that all energy eventually dissipates into heat and will be universally distributed, such that it will be unavailable for useful work. Perhaps, then, the emphasis should be on the ordering properties associated with life processes, and not on chemical or biological properties, if a comprehensive tool for detecting life on Mars is to be developed. If life processes tend to generate order, then order is the product of life processes. Life is not the product of creating order from constituent elements. It would appear, then, that the ordering of abiological (non-biological) and biological matter constituting the ecosystem presupposes life. In other words, life is required for the particular ordering of elements in the biosphere.

Thus, in explaining the organization of the Earth as a life-supporting place, Lovelock hypothesized that Earth itself must be a living entity that organizes its own material conditions, in turn allowing other forms of life to evolve. Clearly, the order of explanation, being reversed as Lovelock argues it must be, is a violation of the principles of experimental science and of mechanistic materialism. Critics might accuse him of using fuzzy concepts, e.g., "the great spirit of Mother Earth" (a criticism of his use of the term "Gaia") as a basis for his hypothesis, partly because the hypothesis cannot be tested. Life, as such, cannot be detected or observed. It cannot, therefore, be measured, making the hypothesis untestable.

But Lovelock is not engaged in poetry. He is attempting to find a language in which to situate his analysis of the standard assumptions in science, a language that would demarcate his theory from standard theories in biology and the life sciences. Lovelock supports his claims by citing evidence from a number of scientific fields. For example, he utilizes geological history (Lovelock 1987: Chapter 2) to demonstrate that the Earth has been in a relatively stable state for millions of years. Rather than undergoing drastic shifts in chemical distributions and temperature, as do many planets, the Earth has undergone relatively slight shifts. From a strictly chemical point of view, concentrations of oxygen, carbon dioxide and methane ought to be much different than they are and should have fluctuated more radically than they have. Some capacity of self-regulation, therefore, must be assumed of the Earth. And since this self-regulation is precisely what life systems do, Lovelock concludes that Earth itself must be a living being.

While ecologists are far from agreeing on his conclusions, Lovelock has challenged the reductionist idea that wholes have no causal efficacy. Although underanalyzed, the idea that the Earth as a whole is a factor in determining how its parts are distributed, concentrated and related seems necessary. Again, we have a situation in which the whole causes organizations of its parts in ways that cannot be analyzed as the sum of the effects of the parts. It is not necessary, however, to suppose that the planet is alive in order to support the idea that the planet as a whole is causally efficacious. Some ecologists, in fact, are prepared to recognize that there is something to this holistic notion that the Earth as a whole, in its "complex web of biological and physical interactions, ... has made our planet habitable" (May 1989: 347).

The idea that holistic causality must be presupposed in order to explain the relationships between its component parts is the critical conclusion. Being presupposed, it is not the sort of thing that can be detected and measured like the components it orders. Lovelock's hypothesis is one in a long history of ideas that espouse the importance of holistic frames of reference. Thinkers of the stature of Benedict Spinoza, Frederick Hegel and Alfred North Whitehead have argued that there could be no parts in relation apart from a whole that forms the ground for their relationships. Even Newton (1756: Letter II, see Koyré 1957: 178), the great mechanist, in a letter to the Reverend Bentley argued that a unifying principle must be presupposed of the universe, for it was inconceivable how brute material objects could act at a distance (through gravity) on one another, apart from some mediating agent causing it to do so. While Newton was primarily concerned with putting God in the picture, what is important for us to note is that the forces organizing and unifying matter cannot be explained solely as properties of the individual parts that make up the whole. Rather, some unifying property of the whole must explain the functioning and distribution of its parts.

Lovelock himself did not seem to appreciate just what he had discovered while writing *Gaia*. In response to critics who accused him of invoking teleology, he tried to show how Gaia is still mechanical by employing the image of "Daisy World," a representation of a mechanistically regulated world maintaining conditions suitable to the survival of daisies. On this world, white and black daisies exist. When the white daisies predominate, they reflect more sunlight than absorb it, cooling the atmosphere. The cooler climate favours the black daisies, so that they proliferate. As they come to dominate, however, they absorb more heat, warming the atmosphere. Since the white daisies are better adapted to higher temperatures, they soon begin to dominate and the cycle repeats itself. Hence, a generally stable temperature can be maintained on a planet in a completely mechanistic system.

Lovelock's attempt to disengage himself from any kind of mystical or animistic cosmology led him to rely on the model of a cybernetic (feedback) mechanism to explain how the Earth self-regulates. The model suggests that the feedback involved in the self-regulating process is like that of a thermostat, entirely mechanical and law-like. However, the model falls short of explaining the data he had collected. It is one thing to explain how the temperature on the Earth has remained relatively constant for millions of years and quite another to explain how an unbalanced distribution of chemicals comes about. Feedback mechanisms cannot be the effective means by which atmospheric chemicals come to exist in an unbalanced state, any more than the temperature-regulating system of the human body explains how sodium and potassium come into relationship to form information transmission mechanisms. Feedback mechanisms of some sort are surely involved in governing how the nervous system operates, once they are in place, but they do not explain how the systems come to be structured and function. Some higher-order cause of integration and distribution is involved. "Life" represents this higher-order cause in Lovelock's explanation and that may be about as clear as he can get, given the conceptual tools available.

To some extent, conceptual clarity is sacrificed when taking holistic/non-mechanistic elements into account in explanations of ecosystem processes. Even if we abandon teleological and animistic explanations, a certain fuzziness in how wholes are causally effective is unavoidable. We cannot model such causal relations on the behaviour of billiard balls nor predict, in a mathematically rigorous way, just how holistic causality operates. As in evolutionary theory, where we talk about "emergent properties" of wholes, Lovelock's analysis of the unequal distribution of chemicals as a consequence of life is an emergent property of the biosphere as a whole. As fuzzy as this may be, it gets fuzzier because the cause of the unequal distribution—life—still remains unanalyzed. In fact, it must remain unanalyzed if it must be presupposed in explaining the unequal distribution. As such, it is related to the antecedent purposiveness that determines the suitability of any evolved structure and function of an organism. We could say, then, that since life is presupposed in the explanation of the most comprehensive structure and function, namely the ecosystem as a whole, it is a cause of purposiveness. It is related to the causal property of the whole.

The notion of a whole or a system as a whole determining distributions of matter runs contrary to reductive explanations. If the existence and function of an organ is dependent on the other parts, and each in turn is dependent on the functioning of the whole organism, which is in turn dependent on the functioning of the whole ecosystem, then there are holistic causes nested within greater wholes. The picture of holistic causes becomes a great deal more complex. Each part and level of organization shares the property of being governed by some unifying principle, which in part determines its function and properties.

Ecology, then, tells us that the function and existence of the parts depend, in some underdetermined way, on the system as a whole. Although no purpose can be specified for their existence, they are, nevertheless, purposive, insofar as they have a function that has had to fit into a pre-established set of conditions existing in its evolutionary history. Most if not all functions interconnect with other functions within the system, forming a network of functions on which each individual and, indeed, the whole depend. Thus, there is a mutual dependency between wholes and parts, lower and higher levels of organization. While it is important to recognize that there is a two-way influencing relationship, our present focus will be on the whole-to-part relationship. The ordering element can be construed as a principle, the principle of adaptation and suitability or fittingness already described in relation to purposiveness.

At each level of organization the conditions of adaptation are different. Since these differing conditions are related to differing types of organization, each level determines different rules according to which systems are to be studied (May 1989: 359). Chemical relations are studied according to different rules than are neurons; these rules differ from those needed to study organisms as wholes, which differ from those needed to study ecosystems as wholes and so on. Clarity of explanation cannot, therefore, be soon expected.

Moreover, there is still much diversity of opinion on what count as the core concepts around which ecology is to be formed as a discipline. J.M. Cherrett (1989) of the British Ecological Society distributed questionnaires to members of the society, including international members. He found that the following concepts were considered the most central and characteristic of ecology: "the ecosystem," "succession," "energy flow," "conservation of resources," "competition," "niche," "materials cycling," "the community," "life-history strategies" and "ecosystem fragility." No concept in the top ten of the aggregate result, however, necessarily appeared in the top ten of any particular respondent. Each, moreover, is indicative of somewhat different commitments to what ought to be studied when examining ecosystems. If it is not clear how we are to go about studying ecosystems, we cannot determine with certainty what basic concepts are to lead our thinking about them or what basic principles are the best to utilize when forming research strategies. Hence, the principle and conditions of adaptation must remain underdetermined and open to different rules at different levels of analysis.

Shrader-Frechette and McCoy (1993) have also argued that there are no universal ecological principles that enjoy support from ecologists, and moreover, no key concepts that are free of ambiguity, disagreement over meaning and inconsistency of use. Key concepts, according to their review of historical and contemporary literature are "community" and "stability" (Shrader-Frechette and McCoy 1993: 7–8). However, neither the meaning nor the operational definitions of these concepts is clear. It is not clear, for instance, what constitutes a community (Shrader-Frechette and McCoy 1993: 24). Do individuals or species count most? Are relationships or interactions between species more important than populations? Should we look at dynamic relationships (interactions) or static ones (typologies)? What temporal and spatial scales should we specify when identifying these communities?

A critical appreciation of ecology would have us understand and accept the limitations to our explanations while, at the same time, recognizing that a degree of systematic understanding is possible. Ecosystems are constituted by discernible but underdetermined patterns. Certain patterns and causal links between parts of ecosystems are discernible, but these patterns and links are not entirely law-like and cannot be completely described. What is important for us philosophically, and as we will see, ethically, is how to deal with the uncertainty and fuzziness presented by the ecological sciences.

It is also important to note how the indeterminacy of ecosystem processes has developed and come to be supported by recent work in chaos theory. James Gleik's popular *Chaos: Making a New Science* (1987) describes how chaos theory has affected science. We have shifted from believing that we can calculate the approximate behaviour of a system, given the approximate initial conditions of a system, to accepting that there exists disorderly behaviour of even simple systems (e.g., the pendulum). This disorderly behaviour acts as a *creative* process (Gleik 1987: 15). Disorder generates complexity of richly organized patterns, sometimes stable and sometimes unstable (Gleik 1987: 43). As Gleik (1987: 41) reports, Galileo argued that, even if two pendula were set into motion, one with a wide swing and the other with a shorter swing, they would swing in perfect coordination with one another. The mathematical mechanistic model predicted that, since the larger pendulum would swing faster than the shorter, it would compensate for having to swing a longer distance. Hence, the two pendula would swing the exact same number of times over the same period of time. Galileo's prediction has proven false, however, even if the experiment is conducted in a vacuum. The reason has to do with changes in angle, which introduce an element of indeterminacy into the relation between the two pendula. Therefore, an elegant formula (linear equation) for describing the pendulum's motion can never quite capture what will actually occur.

Keep in mind that Gleik is describing extremely simple systems at this point. In a system as complex as an ecosystem, it is quite possible that the disorder will be compounded considerably, as it is for weather systems. The point of these remarks is to show that unpredictability is an essential property of ecosystems; so the very nature of the object of study in ecology resists the clear and systematic descriptions that science strives to achieve.

> Chaos is effectively unpredictable long time behavior arising in a deterministic dynamical system because of sensitivity to initial conditions.... For a dynamical system to be chaotic it must have a "large" set of initial conditions which are highly unstable. No matter how precisely you measure the initial condition in these systems, your prediction of its subsequent motion goes radically wrong after a short time. In dynamical systems theory, chaos means irregular fluctuations in a deterministic system. This means the system behaves irregularly because of its own internal logic, not because of random forces acting from outside. (Meiss 2000)

As the emerging scientific inquiry of the Modern world dethroned religious authoritarian and unfalsifiable systems of knowledge, so does ecology dethrone the mechanistic models and simplification methodologies of the Modern world view. Complex systems give rise to indeterminacy. Taken together with the idea that systems as wholes are causally efficacious, indeterminacy means that wholes are basic units of analysis and existence because their contribution to the way things behave cannot be reduced to the sum total of how the parts behave. Wholes, then, determine whether and how parts are organized at various levels in largely unpredictable ways.

Peter Yodzis (1989: 2) points out that, while scientists attempt to describe the world (ecosystems) in as precise and exhaustive terms as possible, searching for and/or imposing patterns onto this search, they also recognize that they are engaged in conceptualization. In other words, they are abstracting from the complexity of ecosystems to determine interesting and effective ways of understanding these systems. Even incomplete and false conceptualizations can yield important discoveries, but no conceptualizations can be expected to reach completion because every attempt at theorizing is a simplification. This is largely a reiteration of what many scientists have come to believe in their post-Newtonian approach to science. Science does not describe the facts, pure and simple. It describes facts, or the objects of inquiry, according to theories and speculations that are used to construct a picture of what the world is and how it operates (see, for example, F.C.S. Northrop in Heisenberg 1958: 5). Indeed, according to scientists such as Heisenberg, the new physics, quantum theory, is not deterministically mechanistic—the world, especially at the subatomic level, does not operate like a machine with complete predictability—but operates according to probabilistic laws. This probability is not random. Subatomic particles act in a directed way toward a potential or an end, such that their behaviour and relationships are not accidental but governed (Heisenberg 1958: 41). Hence, the underdetermined yet purposive characteristics of ecosystems are paralleled in subatomic systems.

What does it mean to be a rational animal in light of these implications? Our capacity to reason or think is better conceived as a function of the organism and, by implication, of ecosystem processes. Given that this capacity involves the ability to think, construct explanations, seek and structure knowledge systems, make decisions and form judgments, it is a creative capacity. Although other wholes may have creative functions, reasoning beings are self-consciously creative beings for whom creative endeavours are problematic. Thought that has to do with perfecting, engineering or dominating the ecosystem may in fact be an aspect of the creative function, but it also leads us into error. A far more sensible way to understand rationality would be to see it as a tool for attuning us to the complexities and tensions that arise in the human-environment relationship. It does so by constructing or creating means by which the relationship can best be structured and the human being's function defined. Rather than functioning straightforwardly as a tool for reductive thinking, reason best functions as an instrument for dialectical thought, creatively integrating opposites to better understand the world and to live in it. The exercise of reason is more coherent when serving to attune us to the manner in which we are dependent on these oppositional ecosystem processes.

When we understand that ecology becomes a foundation for thought, it would be better to use the locution "thinking ecologically," rather than "thinking about ecology." Just as we think mechanistically and reductively when we believe that mechanism is true of the world and that reductive analysis is the principal mode of thought, we can begin to think ecologically when the holistic and oppositional aspects of ecology are infused in how we think. The shift means that ecology is not treated merely as another subject matter but as a foundation for reshaping our world view. It suggests that holism and oppositional interconnectedness become internalized, such that our descriptions, analyses and evaluations are shaped by anticipations of holistic and oppositional relations, much like reductive thinking anticipates being able to analyze whatever object is being investigated into simpler units.

Ecology as Process and Units of Analysis

To this point, discussion of the holistic aspects of ecology has been shaped by the expectations of the "sciences." That is, we have had to show over and against the expectations of more reductive and methodologically strict modes of thinking that the use of holistic concepts is both intelligible and legitimate. It is now appropriate to explore these concepts more directly. I do so by expanding the discussion about the purposive elements associated with evolution and ecology.

Andrew Brennan (1988: Chapter 4) presents a history of approaches to ecology, providing a concise examination of ecology's problems and proposed implications. He examines F.E. Clement's use of "holism" to describe the plant community as a superorganism and ecological processes as successive communities (Brennan 1988: 47). Plant communities function like individual organisms, having a life independent of the lives of the individual organisms. These superorganisms have developed through a succession of communities, which culminate in a terminus, such as a mature forest or grassland. Ecosystems are dynamic processes. Therefore, we cannot gain an adequate understanding of ecosystems using static images of systems. Time, then, must be factored into analyses of ecosystems. Just how much time is needed to study ecosystems adequately has, in fact, become a central problem in ecology (see May 1989: 356, 358).

According to Brennan (1988: 48), in the years after Clement released his theory, A.G. Tansley formulated the notion that ecosystems consist not only of biotic but of abiotic elements (e.g., wind, solar energy and carbon). He saw the plant communities as parts of ecosystems, where ecosystems are the basic units of nature.

Neither Clement's nor Tansley's notions have withstood criticism. Clement's notion of a superorganism, for instance, has been criticized on the grounds that ecological communities do not replicate themselves genetically, as do organisms. Many other dissimilarities between organisms and ecosystems could be cited. Ecosystems do not appear to ingest nutrients and excrete waste material as their individual members do, for example. Tansley's definition of a "basic unit of nature" has been criticized on the grounds that it is difficult, if not impossible, to establish how big the unit is and how long it must exist before it counts as a unit. As we have seen, there still seems to be little agreement in the contemporary scene over what spatial, functional or temporal unit is basic.

Ecologists, as Cherrett (1989) has pointed out, generally are divided on what to identify as a basic unit. Some believe that the fundamental unit is the individual—the individual organism—while others argue that the whole is the fundamental unit. Yet others support the idea that sub-units of the whole (such as populations, niches, rain forests and savannahs) are fundamental. Some take the individual itself as a community of interacting organisms (e.g., E-coli bacteria), where the fundamental unit is something smaller than what we identify as a single organism. This debate over what constitutes a basic unit has become central to the concerns of ecology. It is not only important for sorting out theoretical issues of how we are to conduct research on ecosystems and what we are to look for, it also affects the practical problem of conservation (e.g., whether to protect individuals, species or niches). Do we allow individuals to suffer and die, leaving the weak as prey for predators to keep the larger unit (the herd) genetically strong; or do we protect these individual units?

Despite these legitimate criticisms, neither Clement nor Tansley should be dismissed out of hand. Clement's idea of succession reinforces the notion of process as fundamental to ecosystem identity. Ecosystems are always in the process of becoming something else, a condition that complements the indeterminacy of ecosystems. Tansley's notion of a basic unit should not be entirely rejected either, since it draws attention to the complex interaction between wholes and parts. It is not the ability to identify with certainty which wholes are fundamental that matters so much; rather, it is engaging the problematic that is central to thinking ecologically. The debate itself raises awareness of how interconnected individuals and various levels of organization are. Tensions created in this debate can, under an appropriate mode of thinking, provide an opportunity for thinking holistically by necessitating a different way of understanding the problem of determining basic units.

Rather than using the term "basic unit of nature," I propose using the term "basic unit of analysis" to remain in keeping with the focus on how we think about nature, rather than on what nature is. Recognizing that the determination of a basic unit is problematic is an additional component to recognizing the limits of understanding and the importance of knowing when to shift to different levels of analysis (both reductive and holistic). Judgment, as much as calculation, then, becomes central to the activity of thinking ecologically.

Returning to the examination of the neuron offers an example of how the idea of a unit of analysis can work. If we want to explain the distribution of sodium and potassium in a non-organic context, for instance, we need only refer to chemical laws and mechanisms. If, however, we want to explain the distribution of those same chemicals in a neuron's rest state, we must appeal to a different order of explanation. When examining the properties of the neuron, we are shifting to a different unit of analysis from that of the chemical relation between potassium and sodium. Indeed, we are compelled to do so, since insisting on the chemical unit leads to failure in explanation. Explaining the structure and function of the neuron requires that the unit of analysis (namely, the neuron as a whole) must be assumed to have properties that the chemicals by themselves do not have. Some concepts, such as "sodium pump" and "information transmission," make sense only by assuming the whole neuronal unit and its relationship to other neurons as the basic unit of analysis. Even this shift is insufficient, however. Information transmission presupposes some purposive function of the neuronal network as a whole. Hence, the organism as a whole must be presupposed as a basic unit of analysis in order to explain information transmission as a function.

Lovelock's (1987: 34, 35) examination of the oxygen-carbon dioxide-methane relation shifts the unit of analysis to the earth as a whole. To solve the problem of explaining the distribution of oxygen, carbon and methane, namely that its probability is so low that it approaches zero, Lovelock assumes that a unit of analysis more comprehensive than the laws that govern individual chemicals is needed.

Other metaphors, such as "niche" and "trophic levels," influence how we think about the "unit of analysis." While informative, they are, again, ambiguous and underdetermined (see Schoener 1989). The notion of an ecological niche, as formulated by C. Elton (1927), represents an object's status in a community, the functional role it plays in the broader environmental context (see Brennan 1988: 49). However niches are formed—we can cite competition between species or mutual cooperation—they are multidimensional and extremely complex sets of relations (interrelations). Earlier, more simplistic theories, such as that of Gause (Brennan

1988: 50-51), which focused on species competition for food sources, failed to take into account the fact that some species survived through cooperation, as is indicated by the sheer richness of diversity in some ecosystems (Strong 1980: 275). Though theories that focused on one or a few factors enjoyed some degree of success and popularity (e.g., those concentrating on light distribution, on availability of food sources and on temperature fluctuations [Brennan 1988: 49]), the accepted view on niches is that they are not determined by any single factor (Schoener 1989: 102, 107). Niches involve not only the relation between an organism and its organic and inorganic surroundings, they also involve interactions between each species' members and interspecies relations (e.g., predation). A name we can use to denote this extremely complex and multilevelled environ is "hyperspace."

"Hyperspace" indicates that any theory we apply in describing ecological niches will be incomplete, a partial representation of the complex organizations of ecosystems. As such, the concept "niche" is a conceptual device that enables us to formulate some understanding of ecosystem interrelations and patterns (Schoener 1989: 107) while warning us that understanding will never be complete. It also encompasses the fact that organisms and environments co-evolve, making an organism, in part, a function of the place in which it is suited to live. *Where* something is partly determines *what* it is. Something exists with the characteristics it has because of the suitability of its properties to its place in the environment. Fish are not well suited to an air environment. Human beings are not well suited to a water environment. Bird's beaks are suited to specific types of food stuffs, such that the habitat for one bird species would be unsuitable for another. While the range or size of a niche varies greatly, depending on the factors we are examining and the level of analysis we are adopting, the notions of place and suitability, nevertheless, remain helpful for understanding why various organisms come to be what they are and why they behave as they do. Niche theory reinforces a long-standing idea that human characteristics are largely a function of the geographical regions in which they live. Glacken (1967: 257), for example, spends a number of long chapters describing how thinkers at every stage of Western intellectual history have explained human characteristics, from skin colour to intellectual capacities, in terms of the effects that geographical location has on them. He shows how even the Greeks saw their superior intellectual powers resulting from the purity of the air in Athens. Even the Christian Roger Bacon argued during the Middle Ages that nothing of importance can be known about human beings apart from knowing the places in which they live (Glacken 1967: 283). Much of our sense of who we are, or lack thereof, is grounded in our sense of belonging to a place. Again, if the exact details of niche theory cannot be spelled out, we cannot expect to gain precise understanding of how place affects identity. For detailed information, we are likely to need both experience in different environments and reflection on our own emotional and intellectual states. Niche theory indicates the significance of being able to shift to and formulate different units of analysis. Shifting can disclose or hide important relationships between organisms and their environment, as well as the conditions characterizing our dependency and determining our creativity.

"Trophic level" is perhaps one of the most useful conceptual tools for forming units of analysis to characterize the notion of purposiveness. Ecosystems are systems of energy relations in which energy passes through various levels or configurations called "trophic levels" in forming organizations of nutrients called "the food chain" (Lindeman 1942), or "food web" when the entire set of chains is being considered (Lawton 1989: 43). Organisms, at different levels of the trophic chain, constitute links in a food web. Autotrophs transform inorganic matter into organic composites and aid in the decomposition of matter to form a kind of recycling mechanism. Autotrophs are then consumed by heterotrophs, which form food for higher-level heterotrophs. Thus, a food web is formed. The web itself is somewhat autonomous in the sense that the recycling and reforming of energy enables the system as a whole to be self-sustaining. As Lindeman (1942: 415) suggests, food webs can also be taken as natural units of study, a fundamental ecological unit.

Trophic units, as self-sustaining systems, can be characterized generally as net energy conserving systems. Conservation is not merely a matter of storing quantities of energy for utilization. Trophic systems organize energy into patterns at various levels, which allows us to call the trophic levels a food "chain." Minerals support plant life, which supports animal life. Each of these levels in the chain have their own divisions. These divisions are different organizations of energy, some of which serve as nutrition for certain species but not for others. This differentiation of types of energy patterns means that the food chain is not a mere storehouse of energy as is a gas tank. The way in which energy can be utilized, then, depends as much on the form that energy takes as it does on the availability of raw energy (e.g., sunlight and heat). This is why Lawton, for instance, argues that ecological energetics has little to do with understanding the structure of food webs (1989: 63). Body size, for example, is a more important factor, although it is not entirely clear why this should be the case (Lawton 1989: 64). The structure of ecosystems is largely determined by the specific capacity of species and individuals to act as food producers and/or consumers for one another. The way in which each species configures energy for others to consume is important, since not all forms of energy can be consumed by all species. There is a structure to the sorts of energy configurations that each consumer species can consume. Suitability of types of energy producers and consumers and their interdependency suggest that the type of niche in which a species finds itself is purposive in the sense previously defined. For all species, there is a built-in attraction to some food stuffs and a repulsion or indifference to others. Each species has a discriminating mechanism that determines what it seeks for nutrition. Despite what goes down the throats of some human beings, the same can be said for the human species. The broad conditions of what is suitable for humans to eat and where they can live are set antecedently to any conception we can have of ourselves.

Each of the units of analysis discussed discloses something about the nature of holistic causality to be taken into account when analyzing ecosystems. Holistic causality involves overarching conditions that determine organizations of chemicals, habitats and food relationships as well as suitability conditions for each form of life. The concept of ecosystems as trophic webs is especially fruitful because it describes nutrition hierarchies as patterns of energy relations. It describes a system of nutrient levels in which the higher levels are more dependent on the lower levels than the lower are on the higher. Nevertheless, each is dependent on the others for survival, since the so-called lower levels are dependent on the consumer species to keep their population under control. Each is dependent on the others for its organization and health. Food or trophic webs are integrated relationships between different members of a system that we might call a community, in the sense that they belong to a system of mutual dependencies based on the suitability of each as producer or consumer.

The particular way in which different food sources have evolved has also determined which species can be supported, since each species depends on a suitable food source. Obviously, if no green plants ever evolved, most of the so-called higher organisms would never have evolved. The deer, for instance, could not have evolved into a food source for the wolf. Each food chain has certain suitability conditions that have evolved, enabling the pattern of energy flow to develop. Food chains, then, form purposive relationships between organisms as their behaviour is directed toward consuming and inhabiting certain patterns of energy.

When analyzed at wider levels, a unit of analysis involves dynamic (as opposed to static) patterns of relationships that are constantly changing by forming, dissolving and altering structures and sometimes functions within a region or within the biosphere as a whole. Unlike the static universe of Ptolemy and Aristotle, the creativity of wholes is part of a process of interactions. Both evolution and ecology tell us that all form and function are temporal, part of a comprehensive process that produces patterns both identifiable and indeterminate.

We should expect difficulties with this notion of process because Western thought is predominantly based on static concepts—the idea of unchanging universals—inclining us to expect definiteness, clarity, constancy of meaning and elimination of ambiguity. We tend to formulate concepts in accordance with these anticipations. If we take these anticipations as starting points for thinking ecologically, our strategy will be to show gradually how they need to be transformed. Heisenberg's (1958: 44) explanation of the paradoxes that arise in quantum theory uses a similar strategy. In describing quantum theory, he assumes that he must begin by using concepts from Newtonian physics, which in the end are inadequate for a description of quantum-level physics. Then, by showing how Newtonian anticipations of certainty and clarity in explanations of relations between objects cannot be established, he demonstrates how quantum theory must presuppose just the opposite.

This strategy is not recommended for all thinkers, since not all languages have the propensity toward static representation of the world. Walter Ong describes most oral traditions as utilizing a world-as-event (not a world-as-view) ontology (Smith n.d.: 11, cited in Goulet 1998: 71). Most nouns in the Dene Tha language, for instance, are really nominalized action verbs, indicating that the Dene Tha see the world as being consti-tuted of actions. This is not surprising, given the animistic elements in aboriginal cultures. At the same time, it is somewhat surprising that the languages that are more appropriate for addressing the evolutionary and ecological implications for developing a new world view are those that have been marginalized by the dominance of Greco-Latin languages.

So, while the strategy may not be universally useful, it does point out that there is a possibility for convergence in modes of understanding and that hope for some conclusions that have universal applicability is not lost. For the moment, the following conclusion can be drawn in prepara-tion. The discussion of purposiveness in both evolutionary theory and ecology precludes assumptions about human detachment or independ-ence from ecosystems. Furthermore, we need to shift our thinking to accord with the idea of the world as process and to shift our epistemology to anticipate having to shape what we count as knowledge by holistic and richly textured concepts that admit opposition and ambiguity.

Influences on Contemporary Thought

Andrew Brennan (1988: 28) has drawn a distinction between "scientific" and other forms of ecology. Other forms include those that are intention-ally non-scientific and non-reductionistic, such as deep ecology. Anna Bramwell (1989) draws another distinction, tracing the political progress of the ecological "green" movement from the 1800s onward. She notes that around 1866, Ernst Haeckel (1957) coined the term *oekologie*, in part to challenge his colleagues in biology to adopt a contextual and holistic perspective to explain biological phenomena. He defined ecology as "the science of relations between organisms and their environment" (Haeckel

1957, cited in Bramwell 1989: 40), which was to have an impact on later political and social movements. Bramwell traces the impact of this influence in her historical account of the German "Green Party" fascist politics and of movements in Europe that embraced monistic thinking (that is, viewing the relation between man and nature as one). She demonstrates how ideas often have more widely ranging implications than their authors intend or imagine. The extent to which an emerging scientific concept or approach can affect thought in other areas was seen in the resistance of political and religious authorities to the heliocentric universe during the Copernican revolution. What has developed in the science of ecology likewise has had profound effects on how people think about the world and their relationship to it.

During much of the 1900s, and especially in the post-Second World War economic boom, belief in our ability to engineer the planet dominated as we developed more and more powerful means to force the planet to yield what we demanded. From massive clear-cutting to the alteration of mixed and sustainable indigenous agricultural systems into monocultural, high-energy input farms (as in India's Green Revolution), from the massive exploitation of water systems (e.g., the virtual elimination of the Colorado River to feed California's hunger for water) to the redesign of the environment to meet the demands of a fossil fuel-burning economy, we believed either that the earth could absorb the effects of our exploitation or that we could manage the consequences. We were confident that we could straighten water courses for flood control. We were confident that old growth forests could be replaced by tree plantations and that stocking fish could substitute for the natural regeneration of the stocks we were overexploiting. We confidently carried on using chemicals to control pests, weeds and crop growth/yield rates. In 1962, however, with Rachel Carson's *Silent Spring* a new consciousness emerged. She brought to our attention how our engineering efforts were killing non-human and human life forms alike. Unanticipated effects of chemical interventions became apparent as pesticides made their way through the complex food web. Failures in resource management techniques (e.g., collapsing fisheries, forests and agricultural systems around the world), environment-related health problems, perceived increases in natural disasters and an increasing aesthetic dissatisfaction (e.g., in the viewing of clear cuts) forced us to accept a new environmental consciousness.

As we come to accept that these environmental problems reflect a vast array of interconnected properties of ecosystems, we come to accept the idea of ecosystems as wholes that need to be understood and treated as wholes. In turn, this acceptance has created a new focus on teaching in the universities, on research and even on policy. During my education as an undergraduate, terms associated with ecology and its related disciplines and movements (e.g., human ecology, ecosystem management, ecosystem approach, deep ecology) were not familiar, as they now are. This new ecological consciousness has resulted from environmental management and engineering failures, much like metaphysical and axiological shifts have resulted from failures in dominant analytical systems. Shifting to an ecological perspective has been motivated by a lack of confidence in the human capacity to understand the environment appropriately and to design appropriate tools for controlling the environment. As Roszak (1972) would have it, ecology has helped foster a new way of thinking about our relationship to the environment by offering an alternative way to address the various environmental crises.

Emerging ideas and movements such as restoration ecology and conservation biology have encouraged us to make qualitative changes in how we think about and value the environment. Aldo Leopold's (1964) Land Pyramid, for instance, would have us radically alter our understanding of soil and micro-organisms. They occupy the bottom-most level of the ecological system, while large carnivores and humans occupy the top level in a dependency relationship. In between are plants, insects, birds, rodents and other animals. Each successive layer depends on those below it for food and often for other services, and each in turn furnishes food and services to those above. "Its functioning depends on the cooperation and competition of its diverse parts" (Leopold 1964: 215). We are being asked to invert our understanding of what is important and why it is important. Being at the bottom of the pyramid is not to be of lesser importance (as the Greco-Christian imagery promotes) but of greater importance because what exists at that level supports everything above it.

Three further ideas of interest can be extracted from the idea of the Land Pyramid: 1) the land is not merely soil; 2) by providing food and services, native plants and animals keep the energy circuit open while non-native species may or may not; 3) changes brought about by humans are often of a different order than evolutionary changes and have effects more comprehensive than is intended or foreseen (Leopold 1964: 218). Each idea challenges the Modern system of thinking about the environment by asserting that 1) the land is not a mere object of study and commodification; 2) what has evolved and existed in a particular place is better suited to that place than what humans design to be put there; 3) rational understanding is insufficient for anticipating the consequences of human design and action.

By focusing on maintaining the integrity of the biotic system, Leopold is advocating individual responsibility for the well-being of the land. Conservation of native biota is a primary ethical principle. What motivates us to adopt this responsibility, Leopold argues, is an ethic and an aesthetic: "A thing is right when it tends to preserve integrity, stability, and beauty of the biotic community. It is wrong when it tends otherwise" (1964: 224–25). This ethic is one that Leopold prescribes and, in a way, describes. Many people (see Callicott 1989c [discussed below] and Olver et al. 1995 [discussed in Chapter Six] as examples) have been inspired by Leopold. It is as if he captured their basic ecological sensibilities and formulated them so that they could act on their sensibilities.

Focusing on Leopold's metaphysical commitments for the moment, we can begin to examine how radically he believes our thinking must change. J. Baird Callicott (1989c) is a primary expositor and defender of Leopold's position. He explains that, in contrast to the Modern mechanistic view of nature, ecosystems are energy circuits wherein plants and animals are understood as dissipative structures, enduring only as a result of a continual flow of energy in a system and not as atomic, independently existing entities (Callicott 1986: 311). For Leopold, the land is constituted of interrelated processes. Each member of the biotic community is a flow of energy related to all other flows of energy, and each requires the different dissipative structures to exist. This explanatory scheme is perhaps an even clearer expression of holistic causality. Structuring this energy to form integrated units establishes the discernible patterns that give ecosystems their purposive character. Each dissipative structure is constituted of the same energy as are all other dissipative structures, and so it is, in some way, identical to yet differentiated from the whole. The whole, at the same time, contains the conditions that give rise to differentiation. It follows that every individual in the Land Pyramid is an expression of this condition. For this reason, Leopold can say that the land is not merely soil; indeed it *is* everything else because it is the energy that once constituted other dissipative structures and will *become* the energy constituting yet other dissipative structures.

Purposiveness is related to the structure and function of communities, as Leopold sees "community." His use of this term to describe the relationships between dissipative structures assumes an integrative function of community that is both antecedent to the emergence of evolved species and the development of individuals and shaped by this emergence and development. It is a mutually affecting relationship. As noted, the term "community" has become significant among ecologists, yet it remains ambiguous and vague. I suggest that it is necessarily vague because it attempts to capture for thought something of the order of a first principle in the classical sense. Like Plato's Good, it is that which is necessary to explain the relationship between the forms (primary concepts used in explanation) but cannot itself be explained by those concepts. Unlike Plato's Good, however, ecology tells us that when structures fit or belong to a place they also create new conditions, thereby reconstituting the purposiveness of the places in which they are found.

Leopold, then, represents an important influence on environmental thought, which has directed us toward thinking ecologically. The reformulation of our relationship to the land, however, has left us in a paradox.

In some ways our errors in formulation have been part of an adaptive strategy. Assumptions of superiority, anthropocentrism and the mechanical order of the universe have all aided in our development as the dominant species. We are at a cusp, then, where we are tempted to fall one of two ways rather than trying to remain balanced at the apex. One way is to accept our dominance, however bad the situation in which it has placed us; the other is to accept the tension and struggle with uncertainty.

It would appear that we are headed in the latter direction. The struggle is reflected at the international level at the United Nations. In *Our Common Future*, the U.N.'s World Commission on Environment and Development (WCED) 1987 has tried to address this struggle. Although primarily a forum to advance the principle of the sovereignty of nations and human rights, the WCED makes periodic mention of the unity of humanity and nature. It sponsored the 1992 Earth Summit in Rio de Janeiro at which it struggled to establish a declaration and a new environmental agenda that would recognize how closely linked we are to the environment. Later expressions of this identity, appearing in such publications as *Canada's Green Plan* (Canada 1990) and, more regionally, "The Ecosystem Approach: Theory and Ecosystem Integrity" (Allen et al. 1993), invert the previous world view, which placed our species outside the ecosystem, putting "our species inside the system, not as an outside influence but as a working component" (Allen et al. 1993: 13). Yet the main theme of the WCED's *Our Common Future* (1987), as will be discussed, is to champion the continued exploitation of the land and the industrialization of developing countries to bring them to the same level of prosperity as industrialized countries.

Many attempts to advance ecological thinking have emerged in the deep ecology, social ecology and ecofeminism movements, for whom our reliance on technology to dominate nature is a central concern. Deep ecology focuses on the pursuit of wisdom through intimate awareness and understanding of nature (see Naess 1989; Drengson and Inoue 1995); it addresses the need for epistemic transformation. Deep ecology in part is a response to what is labelled "shallow ecology" (Naess 1972), an inadequate mode of thinking for penetrating to levels of understanding at which disclosure of our connectedness to the non-human world would more spontaneously arise.

The deep ecology movement attempts to integrate metaphysical, epistemological and axiological aspects of ecology to form an ethical orientation toward the earth—one based on a recognition of the intrinsic value of all creatures and of the earth itself as well as the Gandhian practice of non-violent resistance (Naess 1989: 146). Both Arne Naess and Alan Drengson are profoundly influenced by Eastern religious thought, but the deep questioning process need not appeal to these traditions. Indeed, the foundation for Naess' own thinking is what he calls "ecosophy T," where the "T" stands for his Tvergastein, the name of his hut in the Norwegian mountains (1989: 4). Each person will have a different ecosophy (ecological wisdom). Naess, nevertheless, is confident that people will discover a common foundation through the deep questioning process. Supporters of deep ecology recognize the importance of radical shifts in thinking and behaviour, while respecting individual process and individual freedom.

The movement recognizes human ignorance concerning how and why ecosystems work (Naess 1989: 26). Although it accepts that the intellect is the principal instrument through which the human mind acquires understanding, other modes of knowing, such as intuition, emotion and insight, need to form an integral part of what counts as knowledge. These modes allow us to understand ourselves and our relationship to the environment more completely and appropriately. For the supporter of deep ecology, the concept of "intellect" is considerably wider and more comprehensive than tends to be recognized in Western intellectual culture.

Teachings from wilderness experience and other forms of practice (e.g., the martial arts) are often cited as central. Knowing through feeling and through diverse forms of awareness, born not of scepticism but of acceptance and openness, has promoted a study of the connection between deep ecology and indigenous people's environmental consciousness. Some indigenous communities take Western modes of intelligence to be inferior or at least incomplete without a dream world (see Goulet 1998: 181). Dreams are crucial for determining one's sense of personal identity and meaning and can be useful for gathering information about how one ought to act. Similarly, art, personal relationships, music and the like provide outlets for the expression of one's understanding and are crucial for articulating the relationship to the world. Each mode of expression can be a mode of understanding and is valuable in placing us in a context of receptivity to the "information" presented by the environmental context. The most important sort of information for understanding our ecological community relationships is local in character, not universal.

Personal identity questions spawned in the ecological debate have also been connected to aboriginal perspective. The Dene Tha culture views each person as emerging through a process of individuation. Through dreams, vision quests, ceremony and other forms of discipline, the aboriginal person (especially the male) discovers his identity, his animal helper, his vocation in life and, sometimes, his clan. Each element in this process determines a part of who he is both as a person and as a member of the larger community. In the end, each seeker is to recognize himself as this set of special characteristics and functions, created from the oneness of the great spirit. In Ojibway (Anishnaabe) culture, this great spirit is

Kitche Manitou, the Great Mystery. Each person begins as part of the great undifferentiated mystery and gradually becomes differentiated as he or she undergoes the process of individuation (see Morito 1999b). These aspects of aboriginal environmental culture have served as models for many in the environmental movement.

While similar in its demand for sweeping change in perspective and values, social ecology focuses on social change through political recognition of the diversity of life forms and their special place in the ecosystem (see Bookchin 1990, 1991). Resistance to reductionism of any sort is paramount. Social ecology is based on insights taken from biological evolution, and it emphasizes the striving of all living beings to exhibit a self-evolving pattern that gives direction and impetus to life (Bookchin 1991: 365). Opposition to hierarchical social structuring encourages and permits an expanding diversification both in non-human and human communities. Here, the social ecologist is similar to the deep ecologist, insofar as the notion of self-realization is vital (Naess 1989: 8, 9). It is also shared by those who take a more traditional approach. For example, Paul Taylor (1986) argues that all organic beings have a teleological centre that directs them toward maturation and action. They ought, then, to have a right to mature and act according to their *telos* (design or end).

Bookchin (1990) supports the view that ecology requires a dialectical way of understanding the relation between wholes and individuals. An individual's internal or implicit form is actualized or emerges through maturation; individuals are processes of development toward full individuation. Thus, evolutionary and maturational development supports the flourishing of individuals, and society or community structure must be modelled to allow this flourishing to occur. The community that promotes the flourishing of individuals must be respected and maintained.

Ecofeminists criticize the hierarchical social structuring of contemporary society (see Warren 1983). They argue that the "logic of dominance," which is based on patriarchal power structures (male dominance), has been applied equally to nature in the exploitation of natural resources as mere objects for human consumption. The emancipation of women and nature, then, are one in the same process. Understanding the oppression of one helps in understanding the oppression of the other.

The term "logic" is meant to convey the idea that the existence of dominance structures is not haphazard or accidental. These structures are supported by a justificatory world view. Social dominance of one class or gender over another has been justified on the basis of a hierarchical world view that utilizes high/low, intrinsic/instrumental, intellectual/physical dualisms, which assign superior status to the former and inferior status to the latter. The ecofeminist critique of hierarchy aims to undermine dualistic and mechanistic ontologies, with a focus on gender.

Clearly, ecology has had a widespread impact on many areas of thought and social action. Different movements focus on different implications of ecology, but when we see them together we witness how major metaphysical concepts (e.g., holistic causality, purposiveness, interrelatedness and non-detachment) are applied in various spheres of action. Whether or not these movements make proper application of ecological concepts is an issue for later discussion.

An Ecologically Directed Pursuit of Knowledge

The increasing acceptance and influence of ecological approaches have peaked an interest in determining what counts as knowledge under this emerging world view. Answering the question of how a conception of knowledge should be formulated is not easy, especially when the subject matter is fuzzy and largely indeterminate. The idea of probability has been used to substitute for strict deterministic analysis for some contexts (e.g., predicting subatomic motion), but various cultures have made different suggestions. Dreams have been suggested. Those in resource management circles are interested in including field naturalist information and local resident understandings of ecosystems in management plans, and this has been evident in planning activities and policy development.[1] Although the idea of including the traditional environmental knowledge of aboriginal peoples into management policy and decision making has met with considerable resistance (see Howard and Widdowson 1997), co-management and adaptive management regimes are increasingly including aboriginal peoples in management decisions. This inclusion, in part, recognizes multiple forms of knowledge as a mode of "ecological thinking." Although inclusions of this sort are aimed at redressing the injustices perpetrated against aboriginal people rather than responding to epistemic issues, they do influence the kind of knowledge managers are responsible for gathering and including in decision making.

If the reductionistic approach is insufficient, however, do we simply open the floodgates to any approach? To do so would lead to human extinction. Without an appropriate type of knowledge acquisition system in the proper context at the proper time, we die. We cannot switch to intellectual reflection and theory building while an enemy bears down on us and still expect to survive. Likewise, as the weaker species among many others, we would become extinct without analytical and mechanistic ways of thinking to shape tools and weapons. But this is nothing strange. Most people move between different modes of knowing in the contexts of work, family and romantic love. Sometimes empathy with others lets us know that they are suffering and enables us to act appropriately. At other times, we must know through sceptical analysis, as in courts of law.

Thinking ecologically nevertheless involves a core set of ideas about knowledge, which can be introduced at this point and refined later. One idea is that knowledge gained through thinking ecologically must not be directed toward establishing mastery over nature. This idea of mastery, popularized by the Greeks, assumes that a primary function of reason is to control nature. But with evolutionary theory supporting the idea that reason is more an adaptive tool and with ecology telling us that we cannot know environmental conditions sufficiently to master them, the pursuit of knowledge needs to shift onto different foundations. We require a shift in the concept of knowledge from one whose paradigm case is mathematics to one whose aim is to allow us to see and understand as deeply and as comprehensively as possible. This does not mean that simplification and reductive analysis are not vital; it means that they must be recognized as being among a number of possible routes to the kind of knowledge that will attune us to ecosystem processes, our communities and ourselves.

Knowing, then, is ineluctably tied to valuing, insofar as serving a function is of value. As a function of adaptation, knowledge is valued as the pursuit of understanding for purposes of attunement. The acquisition of knowledge is subject to holistic conditions and is concerned with integrating the many forms of knowing that enable us to adapt. Different ways of knowing, then, are best conceived as modes of attunement to the world, each of which is deployed in a different context and for different reasons. Their integration is an art as much as a method. It is an art of weaving the plurality of perspectives, insights and analyses into a coherent grasping of the world. And it is a commitment to finding suitable methods of investigation and rigorously applying them.

Besides the purposiveness of knowledge as a tool of adaptation and attunement and as an integrative activity, knowledge is always problematic. If always limited, then no knowledge claim can expect to attain the status of an absolute. The problematic character of knowledge claims is so by virtue of the tension between two contrary components. On the one hand, we have the relativistic component, generated by the recognition that knowledge claims are value dependent and largely constructed to serve some human end. On the other hand, we must recognize that standards of rigour and falsifications of knowledge claims are possible only because there is a "given" (see Kant 1929[2]). The given, in the classical sense, is "objective" because it cannot be explained in terms of subjective determinants. Some properties or aspects of what we are trying to explain persist, independent of whatever mental or social construction of them we might entertain. This is a vital contribution of science and its methodological approach because it calls us to standards of legitimacy through pursuit of fact. Keeping this problematic in mind is central to attunement and what it means to think ecologically.

Notes

1. My involvement with the Ontario Ministry of Natural Resources during workshops on developing policy on ecosystem management indicates that the ministry is not only open to but desirous of information that field naturalists have acquired. Some discussion has been directed toward recognizing the importance of information gathered idiosyncratically because the usual practice of applying general principles and models of resource management often fails to take account of local peculiarities. For issues concerning location of certain plants and microclimates, local knowledge is becoming recognized as essential.

2. Obviously, a sustained discussion of Kant's notion of the "given" is not appropriate here. It is sufficient to note that in the Introduction, Transcendental Aesthetic, and in the Second Analogy, the notion of the given is related to those aspects of experience upon which we depend for the possibility of experience but which cannot be altered. In other words, the "intuitions" upon which intelligible descriptions and explanations of the world depend are not the product of construction or human valuation. What Kant calls "intuition" is that upon which thought works to form theories, but they cannot be thought about in just any way. For example, in the Second Analogy, Kant recognizes that the sequence of events is "bound down" and cannot be altered by the perceiver. "Givenness" then represents that in experience against which we compare our constructed descriptions and explanations to determine theory reliability, truthfulness or falsity.

Chapter Four

Values and World View

Having seen how world views, their transformation and their systems of knowledge are tied to human valuations, I will now set the stage for a discussion of thinking ecologically about ethics by expanding on the valuational component in world view transitions. The discussion of values thus far has illustrated how the undermining of the hierarchy of being affects the way in which the environment is valued. In this chapter, addressing the nature of values in light of this historical development will involve an investigation of the genesis of values. We saw how, under the Greco-Christian system, environmental values are determined by the Good or God, such that humans are at best the agents who complete these values. In this chapter, our analysis of Modern value theory—which sees environmental values as being conferred by human beings who have taken an interest in the environment—will provide a historical context against which we can envision and construct a model for shifting to an ecological value theory.

The Universality of Value Commitments

Earlier I argued that scientific method is based on a commitment to the values of reliability, public verifiability and the like. It is both historically and conceptually intended to exclude other values in the determination of knowledge acquisition. To assert that science is value neutral, then, is to mask its value commitments and its intent to be exclusionary. I raise this matter for discussion because it is an issue of "misanalysis" parallel to "misidentifying" human nature as fundamentally separate from non-human nature. A critical discussion of assumptions in value theory is, therefore, warranted. Archie Bahm (1993: 7) argues that value theory (axiology)—itself a science—is neglected by scientists; and the subsequent neglect of policy makers to study values has led to confusion and the use of unreliable information regarding what people actually need and want.

Different modes of analysis (e.g., economic, legal, political, sociological, psychological and anthropological) have different underlying values, which direct attention toward different sorts of questions and concerns.

So, to take a psychological point of view is to exclude others, which is to exclude other sorts of values that people might want recognized (e.g., religious or economic). There is nothing untoward about this; it is a necessary simplification for gaining any understanding whatsoever. Even within particular modes, there are different value commitments. Economics, for instance, is primarily concerned with exchange value (money), wealth and gross national products. Analysis directed by this framework suppresses and marginalizes other sorts of economic values, such as maintaining a stable community, subsistence, sharing and need (rather than want). While there are many other reasons for studying values, these reasons are sufficient to demonstrate how neglect of such study can lead to the marginalization both of people and of values that could promote attunement.

In the Greco-Christian era people believed that values were conferred onto the earth by the divine or the gods and that the role of humanity was to recognize these values and then complete and develop them. There were negative values to eradicate; as we have seen in the case of Plato and more ascetic elements of Christianity, the negative value of bodily existence had to be resisted and overcome. Ultimately, recognizing and developing the positive values that God declared the world to have was the mandate of humanity. Forests were cleared, monuments to the divine were erected and vineyards were established in the process of completing God's creation. Wildness (e.g., predators and original forests) had to be eradicated or improved. The effects of the Greco-Christian era on views about environmental values were minimal compared to what occurred during the Modern Era, but it is still important to note how differently the Greco-Christian value orientation was from the animistic. The detachment of the rational mind from the object (nature) permitted the systematic articulation of the human superiority thesis. Coupled with the objectification of nature, assumptions of detachment opened the way to thinking about the environment as value neutral, or at least not valuable until some rational agent (God or man) takes an interest in it and proclaims it to be good or bad.

The connection between intrinsic value and rationality also begins with Socrates and the ancient Greeks. It is one of the most important developments in value theory affecting environmental ethics. The Greeks taught that intrinsic value and its accompanying privilege are owing to the connection between reason and the divine. In the Modern Era, the connection to the divine diminished in importance but that between intrinsic value and rationality remained central. No longer did people believe that value was conferred on the earth by God; rational humans assumed that role. The effects on the ethical sensibilities toward the environment were immense. Belief in the intrinsic value of human individuals formed a pillar for the development of democracy at the same time that it supported a view of the environment as value neutral. Values that permitted the accumulation of human power and control came to dominate values that encouraged obedience to a divine being. A radical change in the sense of community took place, thereby undermining collective values.

The Advent of Liberal Democratic Values

Much of the explicit discussion about values begins in the Modern Era. Greco-Christian (Ptolemaic) hierarchical thinking reached its height with the authority of the Roman papacy, but with the demise of this hierarchical scheme came a political shift to parliamentary democracy (1600s). Rule by monarch and church-led dictatorial rule in Europe began to decline. The so-called "Priesthood of the People," which had its roots in empiricism and the liberalization of academies once controlled by the church, called for the rejection of church authority—the separation of church and state.

Scepticism, the systematic doubting of truth claims, became more influential, especially in academic institutions, which were slowly being released from the dogmatism of the church. The English Civil War (1642–49) greatly contributed to the development of liberalism, as Puritanism and democracy won the battle against aristocratic rule. The result of this and other revolutions (especially the French Revolution) was a secular political system. In a rather provocative move, the Revolution of 1688, as described by John Locke (1960), gave rise to the "priesthood of all believers." This political entity had "no obligation to any government seeking to control an individual for any other reason than his own benefit" (Gould and Truitt 1973: 33). In what Gould and Truitt call the *Agreement of the People* (Putney Debates [November–December, 1647] cited in Gould and Truitt 1973: 33), the "principle of consent" was established to recognize individual interest in the proceedings of government and to give individuals the right to revolt if rulers became corrupt or government became arbitrary.

The advent of democracy paralleled the emergence of the scientific method. What constitutes a legitimate decision and a system of governance became open questions. If God and monarchs were no longer to be recognized as sources of legitimacy, then the community of rational beings was all that remained to fill the role. Where agreement between individuals grounds legitimacy in decision making and governance, individual decision is the source of authority; agreements, in the form of contracts, determine how individuals are to form collectives. Thomas Hobbes' *Leviathan* (1972) argues that individuals agree to forfeit their sovereignty to enjoy the protection of a supreme sovereign (government). John Locke (1960) does not go as far in his *Two Treatises of Government*, since he feels that the right to take up arms against a corrupt sovereign must be built into a democracy's constitution. Jean Jacques Rousseau (1976), in *The Discourse on the Origin of Inequality* and *The Social Contract*, speculates that there once had been a golden period during which human beings enjoyed the best of both worlds of individual freedom and collective security. The development of the arts and sciences required both individual initiative and society's recognition of the contributions. Corruption eventually erupted, owing to natural inequalities. Contracts then had to be formed and enforced to control what otherwise would amount to a tyranny of the human will, at which point individuals would lose their freedom and become slaves. Contract, then, represents the general will of the people as expressed through law.

Despite the different forms contract took, the general view of the time was that, through agreement and contract between individuals, people legitimate government. This new social and political climate demanded that people rethink who they were, as their new-found authority began to strain the relationship between the individual and the state, between the individual and authority. Hobbes' *Leviathan* (1972: 186, pt. 1, ch. 13) describes the life of human beings as one of adversity. Indeed, Hobbes (1972: 189, pt. 1, ch. 14) hardly thinks it worth arguing; he simply asserts that human life is solitary, poor, brutish and short, its relation to nature forbidding, its relation to others a state of war. Adversity or conflict is a basic fact to which the construction of rights and systems of justice is a response. We enter into contracts (or compacts) and assign ourselves rights to overcome such adversity. Paulo Freire makes similar assumptions in proclaiming that human beings cannot be silent but must be nourished by true words that transform the world (1974: 76) in an act of creation, which is, in effect, an act of rebellion against the daily repetition of things (1985: 199). For Freire, the liberal is born in the act of rebellion, in a state of adversity. In *On Liberty*, John Stuart Mill explains that "liberty" means the protection against the tyranny of the political rulers (1947: 1). Wherever we might look among the great progenitors and proponents of liberalism, we find the same assumption of adversity as the moving force that generates normative development.

The beliefs that adversity is the primary fact and that values belong to individual domains of privacy make it appear that what we are, as valuing beings, is everywhere threatened by others and a hostile environment. It is almost automatic to assume that primary values are born in a human being's conflict with unsympathetic nature and other malicious humans.

In North America, where liberalism had it purest start (since it did not have to rid itself of authoritarian and monarchical structures), we have a clear illustration of how the lone individual deals with this hostility by making claims concerning the right to exploit, shape and conquer the land. American history is replete with stories of its heroes conquering the "wild west" and the untamed beast. Nature exists to be conquered and to have its otherwise hostile nature subdued. The idea of laying out stakes to define a boundary was the early method by which pioneers claimed property. A simple act of marking out boundaries was all that was required to carve up natural regions into politically isolated units. Coupled with Darwinian evolutionary theory—the survival of the fittest through natural selection—it would appear that liberal assumptions about conflict, competition and the need for protection identify primary and fundamental truths about how and why human beings form values. Even today, little defence seems necessary for the claim that there is a primary human need for isolation and insularity against the antagonistic influences of nature and other humans. Practically speaking, it is not difficult to see how a person's identity as a rights bearer is formed vis-à-vis conflict. Rights and systems of justice are invented, then, to keep individuals secure within their sphere of privacy. Detachment from the earth and from one another is reinforced by the emerging political and social systems.

The priesthood of all believers and the principle of consent contributed to making individual preference central to axiology (value theory). Two figures in the liberal tradition, John Locke (1600s) and John Stuart Mill (1800s), are key to this shift. In these two philosophers we find the foundations of liberal axiology that persist into the present. The way in which any particular object in the environment acquires value is through the agency of some human being. Human beings confer values onto the environment through the act of taking an interest in some aspect of it. The environment, then, owes its value to human interest.

In *Two Treatises of Government*, Locke states,

> This is certain, That in the beginning, before the desire of having more than Men needed, had altered the intrinsick value of things, which depends only on their usefulness to the Life of Man; or [Men] had agreed, that *a little piece of yellow metal*, which would keep without wasting or decay, should be worth a great piece of Flesh, or a Whole heap of Corn; though Men had a Right to appropriate, by their Labour, each one to himself, as much of the things of Nature, as he could use: Yet this could not be much, nor to the Prejudice of others, where the same plenty was still left, to those who would use the same Industry. (1960: 335–36; original emphasis)

His use of the term "intrinsick" should not be confused with the dominant use of the term, which is that something is valuable in itself. Clearly, as explained above, Locke does not mean to use it this way.

But how do human beings themselves acquire value? As Peter

Singer (1986: 227) explains, for most liberals, they don't; they are simply inherently valuable. Typical Lockeians begin with the assumption that human beings—read rational beings—have intrinsic dignity or intrinsic worth. The most prominent philosopher in the Modern world, Immanuel Kant, is instrumental in entrenching this view. He sets out an ethic that is to form one of the cornerstones of contemporary ethics. In *The Foundations of the Metaphysics of Morals*, Kant (1969: 52–53) argues:

> Man and, in general, every rational being exists as an end in himself and not merely as a means to be arbitrarily used by this or that will.... Beings whose existence does not depend on our will but on nature, if they are not rational beings, have only a relative worth as means and are therefore called "things." On the other hand, rational beings are designated "persons." Such a being is thus an object of respect.

The value of human beings cannot be explained by reference to anything external to them, while non-human beings acquire value only by reference to some external valuer.

John Stuart Mill (1979: 9), in *Utilitarianism*, further argues that the values of the learned and high-cultured are the only values that ought properly to influence the morals and decision-making procedures of society. These persons' values are to be preferred as foundations of value because they are higher and nobler. Nobility is the sort of characteristic that only people with rational capacities can enjoy. Thus, liberals tend to narrow the scope of what can count as a legitimate agent of value conferment to rational beings. In his influential writing *On Liberty* Mill (1947: 11) argues that rationality—the ability to use the intellect to self-correct—is the mark of individuality since it describes the capacities that a being must have in order to be autonomous. When reason is present in an individual, it is sufficient to make that individual a rights bearer. Rationality (interpreted as the ability to understand information, make determinations of truth and falsity and make decisions based on deliberation) becomes the cornerstone of classical liberal axiology. Without rationality, there is no moral status, that is, membership in a moral community. Persons, then, are both unique repositories of rationality and unique creators of value.

This elevated status for rational humans constitutes humanity as the end for which nature exists. It is relatively easy to assume that we are the highest order of creation since no other creature seems able to plan, use its intellect or create value like human beings. For the classical liberal, all values are relative to the valuer, namely, the human agent who takes an interest in an object for one reason or another. In collectives, human beings determine the value of an item through agreements to make that item worth whatever they decide.

When values are conferred onto non-human objects through acts of taking an interest in them, they are "granted" or "bestowed" value. Again, little or no justification for how values get conferred seems important for the originators of liberal value theory. Since an object's value can be contradictory at different times and in relation to different people, it seems obvious that its value is determined entirely by the valuer. To one person, penicillin is a life-giving, healing substance. To another, who wishes to murder someone with a strong allergy to penicillin, it is a deadly toxin. Moreover, at different times, the same person might hold opposite values with respect to penicillin if at one time the desire was to save a friend and at another to kill a foe. The value of penicillin, then, is dependent both on individual interest and context. To be of value, in this sense, is to be instrumental (a means) for accomplishing some end. Instrumental values are fabrications of human agents, much like labels. We label a liquid poisonous not because it is inherently dangerous but because it is dangerous for us. Some property of the liquid is deemed of interest to us because of its effect on us. Values, accordingly, are abstract representations of some human interest, positive or negative, toward an object. From a psychological point of view, it is difficult to see how liberal value theory could be false.

Locke (1960) also introduces the notion of waste into the value framework of classical liberalism. Wasting is considered a morally reprehensible act (see also Hargrove 1989: 69, who makes a similar point in his discussion of Thomas Jefferson's influence on American property law). Not only is taking an interest in an object the basis for an object's value, but not using that object for its obvious instrumental value is considered wrong. That is, not using and exploiting merchantable nature is thought to reduce the amount of value in the world as the resource degenerates. We are obliged to use and exploit, where possible, to improve the economic lot of humankind.

As Hargrove (1989: especially Chapter 4) so graphically describes, the wanton slaughter of non- or less-merchantable resources, e.g., the buffalo, by European settlers and frontiersmen was rampant, but it was considered ethically irrelevant. Slaughter for sport or for trinkets (a horn or tail) was considered both acceptable and expected of the frontiersman. It was inconceivable and soft-minded to be concerned about a buffalo's interest in survival when one was about to kill it. Furthermore, not until it was killed and its parts used for something did the buffalo acquire value. Clearly, the assumption of privileged status was deeply ingrained in the frontier mentality. Today, the professional forester's or civil engineer's judgments about old growth forests and wetlands are remnants of this view. We constantly hear representatives of large forestry corporations stating that saving old growth forests is wasting a valuable timber resource. The forest is not valuable unless used and exploited. Wetlands are wasted areas for the developer because the space they occupy is not being utilized for housing or industry.

Waste and work are of key importance in liberal value theory, not to mention Marxist thought, and are closely related. By mixing our labour with the land, the land acquires worth (Locke 1960: 335). Until we so mix our labour, the land remains virtually worthless, merely potentially valuable. Work, then, is the primary operation that makes taking an interest in something a value-conferring activity. In the act of extracting, shaping, manipulating and exploiting, we create product; something to be used, consumed and enjoyed. If values are born in the enterprising activities of rational human beings, animals cannot properly be said to confer values, even though they do seem to work and take an interest in specific objects in the environment. Work that generates values requires rational planning in accordance with an end (see, for example, Rescher 1969: 9).

Work, in this view, produces something more than value; it produces property. The expenditure of labour energy on the land makes the land, or whatever one labours to produce, one's property. Labour, and the transfer of that which represents labour (money), entitles a person to what is produced or paid for. That property is the sole possession of the labourer, and no external party can legitimately lay claim to it. Hence, the owner also acquires a right or title to the object with which labour is mixed, just as long as no other rational being has mixed his labour with it.

Property rights, accordingly, serve as trumps to override the threat of third parties using or seizing the products of one's labour. The reason for placing such emphasis on individual value-conferring activity, property and individual rights is to protect individuals from tyranny and arbitrary rule (dispossession of property) by others. These rights, moreover, are considered "natural," in the sense that they inhere in the work of rational beings. The value of work is intrinsic to itself.

Values must be protected by the state because, for the liberal democrat, they are generated by individuals and for individuals. If we happen to hold common values, it is only by accident and agreement, and not by nature, that we do so. Rights designed to protect our values are, designed, then, to protect our spheres of independence and privacy. This sphere is insulated against the effects of external interference or intervention. Rights, as a result, isolate the individual from others. When rational individuals claim rights to privacy, they are in effect creating domains of independence in which their freedom to confer values is protected by law and by general moral conviction.

Rights-protected value-conferring activity is principally an act of creating isolated, independent worlds for each individual. What people do on their own property or in their own bedrooms is their own business.

Sometimes, however, agreements are formed to optimize the chances of satisfying commonly held values. Commonly held values serve as the basis for legal rights. Because of commonly held values in protecting property, we agree to pay taxes to support the enforcement of laws because it is in our best interest to agree to such schemes.

Parliamentary systems are formed to manage the process of agreement formulation and to formalize these agreements into conventional rights. Hence, the task of liberal democracy is to form a governing body that ensures the protection of privacy rights. It must govern so as to ensure that the reasons for an individual to stay within the community outweigh the reasons for leaving.

Utility

Liberal axiology has intimate ties to utilitarianism. The roots of utilitarianism can be found in the eudemonistic ethics of the ancient Greeks—the view that the end or goal of moral existence is happiness. Maligned by the church and those who would espouse the virtues of honour, dignity and intellect, the eudemonistic ethic was often seen as belonging to a lower order of morality. Happiness was contrasted with duty (deontological ethics), as determined by the authority of the church and the state. With the demise of the church and the monarchy, utility has become the primary ground for defining goodness, supplanting more deontological notions of duty and obedience to a divine authority or model. The notion of utility has become especially prominent in democratic systems. Where individual will is the measure of value, personal happiness and freedom override duty and obedience as foundations for right and wrong.

Jeremy Bentham (1977), in *An Introduction to the Principles of Morals and Legislation*, states that human beings are governed by two sovereign masters: pain and pleasure. The principle of utility recognizes their sovereignty and takes them as the foundations of ethics and value theory. Utility, consequently, is the property of an object or action to produce benefit, advantage, pleasure or the avoidance of pain. Community interest is just the sum of the utilities of all the members who comprise the community. Deciding what is right and wrong for a community is a matter of adding up the benefits and subtracting the costs of an action. If the benefits outweigh the costs, the action is right.

For Bentham, pleasure is a good in itself, an "intrinsic" good. Those actions and objects that bring the person pleasure or the avoidance of pain are instrumentally valuable as means. Pleasure needs nothing more than itself to explain or justify why it is good. This version of utilitarianism has been called psychological hedonism since it is based on the psychological motivations of pleasure and pain.

Bentham's influence on economics is evident through the extension of the hedonistic calculus to the development of systems of cost-benefit analysis. It is claimed that decisions about right and wrong, determined by weighing the good consequences of an action against the bad, are clear and unambiguous. Decisions can be calculated because the value at issue can be quantified. By weighing the benefits and costs according to the preferences of people, the results appear to be fair and democratic because everyone's preferences are included in the process. Examinations of the market (what people spend money on), surveys, votes, etc., allow us to quantify and measure these preferences. Politicians and policy makers have been eager to employ this approach for their own decision-making schemes. The clarity of the methodology makes the management of decisions and policy relatively straightforward.

In this scheme, all values are treated in the same manner and measured in the same scale. They belong to the same order, and so can be compared according to the weight they carry as indicators of individual and social utility. In assessing which values are to be preferred, the scheme allows for a relative weighting of a value by its proponents, but a basic commensurability between values is assumed.

The assumption that all values can be weighed in the same mechanical way is appealing. In an environmental context, for example, if all values, including economic, social, aesthetic and spiritual, can be measured, the numerical value at the conclusion of the weighing procedure lends clarity, conceptual simplicity and, at least, prima facie fairness to the process. The idea of "willingness to pay" is an example of how all values can be reduced to a single economic value and entered into a decision-making calculus. If people can say how much they are willing to pay to preserve a wilderness park, an economic value can be assigned to it. If they are willing to pay more than the park is worth as a source of minerals or lumber, then the value of exploiting it for resources would be less than the value of protecting it from exploitation; hence, the decision would be to deny exploitation rights to the park.

Even John Stuart Mill's distinction between high and low pleasures can be incorporated into the calculus by using more sophisticated formulations of the calculus, e.g., "what is right is determined by the balance of good over bad, all things considered, over a long period of time." This formulation allows higher-order goods to be included in the calculus and creates stability by qualifying the time frame. The distinction between high and low pleasures can be accommodated; even deontological ethics can be factored in by including duty as one of the goods that people wish to be considered in the calculus, provided that some quantity or numerical value can be assigned to duties. It can accommodate just about any interest or good that people think is worthy of inclusion and, at the same time, foster the freedom that individuals so deeply value.

By far, the dominant view is that only human freedom and values count in this calculus. William Baxter (1995) argues that human freedom and human utility are so deeply entrenched that he finds it impertinent or even imponderable that we should question their centrality and exclusivity. Despite acknowledging the growth in concern for non-human freedom and utility, Baxter argues, "Nevertheless, I think it is the only tenable starting place for analysis for several reasons. First, no other position corresponds to the way most people really think and act—i.e., corresponds to reality" (1995: 382). He makes this statement in defence of excluding non-human beings from the moral community. For interests to be counted in the calculus, they must be capable of being represented in some forum (e.g., election, survey or market). Non-human animals cannot represent their values and cannot, therefore, have their values (if indeed they have values) included in decision making.

At first glance, Baxter's argument seems convincing because he shows how difficult (in his view, impossible) it would be to include non-human beings' utility in calculations. He argues (Baxter 1995: 382) that penguins, or any non-human beings, can have nothing more than instrumental value for humans. Human perspective is all that we know. Other creatures may have forms of representing their values, but we cannot know this to be the case. We can only know how we as human individuals and groups desire and value; it is perverse, therefore, to try to include other forms of life, let alone the whole of the ecosystem, into the calculus of pleasure and pain. Hence, the only sensible proposition is that all but human beings should have value conferred onto them, rather than enjoying intrinsic value. He cannot imagine how any other utilitarian system could be administered.

Baxter's argument belongs to a long-standing tradition that includes not only utilitarians but those who focus on duty (deontologists) as well. Like philosophers before him (e.g., Aquinas, Descartes and Kant), Baxter rejects the proposition that animals can think or feel on the grounds that they cannot communicate as rational human beings do. Typically, those who do not recognize non-human beings as members of the moral community base their arguments on the assumption that rationality requires the use of language. Since non-human animals do not speak, they cannot be rational; ergo, they cannot be members of the moral community. This argument can readily be extended to assert that animals, even if they have a sort of language, cannot be said to engage in rational use of that language, any more than barely articulate humans can be said to be rational. An appeal to Mill's concept of nobility can be used to this effect.

Among its other problems, this approach is chauvinistic because it assumes only one way (the human way) of engaging in rational behaviour and communication. It is also arbitrarily exclusionary in its assumption that there is only one way of receiving evidence about rational behaviour and only one way of acquiring knowledge about the values of others when, in fact, we acquire knowledge about our own and other human values in a plurality of ways. We watch people's behaviour to determine what they "really" value because we often do not trust what they say. We sometimes even surprise ourselves when we act in a manner inconsistent with our avowed values, especially when we have been denying or suppressing what we actually feel and think in order to play a role or hide our true motives from ourselves; these true feelings can come to light when we are placed under stress, for instance. Again, behaviour often tells us what our values are.

An Ecological Approach to Value Theory: The Inverted Scheme

Pursuing this line of criticism leads to the necessity of opening our epistemic commitments in relation to value theory. The predominant theory of value relies on dubious assumptions about how we come to know about values, the extent of conflictual relations, the special status of human valuing agents and what value-conferring activity actually is. If what we are within the emerging holistic ecological scheme is not what the Moderns would have us be, i.e., detached and objective observers, but instead are parts of a causally efficacious whole, then so we are as valuers also. The whole determines, in part, our constitution and purposiveness as valuing beings. What and why we value, therefore, also are determined, in part, by the whole. In light of the dependency of human life and functioning on what has come to be called "environmental integrity," namely, the complex and interdependent processes that form ecosystems, attempts to explain the generation of values without reference to these processes invite error.

Given the emerging understanding of ecological conditions, the assumptions of liberal value theory are proving either too one-sided or false. Consider this: although there is no doubt that conflict persists in our relationship with environmental conditions and other humans, it is false to assert that conflict is fundamental. The purposiveness of our relationship to the integrated ecological conditions and processes that both precede our evolution and determine the preconditions for our existence and exercise of values implies that we are not fundamentally at odds with the environment. The fundamental suitability of our constitutions to the integration of ecological conditions means that conflict is part of the overall integration of opposites.

This idea of integration can be extended. Each of us, as a moral agent, begins as fertilized ovum, and each ovum is the product of an evolutionary process. We undergo maturational processes before we become interest bearers. Our having interests and our ability to confer value are dependent upon these two environmental processes, which are fine-tuned to support our existence. Insofar as we are part of a long evolutionary history and undergo developmental processes similar to other animals, we are parts of the same evolutionary and ecological processes. Our constitutions are dependent on the developmental history of the environment, both as expressions of a species' character and as individuals.

Although rough-hewn, the notion of dependence indicates that certain environmental and evolutionary "causal forces" are at work in shaping our constitutions as valuing beings. The interaction between our ancestor organisms and the environment throughout evolutionary history has largely formed our constitutions. Human valuing is in part a response to environmental demands and exigencies, and our valuing capacities are nested functions within the whole.

We also know that many of our interests vary with the region and climate in which we have evolved. Upon first contact with different cultures, people often find food preferences of the other culture somewhat repulsive. Although we can learn to appreciate other people's culinary delights, our predispositions toward them are determined largely by the environmental context in which we have been raised. Taking the point more deeply, had the atmospheric constituents and evolutionary direction been much different, our interests and needs would now be directed toward much different objects and perhaps in much different ways. We might have evolved exclusively as carnivores or as herbivores, rather than as omnivores. Our valuing of foodstuffs would then be different. If atmospheric chemical balances had been different, we would value a different sort of balance between carbon dioxide, oxygen, nitrogen, etc. Our perceptual organs might have evolved in a different way, such that we would detect the environment in different ways. Likely, then, our brains would have evolved differently, if at all, and our thought patterns might have been radically different than they are. Nothing about our constitutions, including our valuing and thinking functions, exists or operates independent of our evolutionary history and ecosystem processes.

This thought experiment is meant to show how the existence of interests, their characteristics and degrees of intensity are determined in the relation between organism and environment. Obviously, the connection is intimate and causal in the holistic sense described as purposive. Some underlying order and connectedness between our valuations and the way in which the ecosystem is integrated form this causal element. An understanding of the significance of this form of causality can be gained through a comparison with other species. To illustrate, a horse's hunger-needs are directed toward hay, not meat; our hunger-interest is directed toward something other than hay, and sometimes meat. We cannot simply choose or agree to need particular foodstuffs and, therefore, cannot simply choose or agree to be interested in something for which we are not suited. Neither can we choose to have our primitive needs fulfilled in any manner whatsoever because the constitution of those needs demands that we fulfil them in ways that have been pre-set by evolutionary and developmental processes. The constitution of our needs directs the ways in which we become interested in objects long before any rational or deliberative function, such as choice or agreement, arises. Once we reach the rational behaviour stage, most of our valuational activity has already formed. Indeed, all our activities are determined by the antecedent valuational activities of our organic unities, but it is particularly noteworthy that our intellectual activities are motivated and, to a large extent, governed by these activities as well.

The assertion that we as rational beings can order and determine how we are to fulfil our interests must, in light of the preceding, be highly qualified. If our interests are interconnected with ecological processes, our intellectual abilities are constituted as well as limited by the environmental conditions in which we have evolved.[1] Thus, the liberal axiological explanation of the interest-value relation needs to be inverted. The liberal analysis of the relationship has been, from the start, upside down. If human values ultimately derive from evolutionary and ecological processes, the liberal notion that we create value through work, through taking an interest or through agreement is fundamentally mistaken. We may transform valuations through these activities, but we do not create them. Liberal value theory, when based on traditional assertions of a one-way value conferment onto nature, assumptions of conflict and adversarial relations, inverts the ecological scheme, if it does not completely distort it. Correcting the liberal scheme, then, first requires a reconceptualization of the relationship between human valuing agents and the ecosystem.

This critique of liberal value theory points out a new direction for value theory. Key elements to be examined include: 1) the environment is valueless; 2) values in nature are conferred by human rational agents; 3) environmental thinkers have overreacted in showing support for the idea of an objective intrinsic value in nature. The first and second elements are addressed by showing that all valuing is owing to evolutionary and ecological processes and not merely to human rational agents taking an interest. The third element is rather more difficult to address because it seems to run contrary to my overall goal of environmental protection. In this attempt to shift how we think about values, I appeal to work conducted by anthropologists in aboriginal communities to develop a process/ecological model. By contrasting the Western European perspective (which identifies objects) with aboriginal people's perspective (which identifies the same things as events) the significance of shifting to a process model can be drawn out more clearly. This idea of event introduces a further issue, namely, how to reorient our thought and perceptual capacities to identify values, not so much in noun form but in verb form.

Shifting away from the conception of humans as detached, privileged, rational beings has implications for value theory, knowledge and science. All valuations and valuers, being consequences of evolutionary and ecological processes nested within different levels of organization of valuational activity, are parts of a valuational network, such that it becomes impossible to separate the valuer from this network in any radical way. It is false to claim, then, that the environment is valueless without some human agent taking an interest in it. Human valuations take place as ecological processes. Human valuational activity is but one mode of more comprehensive valuational activity. The liberal view that value-conferring activity is one-way assumes a fundamental separateness between the valuing agent and the object valued, which is contrary to the ecological understanding of the relationship. It is similar to the assumption of separateness between the detached observer and the object observed and comes into disrepute in a like manner.

A less abstract examination of the environment-value relationship all but completely undermines the detachment thesis and its accompanying axiology, illustrating that some values are formed independent of people rationally deliberating, working or agreeing about what they are interested in. Consider family values and the deeply held respect for the value of life; these are often not even recognized until they are challenged or threatened. When our children are severely ill or abducted, our concern and motives for acting do not derive from deliberation or work or even agreement; they derive from deeper valuations pertaining to love and care that are evoked, not constructed. These values are often deeply hidden, motivating factors in thought and action; they operate independent of any explicit acknowledgement, deliberate act or work to produce value. When we are prepared to sacrifice job and status to save or protect those whom we love, for example, we are demonstrating that what we truly value often overrides what we explicitly and deliberatively value.

Situations involving family values and repressed or suppressed values—as in the case of the artistically talented person who is forced by family expectation to enter the family business—indicate that many types of values are produced by the deeper elements of the human personality. Irrational behaviour is especially significant. A person who values love or attention in the extreme can exhibit behaviour that defies all reasoned deliberation. Sometimes people sacrifice their reputation, family and job for the sake of love, knowing full well that they are being irrational. Gambling is irrational when cautious, calculated betting is abandoned for a slim chance at high gains. It seems that values are often—indeed, probably mostly—formed independent of rational deliberation or agreement. Empirical evidence can be cited, then, to support the more abstract idea that there are primitive processes at work, forming the values that drive behaviour. Valuational processes precede and underlie the emergence of rational interest-driven behaviour; their function is to orient the rational agent toward taking an interest in particular elements of the environment. Valuational activity may be amenable to rational deliberation, but it is not fundamentally the result of it.

Coupling the idea that values can be unconscious with the idea that they are set antecedently to rational activity, we can claim that underlying all valuational activity are judgments, or quasi-judgments, that an organism makes in determining distinctions between suitable and unsuitable activities, good and bad situations. These primitive judgments direct the organism to be attracted to some objects and repelled by others, to perform certain functions and avoid others. When an organism is attracted to one object rather than another, it is drawn to it because of some property or set of properties it is judged to have and that will satisfy a need. If the object does not satisfy a need, the organism will likely not be drawn to it again; or, if the object is of negative value (e.g., pain-causing, noxious) the organism will learn to avoid that object in the future. Valuations are, among other things, motivations of organisms directing them to adapt.

Human valuers are among the many types of organisms and therefore are one of many types of valuers who exist within a community of valuing beings. The evolutionary interaction between us and other organisms implies that our valuational activity is intimately connected to that of others because our activity has been shaped and defined by the interactions our species has had with other species and the ecosystem. When we make a conscious judgment, or consciously and deliberatively form an interest in something, we are not creating value; we are formulating and shaping valuational activity already taking place. We can admit that sometimes taking an interest in something creates new orders of value, as in the case where the interest in more universal modes of exchange gave rise to the invention of money, which has taken on a value of its own. But we cannot claim that these new orders are created by pure acts of rational deliberation, choice or agreement.

This analysis of values presupposes a process ontology, that is to say, values are processes, not objects. To take the idea of process more into account, we need a theory of *valuing* rather than of *values*. If what we call "values" are not the sorts of things that can be picked out like rocks or trees but rather are expressions of underlying processes, then it would be better to strain language somewhat in order to capture the significance of the distinction than to be clear, where clarity misrepresents the subject of discussion. "Valuing" stands for a process or activity, like running or eating; it is something organisms do rather than have. The point is close to the one cited earlier about the Dene Tha language and its verb-orientation (Goulet 1998). Since the Dene Tha see the world primarily as event and process, as the result of agent actions rather than as a collection of things, most nouns in their language are nominalized action verbs. Similarly, the referring to what are normally called "values" as "valuational activities" or "valuing" draws us away from our tendency to reify or treat processes and events as if they were objects. When the term "value" is used, then, it is meant more as a nominalized expression of the activity of valuing.

According to an ecological perspective, which assumes the interconnectedness of human and non-human, we have room to imagine how a fundamental connection between human and non-human valuational activity is possible; under the Modern world view, no such room for imagination is possible. What Locke would call "conferring value onto nature" (giving nature value or creating value in nature) is, in the ecological scheme, an act of transforming more primitive valuational activity. We are loci of valuational activity, in the sense that we are points through which valuations get organized and synthesized into interests, plans, intentions and the like. This notion of locus implies that we are not independent, isolated units; rather, everything and every process constituting the ecosystem is relevant to who we are, how we value and how our values are formed.

To understand ourselves as loci of valuational activity is to demand a reidentification of ourselves as members of an ecological community. Reidentification requires a reformulation of what it means to be a moral being. Given that we are not detached, superior creators of value, we need to posit a more suitable concept of ourselves. A better one is that, as valuers, we are nested within the more comprehensive valuational activity of ecosystems. Where the predominant value orientation has been toward imposing value and so conquering the resistance of nature, an ecological approach would have us value nature principally as a place of origin and provision. Unlike Hobbes, who assumed that we are essentially alone, such that fear and greed could be considered fundamental to human motivations, we now see that aloneness is not a fundamental fact but a feeling generated under particular circumstances. If the ecosystem is the origin of our structure, function and valuational activity, as well as the provider that satisfies this activity, then aloneness and isolation are not fundamental characteristics of the human condition but are constructed feelings based on a suppression of or ignorance about the basic facts of human existence. Thus, while Hobbes captures a long, developing view about human nature—introduced by the Greeks and brought to its height in later liberal thought—this atomistic conception of human beings can be supported neither by the new metaphysic nor by the new axiological assumptions generated under an ecological world view.

It is difficult to see how the doctrine of intrinsic value can remain intact.[2] There are two aspects to this discussion, one having to do with the exclusion of other than human beings from being accorded intrinsic value (the Modern approach), and the other having to do with the tendency in environmental protection circles to include other than human beings in that accord. By showing that the idea of objective intrinsic value is unintelligible, the Modern exclusionary justifications can no longer be supported. Further, the tendencies of environmentalists to appeal to the objective intrinsic value of the environment can also be shown to be wrong-headed and antithetical to the holistic thinking to which they subscribe. As environmentalists have striven to place non-human beings on an equal footing with human beings, they have been drawn into using the concept of intrinsic value to have non-human beings, species and systems recognized as members of the moral community. By showing how they share properties that are used to assign human beings intrinsic value and, therefore, an inherent right to exist, environmental ethicists sub-scribe to the same inappropriate Modern frame of reference as do their opponents. My intent is to show that this strategy fails from the begin-ning. A new strategy then must be developed to justify moral recognition of the non-human.

When Kant speaks of intrinsic value, he means that the repository of that value (that which contains the value) has value independent of its instrumental value. It has value in itself. The concept is then used to ascribe an inherent right to life and dignity to these repositories. The term "repository" is used to convey the type of object orientation that lies behind our thinking about intrinsic value. "Repository" conjures up the image of a vessel in which values are stored, as if they belong to the vessel. Such imaging fits well with ideas of possession, which, in turn, fit well with the idea that this repository excludes others from challenging or affecting its value. It is an atomistic view of the bearers of value, which is predicated on the assumption that the environment is external to the person as repository. Assuming a fundamental sort of separability of the repository from the external world is critical for this theory of intrinsic value to work.

If each of these assumptions can no longer be supported, however, what can be made of the doctrine of objective intrinsic value? If we accept that who we are and what we are in part are functions of evolutionary process and that we are loci (not repositories) of valuational activity, then nothing of the environment is essentially external to who or what we are. It makes no sense to think of the world and that which generates value as external, except perhaps in some relative or subjective way. All values or, better, valuational activities are fully relational. Accordingly, valuational activity of any one thing owes its existence to the more comprehensive evolutionary and ecological processes that constitute each entity. Obvi-ously, each organism acts to satisfy its values, as if it were a separate entity in competition with other entities. Each organism acts for itself both to satisfy its needs and to grow to maturation. But acting for itself as a locus of valuational activity does not imply that the organism has value in itself, independent of other loci.

One reason to avoid adopting theories of intrinsic value are the traps into which such thinking leads. Paul Taylor's (1986) use of "intrinsic value" is a case in point. Since all creatures have intrinsic value, they have a right to life (Taylor 1986: 368–69). The only condition under which a life can be taken, therefore, is that of necessity. If it is necessary for survival, then, and only then, it is justified to take a life. But with this view, eating is always evil because it violates an inherent right, although it is sometimes justified. Note, however, that what we justify is, in fact, a violation. There is something deeply distressing about a theory that places us in the self-defeating position of being able only to minimize violations rather than actually doing the right thing.

A more fundamental problem with this approach to valuing is found in its allegiance to atomism. It ignores or "misanalyzes" the interconnectedness in the ecosystem of valuational activity. By treating the individual as a repository of value, such theories isolate individual value from the value of all others, which is to ignore the purposive and community conditions that are bases for the existence of all loci of value. In the end, it is best to abandon the notion of objective intrinsic value, which renders senseless the associated dichotomy of intrinsic value versus instrumental value.

The problem for an ecological approach is to determine what concepts to use to recognize the interconnected nature of all valuations. When we do appear to ourselves to be private individuals, what sense can be made of this ecological way of thinking about values? When new world views emerge, they undermine sensibilities. They leave in their wake an uncertainty because the language of the former world view has been shown to be inadequate in capturing the reality being faced. Establishing a new language to capture the new realities cannot be readily accomplished, yet it must be attempted to avoid accusations that the new approach is empty. What follows, then, is necessarily programmatic, sketchy and preliminary.

Under a holistic ecological scheme, we first accept that all elements within the ecosystem contribute to the constitution of our values, such that no ecological event or member of the system is entirely irrelevant to what we are as valuing beings. Some elements may be remotely relevant, but never irrelevant. If all species, non-sentient and non-living beings included, are inseparably linked to the process of generating and satisfying values, then human valuational activity is a part of a more comprehensive system of mutually supporting valuations. To borrow a concept from Holmes Rolston III (1988: 31), ecosystems are sources of valuational activity, as opposed to resources on which such activity takes place. Here, we have another way to contrast the liberal axiological system with the emerging ecological one. We no longer have intrinsically valuable repositories creating value in the world; we have the ecosystem as the source of value. The ecosystem as a whole is an axiological system. Hence, failure to recognize other species as loci of valuational activity and as part of the network of loci that constitute the moral community is a mistake, a factual error. It is not only arbitrarily to exclude relevant sources of our own values, causing us to ignore factors that contribute to their satisfaction, it is to ignore facts about who and what contributes to our identity as moral agents. To value the lives of other species is not an act of altruism or the result of enlightenment; it is demanded of us when we realize that we are one among many loci of valuational activities who owe their existence, natures and satisfaction to one another. It is to recognize that the value of our individuality and uniqueness is shared by every other individual, rational or otherwise.

Re-examining conflict helps to formulate what it means for our valuational activity to be part of a more comprehensive system. As Rolston (1992) points out, nature is rife with disvalue. He cites such activities as predation, parasitism, selfishness, disasters and suffering as examples of disvalue in nature. But he also cites examples of how disvalues precipitate value achievements (Rolston 1992: 275), such as disasters precipitating the achievement of courage or death as the condition for the regeneration of life. When the ecosystem is examined as a whole, disvalue is transmuted into value. Our systems of rights and justice predispose us to think about conflict and disvalue as purely negative. For this reason, we continue to believe that we can and ought to engineer the natural and social environment to overcome need and suffering. We do so by eliminating predators, which we have now found to be essential to ecosystem integrity, and by trying to eliminate disvalue in society—for example, by devaluing inefficiency, negative reinforcements, the less than perfect body and primary producers—thereby marginalizing those who appear to contribute to disvalue. We find, as a result, that in attempting to eliminate a disvalue (such as inefficiency), we also eliminate important values (such as effectiveness). By making workplaces more efficient, we often find that communication is undermined and morale disintegrates, making the workplace a far less effective means of conducting business than it was when less efficiently designed. Efficient extraction of fish stocks has also resulted in the destruction of those stocks on the east coast of Canada and, indeed, worldwide. So, sometimes, what is marked as a disvalue (e.g., inefficiency) precipitates other sorts of values.

Thinking ecologically includes disvalue as part of the network of interrelated valuations. It is a value-rich approach that attempts to understand valuations from many perspectives and many levels of analysis. Finding the means for recognizing the relationship of parts to parts and parts to wholes becomes central to the development of axiology. Earlier discussion of units of analysis showed that, where a unit is irreducible to another, a different level and perhaps type of analysis must be adopted. There, discussion had to do with types of causality. Here, it has to do with how different loci and contexts affect each valuation. At different levels (individual versus part-to-part relation) different sets of assumptions may be required, as for example, when valuing the death of an individual, first from that individual's perspective, and then from a perspective of how the individual's death contributes to the health and balance of relationships in ecosystems (as in predator-prey relationships). At each level, purposiveness informs the analysis of what the valuational activity is. In the case of a death, there is negative value or disvalue for the individual because the event is valued in the context of survival needs and the fear of pain. But it is also of positive value because it is suitable for those who will be nourished as a result of the death. Thus, at the level of individual analysis, the need to survive establishes the value of the death. From the level of the predator-prey relationship, the ecological and evolutionary importance of robust populations establishes the value of the death.

Understanding valuational activity and the interrelationship between different loci and levels at which these loci are organized requires a much more attuned way of thinking than do theories of intrinsic value. In fact, it is incumbent upon us to attune ourselves to the different ways of understanding how this activity operates at different levels; otherwise our axiological beliefs will be ill-informed of the balances and tensions that constitute the integrity of ecosystems. We are likely, then, to destroy these balances and, consequently, the conditions upon which our own identity and valuational activity depend. Seeking ways to understand the contribution of all ecosystem members to the system as a whole and the contribution of the system as a whole to the individual becomes central to the task of thinking ecologically. Value theory, then, needs to be as dialectical as metaphysics and epistemology.

A New Set of Problems

If we accept the above, a new problem arises that the Moderns did not have to face. The Moderns could assume conflict to be basic because there was no compelling reason to think that differences between individuals were ultimately harmonious. A powerful system of analyzing and understanding values has emerged from this set of assumptions. Although unsuccessful, the liberal system does yield ways of managing conflict. It has produced a way of thinking about conflict and competition, resolving conflicts and managing competition. The problem for an ecologically based value theory becomes one of explaining how a dialectical understanding of separateness between human and non-human beings can ultimately be reconciled with the integrity or unity of the whole and how this understanding would result in decision making. If we cannot give a clear account of how all values are to be categorized and prioritized, a different approach to value theory needs to be undertaken. How then can we explain conflict and disvalue as co-primaries with harmony and value?

Part of the explanation appeals to the dialectical opposites that constitute the unity of ecosystems. Dialectical opposites (e.g., the whole-part relationship) work against one another from the perspective of either one of the opposites, but they work in concert from a more comprehensive perspective. In explaining evolution or ecosystem processes, two different orders of causality had to be considered simultaneously to gain an adequate understanding of oppositional relations. We needed to account for part-part mechanical relations and whole-part purposive relations. Tensions between mechanical and purposive relations, then, required resolution. The value-disvalue tension can be similarly modelled. The sodium-potassium relation and how it is an integration of different levels of rules can be revisited for this purpose. Outside the neuron, the sodium/potassium part-part relation obeys chemicals laws; within the neuron in an organism, it becomes a function of the body as a whole and is governed by the demands of the body as a whole. Chemical laws can be said to be subordinated by higher-order laws. At the same time, they are necessary for the possible operation of the higher-order laws. The part-part relation is nested in a more complex system of nested relations, all of which are necessary for the operation of the whole. In a similar manner, human values and disvalues can be considered nested valuational activities in the more comprehensive valuational system. They are not only dependent on the system as a whole, they are functions of the whole.

Now, conflict between valuations owing to divergent needs can also be considered nested within more comprehensive processes. As the function of one organism is exercised, it is likely to come into conflict with other systems that compete for a scarce resource or a mate. The evolutionary notion of competition and the doctrine of the survival of the fittest describe a form of conflict that produces fit individuals; this is one way in which the good of the system as a whole is realized. Once systemic valuations are recognized, a wide range of what were once thought to be competing valuations are seen as systemically complementary valuations. Competition among wolves for a mate tends to generate strong communities of wolves, which are in turn important for maintaining healthy ungulate populations. Apparent competition between hosts and parasites has also come to be seen as important to the overall functioning and health of ecosystems. Mychorizal fungi, once thought to be parasitic on tree roots, have been discovered to be symbiotically integrated with root structures, exchanging nitrogen-fixing functions for a water supply.

Gent et al. (1994) found that diseases, such as Crohn's disease, had a greater incidence in those who were raised in extremely hygienic environments than in those who were not. Those whose immune systems were not exposed to enteric organisms were found to have significantly higher incidents of Crohn's disease because they lacked exposure to organisms that "programmed" the gut's immune system. Usually, obsessive cleaning and sterilization runs together with a revulsion toward dirt and "germs." By failing to appreciate the systemic value of germs, British housewives actually brought about the higher incidence of Crohn's disease.

Conflicts and tensions constitute many of the levels of organization to which we need to respond by shaping the purposiveness that directs valuational activity. From an axiological point of view, they are necessary conditions of valuational activity. From an epistemological point of view, they are opportunities for becoming acquainted with the interrelatedness of all loci. Without conflict, the proper exercise of our capacities and the fulfillment of potentials would not occur. Likewise, disvalue is necessary for the integrity and robustness of the system and individuals.

There is obviously no easy way to attune ourselves to the importance of the value-disvalue tension because exposing ourselves to disvalue and appreciating its ecological function can result in our termination or the termination of others. Clearly, to the degree that we understand these tensions, judgment and decision are involved in determining what we are to do about balancing conflict and cooperation, value and disvalue. To some extent, we can and must decide to what extent disvalue (e.g., disease, conflict, taking of life, suffering) is to be incorporated into our individual and social lives. Where such decisions involve matters of life and death, health and morbidity, they are moral in nature and carry great responsibility. In facing such difficulties, it is tempting to resort to well-tested, though ill-founded, systems of understanding, such as intrinsic value theories.

A related difficulty with the whole-part relationship concerns its association with fascism. Several opponents of the ecosystem approach have warned that it leads to fascist and totalitarian thinking (see, for example, Regan 1989; Marietta 1993). Taking an ecosystemic and functional view of human valuational activity seems to lead to the subordination of human values to ecosystem values; individuals seem to be dispensable for the good of the whole and can be substituted for equally functioning individuals. Individuals are made vulnerable and devalued in holistic schemes. Hence, accusations of misanthropy—as in cases of support for the mass elimination of human beings to ecologically sustainable levels—have been levelled against the proponents of ecological approaches. What happens to the value of individual aspiration? Does it become subordinated to ecosystem values and principles? How will privacy and independence of individuals be affected if the good of the whole is of principal interest?

Indeed, I have used language such as "subordination" but hurrying to the conclusion that this ecosystemic approach to axiology supports fascism is premature. Similar fears abound concerning aborigi-

nal world views and how their collective sense of community undermines individual initiative and value. Typically, such fears are reactions to only one aspect of the world view and a failure to understand
the others. Aboriginal communities typically retain a creative tension
between community and individual concerns. Indeed, individuals are
nothing apart from the community (as is the case in the ecological
world view), but privacy and respect for personal quests are paramount. Recognition of the community as a condition of individuality
implies that the one cannot be thought of in isolation from the other.
Communities obviously are constituted by individuals but not, as
Locke or Rousseau would have it, through contract. Aboriginal communities tend to understand the process of individuation as one that
terminates in the person becoming fully individual through a personal
quest and individual initiative. This process is highly individual and
private, but it is not done without help from esteemed keepers of
wisdom or irrespective of the community. Similarly, the ecological
process of individuation is equally of value to the whole, since the
valuational activity of the whole is as impossible without the nested
valuational activities of the parts as is the valuational activity of the
parts impossible without the whole. Individuals, because they are
creative loci of valuational activity, are not substitutable. To review,
each individual locus synthesizes the valuational activities affecting it
in unique ways, and it does this by virtue of the fact that each has a
distinct history and creates an integration of valuations in a context of
indeterminacy.

Ultimately, the proposed ecological axiology supports respect for
individuals more than does the present liberal axiology. That system,
insofar as it tends to treat people as functional quantities operating
within corporate or market systems, has ironically allowed individuals to
be treated as substitutable functions. They are regarded as ciphers within
a production-consumption system, not as individuals with creative aspirations, emotions and moral commitments. The fact that people are
individuals has been a persistent problem for the dominant class of
economists, which relies on reductive cost-benefit analyses to determine
solutions to environmental problems (see Spash 1999: 431). Those who
begin with the assumption that individuals are atomic units, separate and
private, must find some way to treat them as a unit. Idiosyncratic aspects
of the individual's personality, private concerns, talents, inclinations and
history must be treated as irrelevant in shaping collective values and
institutions. Hence, when collective values are shaped into rights, legislation and policy, the overwhelming tendency is to formulate them as
restrictions on individual freedom. Recognizing collective values—for
example, in formulating responsibilities of governments to ensure national security, order and the rule of law—imposes a restriction or limit

on what a free individual might otherwise do. For the purposes of avoiding chaos, securing property or protecting the value of life, individuals are controlled, organized and studied according to rules, models and methods of analysis (e.g., statistics) that do not recognize individuals as individuals but as types, one of many to be fit into a system. The advertising industry bases its treatment of people on consumer profiles, manipulating behavioural responses designed on a statistical basis. Politicians appeal to polls, rather than to what characterizes respect for individuals—sound individual argument. The law is designed to be blind to individual cases and idiosyncrasy. By assuming atomicity of individuals, therefore, we inevitably fail to treat individuals as individuals. The problem of respecting the parts of the system, then, is at least as great for the liberal system as it is for the ecological approach.

Holistic approaches, however, take recognizing individuals as their primary problem because they begin with the assumption that individuals derive somehow from the whole. The primary task is to determine how each process of individuation is to fit into the whole. Each individual, as in aboriginal cultures, must find an identity and a place within the community structure. It is assumed that each person will contribute something unique to the community, and so part of the quest is to discover what is in the individual's nature to contribute. As each individual pursues his or her own place (for example, through the vision quest), that individuating process shapes and is shaped by community expectation. It may seem ironic that a focus on membership in community should result in greater focus on individuality; it is not so under a classical liberal system. When formulated in the right way, however, holistic approaches demand attention to individuality and particularity as part of solving the puzzle of understanding how the individual is to fit into the community.

A New Way to Think About Anthropocentrism

A further problem for ecological approaches is anthropocentrism. Classical anthropocentrism asserts that all values are conferred onto nature by human rational agents. A more refined version has been broached with William Baxter's (1995) assertion that human beings simply cannot think in any other way than to accept human superiority and privilege. It seems to me true that anthropocentrism, for reasons similar but not identical to those of Baxter, is unavoidable. The position runs contrary to most expectations in environmental thought and ethics. Hence, a gradual formulation of the idea through critique of the main views is warranted. Many who espouse holism and an ecological approach argue that ecocentrism or biocentrism ought to form the foundation for value theory. Typically, the strategy is to undermine anthropocentrism in favour of an ecocentric value theory, since anthropocentrism is identified as the primary cause of the environmental crisis. My strategy is to accept anthropocentrism as ineluctable but to formulate it from an ecological perspective.

As in the beginning stages of all emerging world views, retaining while revising concepts of the old system requires some imagination. We can expect that formulations of an ecological conception of anthropocentrism will go through various iterations. To continue unimaginatively, as Baxter does, would be to act as the counterpart of those who resisted the previous two shifts (i.e., from animistic to Greco-Christian and from Greco-Christian to Modern) against an all too obvious need for change. Not being able to imagine how one could administer a society in which more than human beings had moral status is the same kind of thinking that secured the prejudicial treatment of women and minorities. The sort of imagination needed, however, does not wander aimlessly but is disciplined by a systematic approach to solving the problems with the older theories and to incorporating new discoveries.

A cautionary note also needs to be made concerning rationality since it is so closely connected to anthropocentrism. Although rationality has been tied to mathematical thinking and logic, there is an implicit aspect of rationality that needs to be explicitly identified. Rationality has also acted as critic, not only of propositions and world views but of arguments for restricting the meaning of rationality to that which is mathematical and logical. The very existence of a reasoned account of why knowledge must not be restricted to what conforms to logical principles and the scientific method assumes that rationality includes far more than is captured in mathematical, logical reasoning. There is a more comprehensive rationality at work, an activity of systematic and critical evaluation of ways of understanding. Thus far, rational argument has been used to open understanding to the possibility of alternative ways of knowing. It has done so through destroying received foundations for thought and undermining explanations and world views. If reason has been the tool of empowerment for humans in the domination of the world, it is also the tool disclosing its own weakness. Reason appears as a passion seeking explanation, but only explanations that are complete, exhaustive and systematic. In its detection of incompleteness, it turns against its own constructions, disclosing their weakness. In the moment it recognizes its own incompleteness and limits, it turns against itself, exposing a weakness that is usually hidden by its accomplishments. I wish to make explicit this paradox of reason in order to open the way to understanding attunement as a means for thinking ecologically. Rationality is perhaps best defined as a commitment to a process of understanding and decision making based on as full and systematic an account of the facts, insights and principles of procedure as possible in a given context.

With this view of rationality in mind and rejecting classical anthropocentrism, the retention of anthropocentrism is owing to the fact that it is impossible to eliminate it. Beneath the surface analysis of anthropocentrism lies an inescapable self-interest which, when understood ecologically, changes the face or meaning of anthropocentrism. John Passmore's (1974) argument in defence of anthropocentrism helps identify this underlying self-interest. He argues that we really only need an extension of Western ethical theories to protect the environment. We protect beautiful things because we enjoy them (Passmore 1974: 56). We protect the purity of our water and air because we need them for our health. But we will do so, as Baxter (1995) puts it, in an optimal manner. That is, we will of course pollute and kill penguins or non-human animals as our needs demand, but we will not do so wantonly, as we killed the buffalo, once we understand how they are important for protecting our own interests.

Natural beauty is the sort of value that the rich seek to protect. No doubt, the same rich landowners are also the ones who own the factories and industries that pollute and degrade the environment. This is not an unavoidable problem, however, since we can deal with them by establishing systems of compulsion (legislation) and general acquiescence (Passmore 1974: 64). Agreements between members of this community will be formed to protect the environment as they become informed of the consequences of their behaviour. We can accept that many will try to cheat and get away with pollution to gain an unfair advantage; but the advocates will support systems of fines and punishments for those who would cheat. Each individual will want to protect his or her own well-being but will recognize that it must be accomplished through fair and just means. And to the extent that such environmental problems, such as acid rain, affect everything from the degradation of architectural art to the pollution of lakes that support sport fishing, motives of self-interest will arise to protect wider environments than simply the ones in which the affluent live. In this way, a comprehensive approach to environmental protection will be supported by strong anthropocentric motivations.

On Passmore's assumptions, we could go even further by requiring ecological study as a basis for planning and economics. Since knowledge about ecological processes has become so clearly relevant to protecting our own interests, enlightened self-interest will place a premium on ecological study and planning. We always trade benefits against costs. As we discover the costs of not conducting ecological research and planning, we will accept ecology as necessary to both areas. By doing so, we make human and environmental demands compatible.

Now, on the surface, it appears that Passmore's anthropocentrism merely incorporates ecological concerns into the utilitarian calculus; it does not demand radical changes to the ways in which we structure our values and ethical commitments. The approach is additive, rather than foundational. Recognizing ecological conditions does not imply a change in world view. Passmore's anthropocentrism cum utilitarianism seems to have the capacity to incorporate just about any value or principle into its scheme, just as long as it has utility. The main problem for him is to find a way to weigh its utility and then balance it against other and competing utilities.

I am not interested in defending Passmore's argument any further, but I wish to draw attention to difficulties that emerge as we follow the line of defence. It is clear that self-interest is at the core of his position, but what does it mean to act from self-interest or even from enlightened self-interest? Classical anthropocentrism states that we always act from a perspective of selfish motivations—greed—but this need not be so. We can act from love or benevolence; these may be modes of self-interest, but they yield sets of behaviour that are very different from those produced by greed. Despite the assumption that our motivations are always our own and not someone else's and that there are no non-anthropocentric motives, different sets of behaviours and motivations are conflated under the rubric "anthropocentrism."

At least two distinctions are buried in Passmore's view, distinctions having to do with narrow and wide versions of anthropocentrism. First, the self-interest formulated in terms of the utilitarian cost-benefit scheme fails to distinguish between an individualistic formulation of anthropocentrism and a collective version. Certainly, aboriginal perspectives are anthropocentric in the sense that they are human-centred. But the collective identity of the individual results in profoundly different behaviour than the narrow utilitarian conception would predict or even justify. We might even admit that self-interest motivates the aboriginal seeker, but the sense of self is fundamentally different from the classical utilitarian who takes an atomistic view of the self. If the aboriginal person takes a more organic and communitarian view of the self, the value profile and behaviour that result from following this different metaphysic is not the same as that which results from a narrow utilitarian view. For example, among traditional aboriginal people, and often among those who would not claim to be traditional, distributing the first rewards of a hunt or catch to elders is a communal act (not an individual act of sacrifice). More deeply, as many elders have instructed me, the phrase "all my relations," used so often among aboriginal peoples, indicates an intimate relationship with all beings. Totems, or *dodaems* (e.g., fish, eagle, wolf, bear), are beings from whom members of a clan take their identity. In this context, answering the question "Who am I?" is complex and involves identifying a number of relationships. What it means to be anthropocentric, in this context, is to take the perspective of a human, who understands him- or herself as a function of all these relations. The valuations in which you engage are not straightforward value-conferring activities;

they are the results of knowing yourself to be situated within the valuing activity of both human and non-human beings. Knowing yourself to belong to a wider community of valuing beings makes answering questions about personal identity considerably more complex and more intimately connected to the identity of all things.

Different versions of anthropocentrism can also arise from different ways of knowing. If knowledge acquisition has a much wider base than science or a particular tradition in philosophy prescribes, then anthropocentric approaches to knowledge acquisition can demand to be inclusive of these many windows of understanding. Intuitive, artistic and other modes of apprehending the world or ourselves, such as dreams and insights, conceivably are modes of knowledge acquisition. Each can have and, in some cultures, have had an important epistemic role to play for individuals and for society. Being anthropocentric, then, does not require narrowing the basis for knowledge to any particular version of rationality or utility. Indeed, as the more comprehensive conception of rationality suggests, anthropocentrism involves the capacity to be inclusive of a wide, perhaps indeterminate, range of perspectives and value orientations.

Being anthropocentric is likely different from being feline-centric or elephant-centric because of the different windows of access to the world. As such, claiming to be anthropocentric is not trivial; it marks an important distinction between how we treat and understand ourselves versus other species. We are cut off from the perspectives of others, and we know that we are. Having this knowledge means that we can know that other beings have perspectives and engage in value-driven activity, even though we may not know the quality of experiencing that behaviour. Knowing that but not knowing how such experience occurs places anthropocentric beings in a unique position, having the capacity to understand that there are limits to knowledge claims: limits of access to other perspectives and limits of understanding those other perspectives. When this knowledge of limitation and critical rational capacities are turned toward reflecting on ourselves, we also recognize that there may be limits to our perspective on ourselves, including what is involved in satisfying our self-interest.

If using the suffix "ism" is meant to point out some essential characteristic, anthropocentrism should point out the characteristic that humans are the sort of being for whom self-interest and personal identity are problems. Part of what it means to be anthropocentric is to have a perspective of being engaged in problem solving as a way of determining self-interest and identity. If we are constituted by our relationship to all things and if our value satisfaction is tied to the valuational activity of the whole, then the problematic widens as our perspective widens to recognize our dependency. We cannot know entirely what constitutes ourselves or what is in our best interest. We know this from experience. When we find ourselves in novel situations that expose us to different ways of doing things, or different foodstuffs or medicines, we often discover that our best interest has not been served by our past choices, even when we believed that we were choosing in our own best interest.

All of the key elements captured under "anthropocentrism" are problematic and open to revision. Thinking ecologically about anthropocentrism means radically revising what it means to be a valuer, what one takes to be the properties of utility and how one goes about determining what is in one's best interest. Defining anthropocentrism in the narrow utilitarian manner that dominates today deprives human expectation and self-understanding of a potentially richer and more comprehensive, albeit less precisely defined, perspective and experience. It arbitrarily restricts the purview of human imagination, while robbing the creative process of coming to understand the potential of different perspectives and value orientations.

Another problem with typical formulations of anthropocentrism is evident in Passmore's additive approach. By supplementing narrow anthropocentric policies with ecological information, we run the risk of being too late to employ sufficient protective measures. His argument with respect to beauty illustrates the point. The focus on beauty has tended to devalue swamps, mosquito-breeding marshes and other environmentally necessary features. Our appreciation for beauty, in fact, causes us to overlook, if not eliminate, uglier parts of the ecosystem that are necessary for maintaining balances and stability. We have already drained most of our North American wetlands because we have not been as attuned to their importance as we have that of beautiful areas, such as national parks. Indeed, our wetlands are ecologically more important than many of the features we protect in national parks. Similar criticisms can be made about typical responses to ugly creatures such as toads, fungi, and micro-organisms. We have been too prepared to eliminate these ecosystem contributors on aesthetic grounds. In *Postmodern Wetlands* Rod Giblet (1996) traces attitudes toward wetlands. Our view of the swamp, the "hell" of our Western tradition, parallels Plato's view of Earth as the cold, dark centre of the cosmos; it is that from which evil springs. Giblet shows how this association with wetlands is no accident; it is systemically entrenched through association with the lower elements of creation. Passmore and those who subscribe to the aesthetic foundation for an environmental ethic usually fail to recognize that there is this aesthetic depreciation of ecologically important areas of the environment. By the time an ecological awareness of the importance of wetlands was developed, great and perhaps irreparable damage already had been done. Reliance on aesthetic valuations must be replaced by values more directly influenced by a carefully and problematically formed ecological understanding of how valuations are related.

Narrow anthropocentrism also has led humanity to negatively value predators, especially the wolf and the coyote. But, having eliminated these predators, grazers, such as deer, have proliferated so greatly in some regions that they have to be culled to protect that region's flora and biological stability. Part of the reason for oversight is the attitude that, as privileged beings, we have the right to narrow our way of understanding ecosystems to suit our economic or aesthetic interests. If we begin to understand anthropocentrism as essentially problematic and to prescribe the inclusion of a plurality of perspectives, we would at least remove the justificatory scheme for environmental disasters owing to human arrogance and narrow purview.

Rachel Carson's (1962) *Silent Spring* also demonstrates that a narrow, utilitarian cost-benefit based anthropocentrism fails because costs will not be properly accounted. Indeed, *Silent Spring* should have been taken as a text book in how to cost environmental damage. Despite evidence that the use of chemical pesticides, herbicides and the like was increasing morbidity and mortality rates in both human and non-human beings alike, as well as raising the cost of health care to those poisoned by the chemicals, this evidence was decried by chemical companies in an attempt to discredit Carson. Typically, cost-benefit analysis favours those who can represent their views of cost and benefits most effectively, those who have the greatest financial and political power to do so. Another problem with a narrow, utilitarian anthropocentrism, then, is that it promotes failure to recognize other determinants of social relations that bias how calculations are undertaken and what values are represented (see Spash 1999: 431). Where anthropocentrism is used to justify adopting a narrow purview on an environmental problem, it is not a legitimate use because it truncates and distorts what otherwise would be disclosed by a full exercise of anthropocentrism.

Anthropocentrism, when thought through ecologically, adopts the widest possible purview to be inclusive and to be fully rational (critical). The assertion of privilege is short-sighted. It renders us oblivious to our dependency relation to the ecosystem, much like the relation of the master to his slave. Borrowing from G.W.F. Hegel (1977), the master, in his state of confidence and sense of superiority, thinks himself independent of the slave and in control of his own affairs. The slave, in contrast, proceeds as if dependent and lacking in freedom and control, for he is controlled by his superior. When separated by unforeseen events, however, the master recognizes that he is incapable of fending for himself because he has never learned to do so, having depended all of his life on his slave. The slave, on the other hand, recognizes his greater freedom because he is equipped to survive in the world, having done so both for himself and for his master.

Adopting the attitude of anthropocentric privilege, then, creates delusions of confidence, inviting but not acknowledging error. Even practically speaking, Passmore's confidence in the wisdom of the narrowly self-interested has not been borne out during the period following his writing in 1974. The greenhouse effect has been well researched, and entire communities of scientific experts have announced, even stressed, the need for radical reduction in the production of greenhouse gases. Despite the Kyoto Treaty of 1997, which was to gain compliance from industrialized nations to reduce greenhouse gas emissions to 1990 standards, emissions are on the rise. Despite warnings against clear-cutting and the landslides that have been blamed on the practice, companies continue to practise it and governments to promote it.

An ecologically framed, wide anthropocentrism sometimes supports making use of our rational capacities to impose order onto the environment, for our survival depends on it. We are among the weakest and least adaptive of the animals, apart from our ability to use our reason for the purposes of technological development. But keeping our dependency on the integrity of ecosystem conditions, our ignorance about them and the need to maintain an inclusive purview in dialectical tension with our imposition of order and design both ensures limitation on imposition and directs design toward integration.

All creatures seek to actualize their potential and to exercise their value orientations. Everything is in the process of satisfying some value impulse, either individually or communally. Insofar as this activity is internally related to our own, we need to assume that each creature's valuational activity is reciprocally dependent, despite our ignorance of how this might be the case. In satisfying impulses, there is purposive activity. In the case of hunger, the value impulse is labelled "hunger," and in the case of an animal's development, we call the process "growth" and "maturation." Restraining or restricting these processes results in dissatisfaction and frustration; it negates the purposiveness of the impulse. Allowing such impulses to take their course is akin to what we call "freedom." Acknowledging the freedom-seeking activity of all valuational activities, then, is a first step toward integrating our own activities with ecosystem processes. The desire for freedom that we accord other species is, of course, understood problematically since we can know even less about their desires than we know about our own. But ascribing the desire for freedom to the non-human community is not mere anthropomorphism at work. It is appropriate inasmuch as we are capable of expanding our purview and identifying the valuational activity of others. We know that other species experience hunger, pain and the need to procreate. Failing to acknowledge their capacity for any of these experiences requires a degree of insulation from them. Living closely with other creatures, as we do with other humans, informs us, sometimes all too clearly, of these desires in them.

Consequently, a wide anthropocentrism, guided by ecologically attuned reason, invites breadth of investigation. It treats rigour as a tool of investigation that seeks to understand the consequences of action from a wide range of perspectives. While metaphysical argument has shown that all beings are loci of valuational activity, it does not tell us what the quality of that activity is. For that kind of epistemic access, an attitude of openness and connection to others as a community is required. It is this kind of attitude that brings us to concrete recognition of the value of freedom in other species. Without it, of course, scepticism can play out its course. But this kind of scepticism must admit to inadequacy. Not to have direct and lived experience with other beings in dealing with the exigencies of life is to be bereft of the context in which the kinds of information needed to detect the quality of other beings' valuations can be disclosed. Not to live in such contexts is to lack the ability and subject matter for conducting a proper investigation of the valuational activity of others. It is to be deprived of an experimental context. Without the ability and subject matter to conduct an experiment, the legitimacy of the scientific method cannot be proven. Likewise, without experience with other animals in dealing with the exigencies of life, knowledge of the quality of their valuations cannot be proven.

Notes

1. A more technical and detailed account of the connection between interests and environmental process can be found in Morito 1990.
2. The idea of an intrinsic value has been cause for a great deal of debate in the field of environmental ethics. See John O'Neill's "The Varieties of Intrinsic Value" (1992) for a well-rounded discussion. For present purposes, discussion will be restricted to the formulation "valuable in itself."

Chapter Five

Ecology and Ethics

The relationship between axiology and ethics is a close one. Ethical principles and sensibilities are not derived from axiology, however. Facts about how values are formed and held by people do not tell us what values people ought to hold. Facts about the genesis and prevalence of values do not tell us what is right and what is wrong. This distinction between what is the case and what ought to be the case, the "is-ought" dichotomy, plays an important role. Knowing what other people value does not oblige us to value those things as well. Some people value eliminating certain ethnic groups or the accumulation of wealth, but that does not make it right to do either and it does not place any obligation on us to satisfy those values. Nevertheless, the role of value theory is to inform ethical obligation, since forming ethical obligations is motivated by a need to recognize, satisfy or protect values. Ethics is the system of sensibilities, principles and commitments that we establish to protect the values we identify as critical. Liberals identify freedom, dignity and self-esteem as critical. Herein lies the difficulty: while we must recognize the close connection between statements about the facts concerning values and the ethical systems designed to protect our values, the connection is not straightforward.

Some guidance on how to think ecologically about ethics, however, has been given in previous chapters. Metaphysics, for instance, sets the conditions upon which an ethic must be shaped, e.g., by determining the nature of the person (whether free and responsible, whether a lone individual or part of a collective) and by describing the relationship between people and the environment. Epistemology determines the legitimacy of knowledge claims about metaphysical or axiological propositions or beliefs; it establishes the manner in which these factors can be known or legitimately and intelligibly asserted. Axiology determines the character of the values to be addressed in ethics. Ethics is related to all three areas (metaphysics, epistemology and axiology) because it must refer to each in order to verify or find support for assumptions that it needs to take as basic facts. Ethics, then, is treated as a prescriptive corpus of concepts and principles shaped by how we understand and know ourselves in relation to one another and our environment. Although it has several branches that serve various purposes, it is the prescriptive function that we need to focus on for present purposes. A co-primary function of ethics, beside that of obliging us to become attuned, is to determine what and how values are to be protected and to judge between right and wrong.

In this chapter, I sketch out a system of ethical obligations, taking my lead from Chapter Four regarding the dialectical nature of valuations. This approach departs from traditional, more positivistic approaches to ethical obligation. By "positivistic" I mean the tendency to assert something to be the case, as if its opposite had no claim to legitimacy. For instance, the assertion that happiness and the avoidance of pain are the goods that we seek to protect through ethical principles is often treated as the foundation of utilitarian ethical theory. This excludes pain as an ethical good. But we know ecologically that pain and fear (the lack of happiness) are vital motivations for behaviour, moving us to act in ways that allow ourselves and other animals to survive. "It is wrong to lie" is a classical deontological moral principle that fails to recognize that it might sometimes be good, if not right and obligatory, to lie; consider cases in which an innocent person's life is protected through the act of lying. Positivistic approaches tend to treat the value of opposites as problems for the theory and may try to incorporate these opposites by making provisos to their principles or perhaps by prioritizing principles. The approach, here, is to accept the mutual value of opposites, at least of a fundamental sort, and treat them as belonging to a dialectical relationship to which we must become attuned in order to understand how to make moral decisions.

A rather obvious reason for having to accept a dialectical approach to ethics is nicely captured by Holmes Rolston III (1988). Humans have ethical natures; other animals do not. "The grizzly is not violating human rights when it eats a child, but other humans are if they fail to rescue the victim" (Rolston 1988: 57). Predation is an ecological fact to be affirmed when thinking ecologically. Moral obligation to protect against the predator, then, often runs squarely up against this affirmation. So, it would seem that we have contradictory obligations. This contradiction can be summed up in the contrast between nature and human culture. According to Rolston, then, the human victim has rights only in relation to human culture and other human agents. The antelope has no rights in the wild. Thus, any talk of rights must be understood as culturally determined. However we are to understand our moral relationship to non-human nature, it is not through assuming some natural, ecologically determined right. Later, the issue of natural rights will be addressed, but the ethic under development, here, is not predicated on a belief in such rights. Consequently, ethical perspective, while acknowledging the ethical relevance of non-human, non-moral creatures, must be directed by and formed on some other basis. A number of key positions on animal and environmental ethics will be examined and criticized as a means of shaping this basis.

From an ecological perspective, it is unacceptable to think, in the manner of Albert Schweitzer (1993: 344), that a reverence for the will to live makes it laudable to save an insect from a puddle. Such an act is not "a life devoting itself to life," as he would have it, because life equally requires the taking of life. Schweitzer's ethic would have us praise the rescue of a drowning caribou or the rescue of a deer preyed upon by wolves. Ecologically speaking, however, each rescue and act of protecting deprives another individual or species of the conditions of life. Death, as critical to the food chain, is a co-primary value with life. A Schweitzerian reverence for life is an attempt to undermine ecologically established valuational schemes and the individuals who rely on death. Worse still is the view promoted by Steve Sapontzis, who argues that we ought to prevent predation where we can effect a lower amount of suffering than otherwise would be the case (1984: 36). Sapontzis' and Schweitzer's one-sided ethical approaches fail to understand the ecological fact that, within wild nature, there are no ethical obligations or rights. They make what can be called "category mistakes" by asserting that non-human animals are of a type that can be described as morally good or bad, when preying upon other animalsz. As such, this reverence for life ethic imposes a narrow, anthropocentric valuational scheme, which is no less impositional than the exploitive attitudes of the Modern world view.

Now, the distinction between wild nature and culture is itself controversial since in some cultures there is no distinction. Elders of the Anishnaabe (Ojibway) nation, for example, tell me that the Ojibway language has no word for wilderness or wild nature. The distinction holds no meaning within that language. But, for the moment, the focus is on Western culture, where the distinction is fundamental. Keeping this bias of Western culture in mind, we should take Rolston's point about the absence of rights in natural ecosystems in a somewhat more careful way than he presents it. We can try the following: apart from rational and deliberative activity, there is no consideration of rights and wrongs; but where there is rational activity, potentials for forming a community of moral agents exists. The governing principle of this moral community, in accordance with an ecological formulation of value theory, is the recognition of the need to protect the conditions of freedom and life. Where freedom is understood as the opposite of oppression, it and the value of life are seen as primary expressions of the impulse toward satisfaction of valuational activity. Moral life is born when members of this community recognize these conditions. Struggling with how to recognize and protect these conditions creates an awareness of the world that non-rational creatures do not have. It is plausible to assume, then, that the emergence of moral beings has depended on the emergence of the ability to deliberate, which seems to require the evolution of a brain sufficiently complex to reason, form theories and register facts about its own existence along with facts about its relationships to others.

On this matter, Schweitzer (1993: 345) does offer an important insight. A genuine ethical sensitivity based on ecological thought cannot simply settle for clearly defined ethical principles or rules and then go about compromising them as a method of relieving tensions. Such approaches obscure the "conception of the ethical." For example, when we assert that all beings have an inherent right to live and then go about arguing that, because of necessity, some must die, we invite incoherence. If we seek to do what is right—not to be confused with establishing rights—we must seek to understand the conditions of ethical life before we set out to establish principles for such a life. If Schweitzer had followed his own principle, he would have taken the ecological context more into account before formulating his reverence for life doctrine. One of the contextual ecological features he would have recognized is the dialectical relationships that form ecosystem processes and structures: whole-part, predator-prey, life-death, individual-species relationships. Thinking ecologically about ethical obligation, consequently, means finding some way to respect opposite valuations. So, how we respond ethically to the impulse to protect freedom and life needs to be carefully examined in light of the conditions that give rise to them.

Liberal Ethics and Ecology

In dealing with liberal value theory, it was noted how the one-way value-conferring system fails to acknowledge the ecological and evolutionary context. In the development of liberal democratic principles, this one-way system focuses on individual conferring activity and agreement between individuals to form collective values. Like Schweitzer, classical liberals focus on individuals and on protecting them from harm. Emphasizing freedom from oppression and tolerance for diverse values is also central to liberal ethics. If respect and the capacity to be aware of the many valuational activities at various levels of analysis are coupled with this emphasis, then the basic liberal orientation toward respecting freedom and protecting from harm works well as a starting point for an ecologically determined environmental ethic. The tradition beginning with Jeremy Bentham and John Stuart Mill establishes that it is wrong to discriminate against anyone on morally irrelevant grounds—a principle of non-discrimination designed to protect freedom. This principle matches earlier concerns to ensure inclusion of all loci of valuational activity as relevant to understanding our dependency relationship to ecological conditions, and it will be addressed more fully in later discussions on the work of

Peter Singer. Thus, while liberal metaphysical and axiological frameworks are inappropriate, their ethical principles hold out promise in the establishment of a framework of concepts for the series of iterations that may be necessary for an ecological ethic to take shape.

My strategy, then, is to direct the critique of liberal ethics toward maintaining what is consistent with thinking ecologically and eliminating what is not. Liberal sensibilities can, without ecologically directed reflection, lead to inappropriate conclusions. In "The Case for Animal Rights," for example, Tom Regan (1989) argues that sentient or conscious animals are moral patients whom we are to look after much as we look after children. The reason is that they share the qualities of consciousness, memory and the like; they are experiencing subjects of a life. As subjects of a life, all sentient animals deserve to be protected under the right to life, just as human beings are. To exclude them from protection would be discriminatory on morally irrelevant grounds (for example, just because they are not human). This discrimination would be arbitrary, since not being human is a mere genetic and factual difference that should no more bear on moral worthiness than being tall or plump or white.

Peter Singer (1986), in "All Animals Are Equal," adopts a similar strategy, arguing that we are to look out for the welfare of non-human species because they have an interest in not suffering. The ability to suffer is the morally relevant feature that almost all animals, at least those down to the oyster, possess. If we claim that it is permissible to ignore their suffering, then we again arbitrarily deny them moral worthiness and the right not to suffer. Like Jeremy Bentham, Singer holds that the morally relevant feature of members of a moral community is this ability to suffer and the concomitant desire to avoid suffering.

The approach for both Regan and Singer is to identify a key, morally significant feature that we judge ought to be protected. They then assign a right to life or to liberation for creatures who display these features; we accord them some moral considerability through acknowledging some responsibility to protect them. Both accept restrictions to this extension, limiting protection to those beings displaying sentience or some morally relevant property shared by paradigm cases (namely, humans). Kenneth Goodpaster (1978) takes both to task on this matter. Why stop at subjects of a life or at the ability to suffer? For him, any criterion of inclusion we can imagine selecting will be arbitrary. He argues, in the end, that any self-organizing being should be accorded some degree of moral considerability. Self-organizing activity is the only non-arbitrary, non-discriminatory criterion that we could choose.

Goodpaster likewise employs a paradigm case strategy by identifying what seems to be the key morally significant property in humans, namely self-organizing activity. He then argues that a class of non-human creatures possesses the same properties and concludes that we have illegitimately prejudiced our moral protective sensibilities to exclude some creatures who in fact belong to this class. In "Moral Considerability and Universal Consideration," Tom Birch (1998: 381) asks, "why stop there?" Why this and not some other property? Birch concludes that everything has moral considerability under this logic.

For Regan, Singer and Goodpaster, the moral life is about identifying morally relevant properties and extending protection to creatures who display these properties. But, as Birch points out, this intellectual identification of properties is not what really motivates us to act morally. Somewhere along the line, some root or gut experience motivates us to identify something as having moral considerability, what he calls a "deontic experience" (Birch 1998: 382). When we undergo a deontic experience we do not make some logical connection between a property and its moral considerability. It is not an intellectual act but a feeling of obligation or compulsion to be considerate and protective of another, owing to some deep level of identification with them. We may identify with their need to flourish or to be free of suffering. This experience presents us with a feeling of having to do something to recognize the other. It is this type of experience that, for Birch, brings substance and force to moral life. Our previous discussion on needing direct experience in a community of other beings in order to understand the impulse to freedom allows us to take Birch's criticism further.

The paradigm case strategy fails to engage the proper types of sensibilities needed to understand the conditions of freedom and the need to protect life. This abstract approach, however helpful in ordering and clarifying moral thought, is nevertheless detached from the kind of attunement that is necessary for understanding these conditions. What Regan and Singer are doing is relying on this deontic experience to lend force to their assertion without taking proper account of it. They proceed to distort the moral sense by supposing that moral decision making is really about abstracting from concrete experience and comparing properties of various candidates for inclusion into the moral community with an abstract version of the paradigm case. Both argue that it would then be inconsistent to assign moral protection to the class of human beings and to deny it to other classes that share the same properties. In effect, they are forming a way of thinking about ethics that makes the deontic experience and attunement almost irrelevant. The deontic experience is marginalized by focusing on the formal aspects of class comparison. In fact, the more universally valid they try to make their criteria of inclusion, the less deontic experience matters, since the criteria would apply irrespective of experience.

Now, Regan, Singer and Goodpaster have taken us a long way in opening the liberal community to being aware of a wider moral community, and they have advanced our understanding of how we might respect a more comprehensive set of conditions of freedom and protection from harm. But Birch has identified the importance of the experiential basis of moral life, a basis in feeling and passion. The important contribution Birch makes for present concerns is this: without the basic feelings and passions of having to respond to the needs of freedom and protection from harm, it would be meaningless to try to construct the moral relevance of freedom or suffering. As Walter Berns (1992: 437) argues, laws designed to protect the basic values of a society are united and grounded in deeply held and shared passions to protect freedom; they represent a collectively shared system of values that shape our intuitions, if not our conceptions, of the good. In terms of what is not permissible, these values are not merely negatively defined, as some liberals would assert. Rather they are grounded in a mutual recognition of what it takes to lead a good life: the fulfillment of basic needs, such as the need to have a supportive community, to be treated with dignity and to have a sense of belonging. These needs are, in effect, passions, expressions of positive values. They are pre-rational in the sense that they do not derive from the rational construction of principles and rules but are the underlying motivations for the rational construction of ethical principles and rules. They are recognized and experienced at a pre-theoretical level and supported in trust relationships. Principles would, in fact, be empty apart from the passions and valuations that give them their prescriptive and collective force.

In part, I describe this line of critique to emphasize what has already been introduced with respect to epistemological obligations of thinking ecologically. As in matters pertaining to ways of knowing, ways of thinking about ethics need to recognize the importance of grounding in immediate experience as well as in the theoretical development of principles. Thinking ecologically about ethics requires immediate experience in community to understand the conditions that lead to moral concern. Typically, liberals tend to limit the depth at which ethical analysis is conducted. They truncate their processes of identification of who and what are to be considered morally relevant by focusing on developing universals. By starting with the assumption of individuality and taking the primary problem to be that of treating these individuals as a collective, liberal thought devalues the immediacy of engaged understanding. It would be better, then, to begin with the assumption of community and try to understand how ethical principles shape and are shaped by the individual. Beginning this way draws attention toward the community conditions that bring about concern for freedom and life. By treating the individual as the primary problem, focus is placed on the motivating elements of individuals to determine how they can undergo discipline to respect the community yet be freed to shape the community's understanding of its principles. This suggestion is not significantly different from that represented in the life of Socrates, who both respected the principles of Athenian society by accepting their death sentence yet took it as his responsibility to act as a gadfly in criticizing his community to reform its principles.

By placing immediate engagement at the heart of ethical principle development, we begin to reshape moral concepts. Take "respect" as an example. Felt respect, as opposed to formal respect, is motivated by a need to recognize and protect the dignity of others; a feeling generated not at an abstract level but at an experiential level of sensitivity to the factors contributing to or detracting from the self-esteem of others within the community. Such feelings are connected to a network of related feelings having to do with a sense of worth and acceptance. It is this network of feelings that we seek to protect when establishing principles of conduct that would have us behave so as to guard against injury. Liberals espouse such principles as the harm principle, non-interference, confidentiality and privacy. Each is compatible with protecting this network of feelings and, if Berns is correct, presupposes this network. All too readily, however, liberals tend to apply these principles only in their negative formulation, believing that doing no harm and not interfering with others are sufficient to establish and protect the moral community. When we accept the negative formulation as sufficient for establishing moral rightness and a moral character, we allow even those who have no immediate awareness of dignity and the feelings that are related to it to count as members of the moral community. Even a sociopath or one who has no feelings of respect toward others, for instance, can count as a person who demonstrates respect toward others simply because he or she displays no disrespectful behaviour. Such a person, although not violating any principles, is not aware of the feelings of others and of the modes in which dignity and respect are embodied in action.

This negative formulation of respect falls short in at least two ways. The first is that if all people were sociopaths, the concept of respect would probably not belong to the human vocabulary because there would be no substance to the concept. There are good reasons to believe that the negative formulation is parasitic on the positive. A further weakness of the negative formulation is that, in many cases, it is insufficient in practice. Ignoring someone as you enter the room can signal a lack of respect, especially if it is perceived to be intentional. The need for recognition is often formally acknowledged, where a bow or handshake is considered polite, while the omission is considered a slight or an act of derision. Such omissions can be acts of disrespect. No overt expression of disrespect has occurred, but a clear lack of respect has been demonstrated. Those who are sensitive to the need for recognition and who inadvertently fail to recognize a person will make a concerted effort to apologize or to make recompense for the oversight. Such acts of recompense presuppose the importance and requirement of positive expressions of respect. Where positive demonstrations are required, there is also the expectation that an agent knows what it is to feel respect in the giving of it, owing to the fact that we draw distinctions between genuine and non-genuine expressions. Hence, moral life requires individuals to have a foundation in understanding affirmation of the dignity and freedom of others.

Where the ecological community is concerned, our understanding of moral life and the conditions of freedom must be more inclusive than when considering a human community alone. Just as the human community determines the context and directions for moral development, so too does the ecological community. Obviously the ecological community directs in less determinate ways than does the human and yet, like the human community, the ecological community directs by determining the purposiveness of actions and principles. However, this community constitutes a more fundamental purposiveness than the human because it is that upon which the human community depends and derives its purposiveness.

By reversing the liberal individual-community relationship and expanding the moral community to include the ecological conditions of purposiveness, we have established a quasi-factual set of conditions, which any development of ethical principles must take into account. One way to do this is to examine a further difficulty in liberal thought. As noted earlier, the liberal tendency is to identify holistic thinking as fascist. Tom Regan (1989), in response, focuses his concern for respect on the inherent or intrinsic value of individual subjects of a life. He, Schweitzer (1993) and, to some extent, Singer (1986) criticize humans' treatment of animals in abusive domestic situations or in sport-hunting. It is clear why each would proscribe such activities. Both types of activity violate the inherent right of the individuals who are killed or made to suffer. This position, of course, disallows activities, such as the culling of herds, to protect the health of the whole or of a species. Individuals cannot be sacrificed for the good of the whole, which fascist thinking would allow.

But it is not clear why each would not advocate interfering in the wild to protect the lives of prey, as Sapontzis (1984) does. If non-human animals have the right to life, are we not obliged to intervene to save them against predators? Regan's response to wildlife management is "let them be." But to let them be is to allow predation to continue. It is to allow rights to be violated. So, both Regan and Schweitzer are in a predicament. To let them be is to advocate for the continuation of ecosystem interactions, which include predation, suffering and other forms of premature death. It is to acknowledge predator/prey relations as somehow acceptable. Hence, in the wild, despite being subjects of a life, non-human animals do not have rights, but when living in human contexts, they do.

Regan, especially, seems to understand that predator/prey relations are somehow fundamental and that they override individual rights, but only in the wild. On what grounds can he allow for this exception? If he accepts predator/prey relations as somehow a basic unit of respect, then he is permitting holistic determinants of what is morally right. If he wishes to be consistent with his rejection of holism, he is obliged not to let them be but to intervene to prevent predation and suffering.

This trap occurs, partly because Regan limits the context for analysis of moral considerability. His and others' concern is for the individual as a subject and not for the individual as a member of a species or as a member of an ecosystem. A different trap encountered in wildlife management situations typically arises where populations of ungulates increase beyond the carrying capacity of an ecosystem because natural predators (e.g. wolves) have been eliminated. The resulting damage caused by overgrazing, i.e., elimination of flora and eventually the ungulates themselves, destroys the ecological conditions necessary for survival of the individuals in question. The fact that individual well-being and survival depend on a balanced ecological context and on the health of the whole herd requires that moral consideration of individuals be understood within the context of their membership in a species and in an ecosystem.

So, at least two immediate problems arise. First, the focus on individual rights or welfare leads to failure in identifying what the individual is and its moral context. Identification of individuals exclusively as individuals fails to recognize the identity-determining function of their relationship to others of their species, of the community to which they belong and of the ecological context that gives rise to them and sustains them. An individual does not gain an identity as a lone, isolated atomic unit. Second, insisting on always protecting the individual over and above the collective, as Rolston (1988) points out, can undermine the well-being and even the conditions of existence of that individual, if ecosystem relationships are not kept in balance. It can therefore be self-defeating. Whether the concern be for the survival, the well-being, the dignity or the freedom of an individual, it cannot be satisfied without, at the same time, considering the ecological context in which the individual exists. This consideration expands how we are to understand the ecological community. It not only establishes purposiveness, it is also an identity-determining condition. By taking this into account, part of the identity of the ungulate is that of a prey species. That fact needs to be weighed as carefully as its own desire to survive.

Much of the liberal approach to protecting individuals over species and ecosystems turns on a belief in natural rights; that is, rights are grounded in some naturally occurring property (e.g., being conscious and having a sense of continuation into the future). But do these rights occur in the wild? Rolston contextualizes moral considerability in a way that allows him to address what Regan and others cannot. Clearly, rights do not arise in the wild. Rights arise in cultures that consist of rational individuals. The right to life, then, is to be recognized as arising in the evolution of a cultural context, not a wild context. Animals do not have a right to life in the wild (Rolston 1988: 56). It is difficult to see, then, how rights are natural. Other groundings for natural rights, such as those found in theology or in Kantian ethics, have been shown to fail. It makes more sense to analyze rights as artifacts developed through agreement by human beings to protect values and interests. While Rolston's theory of how the ecological and cultural contexts are related remains unclear, it is more consistent with the ecological facts. Death and violent death are necessary in ecosystems, both because the purposiveness of predators directs them to kill and because balances in ecosystems require death and predation. Hence, the ecological context needs to be held in tension with the cultural context.

Thinking ecologically about ethics demands an ability to deal with the dialectical tension that arises between positive/negative valuational activities (values and disvalues) and between the many levels of organization and units of analysis. Our ethical sensibilities must be attuned to the complexity of the ethical situation, resisting tendencies toward simplification and one-sided thinking. Careful attention needs to be paid to the details of each relationship in order to optimize clarity about each moral situation. Understanding, therefore, needs to be recognized as a precondition of principle development.

Rolston (1988: 88), once again, exemplifies how awareness of a dialectical situation could operate by advancing a notion of reverencing life. Sometimes reverencing life amounts to killing individuals to save a herd; but it can also mean banning killing for vanity, even if it denies so-called higher beings (humans) the right to dress themselves in style. He appeals here to our feelings of disgust toward those who would use others and other animals to satisfy their vanity, as in the wearing of hummingbird feathers on refined European ladies' hats. Failing to kill in order to cull an overpopulated herd and killing for vanity both exemplify an irreverence for life. He argues that this approach is the more suitable one in an ecological context, where principles of stability, integrity and balance operate against a cultural context. In this situation, where there are tensions but no sharp lines between wild ecology and culture, ethics must be based on lived experience and familiarity with the real demands of life, not just the logic of a theory. Rolston (1988: 39) tries to capture this approach in his loosely formulated, general principle "follow nature," that is, "sometimes orient our conduct in accord with value there [in ecological processes]."

We can see why "following nature" is intentionally imprecise; in light of his critique of the simplification, i.e., the reduction of ethical commitments found in other thinkers' approaches to environmental ethics, imprecision follows as an unavoidable response to the complexity and multivariate ecological relationships. The more reductive approaches may offer clarity, but clarity of decision in the face of obscurity of context is ultimately self-defeating. This can take a couple of forms. One we have seen in the self-defeating commitments or lack thereof to individuals in the wild. It also occurs in cases where the intrinsic value of life requires protection by assigning bearers of intrinsic value an inherent right to life. If all creatures must eliminate some other form of life to eat, then they must violate some inherent right to life. For instance, Taylor's (1986) position—that killing and eating are justified only when it is necessary to survive—makes organic existence inescapably evil. Where there is no point to ethical life other than to avoid evil, there is no good to achieve. Either that, or the good to achieve in eating another is counterbalanced by the evil it produces for the eaten. Where there is no good to achieve, ethical principles are not designed to attune ourselves to a good, so that ethics remains nothing more than a restriction on our impetus to act. How this is a motivation to be ethical evades me. In contrast, ecological approaches, such as Rolston's, direct attention toward recognition of the good to be produced, requiring attunement in multivariate ways and at multivariate levels of understanding.

The many contextual determinants of ethical life and the subsequent complexity of that life have led some ethicists to formulate looser, more adaptive approaches. For example, W.D. Ross (1930) and his prima facie system of duties suggest that ethical principles can be designed to adapt to complex situations. Similarly, adaptability of principles needs to be incorporated into an environmental ethic in response to the deeper moral sensibilities and contexts that become relevant in decision making as new situations arise and greater awareness is attained. Adaptability, then, becomes a key principle when following nature. To be attuned is to adapt one's thought, perceptions and judgment to the array of valuations and contexts in the recognition and protection of these valuations.

Freedom

The liberal's commitment to the protection of freedom as a fundamental value is the point at which the greatest convergence between it and the ecological approach occurs. We pursue freedom with a passion in our creative endeavours, and when it is threatened by oppressive regimes, we go to war to protect it. "Freedom" is a term that describes an interest in protecting a wide range of valuations, from the positive to the negative. We act sometimes knowing exactly what it is and what value it has, especially in situations of duress, e.g., war or oppression. Yet in situations of relative peace and affirmation, freedom functions in a strange way in thought and action. Sometimes we can feel trapped in a "good" situation. We have a well-paying job, good family relationships and the like, yet we can feel restless and unfulfilled because we are not developing talents and aspirations that we feel are central to our identity. The entrepreneur or corporate executive who forfeits the life of affluence and influence to pursue an artistic or perhaps backwoods life exemplifies this type of desire for freedom.

While freedom sits at the centre of democratic institutions, its meaning and extension are not entirely clear. One interesting aspect of our commitment to freedom is that we place limits on it by developing principles of non-interference and by advocating for the protection of privacy. Different contexts, however, sometimes demand greater interference and intrusion (as in the case of conscription and national security) to protect the overall freedom of both individuals and nations. So, the meaning of freedom, what it can justify and how it is applied can vary according to context and collective interests. The fact that "freedom" can describe different levels of organization—individuals, communities, regions, states, peoples—suggests that respect for it represents the desire to recognize and protect the sometimes competing valuations and perspectives that vie for moral consideration. The United Nations, in its commitment to national freedom (the autonomy of states), illustrates how commitment to protect one level of organization sometimes conflicts with a commitment to uphold another level (e.g., individual human rights over and against state autonomy). Freedom, then, is a key concept whose application in moral deliberation demands both the recognition of deeply held values and motivations as well as the adaptation of these values in many types of contexts and at multiple levels of organization. "Freedom," when fully analyzed, is itself a thoroughly dialectical concept and, thereby, one well suited to guide us in how to recognize the network of valuations constituting ecological relations.

To understand the positive aspects of freedom, we need to be attuned to individual and collective valuations as well as to the contextual determinants. Framing our moral deliberations in accordance with a respect for freedom places us in a mind-set to make judgments and decisions that "follow" the nature of valuations, rather than simply imposing decisions or merely permitting the exercise of valuations. Following nature, in respect of freedom, disallows dictatorial rule for all valuing beings and organizations, while sometimes requiring informed intervention to ensure that the contextual supports of valuational activity are safeguarded.

If all loci of valuational activity attempt to achieve freedom, then seeking freedom is the sort of activity that humans and non-humans, individuals and systems, hold in common. The search for food, mates and play, the process of maturation and the frustrations encountered in these processes are identifiable as aspects of freedom-seeking activity. In other words, a base sense of freedom applies to all loci of valuational activity. By respecting freedom, then, we enable ourselves to recognize a much wider moral community and establish a base principle for shaping our moral attitudes toward this community.

At this point the problem of epistemic access to this community becomes central. Some may argue that we may know that we are connected but not know how we are connected because we are epistemically barred from communication with other than human beings. Thus far, I have argued only that immediate experience in the community of concern is necessary to be attuned to the factors that give rise to deontic experience. When we understand that such immediacy is an important and foundational aspect of knowledge, we set out to "know" the fear, trust, confidence, affection and language of non-human beings in much the same manner as we do humans. By living with them and interacting in ways that demand that we become aware of their inner workings, we relate intersubjectively. When we are attuned to other animals through spending time with them in the wild or through working with them as friends (as do dog and horse trainers), recognition of their need for freedom becomes concrete (see Hearne 1986). Hearne's work with dogs illustrates a number of possibilities for understanding the motivations of non-human beings, as one gets closer to them. Dogs can be given responsibility proportionate to the degree of trust that has developed between them and their "owner" (Hearne 1986: 21). The right to command a dog, as anyone knows who has tried to command a strange dog, must be earned (Hearne 1986: 47). Such commands must also be coherent (Hearne 1986: 58). The more this type of knowledge increases, the more we come to understand that trust and respect is of as much value for non-human beings as it is for humans. Understanding, in this way, relies on direct acquaintance and experience with other animals.

If we live or interact with other beings, we have no option but to find a way to understand them, both as a species and as individuals. In such a context, we cannot feign ignorance or lack of access because dogs, cats, horses and the like will make their interests, likes, dislikes, inclinations and demands known, either by their actions or by their refusal to act. To remain insulated from the information available in such interactions is to act like the physiologist who cuts the vocal chords of a dog whom he is vivisecting. Cutting the vocal chords, as Evernden (1985: 17) describes, allows the scientist to pretend that the animal is nothing more than the machine of Descartes' philosophy. It allows us to deny and, at the same time, affirm our humanity. We deny our humanity by detaching ourselves from having to react in empathy and disgust to the dog's obvious pain; and we affirm our humanity by showing that we cannot bear to face the obvious pain and violation of the dog. The more acquainted we become with non-human animals, the more attuned we become to their valuational activity; as such we become both attuned to their conditions of freedom and more informed about how to protect these conditions.

Spending time in the wild, depending on it for nourishment and shelter and respecting the territory of predators first teaches us how to see, smell and hear differently than we do in the city. As we look for signs and patterns that indicate where food can be found or when a predator is likely to attack, we become attuned to the land in a way that theoretical understanding cannot provide. Second, when we live in an area and depend on it, we learn what and how to take what we need. We become both careful and respectful as we recognize our dependency relation to the land. The respect comes from identifying others and the land as providers and as members of the web of valuational loci. Their role as provider depends on us respecting their autonomy to grow and to develop according to their own standards of excellence. *Conatus*, a concept used by Spinoza (1949) to indicate an activity toward self-maintenance and self-perfection, is helpful in characterizing these standards. Someone who is aware of the rhythms and conditions that make an ecosystem a provider understands this different order of knowing and how it becomes a requisite manner of knowing.

Knowing the conditions of freedom in non-human nature—knowing how to identify their *conatus* and acknowledging their territory—is entirely possible and, in certain contexts, necessary. If it is possible, then respecting this freedom requires as much of an effort to become attuned to these conditions as it does to become attuned to the conditions of freedom for other human beings. To refuse to try to understand and acknowledge these conditions is to be morally irresponsible, a no less morally reprehensible omission than an outright denial of responsibility to understand and respect conditions of human freedom.

That freedom is directly relevant to descriptions of ecosystems is doubtful, but good reasons for using the concept metaphorically may be in order. Allowing ecosystems to develop and evolve according to their own non-anthropogenic determinants is akin to allowing individual organisms to develop and act according to their own valuations. Engineering environments to some purpose or other denies what that environment would have become and denies other loci the full range of possibilities within that ecosystem. Denying natural succession denies access to the natural history of the system that spawned our valuational activity, thus denying us the full range of information and understanding of how this activity can be satisfied. Highly engineered environments, which entirely replace an existing system, express the values of some loci—some human beings (but not all); they are compatible with the valuations of some opportunistic non-human species, but not many. They completely deny the systemic values of the ecosystem that were once in place. Such environments, either intentionally or implicitly through design, force compliance to a narrow band of special interest group values. Suburbs are examples of how environments are designed to promote the use of automobiles, isolated lifestyles and excessive use of fossil fuels. Such engineered environments completely ignore, rather than respect, pre-existing valuational systems. They force conformity. The aggregate of loci that forms the system, then, can be said to have its freedom denied.

Applying "freedom" to descriptions of ecosystems is not capricious, since terms such as "forcing" the land to yield product (as in high energy input agricultural systems that rely on chemical fertilizers, herbicides and pesticides) are entirely appropriate to describe the elimination of indigenous species and processes. One aspect of the land, e.g., as a holder for crops, is singled out for exploitation, like a slave's ability to perform menial labour. The system of valuations that gives that ecosystem or that person an identity is ignored, eliminated or re-engineered to suit production purposes. By thinking in terms of the freedom of ecosystems, we have a more comprehensive way to capture the moral importance of protecting the system of valuational activities upon which we depend. It is a way to represent the aggregate of loci as a whole and not merely as a sum of the parts. As such, it allows us a way to include the holistic aspect of ecosystems in the moral considerations of ecosystems, and not merely think about them as conditions of purposiveness of the moral community. It is the moral community thought of as a whole.

It should be clear that no simplistic preservationist position is being espoused. The fact that our understanding of ecosystems and our relationships in them are dialectical means that respect for freedom of one may mean the denial of it for another (as in predator-prey relations). Disturbance and intervention are necessary aspects of any creature's activity in what has gone before. Further, the dialectical relationship between the purposiveness of ecosystems (preconditions for our fitting into the ecosystem) and the creative contribution of each member to shaping that purposiveness means that simply leaving systems alone is neither possible nor desirable. What is not acceptable is the unattuned and simplifying eradication of systems and loci. This has both quantitative and qualitative aspects. Some disruptions are compatible with respecting the integrity of ecosystems, until they reach a certain scale (e.g., when low-impact selective logging is replaced by large-scale clearcuts). Some disruptions, such as food hunting, have been part of ecosystem activities for as long as humans have evolved, but altering the constituents of the earth to perform functions that destroy the integrity of individuals and systems (as do nuclear power and weapons) is not acceptable.

The Harm Principle

The foundational concept of freedom and the guiding principle of respect for freedom are closely related to the harm principle. Where there is respect for freedom, there is a corresponding respect for the autonomy of those who can enjoy freedom. It is against this autonomy that the primary harm can be brought, whether by destroying the locus or by injury. Even though the principle is negatively formulated as "avoid doing harm," the ecological context and demands for attunement require that the principle includes an obligation to understand what can bring harm to different loci. And while the principle has its roots in the concern to prevent oppression, the conditions of thinking ecologically require a commitment to recognizing valuations of different loci and levels of organization of loci. Such recognition creates in us an awareness of what will sustain the integrity of autonomous units. An initial formulation of the principle is as follows.

1) Do no harm to the extent that is compatible with protecting the full range of freedoms of other human beings and non-human beings, respecting levels of organization. Focusing on individuals as a first consideration is not meant to prioritize individuality over collectivity or context, since the dialectical nature of ecological thought requires that collective and contextual aspects of the individual's identity be considered together with the harm that may befall it.

2) The principle of equity is connected to the harm principle because there is no prima facie reason for discriminating against any human or non-human being. All valuational loci count in deliberations of harm, such that we are required to become attuned to their particular perspective, needs and ecological contexts. Just as we balance harms and goods for human loci, so too we are to balance harms and goods for non-human loci.

1a) The Precautionary Principle: One other implication of thinking ecologically about the harm principle is that we need to incorporate our inherent ignorance and the opacity of the ecological cum dialectical nature of ethical life into how the harm principle operates. Hence, where information is insufficient to be able to judge harm, err on the side of caution.

While the idea of "leaving alone"—the principle of non-interference—is central to the harm principle, the articulation of the harm principle goes further because it presupposes a responsibility to understand the conditions of freedom for different individuals and species.

According to classical liberal thought, such understanding is not required; hence, the emphasis on spheres of privacy. Respect for privacy is thought to be sufficient to protect freedom. Attunement to different perspectives and needs, however, requires more of a community orientation than it does one based on typical liberal commitments to individualism. Communication and disclosure of need are vital to the operation of the harm principle and are, in fact, central to the principle of non-interference. Since James Rachels' (1975) often republished "Active and Passive Euthanasia," the controversy over the moral equality of acts of omission and acts of commission has made it impossible to ignore the fact that sometimes absence of action is equivalent to presence of action. For instance, not acting to save someone who is drowning can be morally equivalent to killing them. Similarly, by not acting, we could perform the moral equivalent of harming another, as in cases where a child is being bullied by another child and we stand by watching. When we can be the key factors in protecting others' security, dignity, integrity and freedom, our lack of action can be the effective means through which these values and rights are violated. Therefore, not taking appropriate action to understand the values at stake and what it means to victims to be harmed can also be considered in violation of the harm principle. Insofar as we can identify with and know other beings' conditions of freedom, we can know their conditions of harm and are thereby morally obligated to understand what harms we might produce either by acting or by not acting. Therefore, failing to understand these conditions can also be the moral equivalent of interference. For instance, not educating ourselves and remaining uninformed of the consequences of our interventions (e.g., economic development) in different cultures might well bring harm to that culture. By establishing modes of production (e.g., large factories), we may indirectly undermine family and social structures, not to mention conditions of self-esteem and dignity, when workers are displaced by machinery. Attuning ourselves, as an educational commitment, then, is central to satisfying the harm principle. In what follows, I will appeal to a variety of traditions in formulating more fully how attunement enters into the ethical framework. Through criticizing these traditions, I hope to shape a more comprehensive formulation of the harm principle.

The Ethics of Deep Ecology

As we turn to deep ecology as a second backdrop against which to structure an environmental ethic, a critique of the central notion that "all beings have intrinsic values" (Drengson and Inoue 1995: 2) will be useful in shaping the ethics of attunement. When we expand the concept of self to recognize that the ecological system is a more comprehensive Self,[1] of which the ego is a more restricted locus of value, we recognize the possibility that other beings are loci of value and, therefore, have intrinsic value (Drengson and Inoue 1995: 51). Everything within the ecosystem writ large is an end in itself. Kant's view of intrinsic value is being extended to include a wider sense of Self. Deep ecology extends greater protection to a greater number of individuals than would Regan, Singer or Taylor; at the same time, it diminishes the importance of the atomic individual. Each individual is intimately related to all that constitutes the ecosystem. We are mistaken when we try to isolate individuals and treat them as if they are somehow fundamentally independent of one another.

There are further distinctions to be drawn. As Warwick Fox (1990) explains, the notion of intrinsic value, even as espoused by the founder of deep ecology, Arne Naess, is not a technical term. It asserts that the holder of intrinsic value is a value in itself, but no strict definition of this notion is forthcoming. "Intrinsic value" expresses a commitment and a way of seeing, rather than strictly defining the moral rights each being has (Fox 1990: 115). Something with intrinsic value is, indeed, deserving of respect as an end in itself, not merely as a means to further some end. But, since respect of this sort is more an attitude than a formal principle, it does not here yield an inherent right to life as it does in Regan's view. Deep ecology, then, does not extend the principles of the Modern tradition to non-human beings, but it does attempt to extend the moral sensibility of respect for humans to respect for non-humans. Commitment to intrinsic value, in other words, does not yield binding moral principles but aids in engendering an attitude of respect.

Supporters of deep ecology do not extend principles and concepts of moral recognition to include non-human beings in the moral community. This strategy allows supporters to avoid some of the difficulties that many liberal thinkers encounter. One of these difficulties involves the inability of other species to reciprocate respect for others or to act in a morally responsible manner, as rational human beings can. We cannot, therefore, treat them as duty bearers and decision makers. Critics might then respond that without reciprocity, it does not make sense to include other species in the moral community. Countering this, liberals such as Regan draw a distinction between moral patients and agents to show how it is possible for the moral community to have members who cannot reciprocate duties, but who can enjoy rights. Mary Midgeley (1987) has also argued that reciprocity is not necessary for a moral community to exist. Children can enjoy full moral and legal protection against abuse and killing, even though they cannot be expected to honour the duty not to injure or kill.

Both liberal and deep ecological strategies fail in certain contexts, however. We have already discussed the incoherence of the liberal right to life in the wild with respect to predator-prey relationships. Another case involves saving the life of a beached whale. We may or may not be acting in its best interest or in accordance with ecologically sound principles by saving its life. While liberalism would have us save the whale, deep ecology would only tend toward saving it. From an ecological perspective, however, we are best advised to leave it alone and let it die because we cannot know what function and what other lives are preserved by its death. A drowning buffalo or deer with a broken leg surely suffers, but such misfortune is what provides food for other creatures. From an evolutionary perspective, we cannot even determine whether the extermination of an entire species is ultimately good or bad. Certainly, the extermination of some species has made the biosphere compatible for human existence—species that required a non-aerobic atmosphere in which to live had to die for the present system of aerobic metabolizers to evolve. The idea of intrinsic value, then, may actually militate against recognizing the ecological context in which harm to an individual is sometimes necessarily balanced against the good of a species or ecosystem.

More loosely defining intrinsic value allows supporters of deep ecology partially to avoid this difficulty. Unlike the liberal, the deep ecology supporter can identify different units of analysis when determining morally relevant units. Individuals, predator/prey unit and entire ecological niches can be identified as intrinsically valuable units. The set of relations at each of these levels has an autonomy and integrity of its own, which is to be respected because it has intrinsic value. Protecting one unit is not necessarily violating another. According to the tenets of deep ecology (Naess 1989: 29), it is the flourishing of human and non-human life that has intrinsic value. Naess proposes a series of platform principles to describe what is consistent and inconsistent with ascriptions of intrinsic value: maintaining a diversity of life forms, reducing the human population and reducing human interference in the non-human world. The suffering of an individual may, then, be compatible with these principles.

Part of the strength of deep ecological formulations of intrinsic value over traditional liberal ones is that they do not presuppose a radical distinction between one locus of valuational activity and another. Naess does not claim to establish an ethic of binding obligations, so much as a way of seeing the world. He, therefore, need not be as precise about who or what has intrinsic value and how ascriptions of it are to protect its holders. Whereas most doctrines of moral intrinsic value anticipate a rigid internal/external dichotomy between one locus and others, supporters of deep ecology treat the concept as a means for attuning ourselves more keenly to the needs, functions and natures of all creatures. Too much of the traditional liberal form of morality, as seen by these supporters, rides on a belief in the exclusionary force of intrinsic value ascriptions. Deep ecology provides a way to understand that is inclusive and more dialectical than liberal theories. While the liberal can be blinded to the greater harm that may be inflicted on a system or a species when individuals are protected from harm, supporters of deep ecology can be open to weighing possible goods and harms according to how well both individuals and populations flourish.

The deep ecological method is to question assumptions and approaches to understanding as far as thought is capable or until ultimate commitments are reached. This process of questioning is aimed at finding the roots of our ultimate religious or philosophical beliefs (Naess 1995: 11). While the process may seem to be nothing more than one of finding better, more coherent and more consistent explanations, it also involves the totality of human experience, the comprehensive set of factors and motivations that constitute our thought and lives. For this reason, the ultimate beliefs a person adopts are not entirely amenable to logical explanation or justification; they may be largely intuitively grounded. Utilizing meditative and artistic methods, in conjunction with rational techniques, the supporter of deep ecology intends to approximate a "total field" in awareness. This total field is the sum of the factors that constitute a person's knowledge regarding identity, perceptions, motivations, values and relationships.

Scientific knowledge is a specific kind of knowledge that satisfies a limited number of knowledge values. Knowledge gained through intuition, spiritual experience, art and insight is expressive of different values because it is attuned to different sorts of activities and sources of meaning. Together, however, these kinds of knowledge can form as comprehensive an approach to understanding our relationship within the world as seems possible for the human being. At first glance, when we seek awareness in as comprehensive and exhaustive a manner as possible, we have good epistemic reasons for accepting this total field approach. Likewise, there are good reasons for accepting a total field approach to metaphysics, especially in light of holistic ecological, multilevel organizational and cross-cultural expectations. Such an approach should attempt to be comprehensive in the sense that it is attuned to as many aspects of reality and modes of knowing as possible. It should be open to the implications for formulating the human-environment relationship according to the disclosures resulting from such attunement. This comprehensive approach to knowing involves its own form of rigour, which emphasizes what Kant would call the principle of exhaustiveness. It attempts to leave no stone unturned nor any possibly relevant factor unexamined when constructing explanations or ethical systems. This principle militates against those who would, for the sake of clarity and simplicity, reduce ethical life to principled or rule-governed life.

There is a price to pay for committing to this type of rigour, however. Moral judgments tend to be imprecise and lead to unclear theoretical judgments about right and wrong. Inclusion of such a diverse range of perspectives and values creates obscurity and uncertainty, yielding indecision and ambiguity in understanding harm and what we are to protect. Herein lies a classical problem. On the one hand, exhaustiveness demands breadth and inclusiveness of perspective. On the other hand, the values of clarity and parsimony demand narrowness (focus and reduction to a single perspective). This is not the place to settle the issue; but it would appear that some guides can be identified to provide a workable solution in unifying these two expectations. In some respects, the solution to the problem of inclusiveness versus exclusiveness, comprehensiveness versus narrowness, lies in the very nature of rational deliberation itself. A rational person will ask for good reasons for accepting a knowledge source or idea before it is entertained. Claims about values, sources of values and perspectives cannot be introduced willy-nilly. These sources and perspectives must be shown to be necessary or important for an adequate understanding, or we must be shown how our understanding of moral life would be wanting were we to ignore such sources and perspectives. As in the development of new world views, old world views that were found to be wanting could be either modified or augmented until it became necessary to replace them. The strategy is to adapt understanding to the various legitimate demands, while maintaining baseline principles (e.g., democratic, participatory decision making). Adequate moral decision making then becomes a process more than an event or an adherence to principle. It is an acceptance of responsibility for judgments and decisions made in an opaque context as much as it is a commitment to justification procedures.

Balancing these two elements of ethical thought is obviously not a straightforward exercise. Justificatory approaches often appeal to principles and rules that, when obeyed, are seen to excuse the decision maker from responsibility for bad consequences or for not having to understand and be sympathetic to the people affected by the resulting decision. Following the letter of the law as opposed to the spirit of the law is one example of such an approach. However, sometimes judges include a much wider set of ethically relevant conditions when making judgments. Rather than focusing on justificatory narrowness, they seek to be as inclusive of perspectives and values as possible. For instance, in the striking down of the Canadian abortion laws prior to 1988, the Supreme Court (*R. v. Morgentaler*) introduced concepts such as women's perspective on dignity and the self-esteem of women in interpreting the intent of the constitution. In 1990, in a ruling concerning aboriginal rights (*R. v. Sparrow*), the same court mandated taking aboriginal perspective into account when interpreting aboriginal rights, so that the impact of resource management decisions on aboriginal communities would be respected. Such decisions, and in some respects, the operations of common law in general, offer models as to how such a decision-making system can operate. It focuses on judgment, bringing together the demands of clear justification and the opacity of perspectival inclusiveness. In the process of coming to decision, clarity in the expectations of law is established, while considerations of other factors present reasons for modification or even radical interpretation of law.

Returning now to deep ecology, a problem arises because the total field approach does not and perhaps cannot yield an environmental ethic (Naess 1995: 26). It may yield a set of recommended norms, which will be followed when people mature to the point of realizing that their self is really part of a greater Self, connected to all things by way of compassion and recognition of natural beauty; but the approach does not yield the justificatory rigour that seems so important for decision making, the need for standards of legitimacy and justice. Rolston (1988: 58), in contrast, even though he is profoundly influenced by total field thinking, believes that coming to understand the connection to nature generates a sense of duty. He sees prescriptive force emanating from a recognition of intrinsic value. He believes that by understanding what is ecologically the case, a sense of obligation to protect it arises. Here is the rub: How do we get moral obligation from the principles of deep ecology? Is moral life really about self-realization and not about binding obligations? If so, what are the consequences?

The emancipation of women and minorities as well as obligations toward animal welfare have not come to be recognized through processes of self-realization alone, or even principally; rather, they have gained recognition through hard-won battles in the ethical, legislative and legal arenas. Without the force of justified constraint or binding obligations, these developments would not have occurred. Corporations have not voluntarily eliminated lead from fuel, ceased the production of freon (an ozone layer-depleting substance), restricted clear-cutting of old growth forests or ceased killing endangered species because of self-realization. This is not to be cynical, but it is to acknowledge the importance of ethics in society as a constraining force. Development of such legal constraints has been the result largely of having developed strong justificatory ethical arguments using principles such as equality and non-discrimination. Hence, to omit the element of constraint is to leave environmental thought unresponsive to those aspects of human nature that are directed against self-realization: greed, fear, bad faith, obsession with power and dominance. In a sense, it can be argued that it is a denial of attunement to the full range of conditions that moral beings must face. Becoming attuned to others needs and threats of harm without attuning ourselves to what is necessary to apply the harm principle is to fail to understand the conditions of respect for freedom.

Karen Warren (1998), Annie Booth (1997) and Vandana Shiva (1989) and others have identified a connection between the oppression of women and the oppression of nature. Like supporters of deep ecology, many ecofeminists are striving to create an egalitarian society (see Booth 1997: 333) very much along the lines of self-realization and identification with the rest of the world. But the principal issue to address for ecofeminists is the dual oppression of nature and women, an oppression that flies in the face of justice. Justice issues address human-induced evil. However else we are to understand environmental issues, ecofeminists have pointed out that the oppression of women and the oppression of nature are linked fundamentally. This oppression involves violation, outrage, denial of freedom and the perpetration of deliberate harm. We are not dealing merely with a lack of insight, understanding and self-realization, as if through shedding of ignorance we would act in accordance with the good; we are dealing with hatred, aggression, oppressive attitudes of dominance, the evils in the world. For this reason, attunement conceived as enlightenment about self and other is insufficient and one-sided. How the element of constraint is to be built into an ethic of attunement depends largely on our understanding of rationality.

Thinking Ecologically Toward an Environmental Ethic: Further Directions and Tensions

Anthropocentrism, understood ecologically, implies that human loci of valuational activity are situated in the world, are of the world, yet are in possession of special epistemic and decision-making capacities. These capacities can be collectively described as rational capacities, which make us capable of bearing responsibility. Anthropocentrism is also a limiting condition on purview and epistemic access to the world. We cannot experience like a bat or like a snake. We cannot know like a colony of ants or like a dog who follows a trail with its nose. Hence, anthropocentrism marks out a kind of experiential territory beyond which we cannot go. Yet these rational capacities allow us to know that other creatures have their own experiential territory and desire to exercise valuations and that there are certain conditions that have to be met for them to flourish. We are conscious of the fact that we are participants in more comprehensive ecological processes of taking our valuational activity to satisfaction, as do all creatures. Like all other creatures, we seek to protect ourselves from harm so that we can continue in this activity.

Being conscious of facts and conditions and having the capacity to reason distinguishes the anthropocentric locus from other loci. Since these aspects of rationality are linked to the ability to bear responsibility, they constitute us as primary responsibility bearers since they enable us both to engage in justificatory deliberation and to understand more comprehensive relationships and consequences of decisions. Fully exercising this capacity means that we can be and are responsible not only for protecting conditions of freedom but for applying effective means for protecting them. This view of rationality supports entrenching two assumptions about moral life: 1) that in the experience of the moral community there are evils and disvalues that cannot be tolerated; 2) that an important part of the rational response to evil and disvalue is the use of principled constraint where necessary. Reliance on self-actualization or inherent goodness is insufficient as an exercise of attunement. The demands of protection simply require the development of a system of constraints.

If the impetus to protect is a primary impetus of moral life, then a further distinction between the present moral perspective and classical liberalism needs to be drawn. As seen in the Modern world view on anthropocentrism, rationality accords privilege to those to whom it can be ascribed. A more contemporary example of this view can be found in Mary Anne Warren's (1983) "The Moral and Legal Status of Abortion." Being rational, for her, is at the very least a self-evident criterion of moral standing. It is a non-negotiable starting point for assigning values and moral status. Accordingly, abortion can be justified because we can show that the fetus is not rational and therefore has no moral standing.

But given the preceding analysis, Warren's starting point is far from self-evident and is, in fact, perverse when anthropocentrism is understood ecologically. Other philosophers who have insisted on making the same connection between reason and privileged moral considerability have done so by force of agreement, rather than through careful examination of the foundations of moral life. If the foundations of moral life are the passions for freedom in the satisfaction of valuational activity, and the primary impetus of moral life is to protect, then the idea that rationality accords privilege is both forced and rife with chauvinism. Indeed, if one were to examine what is self-evident, one might look to more so-called primitive moral levels where basic moral responses can be identified. Children, for instance, will often protect dolls, dogs and cats before they will protect other human beings. Children often treat their pets and toys with a sense of fairness, but they do not recognize other humans (e.g., playmates) as deserving of the same consideration. In fact, it is often with great effort that children are taught to extend the same consideration to other humans. Although a child's moral sensibilities are not sufficient for developing an ethic, they indicate that what we should consider morally self-evident is unclear. Appealing to rationality as a criterion for excluding others from the community runs contrary to the nature of rationality, when described as a critical tool. Rationality, by virtue of its aim toward comprehensiveness and exhaustiveness, is more coherently connected to the inclusion, than the exclusion, of other beings. As such, it does not have principally to do with privilege and the assigning of rights, but with the assigning of responsibility. This conclusion accords well with Birch's (1998) notion of deontic experience, supporting the idea that an ethic of attunement prescribes duties and responsibilities.

The next obvious question is "For what reasons ought we to protect?" Convergence with liberalism affords an initial direction for answering the question. Liberalism is born in the overthrow of oppression, where oppression can take many forms in relation to *conatus* and multivariate valuational activities. Jeremy Bentham (1977) has argued that what counts morally is not so much rational activity as the ability to suffer. The importance of Bentham's insight, for present purposes, is not his treatment of the ability to suffer as a criterion of moral inclusion but as a way of acknowledging the potential of other valuing beings to suffer and to experience oppression. It connects with the idea of deontic experience by indicating that we have the capacity to identify duties to protect others from violation.

Thinking ecologically, using liberal thought as a launching point, has enabled a clearer formulation of what needs to be protected and to what we respond (i.e., violation) when we protect. Protecting other beings and species is not just a matter of prudentiality. Liberal thought also supports the centrality of integrity as a condition to protect. Of particular interest are the ideas "being a subject of a life" (Regan 1989), "teleological centre" (Taylor 1986), and "self-organizing centre" (Goodpaster 1978). Each implies that all living beings, if not the earth itself, have a sense of integrity (by needing to have their activity conform to pre-established valuations). When deprived of activities that exercise this integrity, individuals undergo perverse behavioural changes and frustrations. Freeing individuals to exercise their *conatus* and allowing conditions that enable this exercise results in flourishing. Anyone who observes a wolf or a bear in the wild and compares it to one in a zoo immediately sees the effects of frustrating *conatus*. Animals, such as predators, sometimes display aberrant pacing behaviour while locked in a cage; others lose the sharpness of their hunting or avoidance skills as they become fat and lazy. Some engage in pathological behaviour; some just die. If we take behaviour and appearance in the wild as our measure of normalcy, we more often than not can immediately recognize pathological behaviour and unhealthy appearance in captive situations. The more attuned we are to wild behaviour through experience in the bush, the better we can see the perversions in captivity or other inappropriate environments. We become aware of conditions and signs of distress in others, not only by setting up objective indicators of distress but by being able to tell the difference between mating calls, expressions of hunger, playful sounds and signals of distress. In other words, we can know these conditions by learning the language of other species. We can then begin to hear expressions of violation.

Even without learning the language of other species, recognition can occur through our interest in healthy plants, animals and ecosystems since our own health and ability to flourish depends on a strong *conatus* in them. We recognize diseased plants and infected livestock as having something of their conditions of well-being and health disrupted or, when done intentionally, violated. We can distinguish between more and less robust *conatus* and, therefore, greater and lesser degrees of violation. Consequently, we can understand that frustrating *conatus* is a form of denying freedom, not in a metaphorical but in a literal sense. The more we understand their language, the more attuned we can be to the manner in which they can be violated. In this way, the process of understanding the frustration of *conatus* in other beings as a violation is neither unintelligible nor perversely anthropomorphic. It is completely rational in the sense that it is mandated and made possible by the critical exercise of reason. The harm principle, then, implies that we have a prima facie obligation to protect all creatures, to respect their freedom-seeking activity and to apply the principle of equality to ensure that their *conatus* is recognized along with all others.

The preceding is the first moment or part of ethical responsibility; the responsibility: to protect from violation. But this is not the complete picture, since protection from violation needs to be dialectically related to the necessity of undermining *conatus*. Taking the other side of the dialectical relationship into account, we need to recognize oppositional relationships and different levels of organization. Those who are a threat to our well-being must be handled differently than those with whom we can live. Those who are a prey species for us and others that are not will again have to be handled differently. Some loci must be consumed and used. Equality applies to how we recognize not only individuals but relations between individuals as well as systems.

Judgment and Decision

Central to human rationality is the capacity to exercise judgment and decision. When an environmental ethic is said to be anthropocentric from an ecological point of view it means that the unique decision-making capacities of human reasoners are expressions of their *conatus*. Judging, deliberating and decision making need to be recognized as distinctive capacities of the human locus. Humans are superior to other animals in this respect and therefore should be seen as taking the lead role as decision-making or responsibility-bearing loci. As Holmes Rolston III points out, however, we are inferior in many other respects. Since anthropocentrism implies not only superiority but limitation on the ability to understand, act and achieve, superiority cannot be dissociated from the value of humility, a value well aligned with the precautionary principle. This superiority, then, is not to be taken in the ancient Greek or

Modern sense. Superiority is not be confused with moral superiority, but it is to be recognized on the basis of real differences between the species. It would simply be unintelligible to say that a blue jay is greedy and ought to be punished for its inferior moral behaviour (Rolston 1988: 67). It would be equally unintelligible to assign the blue jay moral responsibility for developing protective measures for others in the ecological community. On this score, rational human beings need to accept the responsibility of being superior at deliberating, judging and decision making.

In light of the need to attune to the multivariate levels and uncertainty of ecological systems, the rational capacity for judgment and decision become far more central to environmental ethics than simple adherence to principles and formal structures of determining right and wrong. The syllogism is not the primary exercise of reason in this context. The dialectical nature of harm demands comparison between perspectives, between parts and between levels of analysis to determine how best to protect from harm. Obviously, protecting wild processes will involve harm to individuals. Allowing a caribou to drown may be important for the good of the herd or that of a predator. Therefore, we cannot make morally legitimate decisions in a vacuum, disregarding information or failing to understand the perspectives and valuations involved. Giving reasoned accounts for how we understand the perspectives of those affected by our actions and how we can best protect the valuations of individuals and the system, then, is central to the legitimacy of our plans, designs, systems of analysis and even perspective. Something akin to a principle of best effort or reasonable effort to be inclusive in our understanding, analysis and deliberation is necessary to guide our judgments and decisions.

Rational decision makers need to assume a form of hegemony, not owing to privilege, authority or a right to command but owing to the necessity of having to make decisions that affect all creatures and all world systems. We must assume leadership responsibilities because we know ourselves to be decision makers for and of the world. To deny this capacity and position is to deny the significance of the effects we have in the world and our responsibility to protect other creatures from them. In deciding whether to intervene or not to intervene, to protect or to allow to vanish, we are engaged in planning and deciding how the rest of the ecosystem is to be affected. Even though other creatures' behaviour may be said to do the same, we are the only creatures who know that we have this decision-making power that affects all other creatures. There can be no harmonizing with nature or entering into a kind of romantic unity with the ecosystem where these activities are conceived to be innocuous, because such conceptions about our actions deny the dialectical nature of ecosystem relationships and abrogate responsibility for the effects we have on the environment.

A further tension arises at this point. From an ecological point of view, humans are relatively worthless. Indeed, without us, ecosystems would function well, probably better. As those atop the food chain, so to speak, we are dispensable. Microbes and bacteria are far more important for ecosystem functioning than we are. Our superiority, understood within this context, dialectically connects our hegemony with the fact that we are unnecessary. The responsibility connected to our hegemony, then, is not determined by ecological valuations as such, but by the brute fact that however we make decisions, we determine the fate of ecosystems and know that we do.

With what we have called the birth of reason in the transition from animism to the Greco-Christian world view, rationality was seen primarily as an instrument of disclosure. We saw how it enabled humans to understand the world and their place in it in principled, law-like ways. Hegemony, when committed to disclosing the valuational activity of all members of the moral community and to functioning as a responsibility to protect, echoes Taoist and Buddhist notions of leadership. The notion "leading by following," which is central to these philosophies, appropriately describes the type of leadership being proposed. By "following" I mean, as does Rolston (1988: 31), a definition of ourselves in accordance with the polarities of nature, not just defining nature in relation to us. To follow is "to choose a route of submission to nature that utilizes natural laws for our well-being" (Rolston 1988: 37) and "to make its [nature's] value one among our goals; in so doing, our conduct is guided by nature" (Rolston 1988: 41). While I focus on the more paradoxical notion of leading by following, Rolston (1988: 41–42) focuses on following nature:

> Although nature is not a moral agent, and neither its creatures nor ecosystems are moral tutors in interhuman ethics, we often "draw a moral" from reflecting over nature: that is, gain a lesson in living. Nature has a "leading capacity"; it educates, leads us out (Latin: *educere*, to lead out, *educare*, to bring up) to know who and where we are and what our vocation is. Encounter with nature integrates us, protects us from pride, gives a sense of proportion and place, teaches us what to expect and what to be content with. Living well is the catching of certain natural rhythms.

The tone of Rolston's formulation emphasizes the passive and receptive element. Not all decision-making contexts allow for passivity, however, since the dialectical relationship we have to the ecosystem requires the exercise of our own *conatus*, which in turn requires the exercise of our rational capacity for planning and design. Although we have weaker and more vulnerable bodies, our stronger intellects generate a need to go beyond simply following nature—even our own nature—*simpliciter*. We are always in the process of having systematically and by design to order and direct the processes of which we are a part. Our *conatus* involves these conditions of leadership. The idea of following nature, then, must incorporate the hegemonic role into which we are placed.

Some martial arts (e.g., aikido) provide opportunities for experiencing what it means to lead by following. Practitioners do not force an opponent to do as they wish, e.g., by punching or kicking them into submission; they lead the energy (*ki*) of the attack to resolve the aggression in peace. It is turning what would otherwise be a brutal and violent situation into one that promotes mutual recognition and respect. To do this, contact and familiarity with the nature of the attack is required, a situation known as *musubi*. Such contact provides information about how to respond to aggression. Without contact, there is either inappropriate information or no information worth registering.

Becoming attuned in this way is both passive (*yin*) in receiving and becoming aware of the nature of the attack, and active (*yang*) in redirecting the attack and meeting aggression with compassion. It is both adaptive and directive in its process of respecting the attacker while acknowledging one's own values of survival and well-being. Our relationships within ecosystems can become similarly constituted, although not without considerable rethinking and retraining of our epistemic capacities and systems of decision making.

Some forms of agriculture (e.g., no-till farming, organic farming and planting indigenous species) can be considered approximations to leading by following. These methods depend more on the indigenous microbial activity of soils, rain and the natural rhythms of pest infestations and less on massive energy inputs in the form of fertilizers, irrigation and pesticides. They are fostering the rebirth of organic gardens, the use of compost and the like. At the same time, there is an element of transformation that seeks a peaceful accord with what is given by the ecosystem and what people need to survive and flourish.

Ecological restoration projects—such as the removal of concrete embankments and the restoration of riparian zones (i.e., distinctive ecological systems adjacent to river banks), indigenous species and diversity to forests as plantations—are more active forms of leading by following. Unlike agriculture, restoration activity attempts to bring what is indigenous back to a degraded region in our attempt to cohabitate with indigenous species and diversity. Restoration is an iterative and adaptive process and, as such, aids in attuning us to the land.

Restoring ecological functioning to an area, even if it is not a historical, non-anthropogenically altered ecosystem, can teach us how to live with ecological conditions (e.g., water regimes, plant diversity, annoying insects, even predators). Restoration of marshes, nesting sites and drainage systems has both positive and negative value for humans. Mosquitoes breed in abundance, bringing more songbirds to visit; water tables rise, but flooding is more frequent. We gradually learn to adapt to these features by locating further from marshes and flood plains and by building smaller and less obtrusive houses. This kind of learning is progressive as each new insight leads to new restoration development. Marsh zones and riparian restoration can be extended by replacing lawn cover with tall grasses or trees, which in turn may restore other forms of wildlife to which we will learn to adapt. There is nothing terribly odd about the notion of leading by following.

At a more psychological level, accepting and understanding pain provides another mode of leading by following. Pain, in liberal tradition, is treated primarily as a disvalue to be avoided. An ecological understanding of pain, in contrast, would have us treat it as a sub-function within more comprehensive ecological functions, a disvalue within a larger valuational system. Its place within the system of valuations transmutes pain into value through its attuning function. What would be the purpose of pain receptors if not to allow pain to function to our benefit? As an adaptive response to the environment, pain (along with fear) is a means of disclosing suitable environments for various loci and for instructing us how to engage in those environments.

Obviously, when encountered irrationally, pain and fear can engender bad judgments and false views about the object of fear. But by disciplining ourselves to follow pain in the struggle to understand and adapt, we become stronger, more knowledgeable and thereby more capable of guiding ourselves toward satisfaction. Fear and pain provide a perspective that discloses aspects of our environment to which we might otherwise be oblivious (e.g., dangers), and they provide contrasts to aspects with positive values (e.g., safe places) that might otherwise remain unappreciated. Obviously, pain and fear warn us away from things that may cause us injury or bring about premature death. Dealing with pain and fear in the right way can lead to the development of valuable characteristics, such as courage and pride; otherwise, they can lead to cowardice and neurosis. It is, therefore, ethically irresponsible to remove all pain-causing features and dangers of an environment, since it deprives us of the opportunity to become attuned in the fullest way through the discipline of dealing with pain and danger.

The above discussion points to a further and fundamental ethical concern. Leading by following demands that one transmute one's own greed and fear motives into means of attunement and develop a capacity for assuming responsibility. Dealing with pain and danger in the way described requires the same transmuting ability. As the martial arts teach us, our rational capacities and the power endowed us through them are best directed, not outwardly at mastery over the ecosystem, but inwardly at self-mastery. Hegemony is achieved first over ourselves and our unattuned capacities, in which context it is a form of mastery. Applied outwardly, hegemony is achieved in leading by following.

Indeed, if we examine the nature of reason itself, we find that it is far more closely aligned with leading by following and responsibility than it is with mastery and rights. I define reason as the ability to formulate data (information), implement principles, deliberate, logically derive conclusions from premises, systematically relate concepts and critically assess claims. Where reason is associated principally with rights, the connection is forced; where reason is associated with responsibility, the connection is not forced. These functions of reason enable us to bear responsibility and to lead by following; they do not connect to rights in any such way. Moreover, the only way rationality has been connected to the establishing of rights in Western history is through the forced association between reason and intrinsic value. If the connection is forced, then a rights-based environmental ethic is not the appropriate way to develop an environmental ethic. And if we can get a measure of constraint from an ethic of attunement, we do not need a rights-based ethic to generate obligations. A rights approach may serve strategically as a heuristic toward attunement, but there are no fundamental reasons for adopting one.

In summary, reason enables us to lead by following because it allows us to register the identifiable but underdetermined ecological patterns to which we must become attuned in the process of understanding the conditions of our own and others' freedom and *conatus*. It enables us to formulate iteratively better forms of understanding of other loci in the ecological community, which in turn enable us to respect and protect them from the harms that we may impose on them (anthropogenic stress). It enables us to conduct these moral operations dialectically and critically in a continuous process of adaptation to emerging conditions and new disclosures about *conatus* and the conditions of freedom for all creatures. Such use of our reasoning capacity, while constructive, continually seeks to falsify these constructions in the spirit of scientific inquiry. In other words, we always employ our capacities to discover errors, unattuned moral sensibilities and inadequate formulations of moral responsibility. In this way, the construction of moral principles and the more abstract elements of moral reasoning serve the more concrete, namely judgment and decision.

If we consider how dull we have become both perceptually and intellectually with regard to ecosystems, we can also see how an ethic of leading by following is prudent and in our best interest. "Old timers" are often critical of the new technological farmers who have little awareness of the land. New farmers sit all day in sheltered tractors with stereos to help them pass away the hours, and many never even have to touch the soil that they work. In fact, touching the soil is dangerous today, if the lack of microbial activity is any indication. Farmers now have to wear protective clothing when spraying their fields with insecticides, herbicides and fungicides, which render the soil dead and, in effect, a hazard to human health. The soil has become a medium of production and little else, where once it was understood as a living source of life. Farming now requires far less attunement to the rhythms and conditions of ecosystems, since we believe that we can engineer the land for productivity or grow chickens and pigs in factories. We no longer use fallow systems because we believe that we can force the land to yield crops by engineering the plants and by engineering the fertilizers and other chemicals that will yield those crops. We need not restrict our description to plants; animal crops are equally highly engineered. Such practices not only simplify the ecological structures of production, they also simplify the products. Genetic diversity of our seed banks and production animals is decreasing as corporate controllers begin to monopolize the production of seed, chemicals and livestock species. Animals domesticated for purposes of food production are becoming increasingly stupid and unmotivated as absence of *conatus* is engineered into their genetic structure.

Simplification of human attunement and its concomitant dullness are perhaps even more fundamental problems than are the problems of pollution, environmental degradation and the greed that sponsors them. Both shrink the field of potential freedoms that we and other loci can experience. Both shrink the purview of our responsibilities, allowing us to sink into the comfort of anonymity. As such, they promote a laziness in thought. And, while fostering greater efficiency in decision making, they undermine the effectiveness of decision making to protect the basic conditions of freedom.

Hegemony, then, is not only about acknowledging responsibility for the well-being of others and mastery of self, it is also about ensuring the continuance and restoration of an ecological context that saves us from dullness and lack of awareness.

The Land Ethic

"A thing is right when it tends to preserve the integrity, stability and beauty of the biotic community. It is wrong when it tends otherwise" (Leopold 1964: 224–25). Earlier, I discussed the Land Ethic's metaphysical grounding in the notion of the biotic pyramid and the idea that we belong to a community of diverse beings. Acknowledging the symbiotic relationship between land and human beings led Leopold (1964: 204) to conclude that traditional notions of ownership were wrong-headed, and this led him to develop an ethic defined as a limitation on freedom. Initially, at least, Leopold's ethic focused on constraint and protection of the integrity, stability and beauty of the ecological community.

To follow Leopold in this way of thinking is to connect our dependency on the ecological community to the rightness and wrongness of actions. The reasoning follows. Since this integrated community is a community to which we belong as members, we are one among many members. We have evolved as ethical beings, which has helped to ensure our survival because living according to ethical principles creates a cooperative community. People who cooperate have an advantage over others who do not. Ethics, then, generates a community of beings who achieve social organization through recognizing duties to limit the freedom of individuals. Even though non-human members of the biotic community cannot reciprocate duties, nevertheless they are to be protected because of the symbiotic dependency relationship that humans have to them. They can be treated as moral patients in the manner described by Tom Regan (1989). Hence, "the Land Ethic simply enlarges the boundaries of the community to include soils, waters, and animals, or collectively: the land" (Leopold 1964: 204). As J. Baird Callicott (1989a: 67) explains, "if one is a member of the biotic community, then one is also subject to an environmental ethic."

Leopold's approach is another attempt at extending traditional ethical theory to ecosystems and their non-human inhabitants, which it does on an evolutionary foundation. Like Rolston, he wants to derive ethical duties from evolutionary and ecological facts. As Callicott (1989a: 70) notes, this foundation is based on prudence and utilitarian values, and it gains its force from considerations of what makes survival the most likely. Yet Leopold goes far beyond this initial foundation and formulation of the Land Ethic as a limitation on freedom; we need to effect harmonious relationships between humans and the land through love and respect (Callicott 1989a: 70). What Leopold wants is moral force not merely prudential force to ground his ethic.

On the one hand, Leopold suggests that environmental rights are binding in much stronger ways than are utilitarian values of prudence and expediency. On the other hand, most of his argument turns on an evolutionary analysis of ethics as an evolved mode of guidance or community instinct to deal with ecological situations (Leopold 1964: 203). The way we think and make decisions on economic grounds, he argues, is far too lopsided; the only remedy to this situation is to adopt an ethical obligation to the land (Leopold 1964: 214). Ethical obligation, then, is necessary to provide a counterbalance to economic valuations. So, an ambiguity arises where ethics is treated both as a utility and as a deontic responsibility to recognize rights. But from where does the duty come?

Utility and prudence are calculated goods that often come into conflict with duties and rights. Sometimes duty, in fact, is defined as acting not in your best interest, but according to rule, principle or command. Duty is an obligatory action irrespective of what advantage or good it might bring. Both seem to be necessary for making sense of the Land Ethic, which makes it appear somewhat incoherent. Callicott (1989b: 80, 82) reformulates the Land Ethic to address this problem. He focuses on the idea of community as coextensive with a moral collective, which means that the advantages of obeying ethical norms expand and shift as the sense of community expands and shifts. As it became advantageous to shift to new social, economic or political systems, it also became advantageous to adhere to ethical norms that supported these systems because adherence helped these systems become robust. Asserting that we are mere citizens of the land community and that there is a moral right to survive as a species is one idea that helps our own system remain robust. When Leopold (1964: 223) uses the phrase "value in the philosophical sense," Callicott (1989b: 98) interprets this to mean "intrinsic value" or "inherent worth." The right to survive as a species is connected to this inherent worth. Entrenching such a value in our ethical system, once we understand that we depend on the integrity of the ecosystem, makes our system more robust and our survival much more likely. Hence, it would be wrong for wildlife managers not to cull overpopulated herds if they threatened the survival of other species (Callicott 1989b: 84). The Land Ethic has prudential roots and binding force at the same time. So, from a sociobiological perspective, ethics is prudential; from the individual perspective, it is deontological (Callicott 1989b: 99). Since we are generally ignorant of the evolutionary line that generates ethical sensibilities, ethics appear to be deontological; and that's good enough.

There is, however, a fundamental problem with this approach to explaining and justifying ethical principles: it could lead just as easily to the opposite conclusion. Evolution is also marked by the elimination of species and sometimes by massive extinctions, as occurred during the transition from an anaerobic to an aerobic system. If we accept the fact that extinctions and eliminations of other species have been to our advantage, we could very well come to believe that the elimination of other species is also to our advantage. Accepting further eliminations of other animals, then, could be equally supported on an enlightened utilitarian/ evolutionary basis. Evolution is morally neutral or indifferent. Unfortunately, our ethical sensibilities in the Western world and much of the Eastern world have been based on collective fear of wilderness, predators and the like, resulting in justifications for their elimination. Both Callicott and Leopold fail to appreciate the great potential for error in establishing ethical norms and rights by both individuals and collectives. So, explaining the constraint associated with ethical principles as products of evolution undermines the moral force of the Land Ethic.

What I have been proposing is not a derivation of ethical sensibilities and principles from evolutionary and ecological analyses, but an examination of how each informs us about the conditions that constitute the context in which ethical sensibilities are formed. Neither evolution nor ecology completely explain the capacity of reason or our moral sensibilities. Reason has been treated as an emergent capacity that cannot be predicted on the basis of antecedent conditions and that has creative and indeterminate potentials. When we come to experience the deontic constraint that the sense of responsibility brings to our hegemonic roles, it is by force of coherence, not just evolution and community prudentiality. When we come to recognize how all of our rational and perceptual capacities are best integrated around the deontic experience of needing to protect the conditions of freedom, there is a rational compulsion to incorporate an element of constraint into our ethical lives. Although the Land Ethic is valuable as a model for understanding the inverted relationship between humans and other loci of the ecosystem, it fails as a basis for framing the moral sensibilities. Nevertheless, the fact that it points out the need for constraint because of humans' general incapacity to control their behaviour articulates the need for institutional constraints, over and against deep ecological enlightenment approaches.

A further problem arises for the Land Ethic in determining what counts as a rights bearer. On the one hand, the rights bearer is the individual, since it is the individual as repository of intrinsic value who serves as the paradigm case of how we protect moral values. We simply extend this protection to other members, then. On the other hand, it is the system itself, in its integrity and beauty, that also counts as the rights bearer. While Leopold/Callicott want to include all of these rights-bearing units in the Land Ethic, they fail to develop a way of thinking about these levels that avoids the traps of typical liberal thinking. As seen, where the whole is protected, individuals are sacrificed. Where individuals are protected, wholes and their integrity may be threatened. If we formulate protective measures in terms of rights, then we will almost always be doing wrong when acting ethically. This situation is reminiscent of my critique of Taylor (1986).

Invoking the ideas of rights and intrinsic values as fundamental to the Land Ethic is an attempt to introduce old wine into new wineskins, where the ideas are the old wine and the ecological context the wineskins. These ideas are best suited to a world view that understands individuals as atomic and isolated units and that is concerned principally with the protection of individuals. This problem for the Land Ethic reinforces calls for a more dialectical way of recognizing morally legitimate ways of protecting individuals and communities. Moreover, where the focus on rights and intrinsic value advances the assumption of adversarial relationships between individuals and between individuals and systems, we are propelled back to a way of thinking that de-emphasizes and perhaps devalues the interdependence of ecological relationships along with the importance of attuning ourselves to these relationships.

One last criticism helps prepare for examining how we may still draw on the Land Ethic for guidance. Leopold's notion of the biotic community is egalitarian in a too straightforward manner. Human rational agents are not mere citizens of the biotic community due to our inescapable hegemonic role as decision makers. However else we are to understand the relationship between evolution and our ethical nature, it cannot be reduced to a simple matter of ecological survival or adaptability. As rational creatures with different emergent capacities from other loci, our place in the biotic community must be determined by our distinctiveness as much as by our sameness. To ignore this difference is, at minimum, to force human *conatus* into a straightjacket and, more extensively, to invite incoherence into moral thinking—an impediment, rather than an inspiration and guide, to moral thought. If we do not acknowledge the superiority/inferiority dialectic because we are so insistent on egalitarian thinking, we in effect deny the facts.

Despite these criticisms, the Land Ethic can be especially relevant when developing an environmental ethic around the idea of community. Although there is much scientific controversy over the notion of community—namely that it is ambiguous and used inconsistently (see Shrader-Frechette and McCoy 1993: 7)—there are good reasons to retain the concept. Epistemic awareness resulting from direct acquaintance with the rhythms of the land makes us aware that we are indeed members of a living set of relationships. The fact that Leopold, as a wildlife manager, was inspired by his direct and practical relationship to the land gives reason to consider his notions carefully. While we may reject his ethical framework, his familiarity with the land speaks to his having credibility as an attuned thinker. The notion of membership in the biotic community seems to have been inspired by this direct familiarity as a manager and as a hunter. In spite of reservations one might have about his practice of hunting, this juxtaposition of membership and predation is indicative of a dialectical understanding of the community. Ecosystem communities are not governed by laws of harmony and love alone; they are equally governed by competition and disharmony, both of which depend on the integrity of the whole.

Community is defined through individuals interacting in complex systems of communication and mutual influence, as well as through those individuals being shaped and directed by the limits, constraints and exigencies determined by the whole. Moreover, the idea of the Land Pyramid emphasizes our profound dependency on what we at one time thought to be a lower order. As such, it helps us to conceive what it means to invert the valuational scheme assumed in traditional liberal thought. It pushes thought to conceive of ways to understand how our identity is tied into these so-called lower orders. The idea of a pyramid helps to structure how we think about the dependency relationship by placing emphasis on the well-being of systemic priorities, such as soils, microbial life, water and air, first and foremost. It tells us that we need to pay more attention to these elements than we do to our artifacts, for without these elements our artifactual values are nothing. Pyramidal thinking, then, helps to structure thought to attend to what more fundamentally needs to be protected from harm.

Ecosystem Health

When thinking about harm, conditions associated with well-being and health immediately come to mind. Ecosystem health is an idea spawned by those who have recognized the failure of standard economic paradigms to protect the environment (Costanza et al. 1992: 4). Since this idea is partially inspired by the Land Ethic, its formulations are worth exploring. It is also worth exploring because it attempts to develop a comprehensive approach to protection by incorporating multiple values and multiple levels of analysis. To support ecosystem health is to attempt to formulate a comprehensive scheme for dealing with environmental degradation by restoring the processes of a dynamic, self-integrative nature in line with a new ethic of sustainability. Under a single rubric—i.e., health—proponents of the idea attempt to capture our imagination regarding the goals and analytical tools of environmental protection. Ecosystem health presents clearer and more effective operative approaches than other approaches by attaching itself to well-established institutions (e.g., the health professions). Part of its effectiveness has to do with the focus on human health and the belief that humans can flourish while maintaining the life-support functions of ecosystems. The concept is a powerful descriptor that attracts the attention of a large cross-section of stakeholders by attaching our concerns for the well-being of human beings to that of non-human beings and ecosystems. As such, it holds out the promise that we can capture the dual concerns of holism and individualism, ecological and economic well-being. It also supports the demand for constraining measures at every level of organization.

Work on the Toronto waterfront by the Royal Commission on the Future of the Toronto Waterfront focuses on health. The recommendations of the study are based on an ethic "in which progress is measured by the quality, well-being, integrity, and dignity it accords natural, social, and economic systems" (Crombie 1992: xix). This is part and parcel of keeping urban ecosystems in good health. What the Royal Commission calls "regeneration" is an attempt to restore ecological health in terms of usability, aesthetics, wildlife habitat and biological function. Examples of regeneration are the curtailing of the spread of toxic chemicals and the restoration of marshlands. So, at first glance, it would appear that the concept of ecosystem health helps to make an ecological ethic operative.

Regeneration's focus on health (Crombie 1992) pertains to an urban setting and to human well-being. Despite the report's gestures toward the dignity of ecosystems themselves, there is little emphasis on providing operative definitions for recognizing dignity in wild systems. But, as central proponents argue, this may not be a problem. Moreover, even though the model promotes reductive and less attuned modes of analysis than has been suggested is necessary, it does not dismiss holistic concerns. Bryan Norton (1984) thinks that, by rejecting the ascription of intrinsic value to ecosystems and accepting human-considered preferences as sufficient for an environmental ethic, the important perspectives needed in environmental protection will be included in the health approach without its having to be attuned to them. Indeed, for Norton (1991, 1992a), the concerns of those advocating the intrinsic value of ecosystems and non-human species converge with those of anthropocentrists. Thus, the attribution of intrinsic value to ecosystems is redundant. By implication, the concerns that proponents of holism have for the protection of systems as wholes, as well as other species, will occur as a matter of course. At the same time, the approach affords environmental thought clarity and simplicity.

Proponents of the health approach believe it to be holistic and inclusive, thereby accomplishing an inversion of priorities for which an ecological approach calls. According to Norton (1992b: 25):

> These definitions ensure that ecology, not economics, will be the science that provides the basic organization for the new management paradigm because economics is understood as one type of ecological activity, one that takes place within the economic system of one (however dominant) species.

Furthermore, ecosystem health initiatives are to be modelled on the self-organizing characteristics of ecosystems, not as organisms to be accorded intrinsic value (Norton 1992b: 27) but as open systems that self-organize through energy transfer from external systems (dissipative systems) (Norton 1992b: 28). These systems arrive at stability and integrity, as open systems, through creative and self-generating activity, and they remain underdetermined. Their natures, admittedly, can neither be completely described nor their behaviour entirely predicted (Norton 1992b: 31). We can admit that we cannot do better than ecosystems themselves have done in matters of water control and purification, so it is best to leave the natural system in place where possible. Hence, the approach, despite its focus on human health, seems cognizant and incorporative of the wider ecological conditions thus far associated with integrity.

The position is strengthened by what Norton (1992b: 36) considers a third strategy for implementing an ecosystem health model—

experimentalism. The idea is not to predetermine which is the suitable management scheme for ecosystems or how systems must be made to perform. We are not to impose values onto ecosystems; we are to test our values on the basis of how they can be adapted to ecological conditions. Hence, both management schemes and their underlying values are to follow the lead of the indicators of ecological health. Moreover, since health is the sort of concept that evokes a prescriptive response—people not only want to be healthy, they think it is a fundamental right—it provides a constraining measure. With this description, it is difficult to see why ecosystem health cannot serve as the prescriptive focus for an environmental ethic. It offers a fairly elegant set of concepts as a basis for analyzing environmental problems without sacrificing holistic considerations.

There are problems with this reduction to health parameters, however. As David Rapport (1995: 5–6) explains, ecosystem health is a science that turns on the notion that planet Earth is a patient whose breakdown can be diagnosed and healed in a wide variety of senses, which include the biophysical, economic, social and ethical. Several key indicators of ecosystem health have been identified. Healthy ecosystems are free of ecosystem distress syndrome; 2) they are resilient (can recover from perturbations); 3) they are self-sustaining; 4) they do not cause distress to neighbouring systems; 5) they are free from risk factors; 6) they are economically viable; and 7) they sustain healthy human communities (Rapport 1995: 6).

The last two conditions are especially important since they are the primary determinants of ecosystem health assessment. A comprehensive assessment must consider four major elements of regional ecosystems: biophysical integrity, socioeconomic factors, human health and public policy and ethics (Rapport 1995: 7). Appealing to Leopold, Rapport (1995: 9) emphasizes the human element: "To be healthy, land not only had to be free of sickness, but also had to accommodate human needs on a sustainable basis." Thus, a complete assessment includes an assessment of the sustainability of the ecological "services," such as recreational opportunities and wildlife.

Human values and human health are both necessary conditions for ecosystem health and the principal determinants of ecosystem health. That is, ecosystem health is to be measured, not on ecological principles alone, but by criteria of human health conceived biophysically and economically. Both the ecological priority and the ethical components of the paradigm are beginning to recede into the background, despite Norton's assurances to the contrary.

Under the health model, an entirely engineered ecosystem, such as some forest plantations, can meet all seven of Rapport's key indicators of ecosystem health, especially if time scales are not taken seriously into account. Short time scales (i.e., a few human generations) may not reveal how an engineered forest has lost its resiliency. But in the interest of economic health, we may be forced to use shorter time scales since the general tendency of economic analyses is to discount the future. Time frames beyond twenty years or so are unmanageable because we do not know what conditions will exist in the distant future or what human interests will be. Where economic health is measured on the basis of GNP and exchange value, which are usually determined yearly, it is difficult to see how an ecological time frame, which is usually measured geologically in hundreds, thousands or even millions of years, can be taken seriously. It may be that I am not appreciating the potential of the health model to transform economics and the parameters by which economists analyze economic health. But if the critique of the development of environmental economics (e.g., Spash 1999) is correct, that is, if it has not had a significant impact on society's romance with classical economics, then the health model is a tool more for coopting ecological thought than for taking seriously what it identifies as critical for environmental protection.

Further, implementation of the model could be used to justify the elimination of certain types of ecosystems—for example, the destruction of mosquito-populated swamps if it was deemed that the threat of malaria was too great a risk to human health. Many ecological processes and properties are incompatible with human health. Radioactivity, landslides, predation and parasitism could arguably be defined as threats to human health and thereby could be targeted either for elimination or for re-engineering. The point is that the nature of the prescriptive force associated with "health" allows for a wide variety of interventions, which would undermine the importance of keeping tensions in balance, leading by following and applying the harm principle.

Almost all proponents of the idea agree that the concept is vague and that there is a need to specify more rigorously and operationally what the concept means (see also Costanza 1992: 239). At issue is not only the plasticity of the concept but the plasticity of the values that can be applied to defining "health." More importantly, plasticity, together with a strong bias toward exploitive interests and human preference, will tend to reinforce human dominance and an imposition of values rather than an awareness of and respect for other loci of valuational activity. The initial plasticity of the concept is likely to lead to a rigidity in conception as dominant interests come to control the use of the term, even as multinational pharmaceutical companies have come to control research and therapy in human medicine.

While most philosophers, ecologists and ethicists supporting the health model emphasize the importance of self-maintaining, resilient and stable structures, the concept is all too easily coopted by those who would use it toward exploitive ends. We have witnessed criticism of the World Health Organization's (WHO) definition of health—a state of complete physical, social and psychological well-being (see Callahan 1983: 41). Standard criticisms of this view are several. One is that social well-being is determined more by majority opinion and trendy views of health than by objective measures. Thus, we find the notion of mental illness being defined according to social expectation. We call the rapist, the sociopath and even the social dissident "sick." Hence, treating these people for their sickness allows us to incarcerate them, mostly involuntarily, until they come to conform to social expectation. "Health," then, is often used to disguise social engineering as healing.

In the same vein, our definitions of health can license us to re-engineer ecosystems in ways that will force them to produce the economic and health benefits we demand and even to eradicate unhealthy ecosystems, as has been done to swamps. With the present invasive medical model and the dominance of multinational pharmaceutical companies in the business of health care, we would be naive to think that a health model could retain commitments to holism and freedom to exercise the full range of valuations. Genetic research, espoused as medical research, attracts heavy investment by the financial sector because of its market potential. Clearly, the potential for new genetically engineered products is the principal value motivating investments. This relationship between health and engineering for productivity betrays an underlying attitude of dominance, which re-establishes the one-way value-conferring activity that is antithetical to the ecological approach. Pest infestation, fungi and other threats to the economic productivity of the land are, by definition, seen as diseases or illnesses, not as parts of nature's economy. Spruce budworm attacks will not be seen as opportunities for warbler populations to increase; they will be seen as diseases to be eradicated. Since the overwhelming tendency of the dominant medical establishment is to intervene and substitute for natural healing processes, owing both to the Modern scientific approach to analysis and to economic incentives, Norton's maxim of non-intervention can hardly be taken seriously. The health model, then, can readily be coopted by the very powers it is meant to resist.

Other problems with the health model indicate further dangers. A healthy body can function on one kidney, or it can be enhanced for certain purposes through interventive measures, such as nutritional supplements and remedies. A healthy ecosystem, in parallel, could be considered improvable if engineering it would better serve certain functions. Indeed, we sometimes believe that replacing parts of a body enhances its health. Replacing and even substituting parts of an ecosystem might then be seen as requisite, if deemed to improve its function and stability. Clearly, we do not know whether our interventions will produce better results, as ecological and chaos theories have instructed us. Indeed, Faber et al. (1992: 92), in the same volume as Norton (1992b) and Costanza (1992), write that acknowledging our ignorance ought to be at the centre of our determinations of ecosystem health. Despite these warnings and conditions, the idea of making economic and human health inextricably bound to ecosystem health introduces an override factor to the precautionary approach recommended by Faber et al. Human health and economic concerns readily override concerns about uncertainty because of the powerful interests that can rally behind the banner of health. The concept belongs to a tradition of utility maximization because, while health is a good in itself, it is more readily connected to concerns about performance, function and production. We want to be healthy so that we can perform well and work efficiently. We respect people of integrity, but we value healthy people because they can perform certain functions better than non-healthy people. Consequently, health is not so clearly an ethical value, as Norton claims; it is treated more like an instrumental value.

Olver et al. (1995) also anticipate that adopting the medical model is likely to result in the dominance of social and economic expectations over biological and ethical ones. The basic inspirations for the model, as we hear in Costanza and Norton, appear sound. But it also appears that these inspirations, especially respecting holistic concerns, are more closely associated with integrity than with health. Indeed, most supporters of the ecosystem health approach conflate health with integrity. The concept of integrity, unlike the concept of health, is not utility oriented and, as noted, more directly evokes ethical attitudes of respect. It is preferable, then, to draw a distinction between the two, taking integrity, rather than health, as the central concept in establishing basic concepts for an environmental ethic.

Ecosystem Integrity

Henry Regier (1993: 3) states: "A living system exhibits integrity if, when subjected to disturbance, it sustains an organizing, self-correcting capability to recover toward an end-state that is normal and 'good' for that system."

James Kay (1993), a partner with Henry Regier, Laura Westra and James Karr in the development of the notion of ecosystem integrity, emphasizes the resilience of ecosystems, as do proponents of the health model. The full integration of economic and human well-being into the concept of integrity, however, is deliberately omitted. Being more aligned with supporters of deep ecology, proponents of ecosystem integrity stress preservation and protection of wild spaces along with the reintegration of humans with wild spaces, which is in line with the requirements set out by Rolston, namely, leaving ecosystems alone (see, for instance, Westra 1994).

The idea of integrity is also strongly aligned with conservation biology. Core preserves are to be protected by buffer zones in which ecosystem integrity can be maintained. The re-establishment of huge, wild, functional ecosystems replete with large carnivores and their prey is the pinnacle of restoration ecology and human harmonization with nature (Noss 1991). In these ecosystems, roads are either not to be built or are to be eliminated because they are the single most threatening human factor to biodiversity and, therefore, ecosystem integrity. Where roads are already in place, it is important that we allow ecosystems to recover from their perturbations by engaging in restoration activity. Valuational emphasis is placed on the internal determinants of ecosystems by excluding economic and human well-being from the equation. Managing for integrity, then, can be very unlike managing for health of ecosystems. An ecosystem can have full integrity apart from any human valuation and without offering any economic benefit to human beings.

The integrity principle for Westra (1994: 26) can be strongly opposed to the health approach for many reasons already cited (e.g., substitutability of parts, too determined by values of human populations and interests, too limited to human time frames). It is clear that the program to restore ecosystem integrity can conflict with many, if not most, present human values. Living with ecosystem integrity requires a complete reversal of human values to accord more with ecological well-being.

"Integrity" refers to the autonomy of ecosystems. Protecting wildlands by placing buffer zones around wild preserves stresses the fact that we are too ignorant of ecosystem functions and structures to be able intelligently to judge when a system is healthy in its own right. The best principle is to leave wilderness areas alone and to try as much as possible to restore large areas to wilderness, limiting the interventions of human activities to buffer zones. This seems a good way to respect the temporal dimensions of ecosystem functions, satisfy human *conatus* and take uncertainty into account.

Despite our ignorance and uncertainty, integrity, to some extent, can be measured and can be amenable to scientific investigation:

> Integrity obtains when at point C, the system's *optimum capacity* for the greatest possible ongoing development options within its time and location remains undiminished. The greatest possible potentiality for options is also fostered by the greatest possible biodiversity (dependent on contextual natural constraints), as the latter is a necessary but not sufficient component of C. Biodiversity contributes to integrity in at least two ways:
> a. Through genetic potential, based on the size and diversity of populations and their respective gene pools;
> b. Through biodiversity's dimensions as purveyor and locus of

both relational information and communication, of which existing populations and ecosystems manifest and embody only a small proportion. We can only theorize about the immense capacities for diverse qualitative interactions among individuals and species that are not *presently* existing or knowable. (Westra 1994: 25; original emphasis)

Protecting integrity protects *conatus* by protecting the autonomy of systems, whether individual or collective, which allows them to develop according to determinants that are internal to them. It protects against the impositions of an engineering mentality and respects the many loci and levels of organization of ecosystems.

An ethic based on the renaturalization of humans emerges. Restoration ecologists reason that human beings must learn to become indigenous once again. The similarity to Rolston's emphasis on following nature indicates that respecting integrity requires a transformation of ethical sensibilities and principles in a manner that aligns with efforts to become more attuned to ecological processes and conditions. It, therefore, helps inform the process of becoming more aware of our dependency relationship and so responds to demands for greater understanding of this relationship. At the same time, Westra responds to the need for prescriptive force by working out a more formal argument to establish binding ethical principles, which expand upon the moral force in Rolston's arguments. She works out an imperative.

Briefly,[2] Westra (1994: 64) argues that ecosystem integrity is a foundational value because all other values depend on it. This is typical of ecosystem approaches, and so requires no further elaboration. As foundational, it can compete with other foundational values, such as happiness and health. Once more ecologically versed, we will recognize integrity as a foundation and see the validity of raising it to the level of pre-eminence, such that it will become a fundamental value to protect, like freedom. As much as any other value, integrity is universal (Westra 1994: 66), not just because people will see it as such but because people can be shown that it is. Like freedom, we are obliged to protect integrity first with moral principles, then with policy and law. We protect it by protecting the freedom of all creatures to actualize their potentials (*telos*, a close relative of what I have called *conatus*), just as we protect our own freedom to grow and actualize our plans and initiatives. Since the recognition of integrity and its association with the value of freedom is near universal, Westra (1994: 93) claims that it is categorical. Owing to the deep-seated need both individually and collectively to protect this value structure, it has a constraining quality approximating that of an imperative. The categorical imperative, then is: 1a) "Act so that your action will fit within universal natural laws"; and 1b) "Act so that you manifest respect and understanding acceptance of all natural processes and laws" (Westra 1994: 97).

Westra's approach is enticing because it takes into account most of the major ethical parameters that have been established to this point, including the importance of the discernible but underdetermined patterns of ecosystems (see also Westra 1998: xii), the recognition of our dependency relationship and the need for radical change in value theory to account for the holistic element of dependency in the valuational scheme. Her general sketch of how respect for integrity is to be operationalized is attractive because it structures ethical thought in such a way as to guard against the type of cooptation to which "health" is susceptible. It embraces the non-impositional moral commitment to understand the *conatus* of individuals and systems and, at the same time, it addresses the need to provide moral obligation in the form of principled constraints to our behaviour. The idea of protecting core wilderness zones is unambiguous with regard to the types of protective actions we are obliged to take. Protecting wilderness through removing roads and through the renaturalization of human institutions (via restoration projects) concretizes the principle of leading by following.

Unlike some of her detractors, I do not see Westra advancing fascist thinking. She attempts to work out a balance between the holistic and the individualistic aspects of the ecological approach. Indeed, she sees that the "promise" of integrity lies in the openness of debate and discussion about the concept and about stakeholder interests, although it does not allow for a reduction of this discussion to a mere "construct relative to social or cultural preferences" (Westra 1998: 10).

The principle of integrity is, first, a directive to restore harmonious relationships with indigenous species, and second, in the spirit of Leopold, a restriction on freedom. Restoring native biota and reconstructing human relationships with these systems are concrete ways to act on the ethical obligation to understand our dependency on the ecosystem because restoration involves coming to know indigenous species and their relations. In the large picture, living with indigenous biota, as opposed to human-engineered environments, better guarantees human well-being because it better sustains the conditions that give rise to our valuational activity and existence. Restoration projects teach us about the conditions necessary for environmental protection. Unforeseen successes, such as the spontaneous regeneration of amphibian populations and the regeneration of native grasses where none have been planted, can teach us about resilience and about what used to exist in areas that have been degraded or destroyed. The process can restore a sense of wonder as we find native species once again emerge where they might not have been seen for generations.

In one respect, it is vital to preserve wild spaces by keeping humans out, given the present value orientation of this society. We are all too ready to take our all-terrain vehicles into places where we will disturb otherwise undisturbed and fragile systems or sensitive nesting areas. Where the choking and polluting smell of exhaust is the sweet smell of power and excitement to recreational riders, the prescriptive force of the restriction on freedom is at present paramount. Restricting freedom is intelligible and justifiable because too few humans can be expected to act with respect.

While Westra's formal and restrictive approach is vital as well as effective for policy, it falls short when formulating the first thrust of the principle, namely, to restore harmonious relationships with natural ecosystems. The formulation does not take the dialectical relationship between harmony and disharmony sufficiently into account. As I have argued elsewhere (Morito 1999a), the approach inadvertently establishes a new dualism between human (cultural) and wild systems (which are to be protected from human intervention) in a way that inverts the Modern dualism. It idealizes wild systems (rather than rational beings, as Moderns do) and fails to recognize, as thinkers like Leopold and Rolston do, that the wild is also a place of provision. Hunting and fishing, gathering and trapping have been part of the human-nature relationship throughout evolution, but the impact of this fact on Westra's understanding of ecosystems is largely missing. Although I side with her abhorrence of the massive tracks of land used for cattle raising to satisfy our infatuation with meat, much of our dependency on the land has been for meat.

In aboriginal traditions, for instance, the land provides through gathering and hunting activity. These activities are entirely naturalized. Hence, in many if not all North American aboriginal languages, there is no word for "wild." Both Ojibway and Cree teachers and elders have tried to teach me that the lack of a word for "wild" in their languages means that the so-called "wild" for English speakers means to many speakers of aboriginal languages "home" or, better, "the land." The land is that from which "we" come, not merely that which provides. This starting point for thought is significantly different from that of Westra. She, like most wilderness protection advocates, retains a dualism between human cultural development and wild ecosystem development. For the traditional aboriginal person, there is no such dualism. Starting with the assumption that the land and person/culture are one, the aboriginal person is more concerned with understanding how the person becomes individuated from the whole, or how the Great Mystery (Kitche Manitou in Ojibway, Wankan Tanka in Lakota) gives rise to the process of becoming an individual. The practical task in manifesting an understanding of this process is for the individual and the community to undertake the responsibility of guiding each of its members in the process of becoming fully individual—discovering his or her name, animal protector, clan and vocation; females in many aboriginal nations, however, do not have to go through these processes. For this reason, vision quests, sweat lodges and other practices have been developed to shape the person's sense of self and role in the community.

The difference between trying to integrate the individual with the ecosystem whole and trying to individuate the person from the whole can be dramatic. The assumptions and the way in which the world is seen are fundamentally different. Individuation processes, while they seem to be going in the opposite direction of what is called for by the ecosystem approach and holistic thinking, are in fact far more consistent with the approach. When you start with the assumption that you are initially undifferentiated from the whole, what individuation means is very different from what it means when you begin with the assumption that individuals exist as independent units that need to be integrated into the whole. In the latter case, individuation is something to be overcome (or in conflict with the values of the whole), whereas in the former it is something to achieve. But as something to achieve, individuation is a process of shaping oneself in accordance with what is given you to become. Freedom, one aspect of the individuation process, is not the freedom associated with licence or the lack of restriction on choice. It has more to do with realizing *conatus* and discovering purposiveness.

Almost all thinkers in contemporary environmental ethics adopt assumptions that have been entrenched in Western thought for over two thousand years. The retention of the concept of intrinsic value and the atomistic conception of the person that accompanies it exemplifies how this entrenchment persists. Westra and other proponents of holism who retain this idea do not extend the analysis of individuals and wholes enough to take ecological approaches beyond these deeply entrenched assumptions. When we do take the metaphysical implications of ecology far enough, we see that thinking ecologically has far more in common with aboriginal tradition than with Western European tradition.

In part, we do not adopt the principle of integrity in total, despite the many points of agreement, because we wish to advance an alternative understanding of the relationship between personhood and ethical obligation and to go beyond the reliance on intrinsic value. The work on integrity, as I see it, can serve as a heuristic ethic to provide much of the needed constraint in environmental ethics, but, when taken as a foundation, it can lead to further entrenchment of Modern assumptions. The insistence on the use of "intrinsic value" to protect ecosystems and other animals sets up non-ecologically informed conflictual relationships because we begin to view all loci of valuational activity as stakeholders with a right to life and a right to exclude all others from their domains of comfort and safety. This much is fair enough, since it is quite compatible with the idea that privacy of individuals is to be respected. But this mode of thinking assumes all suffering and killing to be morally wrong and assumes relationships between individuals to be adversarial. It is, therefore, compelled to focus too exclusively on part-part relations over and against part-whole relationships and systemic relationships. Examples of how we have inadvertently promoted adversariality where there was little or no previous recognition of such is in the way we have entrenched women's rights in affirmative action, which has led some male supporters of feminism to oppose it. Similarly, children's rights, while designed to protect vulnerable youth from abusive adults, have created greater suspicion and conflict between parents and children. In the end, doctrines of intrinsic value promote thinking about ethics in terms of trumping the interests and privileges of others since each individual repository of intrinsic value is encouraged to define itself as being in conflict with others.

Ethics, Humility and the Great Mystery

In many respects, thinking ecologically about environmental ethics begins with a recognition that our mode of being in the world today is largely that of aliens. Neil Evernden's *Natural Alien* (1985) is a well-taken analysis of the human condition, spawned by existentialist thinkers who have analyzed the absurdity of human existence. His phrase "becoming a perpetual outsider" (Evernden 1985: 31) describes how, in the Modern world view and by virtue of the way they think and the world views they adopt, persons have become estranged from the world in which they belong. We become estranged because we make mistakes in our thinking. As these mistakes developed through the Greco-Christian and Modern world views, we created traps into which our thinking has been confined. Indeed, we have invented and carefully constructed these traps, which, owing to ecology, evolutionary theory, quantum physics and chaos theory, are now in the process of being dismantled. As this dismantling continues to occur, it begins to falsify this seemingly basic fact of the human condition: our sense of alienation begins to dissolve as attunement increases. Certainly, in alternative (e.g., aboriginal) world views, it is far from a given.

We have seen that the key notion of freedom, applied in the form of a principle of respect for autonomy (defined in terms of *conatus*), is as central to an ecologically defined ethic as it is to a liberal ethic. Unlike appeals to intrinsic value, the inverted metaphysical and axiological scheme, wherein the individual is viewed as being in the process of becoming individuated, places far more emphasis on individuals than do traditional modes of thought. With attunement to the conditions of our dependency relationship on ecosystem processes and conditions, a sense of responsibility is generated in the recognition of respect owed to all the members of the ecological community. Hence, an element of constraint, in the form of a deontic recognition, is inherent in this alternative approach. This constraining element placed in a dialectical relationship with the hegemonic role of humans engenders a decision-making principle—lead by following.

Other traditions have been able to establish an ethic of respect without a doctrine of intrinsic value and without the idea that the person is an atomic individual. Buddhist compassion and the Taoist notion of seeing the Tao in all things and so allow them to unfold in their own fashion develop a sensibility that there is a dignity in all things by virtue of their being a part of the One that has spawned us all. For the Chinese, the Tao is the Great Mystery that cannot be spoken, as Yahweh is for the Jews. Likewise, Kitche Manitou is the Great Mystery to which all owe their being. In this recognition of mystery, there is simultaneously a recognition of a great power beyond our comprehension. This sense of mystery generates a sense of humility in the person who acknowledges it. But where there is mystery, there is not complete absence of understanding because we can know why we need to posit or suppose there to be such a ground of our being. Indeed, ecology regenerates a grand mystery with its discernible but underdetermined patterns, its association with the uncertainty principle in quantum physics and chaos theory. From process philosophy, we come to understand that the principal or prior impetus to the formation and constitution of the universe must be a creative force, since our understanding of causal laws is insufficient to explain everything. The creativity of open, dissipative systems in producing order contributes to this way of understanding.

Awareness of one's situatedness before the Great Mystery draws humility and respect together as co-primary moral sensibilities. Sometimes this mystery yields fear, but more often, as with Immanuel Kant (1956: 166), it engenders awe and wonder as we contemplate the greatness of the heavens above and, indeed, the moral law within; ultimately, it brings recognition of a greater power and dependence on the creativeness of this power, which reverberates in our own pursuit of understanding. Once we can think of the ecosystem as our community and this community as the ground of valuational activity—the context created and sustained by this power—then respect for the mystery of this power is grounded.

Aboriginal cultures, once again, illustrate this dimension of respect, as plants and animals that are taken for food are honoured by giving an offering. Traditionally, the offering is also associated with thanksgiving for the life that has been given in sacrifice and, sometimes, in responsibility; many of the stories speak of the responsibility of a living being to give itself. Few professional philosophers are prepared to take their purview this far. Rolston is one who does; Erazim Kohák (1984) is another. In *The Embers and the Stars*, Kohák describes Plato's prisoner who struggles through the stages of *dianoia* (reasoning) to grasp, in direct awareness, the Good (Kohák 1984: xii). If *daionia* fails to attune our sensitivities to this ultimate and to the world around us in all of the ways that have been given us to grasp, then it begins to work in us as do synthetic medicines—designed to help us heal, but ultimately deadening our sensitivity. We fail to get past stage one. Unlike so many technicians of philosophy who limit reason to the tasks of conceptual analysis, criticism and defending positions, Kohák (1984: xi) sees reason as a tool for placing us in a stance of wonder and taking the "sense of lived experience in its primordial immediacy as ... subject matter." Reason does not struggle simply to construct hypotheses or theories, although these come along the way; it has an underlying and perhaps antecedent drive to move us into a position where we are enabled to see clearly.

Seeing clearly is, in this manner, experiencing fully. We find ourselves enmeshed, not so much in the harmony of nature, but in the pulse of nature (Kohák 1984: 6). It is not to pretend that concepts and logic suffice to enable us to understand. Once we understand through having the full range of our capacities opened (through the dialectical process), we measure the legitimacy of our understanding by how well we integrate these capacities to the end of living well. We begin to measure our lives with the falling of the leaves and the growing of the grass. We feel the rhythm of the seasons and prepare ourselves for them. When we come across the remains of a coyote's ruffed grouse meal along a path, we feel the rhythm of predator-prey relations and we stop to note the play of tensions. When attuned to the world in this way, intellect, feeling and emotion are all directed toward attending to the gestalt of the plurality of factors that we cannot identify one by one. The world is seen and understood in a way that is entirely different from the way in which it is seen by the theoretically directed vision of the laboratory or library. This is not to dismiss the laboratory or library modes of understanding; it is to acknowledge that they are limited and reductive ways of understanding. They do not provide access to the pulse of the land or to the experiential whole of having to attune ourselves to the land.

Gaining sight and insight into the greater power and mystery results not only in a respect for the members of the ecological community and its various levels of organization, but in a deepening respect, wherein respect takes on new dimensions. Just as a child gradually learns to appreciate and respect more deeply the power of reason in its technological and explanatory applications—learning more quantitatively and qualitatively about what reason does and can do—so too can respect for the mystery deepen as we attune reason and our other senses to the *conatus* of all things. In the process, we recognize the conditions of freedom, autonomy and excellence, which must be protected for the sake of all.

Thinking ecologically about environmental ethics, then, not only moves us to penetrate to deeper levels of moral sensibility in identifying the deeper grounding of our moral lives, it meets the demands of contemporary moral problems regarding environmental degradation and injustice. It allows for and demands a formulation of moral principles (the harm principle), where deepening sensitivity alone is insufficient. It supports, even requires, constraints and protective measures. It yields concrete prescriptions for guarding against or rectifying harm, in part because such thinking recognizes the concreteness of the era in which we find ourselves and does not theorize about an ideal, atemporal moral world. As such, it does not get trapped into the ideal world thinking so typical of Western traditions. Admittedly, considerably more work needs to be done to develop a full-scale ethic. But for the moment, this sketch of an ethic is sufficient to demonstrate that there are implications for personal moral development and that there are ethical implications for policy and resource management. Even without a deepening consciousness, thinking ecologically establishes an ethic, albeit an inchoate one.

Some proscriptions—because they are easier to develop than prescriptions—have already been mentioned. Trapping for food and clothing is one thing. In certain contexts it is demanded by the valuational activity governing survival behaviour. Selling the products of trapping to serve the vanities of blue-blood New Yorkers, however, is a sign of human degeneration and lack of respect. It violates the *conatus* of the animals killed for no compelling reason and infuses an attitude of disrespect and disregard into our relationships with other animals, treating them merely as decorative and discardable appendages to what are already discardable identities; we can readily shed our identities based on vanity without shedding our humanity and valuational integration with the ecological community. The use of other members of a moral community merely as decoration or as a titillation for our senses are acts of wanton destruction of loci of integrity. Such use undermines the integrity of the valuational system upon which we depend, as well as our own integrity. It undermines the latter by dismissing the capacity to become attuned or by refusing to exercise it. In either case, it truncates the process of reasoning that is directed at achieving full individuation and freedom—that is, the fundamental valuational process. It, thereby, demonstrates a lack of an appropriate protective attitude both to others and to self. Such a mind-set is harmful to the ecological community.

Zoos, as media of entertainment, serve the interests of distraction and deny our intimate connection and debt to other animals. All things being equal, these establishments are morally perverse. Zoos, however, are problematic. Not only have they become significant repositories of endangered species; they have become, in some cases, necessary if we are to have any hope of reintroducing species to and saving those in the wild. Some argue that zoos are justified on these grounds. Similarly, some would argue that using formerly wild animals in circuses is justified on the grounds that loss of habitat has sentenced them to an otherwise miserable death. While such arguments have some moral currency, they indicate a defeatist attitude. Rather than justifying one's abusive and disrespectful actions from within the context of a morally perverse system, thinking ecologically would have us work toward a morally good and robust system, focused on the integrity of individuals and systems together and not principally on justification of acts that are less morally perverse than they might otherwise be.

On a larger scale, the levelling of natural landscapes, the draining of wetlands and the dismantling of entire mountains for aggregate production cannot continue. The increasing spatial scale and decreasing temporal scale—which are products of preferring efficiency of production over effective protection—undermine all aspects of the harm principle, such that such activity is clearly proscribed. Despite hesitations about aligning the protection of integrity with the advocacy of conservation biology and ecological integrity, a strategic proscription required by the harm principle would be to exclude humans from core protected areas. As we grow toward thinking ecologically and producing an ecological economy by learning to live much more attuned to and respectful of ecosystem integrity, we will have to be excluded from these areas unless we are capable of non-disturbance. In the present situation, humans have a long way to go to develop modes of attunement; hence, heuristics need to be adopted to aid transformative learning. Even though some humans traditionally have been able to live in such an attuned and protective mode while altering landscapes and ecosystems, our present dullness and ignorance make it impossible to adopt these as models. Hence, access to wilderness needs to be restricted and the right to access based on deservingness or merit.

Finally, and again only briefly, some application to law is in order, since the concern is over prescriptive force. To anticipate such criticisms, it is worth noting that underlying the constitution of Canada and that of the United States is a respect for basic values of freedom and security (freedom from harm), which is at the same time a respect for the conditions of dignity, self-esteem and identity for individuals as well as members of community. These are basic moral values that provide substance and guidance to the development of law. Indeed, they are the foundations of the rule of law. Insofar as these values ground the development of law, there is no reason to deny that ecosystem integrity as a value and the responsibility for becoming ecologically attuned cannot affect and direct legislation. For instance, just as we issue graduated licenses for new drivers as they incrementally demonstrate competence, so could we issue graduated rights to access wilderness. But we could also finds means to institute attunement curricula into environmental education. As an interim measure, environmental rights serving as trumps against industrial and commercial development interests can be articulated on the grounds that such development undermines the conditions of freedom, along much the same lines as the Canadian Supreme Court rejected the pre-1988 abortion laws.

The argument for constraint leads to a discussion of environmental policy and more politically and legislatively formal expressions of thinking ecologically. What I have tried to show is that an ethic of attunement can operate at both deeply personal levels and at more formal levels where principles and applications to policy need to be developed.

Notes

1. The key strategy in the deep ecology movement has been to develop a respect for nature by expanding our sense of self to include a more comprehensive Self (Drengson and Inoue 1995: 51; Evernden 1985: 47). As we see ourselves as parts or aspects of a larger Self, change in the egoistic conception of self begins to take place. We then become sensitized to the needs of other creatures, who form the basis for the extended Self. Recognizing other ecosystem inhabitants as part of the extended person is a way of seeing the ecosystem as a person to whom respect is owing. Naess develops this idea in detail in works already cited (e.g., 1989: 9), and many supporters of deep ecology have taken this idea as central (see Devall 1995; Anker 1998). Naess sometimes formulates the notion as follows:

   > We "see ourselves in others." Self-realization is hindered if the self-realization of others, with whom we identify, is hindered. Love of our self will fight this obstacle by assisting in the self-realization of others according to the formula, "live and let live." Thus all that can be achieved by altruism—the dutiful moral consideration of others—can be achieved through widening and deepening our self. (1995: 14)

   Or as Devall (1995: 105) describes, "As we discover our ecological self we will joyfully defend and interact with that which we identify; and instead of imposing environmental ethics on people, we will naturally respect, love, honor, and protect that which is our self."

2. I develop a more comprehensive analysis and critique of Westra's work in "Examining Ecosystem Integrity as a Primary Mode of Recognizing the Autonomy of Nature" (Morito 1999a). The details of her argument are well worth understanding, as she uses techniques that have been effective in changing the face of human ethics. Her Kantian approach in establishing a type of categorical imperative, according to which a near universal recognition of the value of integrity generates an imperative to respect integrity as a foundational value, is examined in the article. Despite being impressed with the argument, I see it as falling short of what the insights surrounding the notion of integrity imply. Unfortunately, the description of Westra's work here is truncated and relies on agreement with much of the analysis of the ecological approach that has preceded.

Chapter Six

Ethics and Policy

Ethics and Analytical Failure

Establishing the relationship between environmental values, ethics and policy can begin at many points and in many ways, but the nature of this investigation and the limits of its purview require a considerably restricted discussion. The concern with ethics in environmental policy is driven by a number of factors, not the least of which has been the notable lack of ethical deliberation over the consequences of policy making that is unattuned to conditions of ecosystem integrity, cultural values and effects on marginalized people. Environmental and natural resource policies have been driven by two dominant values: economics and politics. Economic interests in exploitation and waste disposal have often blinded policy and decision makers to the adverse ecological, social and health impacts of exercising these interests. Political conflicts over jurisdiction and land-use planning objectives have led to an inability to deal with impacts of exploitive activity, owing to jurisdictional gridlock and deadlock. Victims of pollution downstream, for instance, could not hold polluters upstream accountable for damages and health costs to their communities. Issues of fairness and the identification of those who should bear the cost of environmental degradation became and remain central issues in environmental management. The publication of Rachel Carson's (1962) *Silent Spring* initiated concern for the modes in which our foods are produced and prepared, while the moonscapes left by clear-cut forestry practices alarmed everyone from tourists to soil scientists.

The method of cost-benefit analysis has been and continues to be the primary approach to resolving issues, while economic values, as defined by the financial sector, continue to dominate the valuational scheme. This dominance either obscures or entirely ignores other sorts of values—heritage, ethical, survival, aesthetic and spiritual—in policy making. As a result, conflict continues to arise over the exclusion of values, necessitating the development of a new ethic of value inclusion to govern environmental policy. Justice issues have also come to the fore, since it has become apparent that the poor bear the costs of degradation while the rich receive the benefits. Third World or developing countries tend to be exploited for their lax environmental regulations and for weak enforcement of the regulations they might have. Deforestation of the Brazilian and Philippine rainforests is a classical example of how utter environmental destruction can go unchecked in jurisdictions of weak or easily manipulated governments. Here in North America, the siting of nuclear waste facilities, garbage dumps, pulp mills and the like is almost always detrimental to the health of a silent minority or ethnic group (especially aboriginal peoples), while those who benefit most in polluting these sites escape responsibility for bearing such costs. Inclusion of diverse voices in the development of policy has, therefore, become a core concern.

In this chapter, I begin to examine some of these demands for an ethic to guide environmental and related policies. Demands for appropriate recognition of values, inclusion of cultural perspectives and justice are my main foci. Infused in this examination are arguments for how an ethic based on thinking ecologically would have us analyze and respond to such demands. Relying on the notion of integrity, the chapter builds toward an ethic of attunement. An examination of the International Joint Commission's commitment to ecosystem integrity, which occurs in Chapter 7, gestures toward this alternative in anticipation of developing a conception of sustainability and conservation as basic policy principles.

We begin examining policy with a statement by J. Baird Callicott (1991: 22):

> The truth is ... that all decisions and all actions are necessarily based both on facts and values. From a practically infinite variety of possibilities, we choose certain ends as well as devise the technical means to achieve them.... Do we want to divert a trout stream into a municipal aqueduct or manage it as a recreational fishery? The choice of ends, such as these, involves values. Ethics or morality—the science of value, so to speak—is therefore inescapable. Ethics may not appear to be operative in routine resource allocation decisions because the prevailing conventional values are simply assumed. They go unnoticed because they are widely shared and built into the system. A proposed new ethic gets labelled as such, and then gets dismissed as insubstantial or just a matter of opinion.

Reeves et al. (1992: abstract) argue:

> The decisions of natural resource managers are not simply scientific issues but involve fundamental questions of ethics. Conflicts in fisheries management, forestry, and other applied sciences arise from social and economic factors that affect natural re-

source values. Administrative processes, cost-benefit analyses, and various management "myths" have been constructed to avoid responsibility for difficult value-based decisions. Through these and other means, individuals and organizational systems tend to "filter" information to minimize conflict. The duty to inform the public of alternative consequences of management actions remains a basic ethical obligation of the resource professional.

Increasingly, thinkers from a variety of disciplines are recognizing that value judgments and ethical decisions are central to environmental policy. Gradually, those who are in positions of influence over environmental policy and management decisions are recognizing that what they do when they manage is advance some and retard (or reject) other values. Two points may be raised in this regard: values are either exercised or suppressed in accordance with ethical commitments; these commitments are more often than not implicit, and their presence is often denied by those making decisions about policy. These points are emphasized because it is important to acknowledge that decisions affecting environmental problems are in fact ethical and that it makes sense to understand them in ethical as much as political, economic or legal terms. How policy decisions advance an ethical commitment, then, needs first to be identified.

The ethical basis of decision making is often overtly denied, largely because of a belief that the predominantly science-based decision-making scheme is value neutral. Despite much work that has been done to show how values are infused in scientific decision-making, many in the resource, business and political arenas remain entrenched in the view that acting on scientific evidence is objective, whereas acting on values/ethics is subjective—a matter of taste, not rational thought. But as Callicott and Reeves et al. suggest, even so-called science-based decision making is not free of bias about what is right and what is wrong. So, the main issue is not whether values should be involved in policy making, but what values should be involved and by what procedure they ought to be included.

Scientific values—reliability, predictability, control, simplification and clarity—are not only epistemic values, they are socially defined values. As seen in some aboriginal communities, reliability and predictability are based on very different sorts of processes, which are in turn based on different attitudes toward control and different conditions of clarity. To insist on scientific values and approaches is to exclude alternative epistemic and value systems, marginalizing an alternative value system and other communities as well. In Canada prior to 1988, when abortion laws were struck down, the Supreme Court's Madam Justice Bertha Wilson identified a violation of a basic human right in the existing abortion law (see *R. v. Morgentaler*). She noted how basic values such as autonomy and self-esteem were being undermined by dominant conceptions of equality, which failed to incorporate women's distinctive understanding of the conditions of autonomy and self-esteem. Abortion law, in effect, marginalized women because it rested on an analytical failure to recognize distinctive conditions of equality. Similar forces of marginalization get played out in environmental policies. It is important to note how in law there are important, even vital, values that motivate the legal mind, at least in democracies. They are based on basic passions for freedom, autonomy, self-esteem and the like. These passions, in turn, equip the legal mind to identify hidden epistemic and value commitments that serve to marginalize people. Justice, then, commits us to analysis of these commitments, whether in law, planning, management or policy.

Nevertheless, resistance to adopting such a critique is strong. Kristin Shrader-Frechette, for example, criticizes ecological approaches, especially the ecosystem integrity approach, because "the normative foundations provided by ecology are basic intuitions. The problem with intuitions is not only that they are vague but also that one either has them or not" (1995: 627). She concludes that intelligent debate cannot be based on such intuitions and, therefore, that the integrity approach will not serve to protect the environment in the adversarial atmosphere of courtrooms. It preaches only to the converted because it is a mere matter of opinion (Shrader-Frechette 1995: 629).

The integrity approach, admittedly, is grounded in a kind of intuition or, more accurately, moral passion; but all ethics is grounded in such passions, which can be considered subjective. These shared moral sensibilities are not "mere" intuitions (that is, they are not capricious and arbitrary); they have some claim to the universal, in the sense of cross-cultural acceptance. They can also be learned in a social and an educational context, as are respect for freedom, dignity and self-esteem. They can be and are foundational for modern democracies. Shrader-Frechette (1995: 623) may be right in her criticism that thinkers like Westra assume too much certainty with regard to ecosystem integrity; we simply do not know what integrity is because ecosystems are constantly changing, undergoing degradation and re-formation. We might not even know whether to focus on thermodynamic theory, systems theory, networks, trophic systems, hierarchical communities or harmonized communities to characterize ecosystem integrity (Shrader-Frechette 1995: 628). But our appreciation for it does not depend on a scientific definition of the concept; it relies on a basic sensibility derived from immediate experience and recognition of the deep dependency we have on the integration of valuational activities that constitute the system. Since our ethical system is grounded in passions, there is no escaping the intuition-base of ethical life. Further, in the real sense that integrity can be seen as a foundational value, when we become attuned to our dependency to the ecosystem, it is not an arbitrary starting point. Like values such as self-esteem, dignity and freedom, integrity may not be as clear and unambiguous as some would like, but it is not clear because it is rich and many-layered. Indeed, adherence to established legal norms and the clear and unambiguous concepts assumed in Canadian abortion laws would have made the overturning of those laws impossible. Neither law nor thinking in environmental policy, then, can afford to retain the status quo if they are to respond to real needs and deal with the roots of the problems we are facing.

Integrity is a many-layered concept and can be used to respond to the many-layered problems faced in environmental policy. It compels us to think about the diversity of values and needs that constitute ecosystem relationships at different levels of organization. It is a morally more adequate response than are demands for clarity, when those demands are based on a desire to make it easier for policy makers and legal minds to set policy and produce decisions. The integrity approach does make decision making more difficult, but it does so, ironically, by requiring greater clarity about the meaning and consequences of policy setting for people with different perspectives and for ecological communities.

If we follow the argument for implementing the harm principle, we find that to know what brings harm is to know the conditions of freedom and well-being of the locus or system under consideration. If there is to be an ethically warranted generalization of what constitutes harm for the purposes of policy and law, it should be developed by people who are attuned to these conditions. A general principle will be fine-textured and not grossly formulated, as is "the avoidance of pain," for instance. It will not be formulated so as to ignore or promote shallow understanding of cultural, heritage, spiritual and other values central to the democratic values of society. At the same time, formulations will not ignore the ecological community or the ecological context that supports the plurality of goods at stake. They will be based on a deep understanding of these values and contexts.

Despite the inherent risk involved in resituating commitments to science in environmental policy, it is important to do so in order to understand what policy is about: the exercise and protection of certain values. If policy is value based, then what goes by the title of science-based policy is actually the method by which certain values are exercised. For this reason, we can apply as much good science as we can produce, yet those recommendations will be ignored or distorted for lack of commitment and political will. Both of these forms of resistance speak to the fact that we need more explicitly and overtly to recognize that policy is about promoting certain values. We then need to reidentify what is being done when there is a lack of political will or commitment. The lack of political will—especially in the U.S.—to comply with the Kyoto Treaty to reduce carbon dioxide (and other greenhouse gas) emissions, despite explicit scientific evidence of the danger of allowing emissions to remain at their present levels, illustrates the point well. Clearly, potential job losses and upheaval in the industrial sector spawn such resistance. Continuing to debate the issue on scientific grounds has become irrelevant. This debate is really about the competition between values. The U.S. is exercising any number of values related to economic prosperity, while most of the rest of the world is concerned about health, ecological stability and threats to people who are suffering the consequences of global warming. To think that policy can be science-based is naive, and it invites analytical failure. Science exercises secondary values that need to be adopted once the more fundamental values are identified and accepted. Science then can determine whether and when these values are being violated (e.g., whether certain increases in airborne particulate matter is the cause of increased mortality and morbidity in lung disease patients).

In a democracy, it is especially important to identify the values that underlie policy because those who dominate in society generally have the power both to determine what values will be recognized and then to use the appearance of democracy to legitimate the ignoring or suppression of other values and voices. If in policy some values are exercised and others are not, then policy developers need to be especially aware of modes of silencing and marginalizing dominated voices. To accomplish this, we need to adopt an analysis that is deep enough to identify how policy either supports or threatens basic democratic values and to formulate these values in ways that ensure the representation of the critical values of freedom and well-being.

Systems of Marginalization

As noted in examining the transition between world views, the adoption of new concepts can alter value priorities (e.g., the value of reason over authority) and sometimes result in complete elimination (e.g., the elimination of experience and direct acquaintance in favour of "objective" methodological approaches to knowledge). Adopting scientific or economic ways of determining values has a similar impact on policy. Of particular importance is the relationship between contemporary scientific/economic values and reductive analysis, which in turn supports the exclusion of values—especially ethnic, women's and tradition-based values—that do not suit or conform to this frame of reference. Aboriginal communities have been among the most victimized when scientific and economic development values are presumed to be objective and, consequently, prevail over spiritual, traditional and community values.

The dominance of scientific and economic values shapes a system of identifying and weighing values that fails systematically to respect conditions of autonomy for many people. Such systems are most poignantly put into service when interests pertaining to hydroelectric projects, logging, uranium mining, agriculture and fishing rights form the focus of government and corporate agendas. Some of the devices central to implementing this system of values are gross national product (GNP) calculations and cost-benefit analyses (CBAs). Where these devices are used by the politically and economically dominant, traditional land and spiritual values are ignored or, more accurately, treated as irrelevant. Traditional aboriginal values, particularly those related to hunting and fishing, typically have been ignored when development and economic values prevail (Morito 2000). Values central to Newfoundland fishing communities were ignored when federal and provincial governments imposed fishing policies that favoured large multinational corporations. After rapacious offshore fishery technologies caused the collapse of both the offshore and inshore cod fishery, some of these communities decided to speak out about what government and industry did to them. One west coast Newfoundland community in the area surrounding Corner Brook produced a video and map to illustrate how their traditional and economic values had been entirely ignored by the Newfoundland and Canadian governments (see Humber Environment Action Group 1996). Their presentation demonstrates how the intangible and non-quantifiable values of the community were undermined and violated as a result of international, national and provincial fisheries policy, which favoured economically based cost-benefit analyses. In this case, the reductive approach to policy became an effective means through which marginalization of the community was justified.

Generally, Modern value systems still are well entrenched, and they demand efficiency and progress, which is reflected in their methods of analysis. Use of these methods have distorted and misrepresented different value systems as economic and dominant political interests place pressure on people to use the dominant system of analysis and a corresponding language to represent their values. Use of the willingness-to-pay strategy,[1] for instance, misrepresent spiritual, community, survival and other values that cannot be costed or that are incommensurable with economic values. Sometimes the distortion comes in a political form, when, according to democratic principles, all values are treated equally because each value holder is counted equally. Counting each value holder equally tends to flatten the relationship between fundamental (e.g., self-esteem), symbolic (e.g., spiritual) and negotiable (e.g., economic and recreational) values, so that they can be weighed equally in the same scale. Many so-called "empirical" approaches tend to yield such flattened profiles when, in principle, values ought to be prioritized and categorized as negotiable versus non-negotiable, fundamental versus non-fundamental; this is a characteristic of constitutional democracies. It is toward these sorts of impositions and methods of approach that we need to turn to see how the policy making-process marginalizes people.

Environmental Policy as an Instrument of Dominance and Eradication

Much of Western ethical tradition has been formed around an ethic of dominance. In this section, I argue that the predominant ethical sensibility operating in environmental policy is an ethic of dominance, which masquerades as an ethic animated by democratic values. While it no longer exists in the blatant forms of genocide and imperialistic wars carried out under Manifest Destiny, the ethic of dominance remains entrenched in agricultural and community development policy. Consider the fact that it is now almost inconceivable for farmers not to treat competing life forms as enemies to be eradicated. Advertising for herbicides and pesticides represents the chemicals as predatorial. They will hunt down and kill the enemy life forms. The suffix "cide" in "herbicide," "fungicide" and "insecticide" betrays this underlying valuation of competing species. In *Ishmael*, Daniel Quinn (1992) cites the beginning of agriculture as the start of the domination ethic. Those who interfere with the subjugation of the land to agricultural production become targets for eradication. Domination through eradication is implicit in the way we think about everything that opposes our domination.

Although Quinn may be extreme in proposing that agriculture is the source of the ethic of dominance—warring peoples surely existed among the hunters and gatherers—his characterization of the agricultural norm rings true, since the development of agriculture has been a major reason for imperialistic colonization of the Americas and India. We often cite greed and fear as the motivations for environmentally devastating activities. Much of environmental ethics, consequently, is designed to curb these motivations, or at least to manage them. For this reason, the audiences of Aldo Leopold and others who espouse an ethic of "limiting freedom" hardly blink an eye when presented with such a conception of ethics. But while greed and fear are motivators, the assumption that our relationship to many plants, predators and other cultures is one of competition allows the justification of eradicating this competition to go without challenge. Quinn's indictment may not apply to all humans, but it does to a great majority of cultures existing today. Very few extant cultures seem to recognize that the relation between ourselves and predators or parasites is dialectical, not one of simple competition. Those whom we call "indigenous peoples" are an exception, however. Many if not most indigenous peoples believe that one cannot eliminate one's competition without violating basic principles of respect and reciprocal dependency.

The close community relationships between species (known often as "peoples") and the identity with other species (since people are identified with their *dodaem* and transmutation from one species to another is assumed possible) proscribe elimination as a strategy for dealing with competition. Other predator species do not kill to eliminate the prey species they hunt; many prey species, such as the gazelle, can continue to graze in the vicinity of the lion that feeds on its cousin. The aboriginal predator must likewise ensure that elimination does not occur.

In contrast, dominant Western European ethical sensibilities, as exercised in North America, Africa, Asia and Central America, have supported either explicit genocide programs (e.g., Manifest Destiny and the conquistadors' genocide of the Maya) or cultural genocide programs (e.g., assimilation and colonization). The explicit purpose has been to eradicate the interference and competition by aboriginal societies and large predators, hence the Indian wars, the reservation system and bounties on the wolf. Deeply entrenched in this mind-set is the assumption of a right to colonize and control.

Previous chapters have shown that this ethic of eradication is rooted in the deeply entrenched metaphysical, epistemological and axiological commitments of the Western tradition. Epistemological commitments to scepticism and scientific rigour further support the interests of eradication since they promote the elimination of forms of knowing that do not conform to scientific values. In narrowing the criteria of legitimacy, scientific scepticism devalues these forms. The tendency toward a narrowing of purview through the elimination of competition, then, is deeply entrenched in Western modes of thought.

A consequence of this narrowing is a type of solipsism: not being able to acknowledge the legitimacy of any claims beyond one's own immediate understanding. Descartes, who has been central to Modern scepticism, found that his scepticism systematically narrowed his purview until he became trapped in a radical form of solipsism; the only thing that truly exists is the "I" who thinks—and then, only when the "I" thinks. This incredible conclusion so clearly was contrary to what was obvious and assumed in practice that Descartes had to construct fantastic theories to show that our ordinary experience actually does have some relationship to what is real. He constructed a theory about how a good God would not deceive us into believing that there is an external world when one does not exist. Guided by the belief that true knowledge must be beyond doubt, Descartes pushed himself until he was able to look at only one aspect of knowledge—the quest for certainty—and was forced to deny the balance of factors that contribute to our lives as knowing beings. Moreover, his insistence that only clear and distinct ideas could count as knowledge implies that we are under obligation to devalue and eliminate ideas representing more holistic or rich contexts and experiences. Similarly, early in the twentieth century, logical positivism attempted to eradicate metaphysical explanations of the world and to place the quantitative scientific approach at the centre of all knowledge. Altogether, this line of thought has led to the development of a perspective predicated on a fear of falling into error rather than on gaining insight and depth of understanding.

When seen as an avoidance of error, the narrowing of purview seems entirely reasonable and prudent. But when compared against other forms of knowing, including forms that are required for everyone in day-to-day living, solipsism is foolish, a product of one-sided thinking. One of the best places to see this type of solipsism at work in policy is in the arena of environmental justice. Unequal distribution of the effects of pollution and environmental degradation has resulted in the poor and other marginalized groups bearing the cost of environmental destruction and the rich taking the balance of the benefits. Siting of waste facilities, downstream/downwind pollution and desertification affect poor and marginalized (e.g., indigenous) communities far more than the communities that benefit from environmental degradation. As growing concern for this inequity has gotten the attention of policy makers, proponents of the dominant economic system have responded with innovative solipsistic thinking.

Leonard and Zeckhauser (1992), for instance, argue that focusing on justice and trying to administer to those who are treated unjustly will produce less justice than letting the economic free-enterprise system operate independent of justice constraints. They reason that there will be a trickle-down effect, in which the wealth of a few will produce an economic system that offers more security, more services and a higher standard of living for the poor and marginalized. Although they must also suffer an increasing gap between themselves and the rich, the poor and unjustly treated will generally be better off than if administrations attended to justice. Administrations are simply too cumbersome and inefficient to be able to deliver justice where it is due. Simplifying the decision-making system and narrowing the purview of justice (by allowing economic motives to play freely) will encourage a better system to emerge.

How feasible is this move? Let us suppose that the claims about government weakness are correct. We still must acknowledge that human beings do not measure their well-being by GNP or by economic wealth alone, or even principally; they measure their well-being by values such as equality, stability, dignity, family cohesion, community support and spiritual wealth. Arguments of the type made by Leonard and Zeckhauser tend to assume either that these values will be satisfied by the trickle-down effect or that these values are irrelevant. In the latter interpretation, valuational solipsism is obvious. In the former, it is hidden. The trickle-down effect argument assumes that increased economic welfare produces an increase in justice and other values. While economic prosperity may result in increased respect for some values, it will just as likely result in a decrease in respect for other values. The more that money becomes the medium through which human relationships are organized, the less that respect for one another, sharing and cooperation are exercised. My research with First Nations shows that many old people trace the problems of their communities to the dominance of money, which has replaced other social currencies, such as respect for elders, sharing work and responsibility for helping neighbours.[2] Blindness to the effect of a money or market economy on the values of communities and other cultures is not necessarily intentional, but it is systemic. Value solipsism may be efficient in managing according to clear goals, but it is ineffective as a tool for satisfying and responding appropriately to people's fundamental values. More importantly, it fails to respect justice, since justice requires its own form of deliberation and adjudication of claims that are fundamentally different from those to which an economic analysis appeals. Aforementioned Supreme Court decisions have demonstrated how terms of reference based on fundamental human and democratic values need to be recognized and decisions need to be based on them in order to be able to claim respect for certain perspectives. Cases that ignore justice issues and those that are attentive to justice issues sometimes produce the same material consequences for victims of injustice, but the former do not demonstrate respect. Values such as human dignity and honour are equally and sometimes more important factors in a just society.

Transformation toward a way of thinking that is inclusive of perspectives, values and methods of recognizing them is critical for developing respectful, just and democratic environmental policies. This transformation must first focus on overcoming solipsism in its various forms. At the root of solipsistic thinking lies a deeply rooted scepticism toward other modes of thought and understanding that suggests that overcoming solipsism requires a balancing of scepticism with openness and receptivity.

Stakeholder Approaches

If we begin with the assumption that all policy development must follow democratic process, principles of inclusion and comprehensiveness in the representation of values, then stakeholder approaches seem good strategies. I will focus here on the approach taken by Shrader-Frechette and McCoy (1993) because it is among the most democratic and sensitive approaches to being inclusive yet it rejects the holistic ecosystem integrity approach. Shrader-Frechette and McCoy advocate a policy- and decision-making scheme that distinguishes between various orders of principles (1993: 242): first order, second order, third order and so on. First-order principles are prima facie obligatory and must be followed; when two or more first-order principles compete with one another, second-order principles adjudicate between them. The first step is to list all competing principles relevant to a particular decision (e.g., whether to preserve the Florida panther and the vast amounts of land needed to do so). Conservation principles, for instance, may compete with development and economic principles (e.g., rights to housing). The process is meant to identify all of the values at stake on the conservation side (e.g., intrinsic value of the panther, recreational values, cultural values and values related to environmental services that would be destroyed by development) and then to weigh them against economic principles (e.g., right to security and profit). If we come to see that the development values cannot compete with the values associated with preservation, the decision is made. But if it is not clear that the economic values are outweighed (e.g., as in cases where economics is connected to needed housing), a second-order principle may have to be devised. Now, Shrader-Frechette and McCoy (1993: 183) believe that a full-cost accounting system, where the full costs of development are disclosed, will likely show that development, in the majority of cases, does not benefit society as a whole but only the developer. Many times, just by tabling and fully analyzing the values at stake and the conditions of their satisfaction, a decision becomes clear. Nevertheless, when first-order principles clash, second-order principles (e.g., fairness, equity and the harm principle) can be devised to adjudicate the debate. Either way, a systematic and clear line of adjudication can be devised to resolve conflicts.

Supposedly, rational communities will eventually reach the point where one alternative clearly becomes the right one, or at least one that is more justifiable than others. Implicit in the model is the belief that there is a final court of appeal, much like a supreme court of a nation is a final arbiter, although the model does not specify what this final arbiter is. The model is well in keeping with moral sensibilities of fairness and is very useful as a dispute-settling mechanism; it could be employed in hearings, public fora, alternative dispute resolution situations and other quasi-legal contexts. I entertain the model, then, as a best approach to a democratic mechanism for developing policy and for decision making for environmental issues. Its strength lies in its initial clarity and conformity to general democratic sensibilities. Moreover, it seems to promote inclusion of all values and renders decisions with sanctioning effectiveness (owing to its legal nature).

Despite their strengths, such approaches are weak in addressing some of the key environmental issues so far identified. My central concern is that stakeholder approaches fail to recognize adequately the silent but vital loci so central to environmental integrity. For instance, Leopold's (1964) discussion of the biotic pyramid indicates that the most vital parts of the ecosystem (the bacteria and so-called lower forms of life) are the ones that traditionally have remained unrecognized and our dependency on them underanalyzed. There are perhaps many unidentified silent loci, which must be heard and properly appreciated, both to satisfy our own valuations and to exercise our hegemonic responsibilities as rational beings. Stakeholder models are, in effect, conflict resolution mechanisms, which represent human interest-bearers as individuals. They are structured to be governed by principles that order competitive relationships between human individuals and groups who can assert their positions over and against one another. This character may be its strength, in some contexts; but in light of the holistic nature of environmental problems and the need to recognize responsibility for protecting silent voices, a more direct form of recognition is required to govern the policy- and decision-making process. Rather than introducing ethical principles somewhere down the line when conflicts arise in a negotiation or hearing process, a sense of ethical responsibility needs to operate from the beginning to ensure proper representation of the whole and the silent.

Further, stakeholder approaches are designed to allow voices capable of representing themselves to be heard and included in the analysis of values, but they tend to treat these voices as data to be collected. They are treated as positions to be adjudicated in some process of fair or equal representation. This process is not precisely a way to recognize and acknowledge vital and fundamental values—a process that requires becoming attuned to suppressed values and voices—because it presupposes that those values worth recognizing will be represented in the process. For voices that are disempowered by the system through marginalization and imposition of ways of knowing, there is no recognition or, alternatively, recognition is left to their champions (e.g., NGOs) who may or may not accurately represent these voices.

By definition, values and voices that are suppressed by the system of analysis cannot be represented adequately, if at all. Where the onus is on the presenter to represent his or her values, but the cultural contexts in which those values acquire their meaning are not recognized and respected, there is no effective voice. As Richardson, Sherman and Gismondi (1993) point out, many so-called stakeholder hearings are designed to restrict the length and the subject matter of questions and responses. The overwhelming emphasis on science as the evidentiary base and economics as the value system implicitly (and sometimes explicitly) biases stakeholder hearings to favour voices that are educated to understand the types of knowledge and systems of analysis recognized in hearings. Those represented, furthermore, tend to be only those who are financially able to be present at these fora. Finally, given that this form of knowledge is based largely on scepticism and reductive forms of thought, such fora do not welcome other forms of representation or tolerate requests to become attuned to cultural and ecological contexts. Such hearings, then, entrench insularity and inhibit attempts to address the injustice of solipsism.

The stakeholder approach remains adversarial (assuming conflict as the basic fact of moral relationships) and classically anthropocentric (no values exist apart from human epistemic agents [Shrader-Frechette and McCoy 1993: 244]). The version of an ecocentric principle in use, e.g., recognizing the intrinsic value of the panther, illustrates how reluctant Shrader-Frechette and McCoy are to take the analysis of ecology beyond its identification as a sub-discipline of biology. In fact, they believe that ecology has almost no value as a means of grounding for an environmental ethic, and that, at most, ecology can offer rules of thumb about whether a region can be preserved and how big a reserve would have to be, given the conservation goals selected. Ecology is not acknowledged as a foundation for human values or identity. This distinction is a watershed for those working in the field of environmental ethics: those who agree with Shrader-Frechette and McCoy see no metaphysical dimension to ecology, and so draw no implications for shifting our world view. There is, therefore, little support for overcoming solipsism at its deeper levels.

Further indication of how such stakeholder approaches contribute to silencing is found in the criticism Shrader-Frechette and McCoy (1993: 243) make of Rolston's work in general. They accuse him of not developing second-order principles to adjudicate between competing values and claims; he does not seem to see the necessity of forming an ethic that recognizes the need for more explicit conflict resolution strategies. But in subscribing to this competitive structure for policy- and decision-making fora, they fail to see the strength and direction of Rolston's arguments: that is, to develop the human reflective capacity and character to accord with the deeper analysis of our dependency relationship to ecological conditions. Their epistemic and valuational solipsism is based on a conception of rigour as formed in law and the experimental sciences. Owing to this solipsism, there is little awareness of the more comprehensive and deeper valuations that need to be recognized when thinking ecologically. Shrader-Frechette and McCoy's approach, therefore, falls short of meeting the conditions of the harm principle.

These criticisms demonstrate our need for a more adequate policy-making framework and foundation if the interests of justice and respect are to be satisfied. It is arguable that adopting the principle of integrity is a better foundation than the previously examined ones (economic and stakeholder approaches). It provides a grounding for a much needed transformative ethic and one that requires a systematic and explicit inclusion of silent voices. It begins with a commitment to the harm principle and, therefore, moves policy in the direction of full disclosure of the values that are pertinent to policy and of the perspectives needed to interpret and respect those values. It does so as a co-primary with other fundamental values, such as freedom and health, both of which demand recognition as bases for defining harm. Recognition, in turn, requires depth of understanding and treatment, not as one among many first-order values and principles but as a foundational value. Other values, then, acquire legitimacy only when shown to be compatible with ecosystem integrity values. At the very least, exercising freedom, health and other values in a way that would undermine integrity would be considered illegitimate, not merely in competition with integrity.

Treating integrity as a primary value implies a demand for human development toward greater attunement to ecosystem integrity. In fact, this consequence is part of the strength of not defining integrity in a straightforward manner. Adopting the principle of integrity promotes both vision-oriented policy and decision making as the latter faces uncertainty and complexity. By not being straightforward and yet committing to the values of integrity and freedom, policy can be set to adapt to advances in understanding and to developments in moral awareness. Policy can be as iterative and as adaptive as human capacity with respect to becoming attuned and accepting responsibility for the protection of the plurality of values. Draconian measures for dealing with oppressive regimes can be eased and finally abandoned, as those regimes democratize; similarly, initially strong measures needed to protect ecosystem integrity can be eased as people's respect for integrity develops. Ambitious goals, such as zero discharge of pollutants, may have to be written into policy, both to reduce pollution and to bring greater awareness to the dependencies and responsibilities we carry. Rigorous tests for determining whether marginalized voices are heard may have to be instituted until a sufficient ethos is developed so as to make the tests superfluous.

The need for adaptive approaches to environmental policy is based in part on the anticipation of disclosures in ecology and on the interactions of different ecological, cultural and other valuational groupings. In other words, setting policy is a process, not an event. Of course, this process must be orderly and rational to mirror the dialectic between chaos/change and order/stability. Within the iterative process, as in constitutional democracies, the basic values of freedom and justice can be protected as foundational, so as to provide order and stability to the process. Thus, the process of adaptation to disclosures is one of becoming attuned to the land and the people, to what is harmful to them and to how best to protect them against harm.

Not only are there ethical reasons for adopting a fundamentally different approach to inclusion of cultural and other valuations; there are legal mandates. Relations with indigenous peoples, according to *R. v. Sparrow*, are not to be based on "sharp dealing" but on fiduciary responsibilities that respect the distinctiveness of aboriginal culture. It is a *sui generis* relationship; it is not to be modeled on traditional (and dominant) modes of negotiation. Partly in response to the fact that aboriginal people have been marginalized through the imposition of a linguistic tradition (that is, through the use of residential schools to eradicate aboriginal languages) and partly because the terms of reference for negotiation favour the dominant sector, the Supreme Court of Canada has mandated that an alternative way of understanding and including aboriginal perspective be developed by government. This is an attempt to avoid distorting the aboriginal voice to suit more competitive negotiation and agreement processes. With expectations similar to "non-sharp dealing," the integrity model can require an alternative mode of recognizing ecosystem integrity and related valuations, even prior to negotiation. There is nothing antidemocratic about requiring a transformation of negotiation processes in order to ensure appropriate recognition of cultural and foundational values, since such protective measures instantiate the principle of protecting the minority and silent voice from the tyranny of the majority and dominant voice.

Concrete modes of protecting ecologically grounded values are also possible. As already indicated, we have prima facie obligations to deny development projects for wilderness areas, partly because the spread of destructive activity has reached disaster proportions and partly because the very activity is typically unattuned to the valuational activity of wilderness areas. These areas ought to be preserved for our own attunement potential and as expressions of respect for non-human loci. Stable buffer zones should also be highly protected from further development since further degradation lowers our own and others' potential for freedom.

Ecological restoration in cities is another clearly prescribed practice, which would enhance the ecological functioning of areas as riparian zones and native biota are restored. The regeneration project of the Toronto waterfront (Crombie 1992) exemplifies how ecologically dysfunctional land can be restored to some degree of functionality for both wildlife and human use. Waterfowl are returning to the area to nest, as humans return to walk, cycle and boat along the shore. The same project would be proscribed for the north shore of Lake Superior or other relatively pristine ecosystems, but in heavily degraded areas such restoration projects have an important, transformative learning value; they promote change in human valuations to respect and appreciate ecological function. Ecological restoration may seem hopelessly romantic if restoration is aimed at reproducing pristine wilderness. But if, with Donald Scherer (1995: 364), we understand restoration to be about re-establishing an equilibrium of biologically similar, similarly interacting, flourishing populations as once existed in a region, we can begin to act effectively on the idea of restoration and integrity. Many communities are experimenting with just such projects, partly to restore ecological functionality and partly to help transform people's understanding of their relationship to ecological function. Such projects promote attunement by putting us into immediate awareness of and contact with ecological conditions. They are also iterative in the sense that they usually require a series of attempts before successful restoration occurs; and they are adaptive in the sense that restoration is adapted to the pressing demands of the urban context and its values. In these areas, some forms of economic development can be compatible with the ecosystem approach because they enhance both thinking ecologically and economic welfare.

Another reason to consider the integrity approach over narrower scientific and in economic approaches is trustworthiness. Scientific expertise in the political domain and economic motivations is often not trustworthy, especially when that expertise is influenced by developers and other economic interests. Recent history is replete with cases of transnational corporations and governments assuring the public of the safety of industrial developments, which later resulted in monumental disaster. The PBB (polybrominated biphenyl) disaster in Michigan in 1973 was just such a case. The PBB disaster was the most widespread and least reported chemical disaster in the Western world; tens of thousands of farm animals died and six million people were contaminated, and yet it took four years for the press to cover the story. The delay was owing to the persistent denials of government officials, who argued that farmers were misinformed and scaremongering when they claimed that their livestock were being killed by the chemical (as reported in Shrader-Frechette and McCoy 1993: 164). The high incidence of Minimata disease among residents near the toxic pulp mill at English River, Ontario, is another such case. Aboriginal communities were subjected to mercuric toxic poisoning for years while the company and government assured them that the mill posed no risk (Hutchison and Wallace 1977). The nuclear energy facilities at Chernobyl and Three Mile Island were touted as safe by the Soviet and U.S. governments respectively. The Chernobyl story, an all too obvious case of broken trust in the government and the science community, was, in effect, the Three Mile Island case carried to its disastrous extreme. Love Canal, a receptacle for tons of toxic waste, was promoted as a safe location for a housing development. When subsequent illness of the residents led to higher incidents of cancer, the area was eventually abandoned. In 1984 disaster followed when the multinational corporation Union Carbide assured the residents of Bhopal, India, that the chemical plant producing toxic pesticides was safe. When a valve gave way and tons of toxic chemicals were released into the atmosphere, between 2000 and 3300 people were killed.

Science, politics and industry is a mixture that cannot always be trusted to yield reliable information. Even when the scientific community is clear about environmental dangers, there is no guarantee that governments and industries will not suppress and distort their findings, as noted earlier in relation to the Kyoto treaty on global warming. Newfoundland's cod stock collapse also exemplifies how the warnings of scientists went unheeded for years by the Newfoundland and Canadian governments.

When we take globalization of the economy into account, we find even more motivations either to coopt or to suppress environmental science. Efficiency objectives and power contraction into a few nations and corporations can be expected to heighten the interests in cooptation and suppression. Where powerful interests and large financial investment are involved, and where there is no deliberate effort to infuse policy with respect for justice, freedom and integrity, there is little reason to trust pronouncements that we must rely on science. In light of globalization, an approach that focuses on effectiveness in respecting values and developing virtues now seems even more indispensable as a foundation for environmental policy.

Since the mode of thinking characteristic of the economically and politically dominant is unabashedly utilitarian, as seen in the Leonard and Zeckhauser position on the trickle-down effect, justice is seen more as a cost to be negotiated rather than a moral principle to be enforced in the protection of the vulnerable and silent. As Milton Friedman (1996) argues, the main objective for corporate executives is to use whatever means available, within the confines of the law, to get what is in their (and their shareholders') best interest. Clearly, corporations will recognize the constraints of the justice system, but they will not recognize justice values as such nor will they commit to understanding these values in terms appropriate to a culture or community. All values are "reduced" to economic values or interpreted as utility values in order to allow these corporations to calculate the costs and benefits of including other forms of values. An ethic that ignores the development of virtues and attunement to the values and perspectives of all voices will serve this corporate solipsism and fail the test of the harm principle.

If these virtues are needed in the process of becoming attuned to the conditions and contexts in which harm is to be recognized, then an ethic that addresses our duty to develop character at a deeper level is indispensable. The virtues, as implied in the concept of hegemony, are a necessary part of an environmental ethic and, therefore, of policy and decision making.

The International Joint Commission

For some (e.g., Shrader-Frechette 1995), focusing on integrity is unreasonable, partly because it is an unattainable goal. Nevertheless, it prescribes workable solutions to environmental problems. Others (e.g., Westra 1994) focus on integrity because it has a long history of acceptance in policy matters. The use of "ecosystem integrity" can be traced through the past three decades: the U.S. *Clean Water Act* in 1972; the Great Lakes Science Advisory Board in 1991; and the "New Constitution of Brazil," the United Nations Commission on Environment and Development, and the World Bank in 1992 (see Westra 1994: 24).

The International Joint Commission (IJC) now utilizes the concept of integrity as well. In its early (1909) incarnation, the IJC was essentially a dispute resolution mechanism between Canada and the United States (see International Joint Commission 1909). In 1978, the Great Lakes Water Quality Agreement—a key component of the *Treaty Between the United States and Great Britain Relating to Boundary Waters, and Questions Arising Between the United States and Canada* (International Joint Commission 1989, which was affirmed and strengthened in 1987—recognized integrity as a core value:

> The purpose of the Parties is to restore and maintain the chemical, physical and biological integrity of the waters of the Great Lakes Basin Ecosystem where the latter is defined as "the interacting components of air, land, water and living organism, including humans, within the drainage basin of the St. Lawrence River"

This statement formed a focus for the Ecological Committee of the International Joint Commission's Science Advisory Board and the Board of Technical Experts of the Great Lakes Fishery Commission, who gathered for the 1988 workshop "Ecosystem Integrity in the Context of Surprise." It reaffirms the rights and obligations of Canada and the United States under the Boundary Waters Treaty (International Joint Commission 1909), which in turn has become a major focus of the Great Lakes Fisheries Commission. In 1987 a protocol was signed to amend the 1978 agreement while retaining the commitment to the integrity of the ecosystem, a commitment to eliminate or reduce to the maximum extent possible the discharge of pollutants into the Great Lakes (International Joint Commission 1989: Article II). Article III (International Joint Commission 1989) commits the IJC to a virtual zero-discharge policy, as it seeks to make the waters "free" of objectionable deposits, pollutants, heat and unwanted nutrients.

Zero discharge involves restoring ecosystems to states in which human health is not endangered by human-made discharges, restoring aesthetic quality and, generally, respecting the life forms that existed and flourished in the region before the heavy impact of human industry and consumption. Clearly, zero discharge is not about to happen. The Great Lakes Quality Agreement does not specify a time period in which restoration is to be achieved. Is this merely an ideological dream, then? Despite the appearance of zero discharge as an unattainable goal and despite criticisms as well as admissions that integrity is not a scientifically clear notion and that it is a valuationally loaded term, the principle of integrity is connected to a commitment to restore a relationship to the ecosystem that both fulfills the deeper needs of human beings and respects other forms of life. It is a vision of a long process through which the ecosystem approach could gradually develop from a piecemeal approach to carrying out the mandate of the Great Lakes Water Quality Agreement into a more comprehensive approach to interpreting the agreement between Canada and the United States (see Allen et al. 1993: 2). A report by the Ecological Committee of the Great Lakes Science Advisory Board (Allen et al. 1993) focuses on how important it is to change our perspective at fundamental levels in order to effect the change from specific to general. For example, it suggests that we change our conception of the ecosystem as a place in which we live to one that sees it as "home," a place that has a distinctly ethical meaning for us. The term can be interpreted on many levels (e.g., personal, community and national), and it has a richness of meaning that indicates a place where we and other creatures go through the process of living (Allen et al. 1993: 10–11). This process is not external to the system, but internal (Allen et al. 1993: 13). What the Ecological Committee is saying, in effect, is that the former Modern world view is no longer appropriate as a basis for environmental and resource management; the ecosystem approach requires a different conception of the person as one who is integrated with all other creatures such that "an insult to them is the same insult to us" (Allen et al. 1993: 14).

As political documents, the IJC's commitments are surprising. The types of change in thought that they have sponsored and their commitment to zero discharge are remarkable in light of the political tone of the day (for example, Ronald Regan's refusal to recognize acid rain sources in the industrial midwest, and George Bush's refusal to sign the biodiversity agreement at the United Nations Rio de Janeiro conference in 1992[3]). Continued commitment to zero discharge, in light of the work that has emerged from the IJC and associated bodies, may not directly determine the environmental policies of the U.S. and Canada, but it is an influence that takes us in an appropriate direction. As a respected body, the IJC places pressure on policy development that would otherwise be lacking.

Commitments of this type are often considered honorific or merely symbolic, expressing good intentions but having no substance. The IJC's commitment to integrity seems somewhat different because, while it recognizes that integrity is not being protected, it continues to foster the types of values that would support the goal of integrity. It resembles the relationship of the legal system to crime. Crime will not be stopped, despite the legal system's commitment to the elimination of crime. Pollution will continue, despite the IJC's or any institution's commitments to eliminate it. Of course, a major difference exists between the IJC and the legal system; the IJC has no executive power to enforce zero discharge since its function is information gathering and dissemination, tendering advice, provision of assistance and possible investigation of complaints through holding public hearings (International Joint Commission 1989: Article VII).

The IJC is principally a conflict-resolution mechanism, but it sponsors remedial action plans (RAPs) as well as public fora and research. It continues to place integrity in a lead position in an attempt to promote a different way of thinking about the environment. Indeed, it attempts to effect a change from thinking about ecology to thinking ecologically. We cannot fault the IJC for failing to bring this change about, since such a transformation requires a comprehensive social change based on education and political will. Nevertheless the commission is having an impact on thinkers, many of whom have been cited in this work and who have in turn had an impact on policy development. The IJC is using the concept of integrity as an inspirational concept and is encouraging the implementation of the principle of integrity in such matters as the export of massive amounts of water from the Great Lakes (see International Joint Commission 2000). Based on both the precautionary principle (in International Joint Commission 2000: 3) and recognition of the fact that the Great Lakes are home to a diversity of plants and animals (International Joint Commission 2000: 5), the IJC continues to reiterate its commitment to integrity and indirectly supports those acting to safeguard integrity. The result is a small but continuous pressure to recognize integrity as a goal to achieve. Given the conceptual work that has been done by IJC subcommittees, the gradual implementation of integrity-achieving programs and activities could have an even more widespread effect.

The IJC is far less committed to engineering intervention than might be expected. Its invocation of the precautionary principle illustrates how leading by following can be implemented, particularly through its emphasis on restoration activity as modeled on unperturbed ecosystems. Looseness and ambiguity in the notion of integrity is, indeed, its important scientific feature because it stimulates scientific imagination in developing research agendas that necessarily begin with total-field visions (for example, of "home"), which in turn help scientists to appreciate and perhaps to begin to understand the wide-ranging implications of their research. Indeed, even the definitions of integrity thus far proposed are based largely on intuition, are not amenable to strict quantification and do not yield strict operative definitions. As such, the scientific mind can be guided to develop progressively more precise and multivariate models as the conditions of ecosystem integrity are disclosed. If, for instance, we were to use reproducing and resilient lake trout (an indigenous species) populations as an indicator of integrity, we would gradually, through the failures and partial success of different models, come to understand the conditions that give rise to thriving populations. We would formulate a series of iterations for modeling these conditions in an attempt to restore them. The result would be a model for sustaining not only the lake trout, but all of the species and non-organic conditions that support it. What begins as an intuition, then, can emerge as a full-blown scientific enterprise that is more effective in generating overall well-being than are narrowly defined policy parameters.

The reason for "integrity's" effectiveness as a lead concept is not owing to its amenability to clarity or strict method; it is owing to the fact that it appeals to deeper values. Integrity, like health and freedom, is a vague term. But like these other two terms, integrity represents something fundamental to the good life, to the honourable life, to the respectful life. It strongly motivates morally and democratically committed persons to become aware and sensitive to the conditions that produce and support such a life. When applied to ecosystems, integrity helps investigators envisage research strategies that are respectful and that contribute to a comprehensive understanding of how systems work. It frees the scientific mind from restriction to narrow experimental agendas and allows it to be more explicitly conscious of the creative elements of research. Respect for ecosystem integrity through passive observation of undisturbed systems and active restoration results in an investigative attitude, which is both open and informed by commitments to responsibility for the plurality of values, both narrow and wide. Integrity is a hybrid concept, informed both by human moral sensibilities and by the conditions that support other loci independent of human intervention or interest. As a hybrid concept, then, integrity directs our attention toward the poles of moral responsibility: the onus to assume leadership in our decision-making capacity, and the obligation to follow the lead of the ecosystem through attuning ourselves to the conditions of well-being for all.

A further indication of its effectiveness in prescribing action is the goal of zero discharge. Optimal pollution goals of utilitarian calculations, despite claims to clarity, are far from clear when one considers all those affected by pollution. Those with high sensitivity to different forms of pollution will say one level is optimal, while those with strong resistance will say another. Those close to and immediately affected will assess optimal pollution in a manner different from those at a distance. Zero-discharge goals, in contrast, demand a fundamental shift in modes of production and consumption, doing so on clear moral grounds: the protection of the health and well-being of people and other loci. They are more comprehensively directed at protecting individuals and systems from harm by placing far more responsibility on decision- and policy-making procedures to be inclusive of the complexity of conditions pertinent to the understanding of harm.

The effectiveness and force of integrity, then, has to do with engaging levels of living, communication and understanding that are deeper than those reached by narrow research, policy or legal agendas; this is prescribed under an ethic of attunement. As such, integrity also prescribes living in a much more connected manner to the environment, which in turn prescribes the sorts of restoration programs supported by the IJC. This may not be concrete in the way expected by narrower approaches—that is, it may not have definite and clear results and prescriptions—but it is concrete in the sense that it promotes living with more robust ecosystems and becoming increasingly aware of their conditions of integrity.

A telling contrast further describes the motivation and effectiveness of integrity. While we may envy those who are rich and powerful, we honour those with integrity. Envying the rich and powerful is a relatively superficial feeling, and the reasons for it can be easily identified. We know that we envy them for the wealth and influence they possess. We also know what to do to satisfy this envy; we attain wealth and power. In contrast, respect for integrity, dignity and wisdom requires a deeper and more complex understanding. People we respect for these qualities may be inscrutable. Perhaps we cannot identify and describe the exact qualities we admire, but we know that we esteem their dependability, their strength of conviction and the good that is generated by the qualities they possess. Moreover, we are willing to undergo tutelage to become like them. We identify what is of value, without being able to define what that value is. When we try to understand why people follow the likes of Gandhi or military commanders who have gained the respect of their troops, we associate them with a kind of forcefulness without being able to explain fully what constitutes that forcefulness. When it is a matter of fundamental values, then, it is contrary to ethical obligation and development to predefine these values and determine exactly how we are to act on them. Insisting on such a definition would betray a philistine character, incapable of understanding this dimension of moral life.

"Ecosystem integrity" belongs to the same language of morality. It, therefore, refers to much more than an intuition. Intuition, if it means "hunch" or guess, is inappropriate. It does not capture how we recognize integrity. Henry Regier (1992: 191) describes integrity as something that is not observable by the non-expert and that does not relate directly to any theoretical or empirical synthesis: "As a conceptual mixture put together according to judgments of knowledgeable observers, it is not 'understandable' in a theoretical sense." It is a general and qualitative concept. We come to recognize ecosystem integrity through direct acquaintance. Recognizing integrity in ecosystems, then, requires much the same kind of attitude and frame of mind as it does in recognizing integrity in people.

While the need for deepening moral consciousness is paramount for the integrity approach to be optimally effective, demands for scientific and legal clarity can serve as "ethical heuristics." Since the science of ecology and especially ecosystem integrity is iterative and adaptive, it indicates that present forms of awareness and investigation will have to be improved as attunement and consequent disclosures about our relationship to the land are improved. As a starting point, anticipating the application of strict rules and principles of clarity will demonstrate their insufficiency through their failure to engender the kind of understanding needed to satisfy the harm principle. Failure in this respect can lead us toward a transformation of moral sensibilities. Buddhist and Taoist philosophical traditions have utilized such progressions through legalistic and rule-governed ways of thinking to bring people toward *satori* (Japanese) or *prajña* (Sanskrit): enlightenment. And if Western thinkers such as Erazim Kohák are right—and right about Plato, moreover—then the point of thinking in the West is also to work through the same criteria for thought in order to get beyond these criteria.

One last comment on the role of ethics in environmental policy and management needs to be made. The fact that policy writers and managers are always advancing some moral norms and denying others makes it important to understand anew what it is that policy does. The advancement of moral and social values should be explicitly recognized and rigorously addressed when developing policy. Now, the principle that representatives of the public interest should not infuse their personal moral bias in their work is a sound one, grounded in the liberation from the dictatorial authorities of the Middle Ages. Hence, an important distinction must be drawn between moralizing, through which decision makers impose their values and moral beliefs onto others, and moral responsibility, through which decision makers uphold the values that make a moral community possible. Moral responsibility necessitates the incorporation of ethical training for policy writers and managers, both in the formal aspects of ethical decision making and in the process of becoming attuned to the valuations of the ecological community and the conditions of harm. Chapter Seven's critique of sustainable development and conservation policies will enable us to understand more concretely how the absence of this ethical dimension leads to injustice and harm.

Notes

1. This strategy attempts to place a monetary value on values that are difficult to quantify, e.g., wilderness and religious values. By asking people how much they would be willing to pay in, say, taxes or park entrance fees to protect a wilderness area from development, decision makers can determine whether it is more economically feasible to log a forest or to preserve it. Further discussion on this strategy will be taken up later.

2. Research funded by Athabasca University Research Fund has enabled me to conduct exploratory research into the sources of conflict and the possibility

of determining a common basis in values for the development of a community constitution. The research cited here took place in the summer of 2000 at the Chippewas of Nawash reserve near Wiarton, Ontario. Some of the interview questions were directed at the impact of residential schools on people's relationship to the land. One surprising feature of the interviews is that many interviewees pointedly mentioned the introduction of money as having undermined community identity and strength.

3. As a newly elected president, George W. Bush announced that the United States would not adhere to the Kyoto protocol, to which the United States agreed in principle under Bill Clinton. The protocol committed the United States to reducing their emissions of greenhouse gases (carbon dioxide) to pre-1990 levels.

Chapter Seven

Sustainable Development, Conservation and Sustainability

Sustainable development and conservation are two central policy concepts whose use illustrates how language, initially intended to articulate protective measures, can be manipulated and used to effect the opposite. Both are central in determining how we think about environmental protection and its relationship to the protection of human values. In this chapter, these two concepts are examined for how they operate in policy and how their adoption undermines the values they are supposed to protect. This inversion of intent shows how old thought patterns remain entrenched, and it helps identify what must be changed in the expectations of policy development to avoid such failures. In this regard, the critique of sustainability and conservation is a model for how to begin an iterative process of thinking ecologically about policy and for defining the role of ethics in policy development. The ways of thinking about environmental problems and the programs generated under the rubric of sustainable development and conservation are many; their meanings are varied and serve a number of different and often incompatible interests. It is important first to sort out these variations.

Beginning with the concept of sustainable development, we can see how community development initiatives, non-governmental organizations, foreign aid and the like are being directed by economic motivations and how language is used to formulate concepts of sustainable development, which in fact promote unsustainable and often destructive activity. I will emphasize the relationship between sustainable development and a use of language that excludes perspectives and voices, resulting in injustice and cooptation.

A briefer discussion on conservation will emphasize the natural resource dimension of environmental issues and sustainability. Here, the predominant focus is "utility value" and how it is formulated to achieve the same inversion of intent. While the same emphases on exclusion and injustice are retained, the conservation focus permits an examination of how language manipulation aids the manipulation of people's values through an infusion of foreign values into the determination of the meaning and interpretation of resources.

211

Rationale for Sustainable Development

Almost everyone today is familiar with the extremes that have awakened our concern for sustainable development: natural resource depletion (e.g., fish stocks and forests), desertification, exceeding the carrying capacity of the land to abate waste and pollution, ozone layer depletion, global warming, increased toxicity and threats of nuclear radiation poisoning. Where overpopulation, deforestation, fisheries collapse, ground water draw-down, soil depletion, erosion, species extinction and elimination of green space are of concern, human survival and economic prosperity are threatened. We have become aware of exceeding the ecosystem's carrying capacity. The primary response to this way of seeing the environmental problem has been to advocate for a reduction in the toll we exact on the environment. Others, however, including the United Nations' World Commission on Environment and Development (WCED) (1987), argue that the problem has as much to do with human and consumption values as with the finite carrying capacity of the earth. Solutions, accordingly, involve the transformation of values, ethics, economic goals and political motivations. It is immediately evident that sustainable development has two, possibly incompatible, motivations; the first insists that a scaling-down approach is all that is required; the second calls for a fundamental change in values.

From a business perspective, carrying capacity is the issue. The primary problem is determining what this capacity is and how we should manage economic activity to allow continued exploitation into the indeterminate future. Those who live on the land and have a different relationship to it—one that involves enriching, non-exploitive relations—see the issue in a very different light. To them, the problem may be how to sustain a respectful and perhaps spiritual relationship with the land.

The best and most accessible place to begin discussing sustainable development is with the WCED, which initiates its discussion of sustainable development on a commitment to ecologically based understanding and to holistic thinking. As it turns out, however, the WCED espouses operative definitions of sustainable development that are quite contrary to its commitments to holistic thinking.

In sustainable development documents and discussions, holistic language underscores the importance of preserving ecosystem integrity. It espouses a commitment to the idea that the enterprises of humanity and the processes of the environment are interconnected and interrelated and that this belief should direct the global community to seek ways to make human enterprises more compatible with ecological integrity. The WCED report *Our Common Future* (1987) is the rallying point of the world political community as it attempts to formulate sustainable development policies in light of the environmental crisis, the price of environmental degradation, the problem of poverty and the unequal distribution of costs and benefits. We are by now all too familiar with statistics like the following: "one fifth of households in many countries hold 50% of the wealth, while the bottom fifth hold just 7%" (WCED 1987: 50); "20% of the world's richest take 60 times more than the bottom 20%" (Wackernagel and Rees 1996: 1). Since the publication of *Our Common Future*, a proliferation of books, scholarly reports and work by non-governmental organizations (NGOs) has connected the distribution of wealth to the environmental problem. Much has also been written and discussed on the connection between the cost of environmental degradation and cost distribution in the field of environmental justice. The poor and marginalized of a society typically bear the costs of degradation because they are most likely to be downstream or downwind from the pollution makers and are most likely to have waste disposal, mine tailing and nuclear waste sites located nearby. Hence, sustainable development appears to have just as much to do with protecting marginalized people and justice as it does with protecting ecosystem integrity.

Human activity, as a process within a particular set of environmental processes, depends on sustaining the environment for its continuance: "Environmental stresses and patterns of economic development are linked to one another.... Thus economics and ecology must be completely integrated in decision-making and law-making processes, not just to protect the environment, but also to protect and promote development" (WCED 1987: 37). Our environmental challenges, therefore, are "interdependent and integrated, requiring comprehensive approaches and popular participation" (WCED 1987: 9). The application of sustainable development "requires a holistic approach focused on ecosystems at national, regional and global levels, with co-ordinated land use and careful planning of water use and forest exploitation" (WCED 1987: 144).

Accordingly, to protect environmental integrity is to protect ourselves and our interests. *Canada's Green Plan for a Healthy Environment* stresses the same holistic viewpoint but goes further: "As a signatory to the United Nations World Charter for Nature, Canada recognizes the inherent right of all species to exist" (Canada 1990: 10). Further, "we exist not simply as individuals, but also as highly active parts of an ecosystem that is itself alive and finite" (Canada 1990: 27). "Nature has an intrinsic value that exceeds its worth in the marketplace. It supports a diversity of life and is essential to our well-being" (Canada 1990: 15). While the Green Plan is not explicitly supported by the current government, subsequent documents continue in the same vein.

It would appear that much of the world community is transforming itself to adopt an ecological world view. The use of the terms "interdependence," "unity," and "oneness," that is, the language of holism, is characteristic of sustainable development policies. The WCED uses holistic terminology to express our need to re-evaluate our consumption and production practices. In their report, holistic language underlines the danger of our present abuse of the environment: "The earth is one" (WCED 1987: 27, 41); genetic diversity is necessary for the normal functioning of ecosystems and biospheres as wholes (WCED 1987: 13). But our economic activities are threatening these diverse wholes, wholes upon which those activities depend. Thus, the report acknowledges that exploitation of the environment changes ecosystems, which are complex and interlinked with other systems. It recommends the minimization of adverse impacts in order to "sustain the ecosystem's overall integrity" (WCED 1987: 45): "We see ... the possibility for a new era of economic growth, one that must be based on policies that sustain and expand the environmental resource base" (WCED 1987: 1). Minimizing impacts and exercising caution are necessary, furthermore, because of the inadequacy of theories to explain these systems. These statements mandate sweeping change in environmental policy, law and, indeed, our ethical orientation toward the earth. It has implications for transformations in education and in personal relations with the environment.

Business and Sustainable Development

It may at first seem strange that business could embrace sustainable development, but in *Changing Course* (Schmidheiny 1992), a publication representing forty-eight chief executive officers of multinational and national corporations, it does so with a passion. Recognition of the dependency relation is front and centre, and the focus on poverty is not far behind (see Schmidheiny 1992: 7). Economic growth, population control, increased efficiency in the use of resources to reduce exploitation and the reduction of pollution are all in keeping with the WCED recommendations. The main engine for change is the market and commitment to full-cost accounting. Full-cost accounting aims at ensuring that the market gives the right signals regarding the prices of goods and services, so that these prices reflect the environmental and social costs that have hitherto been ignored. Examples of such costs are air and water pollution as well the hidden costs to the health care system, which are caused by toxic releases and other environmentally generated health problems. Industry and business do not incur these costs; the public does. A decrease in the availability of clean water contributes to both health and agricultural costs; acid rain damages buildings and vehicles. Social costs include the damage to families and communities dealing with radiation poisoning (for example, the Chernobyl nuclear disaster) and dislocation and feelings of insecurity as neighbourhoods and sometimes whole communities must be evacuated due to toxic spills and other environmental disasters. These are costs that, in the past, have not been borne by those who bring them about. The resolution strategy is to assign a monetary value to these costs and require those who benefit from generating them to bear the costs, a process of internalizing costs. Both producers and consumers will, in the end, bear these costs because internalization will result in increased prices. Hence, those who benefit also pay.

Other types of cost are also recognized, ones which the WCED (1987: 29, 36) identifies as principal costs to humanity: the costs to human rights borne by the poor in industrialized countries and by the poor countries as a whole. Rampant exploitation, which takes advantage of the lax environmental standards of developing nations, has allowed corporations to extract resources and leave or, at least, shirk their responsibility for damages inflicted upon these societies. Costs associated with the breakdown of family-based agriculture and the disenfranchisement of women—problems that arise as multinational corporate investments demand large-scale changes in the modes of production—must also be recognized. Once, agricultural practices were family based, using indigenous species and serving the subsistence needs of the family and community. Now large-scale monoculture operations, designed for export markets, have left women largely without a role to play. This new exploitive approach to agriculture and industry gives rise to sweat shops and child labour because the demands of large-scale export-oriented production require low-cost labour, supported by lax social standards.

In addressing these sorts of costs, business advocates of sustainable development argue for more openness in trade and more efficient use of resources while looking toward long-term investments and being aware of the whole life-cycle of products from the extraction of raw materials to their disposal or the recycling of waste (Schmidheiny 1992: 8). More efficient use of resources can be achieved through technology transfer and through encouraging private ownership (Schmidheiny 1992: 9). Greater use of local entrepreneurship with clear rules and regulations will help bring developing countries to the level of industrialized countries, making trade relationships more competitive, equitable and just. Educating these nations in the skills needed to compete, then, should become a priority.

The Business Council for Sustainable Development acknowledges that the environmental problem is first and foremost an ecological one: overpopulation, the decline in renewable resources, an increased inability of waste "sinks" to absorb pollution, desertification and poverty (Schmidheiny 1992: 18). It also acknowledges the legitimacy of the precautionary principle: "the lack of scientific certainty should not be used as an excuse for postponing measures that prevent major, irreversible environmental degradation" (Schmidheiny 1992: 18). The council appears to adopt the WCED's definition of sustainability: meeting present needs without compromising the needs of future generations. Clean and equitable economic growth constitutes sustainability.

The Business Council for Sustainable Development is also committed to full-cost accounting, that is, internalizing environmental and social
costs. They believe that with internalization, efficiency in the use of
energy will increase and environmental degradation will decrease. Competition will demand it at both the production and the consumption ends.
More efficient and better-made products will become the norm. Moreover, business itself will ensure that the full cost of a product is reflected
in the price through self-regulation. Not only does business have an
interest in self-regulating, it should set the environmental standards as
well as monitor and set pollution-reduction goals because it generally
holds the information on technology and emissions (Schmidheiny 1992:
20). Since government regulation and intervention are more often than
not inefficient and too irregular between countries and regions to attain
standardization, business is in a far better position to regulate.

Clearly, from the business perspective, the "development" in "sustainable development" means "economic growth" (Schmidheiny 1992:
40), which is measured principally by the increase of capital and profitability. Much of this growth can be effected through the increased efficiency of a free and open market system and through open negotiation. In
one respect, the business approach is refreshingly straightforward and
clear. Transparency is a key concept that indicates a commitment to
openness and an acknowledgment that all sides around a negotiation
table represent their own interests. Integrating environmental and social
justice through the equity principle is done through negotiations between
business partners and even competitors as rules of fair competition are set
and all costs are made transparent. Furthermore, equity and social justice
are to be achieved by aiding developing nations in attaining levels of
affluence comparable to the developed world. This will enable them to
compete with industrialized nations in the marketplace and, at the same
time, open new markets. This increased global competition, equity and
economic freedom will, again, lead to greater efficiency in resource development and a decrease in waste. The entrepreneurial spirit will also be
engaged to determine new uses for waste products to effect an overall
decrease in environmental degradation while increasing standards of
living across the globe. Since money is a powerful incentive, it is far more
likely that this program would achieve justice and sound environmental
practice.

A Perverse Assumption

Certain assumptions go unquestioned in this promotion of sustainable
development. What exactly is being sustained here? Business is interested
in sustaining a certain type of relationship with the environment, an
exploitive/extractive one. Moreover, a certain type of interhuman rela-

tionship is being sustained, one defined in terms of the production-consumption relationship. Its primary valuations are determined by the acquisition of capital and the lifestyle that accompanies it. Since this approach is clearly built on classical utilitarian assumptions about our relationship to the environment and each other, human happiness and satisfaction are analyzed as results of wealth accumulation. This assumption, however, is coming increasingly under attack.

Social indicators research is increasingly demonstrating that wealth does not correlate with an increase in happiness or satisfaction with life (see Pearce 1993; Sagoff 1996). Why such social indicator research needs to be done sometimes defies the imagination, when it seems obvious that happiness is often inversely proportional to affluence. The more one acquires, the more one worries about protecting what has been acquired. Home and vehicle security systems are proliferating at an alarming rate, while the financial sector, which spends fortunes to deal with the protection and security of wealth, is also growing in leaps and bounds. Both indicate a parallel growth in the anxiety of the population, as it attempts to erase insecurity and fear. Interestingly we hear reminders from enforcement agencies that crime is in fact on the decline, yet security concerns are increasing. Feelings of insecurity, then, can be traced to the increase in affluence and the widening gap between rich and poor. This factor drives a wedge between wealth accumulation and happiness/satisfaction.

If anything, wealth accumulation and concern over affluence are more closely associated with the need for distraction (e.g., the entertainment industry) than with inherently satisfying activity. Furthermore, the more money becomes the means of commerce, the less free we are to engage in other forms of commerce, such as barter and sharing, which foster trust relationships. Affluence carries fear and suspicion into relationships, causing us to assume that others have ulterior motives for engaging our company. As a result, we are less free to develop relationships on the basis of openness since we are motivated to guard ourselves against the very exploitive motives that we attribute to others. Dissociating affluence from social or individual good is the first step we need to take. Failing to carry out this dissociation supports the de facto dominance of the market-based, corporate economic system. It also denies the legitimacy of other values as determinants of environmental and social policy, not through overt suppression of these values but through an obviating process whereby non-economic and non-market values are generally treated as superfluous, unnecessary and perhaps irrelevant.

It is also important to acknowledge that so much of what passes as values of the affluent are in fact values associated with the avoidance of fear and pain. If we examine how the financial sector has grown and influences people's behaviour we see two underlying motives. Advertising campaigns and the advice of financial advisors use fear and greed as motivating levers of action. It is fear of future insecurity or fear of being seen as irresponsible toward one's children that motivates people to invest in savings plans; it is greed that motivates people to invest in high-risk speculations. As financial security and wealth accumulation increasingly dominate individual and collective consciousness, it begins to appear less intelligible to adopt any values other than monetary ones as a basis for thinking about the conditions of security and happiness. This trend is resulting in a narrowing of people's purview with respect to the plurality of values and the types of relationships for which attunement to their full range of values calls. The trend, then, is tantamount to silencing those who desire to live according to valuations that are more closely, if not essentially, connected to a secure and happy life. It marginalizes other valuations, not only at political and economic levels but at the level of individual consciousness.

The business approach to justice also may serve more to undermine the conditions of freedom and respect than to support them. Michael Redclift (1987) has shown how market-defined measures of development, by their very nature, marginalize many people, especially women and indigenous communities. These groups may measure development differently from the market and in accordance with different values (e.g., community integrity, different modes of exchange and family solidarity). The introduction of market valuations and trade relations often undermines local economies and roles for women, as happens when technology transfers change local modes of production and the goods produced. In a local economy, needed foods are grown and gathered. As Vandana Shiva (1989) has shown in *Staying Alive*, the move toward development in India has virtually destroyed the social infrastructure and turned much of what was once a thriving and balanced ecosystem into wasteland and desert. The primary focus in her writing is the impact development has had on women since their work, which was based principally on subsistence and focused on the local economy, has been devalued and virtually eliminated.

Women's work—such as gathering and farming indigenous species, using manures and composts and gathering from forests—had taken centuries to evolve. A balance had been effected between human needs and ecological processes. With foreign development policy, delivered by what is known as the "green revolution," such practices were replaced by a focus on gross national product (Shiva 1989: 7), agribusiness (the heavy use of chemicals and machinery), monocultures (single crops) and male labour. Reforestation—the process of eliminating non-commercially viable species and replacing them with commercially viable ones (e.g., eucalyptus)—eliminated traditional sources of food and fibre. Women no longer had a role to play since their traditional functions were made irrelevant when men assumed the new task of farming for agribusiness corporations. She calls this process "maldevelopment" because it is both ruinous of the ecosystem and of women's place in it (Shiva 1989: 5).

When economically dominant countries invest in Third World countries (especially when utilizing the International Monetary Fund in the implementation of foreign aid policy), they do so with an emphasis on creating trade relations and transforming indigenous subsistence agriculture to export-oriented commodity production, which, in turn, results in a trend toward monocultures. Communities become dependent on trade, where once their mixed production allowed them to be autonomous. Prior to such foreign aid investments, these countries were almost certainly poorer in terms of monetary wealth (measured in gross domestic product), but they could be said to have been richer in other respects (e.g., their sense of community, place and independence). In these contexts, the business approach to sustainable development is, in effect, an imposition of values of so-called "developed" (Northern) countries onto so-called "developing" (Southern) countries. This is, in the eyes of the disenfranchised, another form of tyranny, brokered through transnational corporations. It is the same imposition of values on collective and individual consciousness that takes place in the industrialized world. It is an imposition that demands compliance to a way of seeing and valuing the world; it is, in fact, an imposition of a world view, largely defined in terms of Modern sensibilities and, therefore, fundamentally opposed to an ecological perspective. It remains unattuned to the valuational activity of those onto whom it imposes its values and, as a result, remains oblivious to the harm it commits.

These measures of development militate against expectations of justice, especially for indigenous cultures, because they are based on the assumption that these cultures are backward and in need of conversion toward a market economy, when in fact they were autonomous and had thriving economies before Northern development models were imposed. The contradiction shows that foreign aid in the form of sustainable development can be a form of colonization in the service of industrialized nations, as they search out sources of cheap labour and natural resources, captive markets and economic dominance.

The idea of internalizing environmental and social costs is suspect to its roots. It is, furthermore, highly unlikely to happen. When the number of parties negotiating prices is large (even more than two), internalization of costs becomes highly unlikely for a number of reasons (Panayotou, cited in Crabbé 1997: 24). With respect to non-point pollution sources (such as exhaust from cars), for instance, it is nearly impossible to identify who the polluters are and, therefore, who should pay for cleanup. Even for point sources, the complexity of causes and effects (e.g., determining whether the effluent from a pulp mill caused a particular person's cancer) is next to impossible. It is, indeed, likely that the majority of environmental costs will remain externalized (ignored) simply because many costs cannot be connected directly to their causes.

Talk about alternative fuel sources has been in the air for well over a decade, indeed since the writing of *Our Common Future* (World Commission on Environment and Development 1987), yet our consumption of fossil fuels continues to climb. The demand for power alone continues to increase as the perceived need for economic growth and productivity climbs. As urban areas grow, the demand for more transportation facilities (principally roads) and a greater supply of electricity rises. Hence, greenhouse gas emissions continue to rise. The contrast between the highly publicized commitment to curbing these emissions (e.g., from the Kyoto treaty) and emission increases indicates that business and government are not committed to the goals of full-cost accounting at all. Considerable doubt can be raised about the possibility of business being able to commit to full-cost accounting and about governments enforcing it. When spokespersons such as Milton Friedman (1996: 222–23) argue that the bottom line for corporate decision makers is to ensure profitability to shareholders, the hope for increased corporate social and environmental responsibility grows rather dim. The logic of the corporation is amoral; so, unless strict government regulations and enforcement measures are in place or unless executive officers are personally morally motivated, externalizing social and environmental costs will remain a strategy for increasing profitability. Moreover, as Hardin (1998: 521) has argued and as countless examples support, cheating will occur as part of this strategy, even where sanctions are in place. If enforcement is weak and the exploitation is of common property, the amoral nature of business thinking and valuing will lead to a continued externalizing of costs where tolerated. That business can be self-regulating and achieve the goals of justice and environmental protection is beyond imagining. In this respect, "sustainable development" is an oxymoron.

As indicated in *Changing Course* (Schmidheiny 1992), and as can readily be affirmed in statements of corporate sector representatives, ethical obligation is identified as legal obligation. According to Friedman (1996), this is the only ethics that business recognizes. Business is simply not in a position to determine principles and means for satisfying principles of social and environmental justice. It cannot be self-regulating nor can it be trusted to internalize costs, not because of its deceptive nature but because so many of its representatives quite explicitly assume that such regulation is not its place. Being a champion for the values of justice and ecological integrity is not in its purview.

Lip Service to Holism and Tolerance for Contradiction

Not only do sustainable development policies fail in addressing justice and demands for cost internalization, their commitment to holistic thinking in preamble statements is not reflected in policy substance. For example, while the WCED report (1987) announces its commitment to holism in preamble, we find that the operative definition of sustainable development is a strategy of limitation on the exploitation of resources, the direction of investments and the orientation of technological development and institutional change. It is imposed as a limiting (not an absolute) principle, which helps us to judge, among other things, to what extent the biosphere can "absorb the effects of human activities" (WCED 1987: 8–9). The report's specific recommendations require no reidentification of ourselves as parts of the environment, as its preamble suggests ought to be the case. It conforms entirely to classical anthropocentric, utilitarian values.

Granted, as a limiting principle and an implementation of holistic thinking, sustainable development is supposed to dampen exploitive energies. It requires a compromise or a decrease in the quantity of exploitation by affluent nations. This constraint is justified by the commitment to protect the interests and rights of future generations (WCED 1987: 43; see also Canada 1990: 15). For Third World nations, the situation seems different. Their loans need to be renegotiated and restructured, and their technology base needs to be expanded (WCED 1987: 87) so that they might better compete with industrialized nations. Indeed, to sustain a world economy, it is essential that global economic growth be revitalized. In practical terms, this means more rapid economic growth in both industrialized and developing countries, freer market access to the products of developing countries, lower interest rates, greater technology transfer and significantly larger capital flows. The overall assessment of the WCED is that the international economy must speed up world growth while respecting the environmental constraints (WCED 1987: 89). The difference between industrialized and developing nations ought, then, to be temporary.

When industrialized nations compromise both with developing nations and with the need to limit exploitation, the claim is that harmony will be produced. This claim is well grounded from industry's point of view, according to Kent Gilbreath (1989). Growing corporate concern for environmental issues is generating economically viable means for reducing pollution and sustaining healthy working conditions. Though to invest in environmentally friendly technology and to conduct research into environmentally safer products naturally reduces profits, such sacrifice in the spirit of compromise produces a common ground among environmental, industrial and social concerns. The result of compromise is a unification of human interest and environmental integrity. Indeed, respect is paid to environmental integrity through compromise; and the extent and methods of reduction, as struck through negotiation, make economic and environmental ends one (Gilbreath 1989: 73).

Rather than advocating for a new way of thinking and for principles that would allow us to develop a more ecologically oriented sense of self and moral sensibilities, sustainable development leads us merely to act more restrictively and prudently. It is enlightened self-interest couched in holistic language. Contrary to Gilbreath's assertions, compromise does not unify; it balances competing threats. If one is about to enter negotiations knowing that a compromise must be struck, the prudent tactic is to ask for more than what one actually wants or needs. To enter into negotiation, in the first place, is to assent to the fact that initial expectations will not be satisfied and that a second line of attack will become necessary. Skill in negotiating, furthermore, is measured by the amount one avoids losing and by how effectively a threat can be packaged against an opponent. Satisfaction, as attained through negotiation, has nothing to do with the mutual understanding of interests and satisfactions of the negotiating parties. It is found in not losing more than one would otherwise lose without the negotiation process. The process defines the opponent's interests as incompatible (competitive) with one's own interests and is motivated by the fear of loss. So, by incorporating the language of holism into preamble, sustainable development policies conflate two incompatible frames of reference or ways of thinking, which allows for the coopting of ecological concepts and principles. The language of holism is utilized, but the substance of holistic thought is absent. As sustainable development approaches to environmental management and protection dominate, then, they silence or render innocuous the voices supporting holistic thought and ecologically based ethics. Hence, the coopting of holistic language results in a continuance of exclusionary practice.

What the WCED calls the "effects of human activities," Paul Ehrlich and John Holdren (1989: 89) call "negative impacts on the environment." Human technological and agricultural activity have a net imbalancing effect (simplification) on the environment through the use of energy and in the production of pollution (Erhlich 1981:10). Such activity is incompatible with environmental integrity because it upsets ecosystemic balances, produces disharmony and destroys what harmony may have existed between human activity and environmental processes. Comparing the IJC commitment to zero discharge with sustainable development policies, as sponsored by business, we see how disparate commitments to ecological integrity and sustainability can be.

The WCED accepts that development and business are ecologically negative in value, but it deems such development harmonious with environmental integrity when it can be "absorbed" by the biosphere. Harmonization criteria are formulated in terms of thresholds beyond which ecosystems cannot recover from human damage (WCED 1987: 33). Pollution, the greenhouse effect, ozone layer depletion and deforestation are, supposedly, disharmonious only when abatement rates or toleration levels are exceeded. Harmonizing is a calculated response to the probability of our activities producing irreversible damage.

When the WCED formulates policies for integrating economic and environmental concerns, it is unambiguous about the meanings of terms it uses. There is no hint that it is calling us to adopt new ways of identifying with the environment, as does the IJC. Thus, phrases such as "if population size and growth are in *harmony* with the changing productive potential of the environment," "challenges are both *interdependent* and *integrated*, requiring comprehensive approaches" and "the normal functioning of the biosphere *as a whole*" (WCED 1987: 9, 13; my emphasis) appropriate holistic language for ulterior motives. Even in its advocating of wildland and genetic diversity preservation, the WCED's reasoning makes no mention of the need for reidentification: we may need these systems for the future commodities they might provide, but what those commodities might be we are presently unaware (WCED 1987: 148, 157). In other words, we need to protect and study wildlands only for potential exploitation. If there was no threat to human economic interests in the complete obliteration of wildlands, there would be no reason not to exhaust whatever resources they might have to offer. This utility-based foundation, therefore, turns sustainable development into a new instrument of domination (Sachs 1993b: xv).

Now, the need for sustainable development is largely based on our ignorance about ecosystems. Since we do not know how genetic diversity and symbiotic relationships between inhabitants and habitat work, we must be prepared to preserve and leave intact large tracks of wilderness. At the very least, we must not exploit beyond the point of recoverability (WCED 1987: 45) because we are ignorant of the number of factors involved in sustaining a resource base. Further, since we do not know how to engineer the environment to create a sustainable resource base, we cannot depend on technological fixes and scientific acumen to undo damages. "Sustainable development" means exploitation that does not backfire. Since the WCED publication (1987) and the 1992 U.N. Conference on the Environment and Development, however, governments and business appear to have concluded that we have overcome much of our ignorance, as they renew their commitment to "developmentalism" (Sachs 1993a: 3). Sachs (1993a) points out how the development agenda has overtaken and supplanted sustainability concerns. Where communities were once in sustainable relationships with their environments but were destroyed through foreign aid and other such programs, new modes of community and economic development have arisen to help cope with that destruction. These new forms of development are predicated on the assumption of economic prosperity, as defined by the dominant sector (Sachs 1993a: 9). More often than not, these forms of development are in fact renewed forms of degradation: oil exploration, clear-cutting logging practices and multinational corporate investment in manufacturing. As corporations and their supporting nations sponsor these new forms of development, they also increase their power and control over developing countries and communities. Again, Sachs (1993a: 10) points out: "'Sustainable development' calls for the conservation of development, not for the conservation of nature."

Contradiction, therefore, lies at the heart of sustainable development policy as applied by the dominant sector, leaving the application of "sustainable development" unprincipled and open to arbitrary decision. The reversal of meanings and intent pays lip service to holism, while effecting just the opposite of what it would mean to think holistically.

Strong and Weak Sustainability

For some, the disparity between these approaches to sustainability and the criticisms brought against sustainable development policies have inspired a distinction between strong and weak sustainability. Weak sustainability assumes that, as long as the aggregate stock of resources and products (capital) does not decrease, development is sustainable. That is, if the net worth of natural resources and industrial production does not decline, then development is sustainable. It follows that substituting manufactured products for natural resources constitutes sustainable development because, if natural resources declined but manufacturing increased, there would be a net equivalence. Weak sustainability assumes that all factors of production are substitutable (Crabbé 1997: 21). Accordingly, a continuation of the wanton destruction of resources would be justified if we could show a corresponding increase in manufacturing (Wackernagel and Rees 1996: 37). This is the sustainable development of business and the WCED. In contrast, strong sustainability would have us maintain natural resources (capital) at a constant, such that we would live off the "interest" or surplus, as measured by the ability of the ecosystem to recover from the perturbations caused by exploitation. "Natural capital" (the raw resources) is not treated as substitutable but as an essential factor of production (Crabbé 1997: 21). Its operative definition is, as a result, more vague, but it internalizes ethical principles, especially equity, between generations of humans (Crabbé 1997: 12).

Strong sustainability distinguishes between growth and development, where "development" applies to social, political and moral development and "growth" is restricted to economics. Economic growth may still be desirable through, for example, increased efficiency of technology, which would allow us to use natural resources (natural capital) more profitably without going beyond the natural carrying capacity of the land. Weak sustainability draws no distinction between growth and development because both are considered measures of exchange of capital.

Where the distinction between strong and weak sustainability is made explicitly, there are reasons to believe that commitments to transformation of thought and values will not turn out to be empty or reverse the intent of holistic language. But even in Wackernagel and Rees' (1996: 9) approach, the use of language favours economic/utilitarian valuations and modes of analysis, which could be turned against their intentions. The thrust of their approach is to draw land area equivalents to our extractive activity. The total amount of energy we consume can be roughly equated to the amount of land required to produce that energy (what they call "the ecological footprint"), such that a measure of the amount of the ecosystem that we use can be determined (Wackernagel and Rees 1996: 67). With this method they show how we in the industrial world each require an enormous amount of land (4.3 hectares) (Wackernagel and Rees 1996: 85) and how a city such as London actually requires twenty times more land than it occupies to feed its needs. The total consumption pattern of the world is calculated to be 30 percent in excess of the natural production capacity of the earth (Wackernagel and Rees 1996: 91).

As effective as such analyses are in drawing our attention to the environmental crisis, they do not address the underlying valuational problems. Wackernagel and Rees try to introduce ethical and valuational concerns, but they do so almost as an addendum. They identify non-material needs, the importance of developing our full potential and transforming the industrial society to serve this end, rather than the end of economic growth. However, their analytical framework adopts an economic form of costing and determining benefits that make it difficult to understand how these other concerns can be factored into the analysis. The approach continues to promote thinking about environmental issues principally in terms of what the environment can absorb (what we can get away with). As such, despite their support for strong sustainability measures, the tool for determining sustainability can be coopted and turned to support weak sustainability. The distinction between weak and strong sustainability indicates that a more explicit ethical grounding is needed for the vision of sustainability, since leaving such matters to the economic and political systems typically results in silencing the ethical dimension of ecological thought. Since these systems strongly tend to externalize non-economic valuations, without a more systematic way to incorporate non-quantifiable values, such as freedom, dignity, respect and recognition of the ecological valuations, the ecological footprint model will fall short of preventing a dismissal or coopting of voices struggling to have these more fundamental values recognized. Although these analytical tools can be an effective means for stimulating awareness of the deeper problems of sustainability and for addressing the quantifiable aspects of attunement, they should not be treated as sufficient measures for satisfying sustainability goals or as sufficient means for thinking ecologically.

The Ethics of Cost-Benefit Analysis

It is clear that cost-benefit analysis (CBA) is the principal and adaptive tool for determining sustainability, and it could take us some distance toward achieving recognition of a wide range of values, including justice. But understanding its roots and underlying commitment to efficiency rather than effectiveness is important for knowing when and how to incorporate such analyses. Environmental cost-benefit analysis stems from the 1940s and '50s, when economists attempted to apply the theory of the firm (corporation) to governments as a basis for evaluating projects. Financial gain of a project (e.g., a dam or a nuclear facility) was weighed against its financial cost, a conceptually simple and efficient tool. Concern for health was eventually calculated into the costs of environmental clean-up and repairing social upheaval (Estrin and Swaigen 1978: 43). Decisions, then, appeared objective and non-partisan, if approval or support for a project was based on a calculation showing benefits to be greater than costs.

The moral value of objectivity (being unbiased and non-arbitrary) in decision making and the apparent fairness of CBA recommend it as an ethically justifiable method, over and above its value as an efficient analytical tool. Costing the treatment of environment-related illness, such as radiation-related diseases, can be done statistically. Examining case studies to determine the likely increase in radiation poisoning and the approximate monetary cost of treatments allows costs to human health and the environment to be quantified. If applied in the same way to all people, this method appears fair, objective and unbiased. In this respect, CBAs are valuable and recommended as a tool of democratic process. The efficiency in policy and decision making expected of CBAs has undermined much of its democratic value, however.

If we ask most people to name a sum of money beyond which they could be considered unreasonable if they would not accept it in exchange for their life, we would get a fairly clear response: no amount of money is acceptable as an equivalent to the value of a human life. Insofar as we assert a fundamental right to life and abhor and criminalize slavery, we deny the legitimacy of monetary valuations of human life. Many aesthetic and spiritual values cannot be costed in the monetary scheme, either. How much money could someone of a religious faith be expected to charge for abandoning their faith? Cost-benefit decision-making principles, because they measure the rectification of injustice and weigh the plurality of values in terms of monetary values, come precariously close to proposing that we are unjust to refuse to abandon our religious beliefs and values for a certain sum of money. The question itself will appear out of order or inappropriate to believers. The assumption that faith can be costed on a monetary scale is by its very nature offensive. For this reason alone, there is good reason to de-couple CBAs and justice/moral issues. Although efficient for decision making, they can be completely ineffective, even violatory, as a means for recognizing certain types of fundamental values.

Cost-benefit analyses violate many human values and, indeed, rights because they view human values on the same plane as commodities to be bought and sold on the market. The act of costing human lives, moral or religious beliefs or spiritual dimensions of life in order to weigh them against economic benefits is precisely to treat them as overhead or production costs. It demonstrates a contempt for moral values, both because it reduces human value to a commodity and because it ignores the distinctive form of decision making that moral values require. Moral judgment requires deliberation on what is right and wrong and how to protect individuals and the community from violations, including violations of treating certain types of values as equivalent to monetary value. We have abolished slavery and child labour on these grounds. We must be careful not to allow for a reintroduction of the same mode of thinking for the sake of efficiency and clarity. Moral principles designed to protect freedom, dignity and self-esteem are non-negotiables; they cannot be traded in the market.

At a legal level, the American Supreme Court decision in *Sierra Club* v. *Morton*) indicated that economic development values are not always commensurable with and cannot always override scenery and historical and wildlife values. Although the Sierra Club failed to win the legal battle to save an ecosystem, having failed to demonstrate that their members would be threatened by development in the particular area of dispute— that is, that direct harm would come to them—the club won something of a moral battle. This decision together with an earlier case—the Scenic Hudson Ruling of 1965 (cited in Barbour 1980: 114)—established that a plaintiff could have standing for a court case, even if no economic interest had been violated. Non-economic values were considered distinct sorts of values, which could have legal purchase. The legal system, then, recognizes that even non-fundamental values (e.g., aesthetic values) ought not always to be recast as economic values but must be treated differently.

In Canada, South Moresby Island in the Queen Charlotte Islands became protected from logging when it was established as a national park and partial Indian reserve. This decision was based on two types of non-economic values, aesthetic/heritage and cultural. In February 1992, the British Columbia government announced the formation of a Commission on Resources and Environment to establish a land use and conflict resolution mechanism as a "grassroots" analysis of multistakeholder interests in setting policy for forestry and land use. This commission was to ensure that non-economic values would be included in the policy- and decision-making process. In 1991, Ontario announced the formation of a Forest Policy Panel to solicit as wide a range of stakeholder views on forestry use and management as possible, partly for the same reason. The Canadian Council of Forestry Ministers (CCFM) upholds a plurality of values, including the intrinsic value of the forests and their spiritual and heritage values (Canadian Council of Forestry Ministers 1992, 1995).

Aboriginal land claims and claims to sovereignty are setting a political and legal precedent for determining how a wider range of values, including non-economic ones, and perspectives are to be incorporated into environmental policy. Canada has recognized aboriginal rights and the validity of land claims in Section 35 of the *Constitution Act, 1982*. Basic human rights to live in accordance with one's cultural values are here recognized independent of economic concerns. Chapter 22 of the United Nations' *Agenda 21* (United Nations 1992) states:

> Indigenous people and their communities shall enjoy the full measure of human rights and fundamental freedoms without hindrance or discrimination.... In view of the interrelationship between the natural environment and its sustainable development and the cultural, social, economic and physical well-being of indigenous people, national and international efforts to implement environmentally sound and sustainable development should recognize, accommodate, promote and strengthen the role of indigenous people and their communities.

Among other elements to be protected are the autonomy and integrity of indigenous communities and cultures and the interrelationship with the land, which is itself recognized as sustainable development. In the legal and political arenas, then, non-monetary, non-quantifiable moral values have been recognized and received into policy. It is false to claim that CBAs better satisfy justice values where direct attempts to do so fail. Moreover, reducing moral decision making to CBA is a recognized perversion of moral decision making.

To understand the sorts of values recognized by the United Nations, we need to develop appropriate and explicit procedures to account for such values. Otherwise, they will be distorted or misrepresented. This procedure involves understanding the different ways of knowing and the context, according to which valuations acquire meaning. The procedure needs to undertake to respect these valuations and determine what types of communication are necessary to understand them.

Again, we gain direction by examining the "willingness to pay" analysis proposed under CBA. By asking people what they would be willing to pay in exchange for protecting a wildlife habitat, for instance, it seems possible to respect the autonomy and range of values of individuals and to provide a quantification analysis for valuing wildlands and other environmental, even community, values. Mark Sagoff (1993: 241), however, has shown that over one half of the people who were asked how much they would be willing to pay to prevent the development of a coal electric generating plant in Wyoming national parks responded with "an infinite amount" or "zero amount." People were not willing to accept the idea of trading dollars for pollution rights.

In another instance, Walt Disney Enterprises' submission to the Forest Service in 1969 to develop Sequoia National Park as a resort (Sagoff 1992: 77) was turned down by the United States Congress. Although the idea was to attract up to 14,000 paying visitors a day, which would make the park pay for itself and provide a profit, and to allow for the exercise of recreation, heritage and aesthetic values, the proposal was rejected on ethical and cultural grounds. Congress rejected economic cost-benefit assessments and denied Disney's assertion that the diverse values at stake were, indeed, compatible just because they could be subjected to quantification analyses.

By answering "zero" and "infinite amount" to the questionnaires reported by Sagoff (1993), respondents defined the question as a non-starter. Such a question should never be asked in the first place. Doing so violates non-negotiable values and expresses a contempt both for these values and for the moral decision-making process. Attempting to quantify and weigh all values in a single calculus distorts how and why people hold certain values and perverts the way we think about moral responsibility.

Now, the perversion of reinterpreting non-negotiable values in terms of monetary values does not imply that fundamental values cannot be quantified in some way or other. For example, in triage situations (emergency situations where large numbers of patients are categorized in order of treatability), physicians and nurses must often weigh the hopes of recovery against the value of life. Among the three triage categories, those on the third tier are given lower priority than those on the first because they stand the least chance of responding positively to treatment. Triage cases demonstrate that we can weigh the value of one life against another in a quasi-quantifiable manner and that sometimes we must do so in order to treat people as fairly and justly as possible.

Weighing fundamental values against one another is not a matter of assigning some exchange or market value to them, however. It is to make a distinctly moral judgment on how best to salvage the values of concern in the most compassionate and just manner possible. At times we are forced to seek some quantification measures to resolve conflicts between fundamental values, but the quantification is not monetarily based. The moral process of weighing values appreciates dilemmas and is not considered valid until the dilemma is clearly understood. But such weighing is not based on the type of calculation typical of CBA because the result is not a definite conclusion but a judgment. Judgment conducted in the context of a struggle to understand and respect is a very different operation from a calculation implemented to provide clear and unambiguous results. As such, judgment requires attunement to the basic values of people and how they experience their satisfaction.

Risk-Benefit Analysis

Risk-benefit analysis (RBA) is another tool for quantifying environmental values, one which goes further in recognizing the plurality of values and the different types of accountability associated with them. It deals more explicitly with the dual concerns of environmental well-being and justice. Like the concept of cost, "risk" carries an ambiguity, which must also be sorted out. Risk-benefit analyses were once based on the assumption that risks could be evaluated in monetary terms. Ian Barbour (1980: 172–73) explains that a much stronger distinction had to be made between costs and risks because human life is characterized by non-monetary values, which can be threatened but not necessarily costed. Some environmental engineers, interestingly, have also recognized the distinction between risk analysis and cost analysis. Richard Conway (1982: xiv) shows how the public concern over hazardous chemicals affects the engineer's decision by determining whether a chemical will be introduced into the market, the constraints on its use, how it is to be transported and its distributional availability. He explains that the hazardous nature of many industrial chemicals is perceived as a threat and not merely a cost. Threats and costs, then, are to be judged differently and by different sectors of society. The engineer may determine how best to produce, transport and store a chemical, and an economist may determine how cost effective these methods might be, but the public is the ultimate judge of whether a particular chemical should be accepted or banned. Banning of chemicals has nothing to do with cost effectiveness; it has to do with whether people are prepared to accept the risk of introducing a chemical into their environment.

According to Conway (1982: xiv), there are two elements to risk assessment: "analysis" and "assessment," and these terms represent distinct elements. Analysis is the collection and examination of scientific and technical data. Assessment includes evaluation of the comprehensive political, social and political factors. As Shrader-Frechette and McCoy (1993) argue, professional or scientific consultants conduct analysis, limiting their role to that of technical adviser regarding considerations of validity and reliability of research results. Since risk, acceptable risk and tolerable levels are matters concerning social values and moral responsibilities, the engineer and research scientist must be careful not to assess acceptability. So, increasingly, public hearings and stakeholder fora are being conducted to assess the risks involved in determining, for instance, acceptable pollution levels. A stakeholder workshop on ambient air quality, sponsored by Environment Canada (Canada, Environment Canada 1997), is a good example. In this workshop, which I attended, public opinion was solicited and supposedly incorporated into the development of risk assessments. Scientific analysis of significant levels of exposure to various pollutants (e.g., when lung-related mortality and morbidity increase, as measured by admissions to hospitals) were presented. Various stakeholders were then given an opportunity to respond to what should be considered an acceptable level. In this case, scientific evidence showed that 15 parts per million (ppm) of particulate matter of a certain size (known as PM5) is the statistically significant point at which morbidity and mortality increase. Industry representatives argued that, with the present technology, 150 ppm was being emitted but, with a fifteen-year technology turn-around time (the time it takes for investments in technology to be cost effective), the next generation of technological innovations would allow industry to reduce PM5 to about 35 ppm. Hence, a fifteen-year target for reducing PM5 would be 35 ppm. Other stakeholders (e.g., the Canadian Lung Association and Health Canada) argued that the target should be set much more aggressively, partly because the cost to the health care system is not borne by industry. As a participant observer, I noted that accepting any level above 15 ppm allows for the killing of people and the violation of their right to security of the person. In this way, different perspectives were introduced, analyzed and finally reported, usually by a team of researchers. Research results and estimates were presented for public commentary and various means of incorporating public input were utilized to "assess" risk.

It has also been recognized that the analytical aspect of risk assessment, defined in terms of probability of outcome, is not calculable in purely scientific and clearly quantifiable terms. Risk may be seen and valued differently by different people and so should be counted differently. On the face of it, risk assessment seems far more responsive to the different valuations relevant to environmental management and policy than is CBA.

Risk assessment is not free of language manipulation, however. Risk, for instance, has often been assessed by comparing the danger value to other forms of activity. The risk of being killed in a nuclear disaster is, according to some, less than the risk we take of being run over by an automobile. It is also less than the risk of dying in a plane crash. If we are prepared to accept a high degree of risk in clearly dangerous situations, then we should be prepared to accept a lesser degree of risk. Proponents of nuclear energy have used this type of argument to show that, given the acceptability of higher forms of risk, lower forms of risk are justifiable.

Comparing situations in this way is perverse because it conflates two very different notions of risk. Plane travel, walking and driving a car are not in themselves dangerous activities because travel and locomotion are not intrinsically dangerous to us. The danger lies in what might happen during travel. Exposure to nuclear radiation is, however, dangerous in itself. Defending the use and production of nuclear energy by using such comparisons would justify exposing people to all sorts of dangerous chemicals and situations, just as long as it could be shown that the risks of dying from such exposure, taken one by one, is less than getting killed in a car accident. Since exposure to nuclear radiation is involuntary, we could also justify exposing someone to a blindfolded firing squad if the probability of them actually hitting their target is lower than or as low as getting hit by a car in daily life.

These types of argument conflate the concepts of risk and hazard. A hazard is something one avoids, by definition, because it is dangerous, unhealthy and injurious. We try to eliminate hazards (Winner 1992: 99). A risk, in contrast, is the sort of thing we are willing to take if there is a potential to gain by taking it. Investing in the stock market or speculating on land are considered risks, as is the use of elaborate plays in a game. We stand to lose money or get scored upon by taking the risk, but we also stand to gain much more than by remaining conservative. As Winner (1992: 101) remarks, risks are endeavours we voluntarily undertake in a calculated response to a given set of obstacles. Hazards and threats are not. When we face a risk, the values associated with risk-taking are mostly positive. Risk-taking involves a virtue of courage and steady nerves. Facing a hazard is not associated with virtues because it is the sort of thing that is to be avoided in the first place. To enter into a hazardous situation is associated not with courage but with foolishness or, perhaps, pathology.

Risk assessment, owing to the tendency toward conflation, can serve as a tool of marginalization. Intercultural risk assessment is of particular concern because of what we might choose as indicators of risk. Suppose we want to determine the risk of a particular pollutant to fish populations in the Great Lakes region. Further, we identify salmon populations and their growth rates as a key indicator of risk because the sports fishery in the region depends on the salmon. It makes sense to focus on the salmon because they are of primary recreational and economic concern. We may find that the pollutant primarily travels to the bottom of the lake and so does not affect the salmon population directly. The risk to the fishery, then, is judged to be minimal and the industry that depends on being able to pollute will be allowed to develop.

Ground and deep water feeders such as white fish, however, will be affected. As one of the traditional food sources and commercial species for the Anishnaabe (Ojibway) communities in the region, white fish are a key indicator. These communities might care little for the salmon and may prefer that they were not planted in the Great Lakes at all (since their presence violates the Creator's intention). By identifying the salmon population for risk assessment, researchers ignore the risk to the aboriginal community and, in effect, support a poisoning of the community. At the same time, they ignore the hazard that the salmon represent to the spiritual beliefs of the community.

Like cost-benefit analyses, risk assessments can hide as much as they reveal about the consequences involved in developments. Risk assessment, like cost-benefit assessment, then, should not be used as justification for a development. Its proper place is in the realm of information gathering, once the concepts of risk are thoroughly identified and understood in light of different values and perspectives. The notion "acceptable risk" should be abandoned since it presupposes some general criterion of acceptability that cannot be determined without knowing what people value and what the effects of a decision will be on those values. If not abandoned, appropriate language should, at least, be used to indicate what is in fact being accepted from the perspective of those who could be affected.

As a collection and examination of technical and scientific data to measure the probability and severity of adverse affects, risk assessment can be a valuable tool in weaning us off damaging and dangerous technologies and modes of development. Since it requires two levels of evaluation and justification, it fits with strong sustainability as an assessment tool. The main problem for the risk analyst, once the physical consequences are estimated, is ensuring that the risks to the network of valuations are not ignored. Further, since ecology is not an exact science and cannot tell us what the consequences of any action will be, risk assessments cannot be precise or complete. Therefore, justification of any proposed action is always underdetermined, and the precautionary principle ought to apply as much to risk assessment as to management decisions.

Discussion of CBAs and RBAs indicates how much thinking ecologically about environmental policy would help structure and supply content. Like the principle of suitability, which is developed to describe the purposiveness presupposed in evolutionary development, a principle of suitability for identifying and analyzing values could be developed to shape the concepts of cost and risk in the process of weighing values. Where the types of frameworks and language are unsuitable, they should be abandoned and restructured in accordance with a deeper understanding of the principle of inclusion and the harm principle.

Sustainable Development and the Third World

Having examined how sustainable development policy can result in the opposite of its avowed intention, a more detailed discussion of how it leads to a cooptation of justice values and a deepening of injustice is in order. Wolfgang Sachs (1993a: 4–5) begins his story of sustainable development with a speech delivered by U.S. President Harry Truman on January 20, 1949. In his speech, the poorer countries, especially those of the South, were called "underdeveloped areas" for the first time. A world view that named North American lifestyle as the standard against which all others are to be measured was then imposed on the rest of the world in the form of foreign aid and trade relations. American foreign policy henceforth was directed at helping all nations compete in the development race. Obviously, the policy mandated not only injection of capital and technology transfers, but a transformation of cultural norms to suit trade relationships with the North (U.S.). The earlier description of the green revolution in India (Shiva 1989) is often used to exemplify the types of alterations in a peoples' culture, society and economic system that are implied by "development."

Although development was supposed to eliminate poverty, it created an entirely new form of poverty. Truman, from his Northern affluent perspective, looked upon the Third World in its mere subsistence lifestyle and judged it as impoverished; but this lifestyle was considered rich by those who could live comfortably, enjoying a sense of place and belonging. But, from the Indian point of view, if it was a type of poverty, that poverty was not necessarily associated with deprivation. After the green revolution, argues Shiva (1989: 10), poverty and deprivation became synonymous. Clearing formerly carefully cultivated forests caused desertification; overirrigation of once rich soils caused salination and depleted water supplies, which could not be replenished due to the destruction of recharge areas (forests). These factors created deprivation, ironically, through injecting capital, and transferring technologies became an instrument of impoverishment.

A second irony, according to Sachs (1993a: 9), is that the North now sees this situation as further opportunity for new forms of development. To relieve community dysfunction, "community or social development" initiatives have been engaged. "Rural development" programs and problems of social justice are to be handled by "equitable development" strategies. All of these measures are, in effect, modes of cultural imperialism, leveraged by a situation brought on by the North's foreign aid policies in the first place.

Shiva (1989: 23) views the profit motive accompanying the development agenda as violating both the ecosystem and justice. Efficiency directives of the profit motive create a situation in which extraction and exploitation destroy the stability of ecosystems and, therefore, the communities dependent on them. Moreover, the imposition of the North's technology and scientific basis for knowledge obviates the indigenous knowledge gained through generations of adaptation to the ecosystem and replaces traditional crops with high-yield strains that require high energy inputs in the form of chemical fertilizers, pesticides or herbicides. Not only are the forests and water supplies depleted to supply the agribusiness demands, but soils are depleted of worms and microbial activity, leaving them virtually incapable of production without external energy input. For those who live with the land, these economic and production efficiencies are perceived as acts of violence against the land; the North's science is seen as the manager of that violence.

The North's type of development is reductive. It reduces the ecosystem to a factory and the people to mere ciphers in the world trade game. Once the chaos of undermining the social system sets in, further reduction of social and ecological values to the North's economic values can hardly be resisted. With this chaos, the North can then position itself as a saviour and deepen the development process. Development, then, is a form of colonization (Shiva 1989: 90) that promises aid and solution while closing off options for communities. This kind of closure leads to uniformity but not to equality. Redclift (1987: 42) argues that what Shiva (1989: 91) calls a uniformity results from assuming a classical economic model in determining the character of what can count as goods (defined in terms of the market). Hence, the valuational perspective of the developer nations is that Third World nations are backward and in need of knowledge input from the developed or industrialized nations (Redclift 1987: 41). Survival or subsistence goods are ignored, partly because they cannot be recognized within the model and partly because of a refusal on the part of the dominant countries to criticize their own colonizing values. They do not see that shifts in the locus of power (especially in the arenas of food production and natural resource management) from local communities to central governments and multinational corporations are acts of colonization (Shiva 1989: 97). Or, if they do see, they choose either to ignore it or to reinterpret their behaviour. Sustainable development, then, has been a tool for coopting, not exercising justice concerns, in a bid to advance the economic colonization interests of the North. Ecology has been coopted under the sustainable development umbrella and the commitment to technology transfer.

Most powerful institutions in the North continue to support sustainable development, although gestures toward restitution for some of the previously mentioned consequences of development are being made. For example, the United Nations held a conference on women and the environment in which many Third World women's concerns were addressed (see Food and Agriculture Organization of the United Nations 1999). The

conference, entitled "High-Level Consultation on Rural Women and Information," was sponsored by the Food and Agriculture Organization
(FAO) of the United Nations and held at the FAO's Rome headquarters on
October 4–6, 1999. It sought to recognize women's contributions to agriculture and to find means for integrating the information they could
provide with other available information so that greater efficiency in food
production could be achieved (Food and Agriculture Organization of the
United Nations 1999). The concerns of women in development seem to be
understood, and concerted effort to be inclusive has been made; but it is
interesting that the issue of men and the values typically espoused by men
are not being addressed. Clearly, the U.N. has no intention of program-
ming sustainable development to diminish the male-dominated sectors of
the economy and return the systems in which women once played key
roles. Words such as "integration," when describing the inclusion of
women, in the end remain synonymous with cooptation or assimilation.

Nicholas Hildyard (1993: 22) points out a number of other poignant
omissions in the U.N.'s efforts to achieve sustainable development, particularly those discussed at the Rio Summit of 1992. While a convention
on biodiversity was discussed, free trade was ignored. Forestry was discussed, but not agribusiness; climate was discussed, but not automobiles.
How the poor might achieve sustainable livelihoods was seen as a crucial
point of discussion, but the silence on how the rich could do so was
deafening. Such omissions betray the intention to continue imposing
Northern values onto the development agenda.

Much the same can be said of the application of sustainable development to North American First Nations. After centuries of disempowering
indigenous peoples and implementing explicit assimilation and even
genocide programs, North American governments continue along the
colonization routes. First by subscribing to the mantra of globalization,
and second by imposing "economic development" and "community development" policies similar to those effected internationally, these governments attempt to enable aboriginal communities to enter into the
market economy. Despite the acknowledgment in Chapter 22 of the
United Nations' *Agenda 21* (1992) that traditional practices of indigenous
peoples are sustainable and models of sustainability, the approach is to
continue assimilating (integrating) these communities into the body economic.

One other important, but necessarily brief, note is that much of the
environmental movement not only has been coopted by governments and
big business but has itself turned into a business or industry of its own.
This process may have begun with Gro Harlem Brundtland's establishment of the WCED's Centre for Our Common Future soon after *Our
Common Future* (World Commission on Environment and Development
1987) was released. The centre's agenda was to promote the messages

contained in the WCED's report by stimulating debate and dialogue on its contents. Increasingly, we find non-governmental organizations (NGOs) developing interests in sustaining themselves as organizations rather than as voices for environmental protection. L. Stark (cited in Finger 1993: 44) notes that NGOs are now seen as collaborators with governments, "providing the services that governments cannot." They act as partners in the dialogue with government and industry and as carriers of responsibility for the environment as well as signs of hope. NGOs such as the World Conservation Union (IUCN), the World Wide Fund for Nature (WWF) and the World Resources Institute (WRI), who are among the best organized and most influential groups, have been incorporated into the sustainable development agenda and are presented as the voice of the NGOs. Marginalization and even silencing of other non-cooperative groups has resulted from this relationship, as has the sponsorship of further industrial development (Finger 1993: 47).

Finger's assertion rings true, as experience with government fora indicates. During the Ambient Air Quality Objectives stakeholder forum, which included a cross-section of stakeholders, the fact that the negotiated goal for reducing particulate matter to 35-50 ppm when 15 ppm was shown to be the threshold for increased morbidity and mortality indicated how much industry ruled the process. At the outset of the meeting, we were instructed that we were not in a negotiation process. Nevertheless, industry's representatives, whose positions were well established and rehearsed, dominated the forum and so managed to control the frame of reference that was to be used. A diagram of circles representing the perspectives to address was produced in which economics by far played the dominant role; social, ethical and legal perspectives were aggregated and allocated a relatively minor role. Not even science could compete with the size of the circle representing the economic perspective. The representatives from Pollution Probe, the Canadian Lung Association and other NGOs largely played into the hands of industry by allowing so much of the talk to be about partnerships and cooperation among sectors. Those groups who tried to represent the interests of the ill and dying were thereby coopted by the process, in effect, to manage the continuation of killing and suffering. Insofar as cooperation continues, these NGOs have become a voice for industry and a handmaiden promoting its agenda. In the end, many of the internal values that motivate concern for human health and well-being were forced into a reinterpretation because external values (economic) were allowed to determine the frame of reference.[1]

Consequently, Third World and NGO considerations reflect the need for a continual vigilance on the policy-making process and on how the ethics of environmental/foreign aid policy is formulated. Sustainability, then, is one of those concepts and policy directives that constantly needs to be assessed and modified through the exercise of thinking ecologically.

Sustainability: Some Necessary Inversions

"What is to be sustained and for whom is it to be sustained?" is one of the many questions presented by the preceding critique. When examining the most influential and ubiquitous formulations of sustainability (i.e., sustainable development), clearly those who wield the greatest economic and political power have the greatest voice in answering the question. Other voices have little influence, not because the values and moral principles that would bring their voices into the policy arena are overtly silenced, as under totalitarian regimes, but because they are misidentified and underanalyzed. Moreover, superficial democratic processes (e.g., voting) promote the perception of fairness and justice for the dominant group, while suppressing it for the dominated groups. Speaking to the deeper motivations and concerns over sustainability, then, requires expanding the analytical base to include the plurality of values and perspectives affected by policy. It also requires a deepening of the analytical process by ensuring that the affected values and relevant moral principles are appropriately understood and included in the process. Respect for other ways of knowing and identifying fundamental values, especially where these values are non-negotiable, needs to be established and entrenched into such processes.

Issues pertaining to sustainability, therefore, are connected to the ethics of attunement as much at national and international policy development levels as at the personal level. Some of the general implications of sustainability are: 1) to determine an alternative to the dominant economic paradigm; 2) to recognize long-standing local knowledge of ecosystem functions; 3) to recognize the economies of long-standing indigenous peoples as they have evolved in sustainable relations with their environment; 4) to become particularly aware of the logic of imperialism operating in policy. More and more ecological science is pointing to the conclusion that we cannot manage ecosystems from the top down but must manage from the bottom up (for example, Shrader-Frechette and McCoy 1993: 1). This approach requires cognizance of locally determined knowledge as much as or more than it requires generalizable knowledge. The same message has come from social and political critics of economic imperialism (see Sachs 1993a; Shiva 1989).

At the same time, however, sustainability involves the development of the dialectical opposite of a more global ethic. Sustainability demands an ethic that exercises the human being's capacity to know, analyze and value in ways that are inclusive of other perspectives and valuations. Since everyone desires to be respected—the main criticism of dominating countries is that they do not respect the values of dominated countries and communities—there is an implicit recognition of a universal ethic. We see at its core a need for recognition of the conditions of freedom (as autonomy). While, in a traditional liberal mode we might call this ethic an ethic of tolerance, we need to go further to think of it as an ethic of inclusion. Tolerance suggests bearing with one another, while inclusion suggests attunement to one another's valuations and interpretations of basic human values (e.g., self-esteem and dignity). With such an ethical bearing, we are far less likely to think about ethical responsibilities in traditional liberal ways, which, in the end, foster acceptance of default modes of analysis (especially economic ones). These default modes are such only because of the dominance of those who employ them. If standards of legitimacy in democratic process were to include responsibility for attunement to other perspectives and values, we would gain some ground in developing a more just and ecologically sound approach to sustainability.

An inversion of the conceptions and principles of sustainable development, then, is in order. In a manner parallel to Leopold's inversion of the biotic pyramid, an ethic of attunement inverts the imperialistic valuations of the dominant society, such that our way of thinking about policy alters in radical ways without abandoning the fundamental concepts of liberal democracy. Acknowledging the more affirming conception of freedom—a non-insular version—helps to show how this inversion can take place. Beginning with an application of the harm principle, as developed in Chapter Five, we would expect that, if the affluent 20 percent of the world were to act on the principle, their 80 percent of the world's consumption would be reduced and their use of 80 percent of the world's pollution sinks would diminish immensely. This reduction would not principally be owing to more equitable distribution of wealth (the WCED approach) but to a reduction in consumption and other forms of exploitation in the developed countries. In North America, we would be as concerned about modeling our relationship to the ecosystem after the relationship of indigenous communities to their systems as we are about aiding the impoverished to reach a level of well-being and sustainability. Rich and poor would be far less radically separated because issues of impoverishment and wealth, not just impoverishment, would be addressed. While environmental policy cannot directly address the consumption habits of North Americans (e.g., by restricting the freedom to consume), it can champion educational efforts to draw attention to the values and ways of coexisting practised by communities that are more ecologically compatible with the ecosystem. Like the IJC, it can promote the restoration of indigenous species and protection of wild spaces. But more importantly with respect to the harm principle, it can more directly devalue consumerism and support more small community-oriented lifestyles. Funding initiatives to research and plan for such development is one way to support the principle.

Foreign policy needs to adopt the approach of leading by following as it attempts to empower ecologically and socially dysfunctional communities to find ways of developing according to their own natures and ecological exigencies. Just as the U.S. is prepared to develop and enforce economic sanction policies against Cuba and other nations, ostensibly with moral justification, so could it, and all democratic countries respecting freedom, institute policies that would identify current development agendas as harmful both to other people and ecosystems. However unlikely they are to succeed, attempts at leading by following and intervening where necessary to protect local autonomy from oppressors are central to respecting conditions of community freedom and adhering to the harm principle.

Inverting the dominant and negative version of the harm principle to a positive principle would highlight our responsibility to be cognizant of the particular characteristics of the communities affected by environmental and foreign aid policies. Being more supportive of the precautionary principle, in itself, would go a long way toward reducing harm to the ecosystem and communities, but we need to go further by developing the positive version of the harm principle.

A few gestures toward inversion of our ways of understanding and policy priorities do hold some promise. Despite its overall commitment to the WCED version of sustainable development, the OSEM (Ontario Society of Environmental Management) states in its Principle 5: "Sustainable development must not endanger the natural systems that support life on Earth; the atmosphere, the waters, the soils, and living beings" (Nelson and Edsvik 1990). After articulating its commitments to full-cost accounting and living off the interest, rather than the capital, of the land, the Ontario Round Table on Environment and Economics (1992) states: "The quality of social and economic development must take precedence over quantity"; "We must respect nature and the rights of future generations." In 1994, this principle was supplemented as follows: "A sustainable community is one which has respect for other life forms and supports biodiversity" (Ontario Round Table on Environment and Economics 1994). Here, we have a sustainable development policy statement that seems to align well with the concerns of sustainability.

The apparent alignment is betrayed in the way sustainable development initiatives are evaluated, however. Performance evaluations—analyses of how well policies and programs have achieved their objectives and satisfied their principles—of sustainable development have begun to recognize this ethical problem, albeit sporadically and superficially. In one of the most thorough evaluations of sustainable development initiatives initiated by the WCED report (1987), an initiative known as the Bellagio Project (Hardi and Zdan 1997), the International Institute for Sustainable Development (IISD) attempts to respond to the U.N.'s call for devices to measure the progress of sustainable development policies around the world. The Bellagio Project ostensibly is predicated on three holistic principles: that analyses must consider systems, including human and ecosystems as wholes; that both economic and non-economic elements be factored in; and that such elements as poverty and dependency on ecosystems be considered essential. It denies exclusive reliance on GNP measures for assessing progress and considers justice and gender issues to be critical. Acknowledging that sustainable development is values-based across a wide spectrum, the IISD recognizes that the process of evaluation is normative in an ethically fundamental way. At the same time, measurement must be based on clearly defined indicators (Hardi and Zdan 1997: 13, 16, 17).

Like the World Commission on the Environment and Development, the Bellagio Project, in its report, acknowledges the need for deeper ethical transformation in policy and evaluation and it hints at the need for inversion. However, there remains either considerable resistance to or lack of understanding about the ethical dimension. In two of the case studies presented in the report (i.e., Costa Rica and Ontario Hydro), economic competitiveness is identified as a key element for sustainability. Competitiveness is just another word for economic growth. This analysis is well in keeping with the principle of externalizing environmental and social costs. Nothing much has changed. Economic growth remains the focus, while the other, so-called central, democratic values remain marginalized in the evaluation.

However, in other cases (i.e., evaluations of the government of British Columbia), far more emphasis is placed on ecosystem sustainability and on the coordination of governmental and public participation (Hardi and Zdan 1997: 38).

> For this assessment, human well-being is defined as a healthy population living in a thriving set of communities with established and respected systems of governance, justice, education, and social support; a prosperous and vibrant economy; a well-built infrastructure; flourishing arts, cultural and recreational activities; and opportunities for citizen involvement in decision-making processes affecting their interests. (Hardi and Zdan 1997: 41)

Economic growth remains important, but commitments to noneconomic values steer the focus away from growth and onto other conditions of community wellbeing. Hardi and Zdan are also concerned to include those elements of productivity that are not included in the GDP (e.g., women's unpaid work) (1997: 42).

> [Further,] in this project, ecosystem well-being is defined as a condition in which ecosystems maintain their diversity, produc-

tivity and resilience, such that they are able to provide a wide range of choices and opportunities for the future and are able to adapt to forces of change. Ecosystem well-being does not imply keeping things as they are today or returning to how they were 200 years ago. Rather, it implies maintaining the evolutionary capacity of the ecosystem. (Hardi and Zdan 1997: 42)

In the IISD/Bellagio report, we can see how economic development and sustainability criteria vie for prominence and how the definition and assessment of sustainability remains ambiguous. At the same time, the ten-year interim between the WCED (1987) and the IISD (Hardi and Zdan 1997) reports indicates that some movement toward a more ethically sound and inverted approach to sustainability is occurring. Nevertheless, with this progress comes dangers that the Bellagio report does not identify. We have seen how difficult it is to recognize and acknowledge the multiplicity of values and their contexts. How economic, ecological, moral, political and other values are weighed, which ones are included and how they are included are questions that are not clearly answered in the report. Missing in all assessments is a thorough analysis of the values involved. For an analysis that recognizes possible harms to communities and ecosystems to be possible, the values to be recognized must be appropriately identified, categorized and prioritized. Evaluations of sustainability must be preceded by an analysis of the frames of reference and methods used to identify the values to be protected. Without this analysis, coopting, ignoring or perverting of the ethical dimension is almost certain to recur. Since it is insufficient simply to add an ethical component to the other analytical components, part of the inversion needed is to ensure that ethics is not treated as an add-on but as a foundation.

Part of the process of attuning policy to values once identified is to understand them according to appropriate categories. Having seen how misanalysis and violation of values can occur through the adoption of CBA or RBA and through making assumptions about what development is about, it becomes important to ensure that values are properly categorized (e.g., as negotiable versus non-negotiable, spiritual versus economic, culturally specific versus universal, etc.). Last, prioritizing the values according to how fundamental and peripheral they are becomes necessary in light of the tendency of decision makers and policy-making devices (e.g., stakeholder processes) to treat all values with equal weight.

While the IISD thought to bring values analysis experts into the assessment, the manner in which those values were identified, categorized and prioritized failed to give some of those values thorough and appropriate analysis. Including women's perspectives through consultation with women was intended to integrate them with other perspectives.

But doing so without addressing the problem of the dominant male perspective on resource development achieves little more than the incorporation of women's concerns into male-dominated schemes. Women's values were included, and they were recognized insofar as they could contribute to the male-oriented prescriptions for development, but they were not recognized in their own right. The manner in which women's values are proposed to be incorporated does not involve fundamental levels of analysis.

Conditions Necessary for Full Values Analysis

A full values analysis involves not only analysis of marginalized people's values, but an analysis of the presuppositions of the system already in place and the manner in which it forces reinterpretation of marginalized values. Omitting such analyses, by neglecting to analyze dominant male valuations or valuations underlying technology transfer and capital injection strategies, also injects the seeds of analytical failure.

The IISD's use of value analysis experts in its evaluation is a step in the right direction. The result, however, was not an analysis of pre-established cultural and world view prejudices; this was partly owing to the absence of appropriate experts who could provide the analysis. Those who are capable of understanding where these prejudices lie and how to detect when they are actually being imposed and being used to steer the way in which sustainability initiatives are being conceived and evaluated need to be included as front-line analysts. Typically, those who are identified for values analysis are economists, sociologists, lawyers, anthropologists and ethicists. Each, however, carries professional bias instilled during training; and where they are selected from the same cultural pool, they are likely to carry cultural bias into the analysis. Owing to the limits and purposes of their training, each may be particularly unsuitable for understanding the cultural, communal and ecological contexts that need to be recognized and acknowledged. A general capacity for rigour and an openness and self-critical attitude are crucial for guiding analysis in a respectful, sensitive, disciplined way. It is, indeed, the tension between reductive rigour and self-critical openness that allows for the penetration into the nature of diverse valuations that is necessary for evaluation of sustainability. This type of rigour requires analysts who are capable of keeping dialectical opposites in tension. Who counts as an expert, consequently, is likely to have to shift from one who is narrowly specialized to one who is specialized but trained to be aware of fundamental and more comprehensive valuations. The types of ethicists needed are cross-culturally aware and attuned to the multiplicity of valuations and levels of organization of valuations. Ethical experts must be versed in the difficulties of cross-cultural understanding and moral commitments to see what the more universal moral values mean to the variety of cultures and how they apply across cultures.

At least one substantive recommendation is suggested by the discussion thus far. In the attempt to overcome reductionistic thinking and its tendency to eliminate certain kinds of values, policy should also begin addressing the insularity and dominance (e.g., economic, male, North) values that govern so much thinking in environmental policy. Acting on these values, in effect and by virtue of acts of omission, deprives people of their culturally distinctive voices. It similarly deprives us of experiences that attune us to the rhythms of the land and of the deep sense of belonging, wonder and health that such experiences bring. If we are to begin seeing the land as "home," as proponents of ecosystem integrity suggest, we need to detach these insularity and dominance values from policy. We need then to ensure that our policy makers themselves are not committed to insularity values, since this militates against the capacity to be attuned to the multivariate conditions of ecological and cultural valuations.

With an appropriate value inversion, policy development will be reshaped to prevent the deprivation of opportunities to develop capacities of adaptation and attunement, which, in turn, militates against the dullness of our senses and intellect. We shrink our capacities and identity-determining conditions so that we become incapacitated, for example, in relating to other cultures and even other people in our own cultures as expectations of insularity continue to mount. Insularity values are further motivated by fear, and they are satisfied through engineering the environment to eliminate fear-causing elements.

Vandana Shiva (1989) argues that familiarity with local processes, through direct experiencing of the rhythms of the land and its conditions of well-being, cannot be replaced by global or universal techniques of environmental management; yet that is precisely what happens in foreign aid projects. Further, vast data sets are not necessary for this type of sustainability, and efficiency in the modes of production and distribution is not the most important value to be satisfied. But this research remains the type that generally is funded.

Work in locally evolved economies is often valued in a manner quite distinct from how Locke would have us value it. Work is principally an activity of connecting to the land, not an activity of acquisition. Acquisition is obviously involved in the consumption of the goods for which people work, but this type of acquisition is not an act of creating property or value. As an act of connecting to the land, work is an expression of the understanding of the rhythms and conditions that the land sets and of identifying with the land as a home, a provider. The land is seen as giving, rather than yielding; it is a place from which value is received, rather than a raw material upon which work confers value. Unlike technologically imposing and dependent work, which seeks to control the conditions of production and create insularity against the land, this connected work seeks to become attuned to the conditions of ecological production; it is a result of a readiness to adapt. Learning how to read the environment's indicators for when and where to fish or hunt, when and how to plant and when to leave fields fallow are examples of such ways. These ways starkly contrast with the use of fish finders and infrared detectors, the engineering of crops to increase growing time and yield and the continuous use of external energy to force production from fields.

Work, then, can become a principal means for attuning us to the conditions of sustainability. The localization of knowledge and production connected to attuned work sensitizes us more immediately to ideas such as the ecological footprint. It does so without the use of massive data sets or reams of formal and expensive research. Those who have not forgotten or who have not failed to experience work of this nature understand the value of being able to produce what is needed to survive or subsist. We are rewarded not by money—a mere substitute for work—but by the satisfaction felt in our bodies as we eat what we have grown or gathered and as we use what we have produced. Indeed, the appreciation is felt in our bodies as fatigue and hunger are dissipated by the fruits of our work. This feeling is not only one of relief but of strengthening, as our bodies become harder and better adapted to work. It may be that only in this type of connection to the land can we properly develop a respect for the land. Genuine respect for people is established and grows only when we engage them as individuals by becoming familiar with their abilities and character; otherwise, respect is merely nominal. Similarly, respect for the land is concretely established through direct acquaintance with it. Such respect is generated in taking from the land; but this taking is not done with the attitude of deservingness, as if we had a right to take; it is taken in full recognition that what the land provides is given to us.

The import of reviewing these conditions of sustainability for policy is that we need to infuse into policy the ways of understanding, knowing and valuing that come from direct acquaintance with the land as a provider. One way to do this is to require those who are commissioned to write policy to have such a background as a qualification for policy development.

Tools, whether physical or intellectual, should first be properly identified as a means for satisfying the underlying valuations of sustainability, enabling us to exercise the virtues and epistemic responsibilities for which sustainability calls. To count as a sustainable technology, then, a device needs to promote awareness of the land's rhythms; it must not mask them or insulate us from them. In fact, some technologies help us to become aware in ways that might not have been available to us previously. Those that aid our ability to observe (e.g., the telescope and microscope) can greatly enhance our appreciation of the conditions of sustainability and the complexity of the systems upon which we depend. Technologies needed to produce these instruments may require great energy inputs, and therefore some environmental harm, but the value gained as weighed against the disvalues produced can enhance our ability to become attuned and help us progress toward living with one another and ecosystem integrity.

Sustainability is a historically situated concept, much like the concepts of infinity, democracy, scientific method and the detached observer. These sorts of concepts are often inchoately formed in earlier world views and develop more fully as problems with the old world view become more explicit and the need for a new world view is recognized. Similarly, sustainability is formed in the historical context of the need for a shift in world view and for value inversions. Failure to identify this element is a failure to bring thought to the level required to address the critical issues that spawn the concern for sustainability.

Accordingly, it is fine to work toward enhancing quality of life for all—alternative fuel and transportation technologies, greater health awareness, more natural and aesthetically pleasing cities, non-motorized boating and the like. But all measures will achieve little more than the imposition of restrictions on assumed human greed and arrogance if emphasis on attunement and moral character is not made. If environmental policy is to begin addressing moral character, it must also strive to educate the population and not just to reduce harm to the physical environment; it must be inclusive of aspects of harm to the psyche and all loci of valuational activities. We cannot sacrifice concern for harm done to wholes in favour of the clearer and more manageable concern for harm to individuals. If both are relevant to the web of loci that constitute the ecological community, then all individual loci and the nets of relations to which they belong must be admitted to the sphere of concern for sustainability.

Were development to be conceived as a development of the person toward attunement and respect, sustainable development might not be an offense but a comprehensive measure of sustainability. It could help us work toward new forms of autonomous community development, empowering communities to develop low-impact technologies and modes of production that would protect rather than undermine the many valuational activities of all loci. Although they are not the most competitive and wealth-generating practices available, low-impact logging with small machinery or horses and value-added industry development (e.g., chip board manufacturing, carpentry shops and furniture making) would go a long way toward establishing communities whose individuals are interconnected economically and, therefore, motivated to be much more attuned to one another and to the land than are communities dominated by large industries, which promote insularity. Wealth in such "developed" communities is measured not only by income but by the security found in neighbourliness, mutual concern, readiness to help, sharing, connection to the land and, likely, more rewarding work.

Policy can be effective in bringing about such transformations in communities, not by forcing compliance but by supporting the values that already exist. The ecosystem integrity model can serve this end because almost everything it recommends protects some core value that people hold, however suppressed and distorted.

Conservation

Conservation, like sustainability, is a key environmental management concept; and like sustainability, it is ambiguous and prone to use as a tool of marginalization and cooptation. Many definitions of conservation have been proposed, each presupposing a world view and sets of values to be satisfied. Conservation is centred on natural resource management and utility. Focusing on it thereby helps to emphasize environmental policy and its underlying assumptions about use-value and thinking about the land as a resource. The debate over sustainable development and sustainability discloses elements of our ethical relationship to the ecosystem, which links closely with communities, but it does not focus as closely on the notions of resource and utility as does conservation. Obviously, utility values are critical to well-being, but the ways in which they have been understood as foundations for ethical sensibilities have distorted our relationship to ecological conditions of well-being. We then need to understand anew what utility is in light of thinking ecologically.

Debate over what constitutes conservation is traceable to the turn of the century. At that time, John Muir (who founded the Sierra Club in 1892) and Gifford Pinchot (who became the first head of the U.S. Forest Service in 1905) each pressed Theodore Roosevelt to support their divergent wildland policies; the former pressing for absolute protectionist policies, the latter for wise scientific management policies (see Taylor 1992; Olver et al. 1995). Pinchot's program was received while Muir's receded to counterestablishment status. Both believed themselves to be advocating conservation policies.

In the early stages, conservation movements were motivated by the growing fear that stocks of renewable resources and quantities of non-renewable resources were being depleted at alarming rates (see Van Hise 1910). Cain (1977: 186), in the *Encyclopedia of Environmental Science,* traces the origins of concern to socially harmful waste, which, even though good for business, violates certain social values. He focuses on pollution and wanton, inefficient use of natural resources. Fosberg (1970: 215) cites the same reasons but formulates them as a concern for greater frugality in the reduction of waste. Prodigal exploitation has led to the destruction of once beautiful landscapes. Early versions of sustainable development policies reflected this view of conservation as "the management of human use of the biosphere so that it may yield the greatest sustainable benefit to present generations while maintaining its potential to meet the needs and aspirations of future generations" (International Union for Conservation of Nature and Natural Resources 1980: sect. 1.4). Conservation embraces preservation, maintenance, sustainable utilization, restoration and enhancement (International Union for Conservation of Nature and Natural Resources 1980: sect. 1.4). A wide range of goals and values can, therefore, be at stake when people support conservation.

Many concerns were brought into the arena as the conservation movement grew: inefficient use of natural resources (waste), loss of natural resources (overexploitation), socially ill effects of production and extraction (pollution), the loss of natural beauty (aesthetics) and the rights of future generations. Other concerns are being added to this mix: preservation of wild spaces for their own sake (intrinsic value) and restoration of wild, semi-wild and marginally wild spaces to restore ecological function. In the face of such diverse values, some have attempted to offer a general definition of conservation. Cain (1977: 185) suggests that it is "the maximization over time of the net social benefits in goods and services from natural resources." Fosberg (1970: 214) considers conservation to be the "preservation of man's environment in a condition to fulfill his needs for a healthy and satisfying life." Van Hise (1910: 117) argues: "It is the aim of conservation to reduce the intensity of struggle for existence, to make the situation more favorable, to reduce mere subsistence to subordinate place, and thus give an opportunity for development to a higher intellectual and spiritual level." The latter two advocate Pinchot's utilitarian version of conservation, namely, that "conservation is the use of natural resources for the greatest good for the greatest number for the longest time" (1947: 326).

Conservation can be an act of protecting a diverse and conflicting range of valuations. All policies and decisions advance some values and ethical commitments and, in so doing, ignore or even demonize others. Building a dam for flood control and recreation satisfies the values of one sector of society and can be justified on grounds of safety for those living along flood plains. It may also have economic justifications, if it can be used for hydroelectricity generation or if it offers new revenue-generating recreational activity. But dams violate other values for those who depend on flood regimes, for downstream users whose water supply may be curtailed and for those who value indigenous fish species that require a non-obstructed river for habitat and spawning. It often has been the case that dams destroy the sacred burial grounds of indigenous peoples and ruin heritage values for those whose private and secret places used to be where water now stands. Yet "conservation" is usually used without much concern for the diversity of meanings associated with it. We say that we conserve (e.g., energy and resources) to save for later use, to preserve (e.g., old-growth forests) so that resources cannot be used, to alter for special use (e.g., recreation) and to manage (e.g., water regimes and game species). Sometimes conservation entails highly intrusive management and at other times no management at all.

Contributing to the problem of defining and characterizing what it is to conserve is the unavoidable uncertainty in the complexity of relationships and dialectical nature of ecosystem approaches. The measures required to aid conservation cannot be determined with as much clarity as we might like. Shrader-Frechette and McCoy (1993: 53–54) show how a variety of conservation strategies could be recommended, depending on how concepts are defined and which concepts are chosen as key for determining strategies. If we focus on species, we still have a number of options from which to choose. Do we focus on a single species? Do we try to maintain a constant population, or do we let populations vary? Do we focus on an unbroken population, in which all members are contained in one geographic area where they can interact freely, or do we focus on broken populations in which members are somewhat isolated in relatively unrelated geographic locations where they may or may not interact periodically with other areas. Sometimes broken populations are more stable because they can better resist the effects of invasions of predators, parasites and diseases, whereas an unbroken population may be completely exterminated by an invasion. If we choose the wrong spatial scale, which is more or less arbitrary at any rate, for a very long time we may remain unaware of the stability of a population that uses a vast range and never one management area (e.g., migratory populations). Uncertainty, then, implies that the science of ecology can advise managers of conservation strategies, but it cannot offer incontrovertible evidence and justification for a policy.

Conserving and protecting utility, even with respect to a single value, is necessarily complex, such that we are unsure of how to identify the object of utility. According to the Modern world view (as represented, for example, by Locke) the object of utility is uncontroversially identifiable; it is whatever object we choose or agree to value. Ecologically, however, choosing to value one thing involves a network of related valuations. For instance, choosing to value a forest for its timber value cannot be divorced from valuing it as a carbon sink (i.e., a repository for carbon, which is important for maintaining atmospheric carbon dioxide levels), as a water charge area and as a habitat area. We are beginning to recognize that any judgment or decision about utility involves a system of relations of supporting values and ecosystem conditions as well as implications for other values. Thus, what we initially choose to be of value, for example, gold, may in fact turn out to be of negative value or disvalue if acquiring it requires polluting rivers and violating health values. We are beginning to accept the dialectical nature of valuations: oil has utility in relation to transportation, heating and lubrication; but it is of negative value (negative utility) in relation to the destruction of the environment needed to extract it, the pollution its use causes and the hazard it becomes when spilled.

If we properly identify what we are doing when implementing conservation policies, then we realize that we cannot protect one value or set of values without, at the same time, protecting other related values. This fact has been hidden, much like the fact that all conservation advances some value or other, largely because we could avoid the consequences of narrow thinking. We could move on when resources ran out. We could ignore water pollution when the scale was small, situate ourselves upstream from the pollution or rely on victims to be silent. We could ignore the health costs of pollution in establishing conservation policy, as long as the health system absorbed these costs. We could switch to different kinds of resources once we exhausted ones we had formerly exploited (e.g., switching to shrimp and lower-grade fish once the East Coast cod fishery had collapsed). Today, most of these strategies cannot be expected to work. Hence, when thinking about conservation, systems of relations need to be acknowledged and the implications of this acknowledgment must be addressed explicitly. In this way, the changes in conservation thinking over the last one hundred years mirrors the need to develop a holistic, ecological world view as a basis for thinking about policy.

One important aspect of conservation policy is adaptability. To take proper account of the network of valuations, the ecosystem conditions that support them and the uncertainties that arise in holistic contexts, we need to be able to adapt our policies and thinking about what needs to be conserved. Unanticipated consequences present a challenge to adapt to changes in physical conditions and to social conditions, as new impacts on systems become evident. Deforestation leading to desertification and many other ill consequences of anthropogenic interventions (e.g., ozone layer depletion and global warming) can be cited as indicators. Unless we adapt early to such consequences, we will most assuredly undermine and violate a large number of valuations. Conservation policy, then, necessarily invokes the precautionary principle when adapting to undermined and violated valuations.

Since we are able to discern some patterns of ecosystems, it is possible to use ecological concepts and principles as heuristics for resource conservation (Shrader-Frechette and McCoy 1993: 54–55). We can learn from imprecision and error in a progressive and adaptive manner. Adaptivity in conservation strategies assumes ecosystem relationships to be discernible but underdetermined. Developing conservation policy can be grounded in pattern discernment, then, but it must remain adaptive to the changes in those patterns.

The diverse range of motivations and levels of analysis that a conservation policy needs to take into account allows for diverse kinds of prescriptions, even within the ecosystem approach. Justifying protection of core wilderness areas is relatively unproblematic because protecting all that remains still will not sufficiently protect the full range of values pertinent to freedom and attunement. Too few people have any understanding of wilderness, let alone access to it. In this case, leaving alone is the primary principle, although sometimes intervention may be the best way to apply the harm and precautionary principles. For example, sometimes suppression of fires may be necessary if there are no places left for fleeing wildlife to go. Buffer zones are another matter. Where restoration is part of the conservation goal, the extent of restoration to indigenous species, spatial dimensions and the degree of functionality to restore are choices that involve a wide range of factors, including economic feasibility and safety. In this context, there are obligations to control for certain environmental qualities, but since the values to be protected are so wide-ranging, there is no clear set of obligations to be derived from these values. To try to protect all values and all senses of utility is to resign policy to incoherence and hopeless confusion. As some of the most important sustainable development policies have proven, the tendency to conflate all values, asserting that they can all be recognized and satisfied through democratic process, results in confusion and default to economic values or to the values of those who dominate.

Herfindahl (1960: 233) has identified the problem with setting conservation policy as a conceptual one; deeply contradictory expectations, owing to a desire to appropriate into conservation policy the diverse views of special interest groups, made early and many present-day conservation definitions incoherent. John Livingston (1981: 25) reiterates this conviction in *The Fallacy of Wildlife Conservation* by showing how the idea of wildlife conservation through husbandry is precisely non-preservationist. Twenty years later, he repeats Herfindahl's indictment against proponents of wildlife conservation. Confusion persists because of the conflation of contradictory expectations into the conservation agenda. And this conflation persists through to the present, as indicated in official documents such as *Canada's Green Plan* (Canada 1990), *Sustainable Forests* (Canadian Council of Forestry Ministers 1992) and *Our Common Future* (WCED 1987). All list the many values to be recognized in government environmental policy, but none commit to a coherent approach to understanding how contradictory values are to be recognized. The exception among the sources examined is the International Joint Commission (2000). Its prioritizing of integrity as a fundamental concern makes it a suitable foundation for conservation policy because it treats contradictory values in a systematic way. While accepting ecological and evolutionary oppositional values as necessary to integrity, it also treats human values as parts of that system. We need to be informed about the opposition between values and manage accordingly, which, it turns out, best achieves freedom for human beings.

In contrast, the International Union for Conservation of Nature and Natural Resources in its *World Conservation Strategy* (1980: sect. 1.4) conflates disparate values. It defines conservation as

> the management of human use of the biosphere so that it may yield the greatest sustainable benefit to present generations while maintaining its potential to meet the needs and aspirations of future generations. Thus conservation is positive, embracing preservation, maintenance, sustainable utilization, restoration and enhancement of the natural environment.

This commitment to benefit, utilization and enhancement may seem democratic and pluralistic, but the incoherence and lack of focus favour those who can dominate the policy arena: those with powerful economic and social influence. Olver, Shuter and Minns (1995), three scientists working with (or retired from) the Ontario Ministry of Natural Resources and the federal Department of Fisheries and Oceans, have argued for the need to extricate conservation policy from economic and social directives and to place the primary emphasis on biological directives. They have seen how the dominant economic and social influences have either overridden or coopted the biological perspective, resulting in the present ecologically dysfunctional systems. What they witness in the Great Lakes fisheries is a conservation emphasis on exotic species (e.g., pacific salmon) and massive intrusions of recreational fishers who are more concerned about values pertinent to sports than to ecosystem integrity. To support the recreational fishery, massive numbers of salmon are introduced into the Great Lake system every year in the name of conservation. This management initiative is in direct conflict with the focus on indigenous species (Olver et al. 1995: 1588). For this reason a more directed and explicit commitment to an ecosystem approach is needed.

Olver et al. (1995: 1586) subscribe to the Land Ethic of Aldo Leopold in an effort to provide a foundation for their conservation ethic. This move is seen as a radical departure from the traditional utilitarian and romantic approaches they hope to displace (Olver et al. 1995: 1587) since neither is adequately grounded ecologically. Further, following Mangel et al. (1996: 338), they recognize that the new era of developing management and conservation ethics is marked by a commitment to an open, fair and comprehensive dialogue about values, perspectives and commitments. But this openness cannot engender a mere aggregate of valuations. Effective conservation demands understanding and taking account of the motives, interests and values of all users and stakeholders, but not by simply averaging their positions (Mangel et al. 1996: 349). As such, this ecological approach is an advance, insofar as it attempts to avoid the confusion and default to narrow utilitarian economic parameters and the simplistic democratic process of aggregating preferences. Its focus on biological criteria for conservation, then, is a way to direct attention away from the exploitive and special interest group criteria of conservation and onto more ecologically based criteria, in the interest of achieving some degree of coherence in conservation policy.

Olver et al. and Mangel et al. attempt to establish new balances between the plurality of valuations by adopting the idea of integrity. Ecological values, then, become foundational for conservation, such that humans derive social, economic, recreational and cultural benefits in a sustainable manner. In their own way, they support the general strategy of inverting the valuational system and the assumptions of the Modern world view.

The appeal to science's ability to "provide objective validation of those assumptions about the real world that underlie any particular valuation procedure" (Olver et al. 1995: 1586) is also appealing because it uses science as a tool for determining feasibility, not as the foundation for decision making. Biology and ecology can disclose whether particular conservation ethics and strategies can meet with success by judging whether they have taken the physical constraints of ecosystem integrity sufficiently into account. The ideas that integrity (not utility or particular values) is the primary value and that science can test whether a policy or activity satisfies conditions of integrity provide a route to coherence and avoidance of economics as the primary valuational system. Their primary focus, which is protecting indigenous places and indigenous species (Olver et al. 1995: 1587), is in keeping with the ecosystem approach and demonstrates support for an explicit ethical grounding for conservation policy, which, at the same time, recognizes the need to shape democratic process in accordance with ecological conditions.

As supportive as such approaches may be, they are not sufficient to address the valuational issues that arise for policy makers. In dealing with the full range of valuations, Olver et al., who follow Mangel et al. on the matter of values analysis (see Shuter et al. 1997: 2725), explicitly commit to developing a conservation ethic in an open and comprehensive manner. To satisfy this commitment, the full range of skills from the natural and social sciences must be brought to bear on conservation problems (Mangel et al. 1996: 348). Relying on experts in the social sciences to determine how to address the problem of identifying values relevant to conservation is fair enough, but this reliance can also result in the same mistakes that have been mentioned with respect to Third World nations and other marginalized communities. As important as experts are for analysis, more often than not they are also academics and consultants, who are rarely attuned to the land in intimate ways. Launching an invective against academics is not what I have in mind. But experts who are most attuned to the expectations of their colleagues and disciplinary expectations often impose interpretations and frames of reference for identifying values rather than becoming attuned to the actual meaning of the values people hold and their contextual significance. Similarly, ecologists are rarely attuned to the systems they study, depending principally on detached methods of inquiry rather than on the full range of their senses and reason. Experts, then, restrict the voices and types of understanding needed for attunement, leading almost inevitably to the further marginalization of voices and perspectives.

Muktuk and Terms of Reference

In their article "Traditional Knowledge Threatens Environmental Assessment," Albert Howard and Frances Widdowson (1997) argue against acceptance of indigenous peoples' traditional knowledge into resource management policy, partly because it would and does undermine conservation and other environmental policies of the government of the Northwest Territories. Widdowson, a senior bureaucrat, is concerned by a case in which an indigenous community harvested a species of whale on the endangered list, a practice banned for conservation reasons. The hunters claim that the whale offered itself so that a dying elder could have one last taste of *muktuk*, an appeal to traditional environmental knowledge and practice. Howard and Widdowson reject this appeal on the grounds that accepting such justifications would open the door to any and every justification that indigenous people might give on the basis of religion or tradition. We would be reverting back to the system of capricious religious authority against which democratic societies have fought so long and hard to free themselves (Howard and Widdowson 1997: 34).

All democracies, indeed, must guard against arbitrary decision making and policy that allows religious authority to determine what is acceptable. However, before condemning a practice, the context in which that practice takes place has to be understood. If that practice belongs to a system about which we are ignorant but which is systematic and principled, then epistemically and morally we are responsible for becoming cognizant of that system. When the original defenders of democracy were fighting the arbitrary rule of the church and monarchies, that system was clear in their minds since they had been part of it and had been victimized by it. By being part of that system, they had legitimacy when criticizing it. When observing a foreign system, however, such familiarity must be gained through study. Study of this sort requires one to understand the frame of reference (e.g., standards of excellence and rules of evidence) according to which thinking is judged as good or bad and decisions judged as right or wrong. While the process is complex and perhaps arduous, it is important to note how members of a minority or dominated society need precisely to do this when encountering the dominant society. Members of the dominant society are not pressed to examine their own system because they have been raised in it, such that their sensibilities are habituated to the processes and frame of reference of that system; they know unreflectively how to work within it. Members of the dominated or minority society must understand explicitly what the frame of reference for the dominant society is.

Suppose, for instance, that a foreigner were to come from a system in which all decisions were based on consensus, such that voting and consulting with the general population was considered unimaginable. Our system of voting and public consultation would appear entirely arbitrary and irrational, largely unpredictable and unreliable. Without understanding our history and the process of becoming free of church/monarchical arbitrary rule for the protection of the individual, our democratic system surely would seem the product of muddled thinking. What may appear irrational from the dominant society's point of view, then, may in fact be more rational and more coherent than its own. The epistemological irresponsibility in judging another culture by the standards of one's own is in not examining the possibility that the indigenous system has internal coherence and its own system of controls. The moral error is in simply judging the indigenous system as unworthy of recognition, thereby, *a priori* depriving the community of autonomy.

Like many, Howard and Widdowson have imposed their culturally and professionally grounded sensibilities onto their perceptions of the indigenous community, rather than judging an attuned perspective of the system of traditional environmental knowledge. We must ask: What is the system of internal controls? What are the values and ethical commitments that these controls invoke? How do these elements affect perception and judgment? How does an elder become an elder and what is the nature of his or her authority in the community? What does it mean to have such authority? Is "authority" even the right word to use when describing the role of the elder? What does it mean for the whale to give itself? Without answering these sorts of questions, we cannot claim to understand the frame of reference being judged. We cannot democratically proceed to accept or to change these practices through policy or negotiation.

One of the prevailing and deeply entrenched concepts of conservation operating today is that of checks and balances. The assumption is that developers and industrialists work from a motivation of greed, which requires control. Part of the liberal sensibility is the assumption that human beings are infinite acquisitors and will exploit endlessly unless controlled by external forces. Obviously, suspicion of others becomes a primary reason to control people's behaviour in the effort to conserve natural resources.

But if different cosmologies and value systems are at work in indigenous peoples' perspectives, then different sets of assumptions and sensibilities are also involved. Where the aboriginal cosmology has thousands of years of history, it cannot be dismissed as irrelevant in determining how knowledge is to be gained and how it is to be exercised. And in light of the monumental failures of non-native policy in just about every area of environmental protection, we have good reason to believe that the criticism of indigenous people's ways of managing the ecosystem are based more on a refusal to exercise epistemic responsibility of understanding the ways of indigenous people than on evidence that these ways are irresponsible and environmentally disastrous. At a deeper level, conservation policy reflects a lack of respect for indigenous cultures and perpetuates colonization. Where the dominant society imposes conditions of legitimacy based on cultural biases, it fails to recognize the conditions of autonomy, self-esteem, integrity and other fundamental values of the dominated society.

Even a brief and superficial look at indigenous systems reveals that they have standards of legitimacy for environmental management, which have long been obscured by Western romantic notions of the noble savage. Indigenous peoples were not the noble savage of European fantasy, but they had to develop stories and myths as means for communicating codes of responsibility for the land, precisely because there was greed and violation of the Creator's work. John Borrows (1997), an Anishnaabe, explains that the aboriginal was not some kind of noble savage living in harmony with the land; this could not be the case, since aboriginal stories and ceremonies necessarily carry instructions and warnings about greed and irresponsible activity. The sense of moral responsibility, then, was deeply ingrained in the culture and traditional environmental knowledge of the people, justifying a system of sanctions when people took too much or destroyed wantonly. Aboriginal tradition, then, is culturally conservationist, not genetically conservationist. As such, traditional environmental knowledge includes many laws to curb and to control greed and blindness to destruction. Failing to respect this cultural grounding means dismissing a perhaps superior concept of conservation or, better, an approach to protecting the valuational system that we call the "ecological community." Silencing the indigenous voice, then, means silencing a potentially vital teaching voice, which can offer guidance in the struggle to find a way of living with integrity and of becoming educated in the dialectics of attunement.

Conservation for Whom and for What Values?

The above examination shows that we need to ask the question "For whom is conservation of value?" It is becoming increasingly clear that conservation and sustainability efforts (under the guise of sustainable development) often result in marginalization for some groups or communities, since both can be used to manipulate and disempower as much as to protect. Striving for coherence can contribute to this process. But as arguments supporting the centrality of integrity suggest, some convergence between the two expectations is possible.

The concept of sustainability emphasizes systemic and holistic valuations, whereas conservation has tended to emphasize use values or utility. The formulation of "utility" predominantly has been reductive, since the debate has been largely over utility versus spiritual and other values. Without radical changes in how we understand utility, conservation policy initiatives will likely continue in this reductive, exclusionary vein. Thus, utility like sustainability needs to be formulated in an appropriate cross-cultural, cross-sectoral and cross-gendered manner. Once we accept that conservation is about protecting not only resources as defined in this manner, we come to acknowledge that it is also about protecting communities and ways of valuing, perceiving, feeling and relating to others.

When utility is so formulated, other near universal values can be identified as targets for conservation. The appeal to use values recognizes the need for survival and thriving. Robustness and strength (physical and psychological) then become clearly valued. As such, what we want to conserve are the conditions that enable such strength. In contrast to insularity values, which promote weakness (inability), use values direct attention toward strengthening and enabling conditions. Hence, we have a vital interest in conserving a diversity of environments that call all of our capacities into action. Where we are not able to engage such environments, our awareness shrinks. We become deficient in our ability to use our environment and deficient in our ability to teach our children how to exercise their *conatus* and to recognize it in others. We become confused about what we are and how we are to act when we know that adapting to ecosystem conditions is necessary for identity, strength, awareness and health. We see this consequence in the debate over national parks, which are supposed to be monuments to our natural heritage. As more compromise is made for tourists who demand safe experiences when encountering the wild, we find highways in national parks being widened and improved; fences being erected to prevent wildlife from entering the highway; roads, bridges and facilities constructed to allow for safe access to "wilderness" areas; and removal of predators from populated areas. Once wilderness values are compromised in this way, ecological, psychological and social dysfunction increase. The result is an increasingly systemic deprivation of the conditions of attunement necessary to satisfy the demands of respect for persons and ecosystems.

As Mangel et al. (1996) point out, simply adding or including a more comprehensive set of values or voices in thinking about conservation will not result in the kind of transformation implied in thinking ecologically. No doubt we need heuristic devices to help us in the transformation process. This book has identified some of these devices in the integrity project and in the proposal to develop a fuller system of values analysis. Rethinking liberal notions of freedom and radically rethinking the meaning and application of the harm principle are others. But ecosystem integrity becomes the central focus for conservation because it is the necessary condition for developing and sustaining all of the fundamental values of a just and democratic system.

Like sustainability, conservation aims at protecting all loci of valuational activities and all levels of organization. But while conservation attends to resources and utility, sustainability draws attention to the conditions of dependency. Since conservation is about use and utility, it focuses our attention more on the extractive aspects of human activity. Sustainability helps attune us to the supportive elements of our relationship to the environment, but conservation provides the dialectical opposite, attuning us to the utility relationship we have to the environment. Borrowing from Taoism, again, conservation is the *yang* moment in thinking ecologically, where sustainability is the *yin*. Extraction, killing and causing suffering is part of our function in the ecosystem. Conservation and the need for developing conservation policy reminds of us of this fact.

Conclusion

The full exercise of reason in the development of ecological thought moves us toward thinking about sustainability and conservation, both in terms of management and in terms of thankfulness. Both sustainability and conservation have, as a grounding assumption, the purposiveness of the ecological conditions upon which we depend. In this dependency relationship, which engenders an attitude of respect, we recognize that we are in a relationship of provision, where the various communities constituting the ecosystem are the providers. We also recognize that we are takers, actively designing ways of using the ecosystem to satisfy a plurality of values. When we accept and fully understand our dependency relation, we adopt a proper attitude: not of assuming deservingness or a right to exploit, but of thankfulness. While some would consider human beings a cancer or plague upon the earth, creatures who deserve to feel guilty because of the suffering and killing they impose on the earth, a balanced perspective is grateful for what is given and is not remorseful for having to take what is provided. While we have largely forgotten how to be thankful—we turn even Thanksgiving Day into an opportunity for economic gain and special sports events—there remain models for helping in the exercise of thankfulness. One model that we can affirm is the indigenous peoples' practice of spreading the first gathered seeds onto the land around which harvesting takes place, offering tobacco in thanksgiving and giving the first products of the hunt to those in need. As antithetical to the designs of business and industry as this suggestion may be, it is not inconceivable. We have perverted Thanksgiving Day and rejected Sunday as a day of rest, but there are still shadows of thankfulness in Western culture, and these inform us that thankfulness is still a possibility.

Where ecological attunement is recognized as vital, it is not difficult to imagine incorporating thankfulness into our lives, even at institutional levels. Attunement requires moments of silence as we engage our receptive capacities to attend to all that is given. But it also requires moments of action through which we test our intentions for suitability. By slowing ourselves to be aware of the rhythms of the land and the dependency we have on them, we allow ourselves to recognize that taking is a mode of attunement to the land. All planning, intending, designing, even commanding with respect to taking from ecosystems demands that we first obey their laws. Ironically, citing Bacon (1955: Aphorism III) seems appropriate by way of conclusion: "Nature to be commanded must be obeyed." Recasting this dependency relationship between command and obedience in light of thinking ecologically would have it thus: "Nature to be used must be received in thanksgiving."

Note

1. I wish to qualify these remarks as descriptive of the stakeholder consultation process to the termination of the Toronto meetings. During the writing of this book, an announcement was made by Environment Canada that Canada's ministers of the environment and of health declared particulate matter less than or equal to 10 microns to be toxic under the *Canadian Environment Protection Act* (see Environment Canada 2000; or *The Canada Gazette, Part 1*, Vol. 134, No. 22 [27 May 2000]). Whether this change was the result of policy makers rejecting the dominance of economic terms of reference or weighing justice concerns more heavily, I am uncertain. It is unlikely that industry brought the targets to their present levels. Although anecdotal, part of my speculated explanation is that several of the government analysts involved in organizing and presenting the data and results of the stakeholder meetings to deputy ministers and ministers became concerned about the stakeholder process after realizing how much industry had dominated. During informal conversations, several indicated that they had moral concerns with the process and invited me to submit a critique of the process to that effect. It would seem that it was the conscientiousness and virtue of individuals responsible for conducting the forum that resulted in this decrease, not the forum itself.

Bibliography

Aeschylus. 1988. *The Oresteia.* Ed. Harold Bloom. New York : Chelsea House.

Allen, Timothy F., Bruce L. Bandurski, and Anthony W. King. 1993. "The Ecosystem Approach: Theory and Ecosystem Integrity." Report to the Great Lakes Science Advisory Board of the International Joint Commission: Initial Report of a Multi-Year Project of the Ecological Committee. Project #32.1.4 of the Science Advisory Board's Workplan. Ministry of Natural Resources Workshop. June. Windsor, ON: Great Lakes Science Advisory Board.

Anker, Peder. 1998. "Ecosophy: An Outline of Its Metaethics." *The Trumpeter* 15 (1). On-line at <http:\\trumpeter.athabascau.ca>. Accessed July 15, 2002.

Aquinas, Thomas. 1993. "Differences Between Rational and Other Creatures." In Susan J. Armstrong and Richard G. Botzler (eds.), *Environmental Ethics: Divergence and Convergence.* New York: McGraw, 278–80.

Aristotle. 1939. *On the Heavens.* Trans. W.K.C. Guthrie. Cambridge: Harvard University Press.

_____. 1962. *Nicomachean Ethics.* Trans. Martin Ostwald. Indianapolis: Bobbs.

Armstrong, Susan J., and Richard G. Botzler, eds. 1993. *Environmental Ethics: Divergence and Convergence.* New York: McGraw.

Aurelius, Marcus. 1964. *Meditations.* Trans. A.S.L. Farquarson. London: Dent.

Bacon, Francis. 1955. *The New Organon.* In Hugh G. Dick (ed.), *Selected Writings of Francis Bacon.* New York: Modern Library.

Bahm, Archie J. 1993. *Axiology: The Science of Values.* Atlanta: Editions Rodopi.

Barbour, Ian. 1980. *Technology, Environment, and Human Values.* New York: Praeger.

Baxter, William F. 1995. "People or Penguins." In Christine Pierce and Donald Van De Veer (eds.), *People, Penguins and Plastic Trees.* 2nd ed. New York: Wadsworth, 381–84.

Beauchamp, Tom, and James Childress. 1989. *Principles of Biomedical Ethics.* New York: Oxford University Press.

Bentall, Richard. 1992. "A Proposal to Classify Happiness as a Psychiatric Disorder." *Journal of Medical Ethics* 18: 94–98.

Bentham, Jeremy. 1977. *An Introduction to the Principles of Morals and Legislation.* In Robert E. Dewey and Robert H. Hurlbutt III (eds.), *An Introduction to Ethics.* New York: New York Publishing, 226–33.

Berger, Thomas. 1988. *Northern Frontier Northern Homeland: The Report of the Mackenzie Valley Pipeline Inquiry.* Rev. ed. Toronto: Douglas and McIntyre.

Berns, Walter. 1992. "Defending the Death Penalty." In Wesley Cragg (ed.), *Contemporary Moral Issues.* 3rd ed. Toronto: McGraw, 433–41.

Birch, Thomas H. 1998. "Moral Considerability and Universal Consideration."

In Susan J. Armstrong and Richard G. Botzler (eds.), *Environmental Ethics: Divergence and Convergence*. 2nd ed. New York: McGraw, 380–90.

Black Elk, Wallace H., and William S. Lyon. 1991. *Black Elk: The Sacred Ways of a Lakota*. San Francisco: HarperSanFrancisco.

Bookchin, Murray. 1990. *The Philosophy of Social Ecology: Essays on Dialectical Naturalism*. Montreal: Black Rose.

_____. 1991. *The Ecology of Freedom: The Emergence and Dissolution of Hierarchy*. Montreal: Black Rose.

Booth, Annie. 1997. "An Overview of Ecofeminism." In Alex Wellington, Allen Greenbaum and Wesley Cragg (eds.), *Canadian Issues in Applied Environmental Ethics*. Toronto: Broadview, 330–51.

Booth, Annie, and Harvey M. Jacobs. 1993. "Ties that Bind: Native American Beliefs as a Foundation for Environmental Consciousness." *Environmental Ethics* 12 (Spring): 27–43.

Borrows, John. 1997. "Living Between Water and Rocks: First Nations, the Environment and Democracy." *University of Toronto Law Journal* 47: 417–68.

Bowler, Peter J. 1989. *Evolution: The History of an Idea*. Berkeley: University of California Press.

Bramwell, Anna. 1989. *Ecology in the 20th Century: A History*. New Haven, CT: Yale University Press.

Brennan, Andrew. 1988. *Thinking About Nature*. Athens, GA: University of Georgia Press.

Browne, Sir Thomas. 1956. *Religio Medici and Other Works*. Gateway ed. Los Angeles: Henry Regney.

Bruno, Giordano. 1907. *La Cena de la Ceneri*. In G. Gentile (ed.), *Opere Italiane: Vol. I*. 1923–27. Bari: Laterza.

Burnet, John. 1957. *Early Greek Philosophy*. New York: Meridian.

Cain, Stanley A. 1977. "Conservation of Resources." In S.P. Parker (ed.), *Encyclopedia of Environmental Science*. Toronto: McGraw, 185–88.

Callahan, Daniel. 1983. "The WHO Definition of Health." In J.E. Thomas (ed.), *Medical Ethics and Human Life*. Toronto: Samuel Stevens.

Callicott, J. Baird. 1986. "The Metaphysical Implications of Ecology." *Environmental Ethics* 8 (4): 301–16.

_____. 1989a. "Elements of an Environmental Ethic: Moral Considerability and the Biotic Community." In *In Defense of the Land Ethic*. New York: State University of New York Press, 63–73.

_____. 1989b. "The Conceptual Foundations of the Land Ethic." In *In Defense of the Land Ethic*. New York: State University of New York Press, 75–99.

_____. 1989c. *In Defense of the Land Ethic*. New York: State University of New York Press.

_____. 1991. "Conservation Ethics and Fishery Management." *Fisheries* 16: 22–28.

Canada. 1990. *Canada's Green Plan for a Healthy Environment*. Ottawa: Government of Canada.

Canada, Environment Canada. 1997. Workshop on "National Ambient Air Quality Objectives." December 1–2. Downsview, ON.

Canadian Council of Forestry Ministers. 1992. *Sustainable Forests: A Canadian Commitment*. Hull, PQ: National Forest Strategy.

_____. 1995. "Defining Sustainable Forest Management: A Canadian Approach to Criteria and Indicators." Ottawa, ON: Canadian Forest Service, Natural

Resources Canada.

Carson, Rachel. 1962. *Silent Spring*. Boston: Houghton.

Cheney, Jim. 1987. "Ecofeminism and Deep Ecology." *Environmental Ethics* 9 (2): 115–45.

Cherrett, J.M., ed. 1989. *Ecological Concepts: The Contribution of Ecology to an Understanding of the Natural World*. Oxford: Blackwell Scientific.

Churchill, Larry, and José Jorge Siman. 1983. "Abortion and the Rhetoric of Individual Rights." In John Thomas (ed.), *Medical Ethics and Human Life*. Toronto: Samuel Stevens, 117–25.

Clements, F.E. 1905. *Research Methods in Ecology*. Lincoln, NE: University.

Conway, Richard A. 1982. *Environmental Risk Analysis for Chemicals*. New York: Van Nostrand Reinhold.

Copernicus, Nicholas. 1947. *De Revolutionibus Orbium Coelestium*. Trans. John F. Dobson and Selig Brodetsky. *Occasional Notes of the Royal Astronomical Society: Vols. 2, 10*. London: Royal Astronomical Society.

Copleston, Frederick. 1962. *History of Philosophy: Vol. 1*. New York: Image.

Costanza, Robert. 1992. "Toward an Operational Definition of Ecosystem Health." In Robert Costanza, Bryan G. Norton and Benjamin D. Haskell (eds.), *Ecosystem Health: New Goals for Environmental Management*. Washington, DC: Island.

Costanza, Robert, Bryan G. Norton, and Benjamin D. Haskell. 1992. *Ecosystem Health: New Goals for Environmental Management*. Washington, DC: Island.

Court, Thijs de la. 1990. *Beyond Brundtland: Green Development in the 1990s*. New York: New Horizons.

Crabbé, Philippe. 1997. *Sustainable Development: Concepts, Measures, Market and Policy Failures at the Open Economy, Industry and Firm Levels*. Occasional Paper Number 16. October. Ottawa: Industry Canada.

Cragg, Wesley. 1997. "Values Mapping Workshop." October 15–17. Eaton Hall Inn. Toronto, ON.

Crombie, David. 1992. *Regeneration: Toronto's Waterfront and the Sustainable City: Final Report*. Toronto: Royal Commission on the Future of the Toronto Waterfront.

Darwin, Charles. 1972. *Descent of Man and Selection in Relation to Sex*. 2 vols. New York: AMS.

Davis, Nancy Ann. 1990. "Moral Theorizing and Moral Practice." A Paper Presented at the Conference "Moral Philosophy in the Public Domain." June. University of British Columbia, Vancouver.

Deen (Samarrai), Mawil Y. 1993. "Islamic Environmental Ethics, Law and Society." In Susan J. Armstrong and Richard G. Botzler (eds.), *Environmental Ethics: Divergence and Convergence*. New York: McGraw, 527–34.

de Silva, Lily. 1998. "The Buddhist Attitude Toward Nature." In Susan J. Armstrong and Richard G. Botzler (eds.), *Environmental Ethics: Divergence and Convergence*. New York: McGraw.

Descartes, René. 1905. *Principia Philosophiae*. In René Descartes, *Oeuvres, Vol. 3*. Paris: Adam Tannery.

_____. 1975a. *Meditations*. In René Descartes, *The Philosophical Works of Descartes, Vol. 1*. Trans. Elizabeth S. Haldane and G.R.T. Ross. London: Cambridge University Press, 131–200.

_____. 1975b. *Discourse on Method*. In René Descartes, *The Philosophical Works of*

Descartes, Vol. 1. Trans. Elizabeth S. Haldane and G.R.T. Ross. London: Cambridge University Press, 115–18.

Devall, Bill. 1995. "The Ecological Self." In Alan Drengson and Yuichi Inoue (eds.), *The Deep Ecology Movement: An Introductory Anthology.* Berkeley, CA: North Atlantic, 101–23.

Devall, Bill, and George Sessions. 1985. *Deep Ecology.* Salt Lake City, UT: Peregrine Smith.

Dickason, Olive P. 1997. *Myth of the Savage and the Beginnings of French Colonialism in the Americas.* Edmonton, AB: University of Alberta Press.

Donne, John. 1929. "Ignatius His Conclave." In John Hayward (ed.), *Complete Poetry and Selected Prose of John Donne.* Bloomsbury: Nonesuch.

Drengson, Alan. 1989. *Beyond Environmental Crisis: From Technocrat to Planetary Person.* New York: Peter Lang.

Drengson, Alan, and Yuichi Inoue, eds. 1995. *The Deep Ecology Movement: An Introductory Anthology.* Berkeley, CA: North Atlantic.

Ehrlich, Paul. 1981. "Human Population and the Global Environment." In B.J. Skinner (ed.), *Use and Misuse of Earth's Surface.* California: William Kaufman.

Ehrlich, Paul, and John Holdren. 1989. "Impact on Population Growth." In T.D. Goldfarb (ed.), *Taking Sides: Clashing Views on Controversial Environmental Issues.* 3rd ed. Guilford, CT: Dushkin, 88–95.

Eliade, Mircea. 1978. *A History of Religious Ideas, Vol. 1: From the Stone Age to the Eleusinian Mysteries.* Trans. Willard R. Trask. Chicago: University of Chicago Press.

Ellul, Jacques. 1964. *The Technological Society.* Trans. John Wilkinson. New York: Vintage.

Elton, C. 1927. *Animal Ecology.* New York: Macmillan.

Environment Canada. 2000. "Particulate Matter (PM < 10)." On-line at <http://www.ec.gc.ca/air/p-matter_e.shtml>. Accessed July 15, 2002.

Estrin, David, and John Swaigen. 1978. *Environment on Trial: A Handbook of Ontario Environmental Law.* 2nd ed. Toronto: Canadian Environmental Law Research Foundation.

Evernden, Neil. 1985. *The Natural Alien: Humankind and the Environment.* Toronto: University of Toronto Press.

_____. 1993. "Nature in Industrial Society." In Susan J. Armstrong and Richard G. Botzler (eds.), *Environmental Ethics: Divergence and Convergence.* New York: McGraw, 209–17.

Faber, Malte, Reiner Manstetten, and John Proops. 1992. "Toward an Open Future: Ignorance Novelty and Evolution." In Robert Costanza, Bryan G. Norton and Benjamin D. Haskell (eds.), *Ecosystem Health: New Goals for Environmental Management.* Washington, DC: Island, 72–96.

Feibleman, James K. 1972. *Scientific Method: The Hypothetico-Experimental Laboratory Procedure of the Physical Sciences.* The Hague: Martinus Nijhoff.

Finger, Matthias. 1993. "Politics of the UNCED Process." In Wolfgang Sachs (ed.), *Global Ecology: A New Arena of Political Conflict.* Halifax, NS: Fernwood, 36–48.

Fisher, Roger, and William Ury. 1991. *Getting to Yes.* 2nd ed. New York: Penguin.

Food and Agriculture Organization of the United Nations. 1999. Conference on "High-Level Consultation on Rural Women and Information." October 4–6. Rome. On-line at <http://www.fao.org/gender/highlcon/default.htm>.

Accessed July 15, 2002.

Fosberg, F.R. 1970. "Conservation." In P. Gray (ed.), *The Encyclopedia of the Biological Sciences.* Toronto: Van Nostrand Reinhold, 214–17.

Fox, Warwick. 1990. *Toward a Transpersonal Ecology: Developing New Foundations for Environmentalism.* Boston: Shambala.

Freire, Paulo. 1974. *Pedagogy of the Oppressed.* New York: Seabury.

———. 1985. *The Politics of Education.* South Hadley, MA: Bergin and Garvey.

Friedman, Milton. 1996. "The Social Responsibility of Business Is to Increase Its Profits." In Thomas Donaldson and Patricia H. Werhane (eds.), *Ethical Issues in Business: A Philosophical Approach.* Upper Saddle River, NJ: Prentice, 222–27.

Frodeman, Robert. "A Sense of the Whole: Toward an Understanding of Acid Mine Drainage in the West." In Robert Frodeman (ed.), *Earth Matters: The Earth Sciences, Philosophy, and the Claims of Community.* Upper Saddle River, NJ: Prentice, 119–39.

Gause, G.F. 1934. *The Struggle for Existence.* Baltimore, MD: Williams and Wilkins.

Gent, A.E., M.D. Hellier, R.H. Grace, E.T. Swarbrick, and D. Coggan. 1994. "Inflammatory Bowel Disease and Domestic Hygiene in Infancy." *Lancet* 343: 766–67.

Giblet, Rodney James. 1996. *Postmodern Wetlands: Culture, History, Ecology.* Edinburgh: Edinburgh University Press.

Gilbreath, Kent. 1989. "Industry's Environmental Attitudes." In Theodore D. Goldfarb (ed.), *Taking Sides: Clashing Views on Controversial Environmental Issues.* 3rd ed. Guilford, CT: Dushkin, 72–76.

Glacken, Clarence. 1967. *Traces on the Rhodian Shore.* Berkeley, CA: University of California Press.

Gleik, James. 1987. *Chaos: Making a New Science.* New York: Penguin.

Goodpaster, Kenneth. 1978. "On Being Morally Considerable." *Journal of Philosophy* 78: 308–25.

Gould, J.A., and W.H. Truitt. 1973. *Political Ideologies.* New York: Macmillan.

Goulet, Jean-Guy. 1998. *Ways of Knowing: Experience, Knowledge and Power Among the Dene Tha.* Vancouver: University of British Columbia Press.

Graves, Robert. 1996. *The Greek Myths: Vol. II.* London: Folio Society.

Haeckel, Ernst. 1957. *Generelle Morphologie.* In R.C. Stauffer, "Haeckel, Darwin and Ecology." *Quarterly Review of Biology* 32: 138–44.

Haldane, J.B.S. 1996. *The Causes of Evolution.* Ithaca, NY: Cornell University Press.

Hale, Sir Matthew. 1677. *The Primitive Origination of Mankind.* London: Printed by W. Godbin for W. Shrowsbery.

Hardi, Péter, and Terrence Zdan, eds. 1997. *Assessing Sustainable Development: Principles in Practice.* Winnipeg: International Institute for Sustainable Development.

Hardin, Garret. 1983. "Living on a Lifeboat." In Jan Narveson (ed.), *Moral Issues.* Toronto: Oxford University Press, 167–78.

———. 1998. "Tragedy of the Commons." In Susan J. Armstrong and Richard G. Botzler (eds.), *Environmental Ethics: Divergence and Convergence.* 2nd ed. New York: McGraw, 520–40.

Hargrove, Eugene. 1989. *Foundations of Environmental Ethics.* Englewood Cliffs, NJ: Prentice.

Haywood, Richard M. 1971. *The Ancient World.* New York: David McKay.

Hearne, Vicki. 1986. *Adam's Task: Calling Animals By Name.* New York: Knopf.

Hegel, G.W.F. 1977. *Phenomenology of Spirit.* Trans. J.N. Findlay. Oxford: Clarendon.

Heisenberg, Werner. 1958. *Physics and Philosophy: The Revolution in Modern Science.* New York: Harper.

Herfindahl, Orris C. 1960. "What Is Conservation." In Ian Burton and Robert W. Kates (eds.), *Readings in Resource Management and Conservation.* Chicago: University of Chicago Press.

Hildyard, Nicholas. 1993. "Foxes in Charge of the Chickens." In Wolfgang Sachs (ed.), *Global Ecology: A New Arena of Political Conflict.* Halifax, NS: Fernwood, 22–35.

Hobbes, Thomas. 1972. *Leviathan.* Baltimore: Penguin.

Holbrook, Daniel. 1990. "Deep Ecology: Fact, Value, or Ideology." *Methodology and Science* 23 (3): 130–41.

Hough, Michael. 1990. *Out of Place: Restoring Identity to the Regional Landscape.* New Haven, CT: Yale University Press.

_____. 1992. "Design for Nature in the Urban Fabric." Plenary Lecture. Society for Ecological Restoration. August. Waterloo, ON.

Howard, Albert, and Frances Widdowson. 1997. "Traditional Knowledge Threatens Environmental Assessment." *Policy Options* March: 34–36.

Humber Environment Action Group. 1996. *A Guide to Community Values Mapping and a Photo Documentation of Community Values in the Outer Bay of Islands (Video and Workbook).* Corner Brook, NF: Humber Environment Action Group.

Hume, David. 1968. *A Treatise Concerning Human Understanding.* Everyman ed. Dutton, NY: Dent.

Hutchison, George, and Dick Wallace. 1977. *Grassy Narrows.* Toronto: Van Nostrand Reinhold.

Huxley, Aldous. 1964. *Brave New World.* London: Chatto and Windus.

International Joint Commission. 1909. *Treaty Between the United States and Great Britain Relating to Boundary Waters, and Questions Arising Between the United States and Canada.* On-line at <http://www.ijc.org/ijcweb-e.html>. Search under "Who We Are"; "Boundary Waters Treaty." Accessed July 15, 2002.

_____. 1989. "Great Lakes Water Quality Agreement of 1978." May 8. On-line at <http://www.ijc.org/ijcweb-e.html>. Search under "Who We Are"; "Great Lakes Water Quality Agreement." Accessed July 15, 2002.

_____. 2000. "Protection of the Waters of the Great Lakes: Final Report to the Governments of Canada and the United States," Report submitted February 22. On-line at <http://www.ijc.org/ijcweb-e.html>. Search under "Publications"; "IJC Reports"; "Other IJC Reports"; "Protection of the Waters of the Great Lakes."Accessed July 15, 2002.

International Union for Conservation of Nature and Natural Resources. 1980. *World Conservation Strategy: Living Resource Conservation for Sustainable Development.* Gland, Switz.: International Union for Conservation of Nature and Natural Resources.

Ip, Po-Keung. 1998. "Taoism and the Foundations of Environmental Ethics." In Susan J. Armstrong and Richard G. Botzler (eds.), *Environmental Ethics: Divergence and Convergence.* 2nd ed. New York: McGraw, 290–96.

Jefferson, Thomas. 1975. "Notes on the State of Virginia." In Merrill D. Peterson (ed.), *The Portable Thomas Jefferson.* New York: Viking.

Johnson, Francis R., and Sanford V. Larkey. 1934. "Thomas Digges, the Copernican System and the Idea of the Infinity of the Universe." *The Huntington Library Bulletin* 5.

Johnston, Basil. 1994. *Ojibway Heritage*. Toronto: McClelland and Stewart.

Kant, Immanuel. 1929. *The Critique of Pure Reason*. Trans. Norman Kemp Smith. New York: St. Martin's.

_____. 1956. *Critique of Practical Reason*. Indianapolis: Bobbs.

_____. 1969. *The Foundations of the Metaphysics of Morals*. Trans. Lewis White Beck. Indianapolis: Bobbs.

_____. 1993. "Duties to Animals." In Susan J. Armstrong and Richard G. Botzler (eds.), *Environmental Ethics: Divergence and Convergence*. 2nd ed. New York: McGraw, 312–13.

Karr, James R. 1993. "Measuring Biological Integrity: Lessons from Streams." In Stephen Woodley, James Kay and George Francis (eds.), *Ecological Integrity and the Management of Ecosystems*. Delray Beach, FL: St. Lucie, 83–104.

Katz, Eric. 1985. "Organism, Community, and the 'Substitution Problem.'" *Environmental Ethics* 7 (4): 241–56.

Kay, James. 1993. "On the Nature of Ecological Integrity: Some Closing Comments." In S. Woodley, J. Kay and G. Francis (eds.), *Ecological Integrity and the Management of Ecosystems*. Delray Beach, FL: St. Lucie, 201–12.

Kohák, Erazim. 1984. *The Embers and the Stars: A Philosophical Inquiry into the Moral Sense of Nature*. Chicago: University of Chicago Press.

Koyré, Alexandre. 1957. *From the Closed World to the Infinite Universe*. Baltimore, MD: Johns Hopkins.

Kuhn, Thomas. 1970. *The Structure of Scientific Revolutions*. 2nd ed. Chicago: University of Chicago Press.

_____. 1985. *The Copernican Revolution: Planetary Astronomy in the Development of Western Thought*. Cambridge, MA: Harvard University Press.

Lawton, J.H. 1989. "Food Webs." In J.M. Cherrett (ed.) *Ecological Concepts: The Contribution of Ecology to an Understanding of the Natural World*. Oxford: Blackwell Scientific, 43–78.

Lee, Shonh S. "Mathematical Modeling for Prediction of Chemical Fate." In Richard Conway (ed.), *Environmental Risk Analysis for Chemicals*. New York: Van Nostrand Reinhold, 241–56.

Leonard, Herman B., and Richard J. Zeckhauser. 1992. "Cost-Benefit Analysis Defended." In Claudia Mills (ed.), *Values and Public Policy*. Orlando, FL: Harcourt, 80–85.

Leopold, Aldo. 1964. *Sand County Almanac: And Sketches Here and There*. New York: Oxford University Press.

Lewis, Stephen. 1988. Keynote address for a Symposium on Sustainable Development. In *Planning for Sustainable Development: A Resource Book*. Vancouver: University of British Columbia, School of Community and Regional Planning.

Lindeman, R.L. 1942. "The Trophic Dynamic Aspect of Ecology." *Ecology* 23: 399–418.

Livingston, John. 1981. *The Fallacy of Wildlife Conservation*. Toronto: McClelland and Stewart.

Locke, John. 1960. *Two Treatises of Government*. New York: New American Library.

Lovelock, James. 1987. *Gaia*. Oxford: Oxford University Press.

Mangel, Marc, et al. 1996. "Principles for the Conservation of Wild Living Resources." *Ecological Applications* 6 (2): 338–62.

Marietta, Jr., Don. 1993. "Environmental Holism and Individuals." In Susan J. Armstrong and Richard G. Botzler (eds.), *Environmental Ethics: Divergence and Convergence*. New York: McGraw, 405–10.

———. 1994. *For People and the Planet: Holism and Humanism in Environmental Ethics*. Philadelphia: Temple University Press.

May, R.M. 1989. "Levels of Organization in Ecology." In J.M. Cherrett (ed.), *Ecological Concepts: The Contribution of Ecology to an Understanding of the Natural World*. Oxford: Blackwell Scientific, 339–63.

McHarg, Ian L. 1970. "Values, Process, and Form." In Robert Disch (ed.), *The Ecological Conscience: Values for Survival*. Englewood Cliffs, NJ: Prentice, 21–36.

McKeon, Richard, ed. 1941. *The Basic Works of Aristotle*. New York: Random House.

McPherson, Dennis H., and J. Douglas Rabb. 1993. *Indian from the Inside: A Study of Ethno-Metaphysics*. Occasional Paper Number 14. Thunder Bay, ON: Lakehead University, Centre for Northern Studies.

Meiss, James D. 2000. "sci.nonlinear FAQ." On-line at <http://amath.colorado.edu/faculty/jdm/faq-[2].html#Heading12>. Accessed July 15, 2002.

Midgeley, Mary. 1987. "Duties Concerning Islands." In Wesley Cragg (ed.), *Contemporary Moral Issues*. Toronto: McGraw, 434–36.

Mill, J.S. 1947. *On Liberty*. Northbrook, IL: AHM.

———. 1979. *Utilitarianism*. Ed. George Sher. Indianapolis: Hackett.

Momaday, Scott M. 1997. *The Man Made of Words*. New York: St. Martin's.

More, Sir Thomas. 1965. *Utopia*. New York: Penguin.

Morito, Bruce. 1990. "Holism, Learned Ignorance and Policy: A Case Against Sustainable Development." A Paper Presented at the Conference "Moral Philosophy and the Public Domain." June 7–9. University of British Columbia, Vancouver.

———. 1993. "Holism, Interest-Identity, and Value." *Journal of Value Inquiry* 27: 49–62.

———. 1995. "Value, Metaphysics, and Anthropocentrism." *Environmental Values* 4: 31–47.

———. 1999a. "Examining Ecosystem Integrity as a Primary Mode of Recognizing the Autonomy of Nature." *Environmental Ethics* 21 (1): 59–73.

———. 1999b. "The Rule of Law and Aboriginal Rights: The Case of the Chippewas of Nawash." *The Canadian Journal of Native Studies* 19 (2): 263–88.

———. 2000. "Language, Sustainable Development and Indigenous Peoples: An Ethical Perspective." *Ethics and Environment* 5 (1): 47–60.

Mumford, Lewis. 1970. *The Myth of the Machine: The Pentagon of Power*. New York: Harcourt.

Naess, Arne. 1972. "The Shallow and Deep, Long-range Ecology Movement." *Inquiry* 16: 95–100.

———. 1989. *Ecology, Community and Lifestyle*. Ed./Trans. David Rothenberg. Cambridge: Cambridge University Press.

———. 1995. "The Apron Diagram." In Alan Drengson and Yuichi Inoue (eds.), *The Deep Ecology Movement: An Introductory Anthology*. Berkeley, CA: North

Atlantic, 10–12.

Neihardt, John G. 1979. *Black Elk Speaks: Being the Story of a Holy Man of the Oglala Sioux*. Lincoln, NE: University of Nebraska Press.

Nelson, J.G., and H. Edsvik. 1990. "Sustainable Development, Conservation Strategies, and Heritage." *Alternatives* 16 (4): 62–71.

Neville, Robert. 1992. "Sterilizing the Mildly Mentally Retarded Without Their Consent." In Thomas Mappes and Jane Zembatty (eds.), *Biomedical Ethics*. 3rd ed. New York: McGraw, 295–98.

Newton, Sir Isaac. 1756. "Four Letters from Sir Isaac Newton to the Reverend Dr. Bentley." Letter 2; January 17, 1692–93. London. In Alexandre Koyré, *From the Closed World to the Infinite Universe*. Baltimore, MD: Johns Hopkins, 1957.

Norton, Bryan. 1984. "Environmental Ethics and Weak Anthropocentrism." *Environmental Ethics* 6 (3): 131–48.

_____. 1991. *Toward Unity Among Environmentalists*. New York: Oxford University Press.

_____. 1992a. "Epistemology and Environmental Value." *Monist* 75: 208–26.

_____. 1992b. "A New Paradigm for Environmental Management." In Robert Costanza, Bryan G. Norton and Benjamin D. Haskell (eds.), *Ecosystem Health: New Goals for Environmental Management*. Washington, DC: Island, 23–41.

Noss, Reed. 1991. "Wilderness Recovery: Thinking Big in Restoration Ecology." *The Environmental Professional* 13: 225–34.

Ockham, William of. 1957. *Ockham: Philosophical Writings*. Toronto: Thomas Nelson and Sons.

Olver, C.H., B.J. Shuter, and C.K. Minns. 1995. "Toward a Definition of Conservation Principles for Fisheries Management." *Canadian Journal of Fisheries and Aquatic Science* 52: 1584–94.

O'Neill, John. 1992. "The Varieties of Intrinsic Value." *The Monist* 75 (2): 119–37.

Ong, Walter J. 1969. "World as View and World as Event." *American Anthropologist* 71 (4): 634–47.

Ontario Round Table on Environment and Economics. 1992. "Six Principles of Sustainable Development." On-line at <http://www.brocku.ca/epi/sustainability/ORTEE92.HTM>. Accessed July 15, 2002.

_____. 1994. "Sustainability Principles." On-line at <http://www.brocku.ca/epi/sustainability/ORTEE.HTM>. Accessed July 15, 2002.

Overholt, Thomas W., and J. Baird Callicott. 1982. *Clothed in Fur and Other Tales: An Introduction to an Ojibwa World View*. Lanham, MD: University Press of America.

Passmore, John. 1974. *Man's Responsibility for Nature: Ecological Problems and Western Culture*. New York: Scribner's.

Pearce, D.W. 1993. *World Without End*. London: Oxford University Press.

Philo [Philo Judaeus]. 1929. "On the Account of the World's Creation Given by Moses." In *Philo, Vol. 1*. Trans. G.H. Whitaker. London: Heinemann; New York: Putnam's.

Pinchot, Gifford. 1947. *Breaking New Ground*. New York: Harcourt.

Plato. 1973. *Timaeus*. Trans. Benjamin Jowett. In Edith Hamilton and Huntington Cairns (eds.), *Plato: The Collected Dialogues*. Princeton, NJ: Princeton University Press, 1151–211.

_____. 1974. *The Republic*. Trans. G.M.A. Grube. Indianapolis: Hackett.

_____. 1977. *The Phaedo*. Trans. G.M.A. Grube. Indianapolis: Hackett.

Plotinus. 1956. *The Enneads.* 2nd ed. Trans. Stephen MacKenna. London: Faber.
Popper, Sir Karl R. 1961. *The Logic of Scientific Discovery.* New York: Basic.
Pritchard, P.H. 1982. "Model Ecosystems." In Richard A. Conway (ed.), *Environmental Risk Analysis for Chemicals.* New York: Van Nostrand Reinhold, 257–353.
Quinn, Daniel. 1992. *Ishmael.* New York: Bantam.
R. v. Sparrow, [1990] 1 Supreme Court Reports 1075
R. v. Van der Peet, [1996] 2 S.C.R. 507
R. v. Morgentaler, [1988] 1 S.C.R. 30
Rachels, James. 1975. "Active and Passive Euthanasia." *New England Journal of Medicine* 292 (2): 78–80.
Rapport, David. 1989. "What Constitutes Ecosystem Health." *Perspectives in Biology and Medicine* 33 (1): 120–32.
_____. 1995. "Ecosystem Health: Exploring the Territory." *Ecosystem Health* 1 (1): 5–13.
Rapport, David, J.H.A. Regier, and T.C. Hutchinson. 1985. "Ecosystem Behavior Under Stress." *The American Naturalist* 125 (5): 617–40.
Redclift, Michael. 1987. *Sustainable Development: Exploring the Contradictions.* London: Methuen.
Reeves, Gordon H., Daniel L. Bottom, and Martha H. Brookes. 1992. *Ethical Questions for Resource Managers.* Pacific Northwest Research Station, General Technical Report PNW-GTR-288. Portland, OR: U.S. Department of Agriculture Forest Service.
Reference Encyclopedia. 1998. New York: Oxford University Press.
Regan, Tom. 1989. "The Case for Animal Rights." In James Rachels (ed.), *The Right Thing to Do.* New York: Random, 211–25.
Regier, Henry. 1990. "Integrity and Surprise in the Great Lakes Basin Ecosystem." In Great Lakes Fisheries Commission Special Publications 90–4, *An Ecosystem Approach to the Integrity of the Great Lakes in Turbulent Times.* Ann Arbor, MI: Great Lakes Commission, 17–36.
_____. 1992. "Indicators of Ecosystem Integrity." In D.H. McKenzie, D.E. Hyatt and V.J. McDonald (eds.), *Ecological Indicators.* Fort Lauderdale, FL: Elsevier, 183–200.
_____. 1993. "The Notion of Natural and Cultural Integrity." In S. Woodley, J. Kay and G. Francis (eds.), *Ecological Integrity and the Management of Ecosystems.* Delray Beach, FL: St. Lucie, 3–18.
Rescher, Nicholas. 1969. *Value Theory.* Englewood Cliffs, NJ: Prentice.
Richardson, Mary, Joan Sherman, and Michael Gismondi. 1993. *Winning Back the Words.* Toronto: Garamond.
Robinson, John Mansley. 1968. *An Introduction to Early Greek Philosophy.* Boston: Houghton.
Rolston, III, Holmes. 1986. *Philosophy Gone Wild: Essays in Environmental Ethics.* Buffalo, NY: Prometheus.
_____. 1988. *Environmental Ethics: Duties and Values in the Natural World.* Philadelphia: Temple University Press.
_____. 1992. "Disvalues in Nature." *The Monist* 75: 250–78.
Rosen, Edward. 1973. "Cosmology from Antiquity to 1850." In Charles E. Pettee and Laurie Sullivan (eds.), *Dictionary of the History of Ideas: Studies of Selected Pivotal Ideas: Vol. 1.* New York: Scribner's, 535–54.

Ross, Rupert. 1992. *Dancing with a Ghost: Exploring Indian Reality.* Toronto: Reed.

Ross, Stephen David. *1971. The Scientific Process.* The Hague: Martinus Nijhoff.

Ross, W.D. 1930. *The Right and the Good.* Oxford: Clarendon.

Roszak, Theodore. 1972. *Where the Wasteland Ends.* Garden City, NY: Doubleday.

Rousseau, Jean Jacques. 1976. *Discourse on the Origin of Inequality.* In Jean Jacques Rousseau, *The Social Contract and The Discourse on the Origin of Inequality.* New York: Washington Square.

Sachs, Wolfgang. 1993a. "Global Ecology and the Shadow of Development." In Wolfgang Sachs (ed.), *Global Ecology: A New Arena of Political Conflict.* Halifax, NS: Fernwood.

_____, ed. 1993b. *Global Ecology: A New Arena of Political Conflict.* Halifax, NS: Fernwood.

Sagoff, Mark. 1992. "The Limits of Cost-Benefit Analysis." In Claudia Mills (ed.), *Values and Public Policy.* Orlando, FL: Harcourt, 76–79.

_____. 1993. "Some Problems with Environmental Economics." In Susan J. Armstrong and Richard G. Botzler (eds.), *Environmental Ethics: Divergence and Convergence.* New York: McGraw, 238–44.

_____. 1996. "On the Value of Endangers and Other Species." *Environmental Management* 20: 1–16.

Sapontzis, Steve F. 1984. "Predation," *Ethics and Animals* 5 (2): 27–38.

Sartre, Jean Paul. 1943. *Being and Nothingness: An Essay on Phenomenological Ontology.* Trans. Hazel E. Barnes. London: Methuen.

_____. 1974. "The Humanism of Existentialism." In Jean Paul Sartre, *Essays in Existentialism.* Secaucus, NJ: Citadel, 31–62.

Scherer, Donald. 1995. "Evolution, Human Living, and the Practice of Ecological Restoration." *Environmental Ethics* 17 (4): 359–79.

Schmidheiny, Stephan. 1992. *Changing Course: A Global Business Perspective on Development and the Environment: Executive Summary.* Cambridge, MA: MIT.

Schoener, T.W. 1989. "The Ecological Niche." In J.M. Cherrett (ed.), *Ecological Concepts: The Contribution of Ecology to an Understanding of the Natural World.* Oxford: Blackwell Scientific, 79–113.

Schweitzer, Albert. 1993. "The Ethics of Reverence for Life." In Susan J. Armstrong and Richard G. Botzler (eds.), *Environmental Ethics: Divergence and Convergence.* New York: McGraw, 342–53.

Shiva, Vandana. 1989. *Staying Alive: Women Ecology and Development.* London: Zed.

Shrader-Frechette, Kristin. 1991. *Environmental Ethics.* 2nd ed. Pacific Grove, CA: Boxwood.

_____. 1995. "Practical Ecology and Foundations for Environmental Ethics." *Journal of Philosophy* 92 (12): 621–35.

Shrader-Frechette, Kristin, and E.D. McCoy. 1993. *Method in Ecology: Strategies for Conservation.* Cambridge: Cambridge University Press.

Shuter, B.J., C.K. Minns, and C.H. Olver. 1997. "Reply: Toward a Definition of Conservation Principles for Fisheries Management." *Canadian Journal of Fisheries and Aquatic Sciences* 54: 2724–25.

Sierra Club v. *Morton*, 405 US 727 (1972)

Singer, Peter. 1986. "All Animals Are Equal." In Peter Singer (ed.), *Applied Ethics.* Oxford: Oxford University Press, 215–28.

Skinner, B.F. 1971. *Beyond Freedom and Dignity.* New York: Bantam.

_____. 1976. *Walden II*. New York: Macmillan.

Smith, David M. n.d. "An Athapaskan Way of Knowing: Chippewyan Ontology." Unpublished manuscript.

Snell, Bruno. 1982. *The Discovery of the Mind in Greek Philosophy and Literature*. New York: Dover.

Spash, Clive L. 1999. "The Development of Environmental Thinking in Economics." *Environmental Values* 8: 413–35.

Spinoza, Benedict. 1949. *Ethics and On the Improvement of the Understanding*. New York: Hafner.

Stark, L. 1990. *Signs of Hope: Working Towards Our Common Future*. Oxford: Oxford University Press.

Stevenson, Leslie. 1993. "Is Scientific Research Value Neutral?" In Susan J. Armstrong and Richard G. Botzler (eds.), *Environmental Ethics: Divergence and Convergence*. New York: McGraw, 9–16.

Strong, Jr., D.R. 1980. "Null Hypotheses in Ecology." *Synthese* 43: 271–85.

Suzuki, D.T. 1985. *Essays in Zen Buddhism: Second Series*. York Beach, ME: Samuel Wiser.

Sylvan, Richard. n.d. "A Critique of (Wild) Western Deep Ecology: A Response to Warwick Fox's Response to an Earlier Critique." Unpublished paper.

Tansley, A.G. 1935. *Introduction to Plant Ecology*. London: Allen.

Taylor, Duncan. 1992. "Disagreeing on the Basics: Environmental Debates Reflect Competing World Views." *Alternatives* 18 (3): 26–33.

Taylor, Paul. 1986. *Respect for Nature: A Theory of Environmental Ethics*. Princeton, NJ: Princeton University Press.

Trudeau, Pierre Elliott. 1987. "Remarks on Aboriginal and Treaty Rights." In Wesley Cragg (ed.), *Contemporary Moral Issues*. Toronto: McGraw, 267–68.

United Nations. 1992. *Agenda 21*. July. On-line at <gopher://gopher.undp.org/00/unconfs/UNCED/English/a21_02>. Accessed July 1997.

Van Hise, Charles R. 1910. "Conservation and Mankind." In Charles R. Van Hise, *The Conservation of Natural Resources in the Unites States*. New York: Macmillan.

Wackernagel, Mathis, and William Rees. 1996. *Our Ecological Footprint: Reducing Human Impact on the Earth*. Gabriola Island, BC: New Society.

Waring, R.H. 1989. "Ecosystems: Fluxes of Matter and Energy." In J.M. Cherrett (ed.), *Ecological Concepts: The Contribution of Ecology to an Understanding of the Natural World*. Oxford: Blackwell Scientific, 17–41.

Warren, Karen J. 1998. "The Power and the Promise of Ecological Feminism." In Susan J. Armstrong and Richard G. Botzler (eds.), *Environmental Ethics: Divergence and Convergence*. 2nd ed. New York: McGraw, 471–80.

Warren, Mary Anne. 1983. "The Moral and Legal Status of Abortion." In J. Thomas (ed.), *Medical Ethics and Human Life*. Toronto: Samuel Stevens.

Westra, Laura. 1994. *An Environmental Proposal for Ethics: The Principle of Integrity*. Savage, MD: Rowman & Littlefield.

_____. 1998. *Living in Integrity: A Global Ethic to Restore a Fragmented Earth*. Lanham, MD: Rowman & Littlefield.

White, Jr., Lynn. 1967. "The Historical Roots of Our Ecological Crisis." *Science* 155: 1203–07.

Whitehead, Alfred North. 1929. *Process and Reality*. New York: Harper Torch.

Wilson, Bryan. 1988. Introduction. In Brenda Almond and Bryan Wilson (eds.), *Values*. Atlantic Highlands, NJ: Humanities, 1–10.

Winner, Langdon. 1992. "The Risk of Talking About Risk." In Claudia Mills (ed.), *Values and Public Policy*. Orlando, FL: Harcourt, 98–102.

Woodley, Stephen, James Kay, and George Francis. 1993. *Ecological Integrity and the Management of Ecosystems*. Delray Beach, FL: St. Lucie.

World Commission on Environment and Development. 1987. *Our Common Future*. New York: Oxford.

Worster, Donald. 1990. "The Ecology of Order and Chaos." *Environmental History Review* 14: 1–18.

Yodzis, Peter. 1989. *Introduction to Theoretical Ecology*. New York: Harper.

Index

adaptation/adaptive, 63, 68, 94, 161, 201, 245, 250
aedificare, 30
allodial rights, 35
Ambient Air Quality Objectives, 237, 259
analytic failure, 188, 190, 243
animism, 14-20
    aboriginal, 15-17
    ancient times, 15
    critique and elimination of, 20-21, 30
Anishnaabe, 16, 91, 133, 177, 233
anomaly, 41, 62-63
anthropocentrism, 90, 121-129, 133, 154, 221
anthropomorphism, 128
Aristotle, 33
    and finite cosmos, 24, 41, 43
    Nicomachean Ethics, 33
atman and *anatman*, 37
attunement, 8, 94, 98, 136, 142, 143-45, 148, 150, 153, 161, 181, 183, 186, 201, 207-208, 218, 238, 244, 246, 254, 259
authority, 56
    as ground of knowledge, 23
axiology
    and work, 104, 110-11, 244-45
    hierarchy, 26-27, 55
    intrinsic value, 90, 101-102, 105, 107, 113, 114, 149, 153, 165, 169, 213, 248

instrumental value, 102-103, 107, 173
inverted scheme, 108-117, 167, 239, 244, 253
liberalism, 99-108, 142
negative value, 116, 155
sources of value, 58, 102, 115
utilitarian, 105, 164, 202, 211, 217, 221, 225
world as valueless, 49

Bacon, Sir Francis, 46, 259
Bacon, Roger, 83
Bahm, Archie, 97
Baxter, William, 107, 121-122
Bellagio Project, 240-43
Bentham, Jeremy, 105, 134-35, 156
Berkeley, Bishop George, 56
Berns, Walter, 137
Birch, Tom, 136, 156
Black Elk, 18, 37
Bookchin, Murray, 92
Booth, Annie, 153
Brennan, Andrew, 1, 80
Browne, Thomas, 53
Bruno, Giordano, 40, 41
Buddhism, 19, 159, 180, 208

Callicott, J. Baird, 164-65, 186-87
Carson, Rachel, 87, 127, 185
chaos theory, 73, 78, 179
ch'i, 18-19
Christianity, 29, 53

and colonialism, 31
critique of, 29-30
chthonic gods, 20
Clements, F.E., 80
colonialism, 31, 36
community, 115, 137, 166
    and ecology, 77, 80, 89, 139,
    167, 256
    moral, 102, 138, 146
conatus, 145, 156-57, 159, 174-75,
    178-79, 182
conflict, 108, 116
    assumed in liberalism, 101
cooptation, 171, 202, 222, 234-37,
    247, 252
conservation, 81, 88, 186, 247-59,
    224
    biology, 174, 183
Copernican Revolution, Chapter
    Two, 39-59
cosmology
    aboriginal, 120, 124
    Christian, 28
    Copernican, 39-45,
    Ptolemaic, 24, 47, 55
    two-sphere universe, 40
cost-benefit analysis (CBA), 106,
    127, 185, 187, 191, 226-30
creativity, 78, 85, 180

Darwin, Charles, 61, 63-64,101
democracy, 2, 6, 98-99, 105, 188,
    190, 195, 196, 226, 238
Democritus, 47
Dene Tha, 18, 86, 91, 112
deontic experience, 136, 164, 179
Descartes, René, 32, 43, 44, 54, 56,
    62, 144, 193
detachment, 8, 52, 65, 70, 101,
    111, 136
dialectics, 117-118, 132, 143, 146,
    151, 159, 166, 177, 181, 192,
    199, 238, 243, 256
Digges, Thomas, 40

dissipative structures, 89, 169
divided line, 26-27, 36, 56
Donne, John, 52
dreams, 18, 91
dualism, 92, 177
    between physical and mental,
    19, 26-27, 29, 62, 65
    between self and other, 52, 64

Earth
    as centre of cosmos, 24, 39
    as dark place, 25
    as test of mettle, 29-30
ecological
    as necessary for explanation,
    71-80
    as underdetermined, 72, 77-80
    footprint, 225
    thinking, 9, 80, 94, 117, 121,
    186, 205, 258
    world view, 113, 250
    relation to ethics, Chapter
    Five
ecology (*oikemene*), 27, 30, 86, 179
    and competition, 83, 167
    and cooperation, 83, 167
    and fascism, 87, 119, 139
    and feminism, 92, 153-54
    deep, 86, 90-91, 148-54, 184
    restoration, 88, 160-61, 168,
    174, 203, 205, 207, 248
    social, 92
ecosystem health, 168-73
ecosystem integrity, 116-117, 146,
    169, 173-79, 183, 186, 189,
    199, 202-203, 206, 212, 247,
    252
efficiency, 202
Eleatic philosophers, 23
Elton, C., 82
emergent properties, 76
Enlightenment, the, 54, 56
entropy, 73
Erinnyes, 21

eros, 25
ether theory, 43
Eumenides (See Errinyes)
exclusion, 8, 55, 70, 97, 107,113,
    150, 155, 185, 190, 222
exhaustiveness, principle of, 151-
    52, 155
Evernden, Neil, 144, 179
evolution, 61-70, 179

flourishing, 92,
food web (chain) (See trophic
    level)
Fox, Warwick, 149
fragmentation, 51, 57
freedom, 106, 107, 128, 131, 133,
    137, 142-48, 163, 172, 175-78,
    188, 189, 199-200, 202, 218,
    225, 251
    from authority/oppression,
    52-53, 91,100, 120, 134, 154,
    156, 157
    from corporeal existence, 30
    vs. determinism, 27-28
Friere, Paulo, 100
full-cost accounting, 196, 220

Gaia hypothesis, 1, 3, 73-76
Galileo, 43, 78
Gause, G.F., 82
geology, 61, 63, 74
Gilbreath, Kent, 221-22
Gleik, James, 78
Goodpaster, Kenneth, 135
Great Chain of Being, 29, 32, 40
Great Spirit (Mystery), 16, 19, 91-
    92, 177, 180
Green Plan, Canada, 90
green revolution, 218, 234
gross national product (GNP),
    171, 191, 194, 241

Haeckel, Ernst, 86
Hale, Matthew, 53

harm, 168, 189, 206, 208
    principle, 147-54, 157, 182,
    198, 233, 239-40, 258
Hegel, G.W.F., 75, 127
hegemony, 158, 160, 162, 167, 197,
    202, 206
Heisenberg, Werner, 61, 65, 79, 86
Hobbes, Thomas, 113
holism, 71, 140, 168, 172, 212, 214,
    250, 257
    and causality, 76
    approach, 8, 68-69, 121, 240-
    41
    need for, 67
Homer, 20-21
Hough, Michael, 11, 51
Hume, David, 56

immanence, 19
immediate experience, 137,
    144,188
inclusion, 8, 10, 186, 200, 206
incommensurability, 191
indeterminacy, 78, 120, 174
    principle of, 65
individualism, 99, 121, 124, 148,
    168, 213
individuation , 89, 120, 177-78
Industrial Revolution, 47
infinity, 40
International Joint Commission
    (IJC), 186, 202-208, 222, 239,
    251
intrinsic value (See axiology)
Ionian philosophers, 22

Jefferson, Thomas, 35
Jouvency, Joseph, 31
judgment, 112, 119, 143, 157-63
justice, environmental, 220

Kant, Immanuel, 55, 94, 114, 180
Karr, James, 12, 173
Kay, James, 173

Kepler, Johannes, 44
ki (See *ch'i*)
Kitche Manitou (See Great Spirit)
Kohák, Erazim, 180, 208
Kyoto Treaty, 128, 190, 202, 209,
    220

Lakota, 18
Land Ethic, 163-68, 252
law-governed cosmos, 24-5
leading by following, 11, 160-62,
    171, 176, 205, 239-40
Leonard, Herman B., 194, 202
Leopold, Aldo, 88-89, 163-68, 170,
    192, 196, 239, 252
levels of explanation (organiza-
    tion), 69, 76, 117, 119, 147,
    175, 181, 189
liberalism, 99-108, 131, 134, 138,
    149
life (presupposed), 74-75
Locke, John, 56, 99, 101,103, 244,
    249
locus of valuational activity, 113,
    145
Lovelock, James, 1, 73-76, 82
Lucretius, 28

Manifest Destiny, 34, 193
marginalization, 8, 185-192, 197,
    212, 218, 232, 243, 247, 254
martial arts, 160
materio-mechanism, 45-49, 55, 62
    critique of, 65, 90
McHarg, Ian, L., 29
metaphysics, denial of, 46
Midgeley, Mary, 149
Mill, John Stuart, 101, 102, 106,
    134
mind
    and rationality, 22-24
    status of, 15, 29
Monroe doctrine, 35
moral considerability, 102, 135-36,

140, 155
Muir, John, 247
muktuk, 254-55
myth, 16-17

Naess, Arne, 90-91, 149, 184
neuron, 66, 82, 118
Newton, Sir Isaac, 44, 45, 75
normalization, 6
Norton, Bryan, 169, 173

observer status, 23, 52, 54
occult qualities, 45
oikemene (See ecology)
Ojibway (see Anishnaabe)
Origen, 29

pain, 161
Passmore, John, 123-126, 128
patriarchy and devaluing of
    feminine, 21
personhood (See self)
Philo, 29
Pinchott, Gifford, 35, 247
place, 18, 83, 204
Plato, 36, 54, 62, 89, 126
    Phaedo, 22, 26-27, 29
    Republic, 29, 34
    Timaeus, 24
precautionary principle, 147, 205,
    215, 233, 240, 250
priesthood of the people, 99
pre-Socratics
process, 61, 63, 85, 112, 199
progress, 54
Ptolemaic
    cosmology (see world view,
    Ptolemaic)
    value system, 24-27, 55, 99
purposiveness, 27, 61, 68, 71, 82,
    85, 89, 108, 109, 115, 117, 119,
    128, 139-40, 146, 258
Pythagoras, 21

Rachels, James, 148
Rapport, David, 170
rationality, 23, 69, 155, 158
   and feminism, 36, 55
   and mathematics, 21-22,
   and power, 33, 48, 53, 54-55
   as intrinsically valuable, 25,
     55, 98, 178
   as source of value, 58
   as tool of attunement, 79-80,
     133, 152, 166
   critique of, 13, 79, 122
   radicalisation of, 11, 13, 79,
     112, 125, 166
   vs. animism, 29
reductionism, 48
Rees, William, 225
Regan, Tom, 135, 139, 149
Regier, Henry, 173, 207
repository model, 114
respect, 18, 138, 139, 143, 146-47,
   149, 160, 164, 173, 179-81,
   183, 203, 206-207, 218, 225,
   245, 258
responsibility, as ethically primary, 154, 157
retrograde motion, 42
right of discovery, 31
risk-benefit analysis, 230-33
Rio de Janeiro, UNCED Conference, 7, 90, 204, 236
Rolston III, Holmes, 115, 132,
   140-42, 153, 157, 159, 164,
   173, 175, 180, 198
Roosevelt, Theodore, 35, 88
roses and the rabbits, 20
Ross, W.D., 142
Roszak, Theodore, 71-72
Rousseau, Jean Jacques, 55, 100
Royal Commission on the Future
   of the Toronto Waterfront,
   168, 200

Sagoff, Mark, 229

Sapontzis, Steve, 133, 139
scepticism, 50, 91
Schweitzer, Albert, 133-34, 139
scientific method, 46, 49-50, 57,
   65, 71
self, 178
   -interest, 123-125
   -mastery, 162
self-regulation, 74, 156
senescence, 29
Shiva, Vandana, 153, 218, 244
Shrader-Frechette, Kristin, 188,
   195,
   and McCoy, E.D., 77, 195-97,
   249
Singer, Peter, 102, 135, 139
Socrates, 22, 34
solipsism, 193-95, 198
soul (See mind, eternal)
space, 18, 43-44
Spinoza, Benedict, 75, 145
stakeholder approaches, 195-202,
   228, 231, 259
structure and function, 68
suitability, 68, 70, 85, 109, 233
Supreme Court, Canada, 31, 187,
   199-200
sustainability, 186, 211-47
   strong, 224-26
   weak, 224-26

sustainable development, 211-38
   Business Council for, 213-216

Tansley, A.G., 81
Taylor, Paul, 92, 115, 142, 166
Taoism, 159, 180, 208
teleology, 14, 156
   and Gaia hypothesis, 15
   versus evolution, 15
traditional environmental knowledge, 254-56
trickle-down effect, 194, 202
trophic level, 84-85

unit of analysis, 79-86
United Nations
    Agenda 21, 228, 236
    WCED, 90, 212-14, 220-23,
    236

values analysis, 242-47, 253, 258
vacuum, 43

Warren, Karen J., 36, 153
Warren, Mary Anne, 155
waste, 103-104, 216, 248
Westra, Laura, 173-78, 184
White, Lynn jr., 29-30
Whitehead, Alfred North, 75
wilderness, 5, 98,101, 165, 169,

176-77, 200, 223, 248, 251
world view
    animistic,13-21
    Copernican, 39-45
    mechanistic, 22
    Modern, Chapter Two, 204,
    219, 249, 253
    Ptolemaic, 21-28
    modelling, 11
Wackernagel, Mathis, 225
Yodzis, Peter, 79

Zeckhauser, Richard J. (See
    Leonard, Herman B.)
zoos, 182